Vol. 1
Story & Art by
Ayumi Komura

Mixed Vegetables

Volume 1
CONTENTS

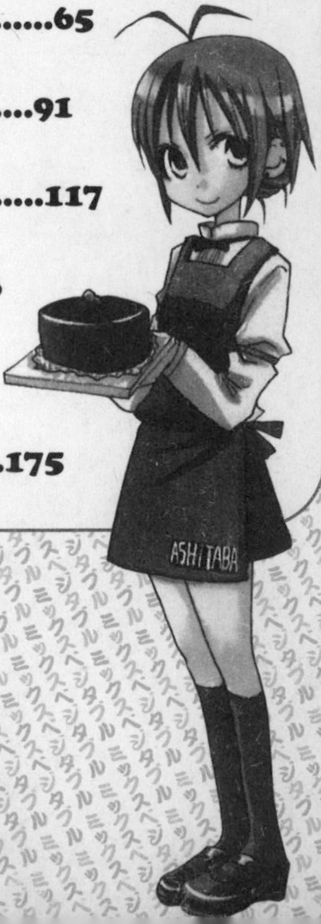

ASHITABA

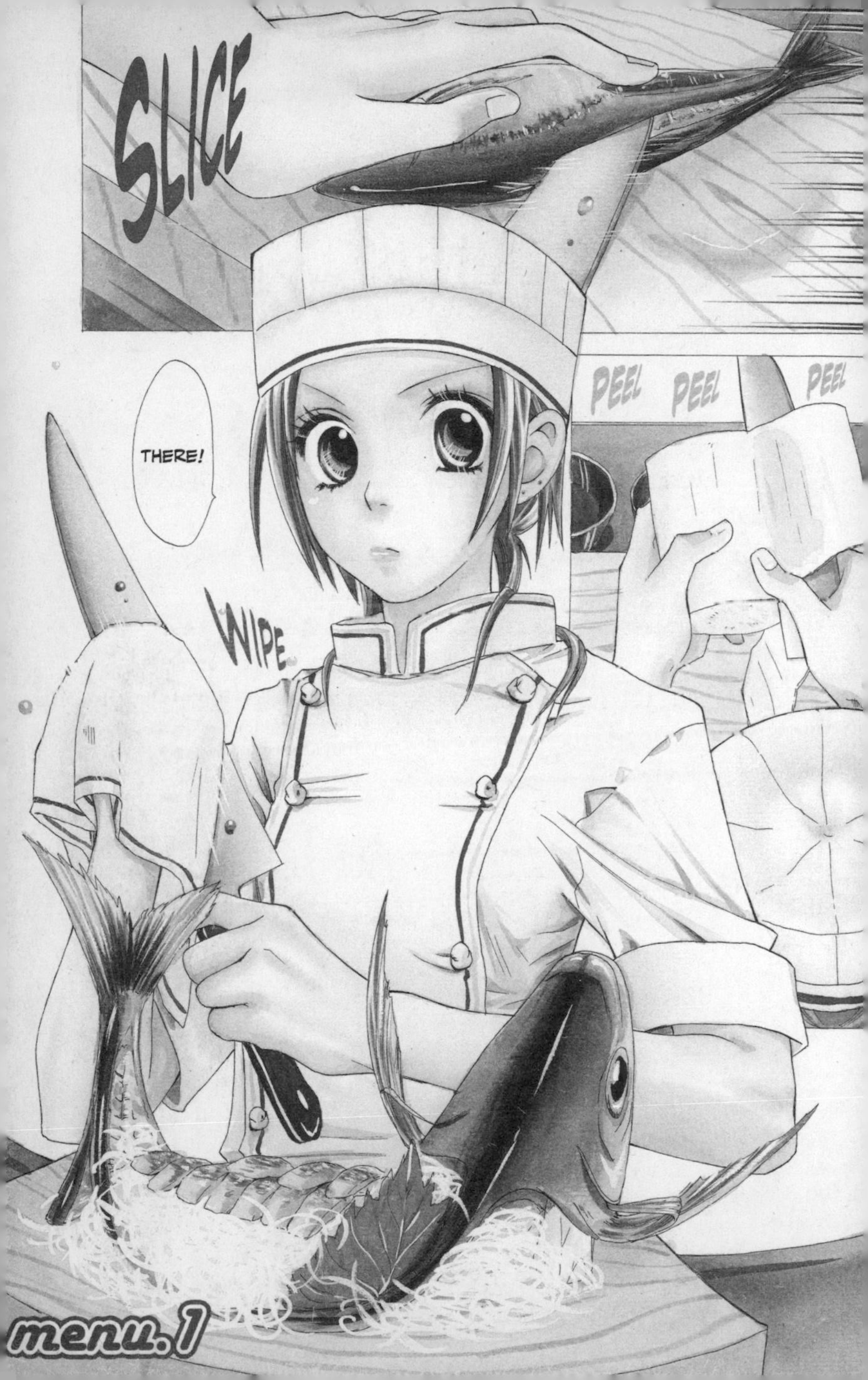
SLICE
PEEL
PEEL
PEEL
THERE!
WIPE
menu.1

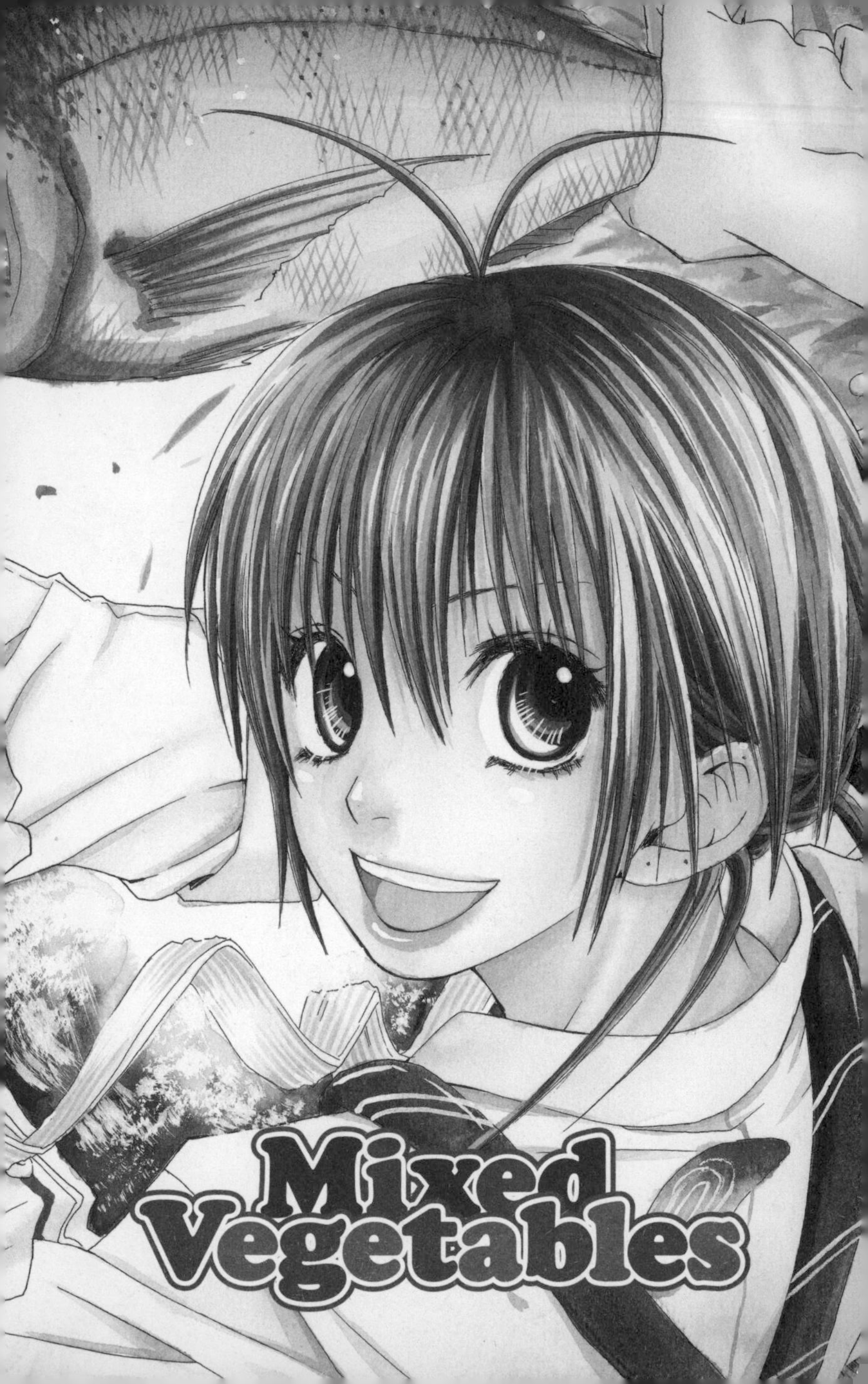
Mixed
Vegetables

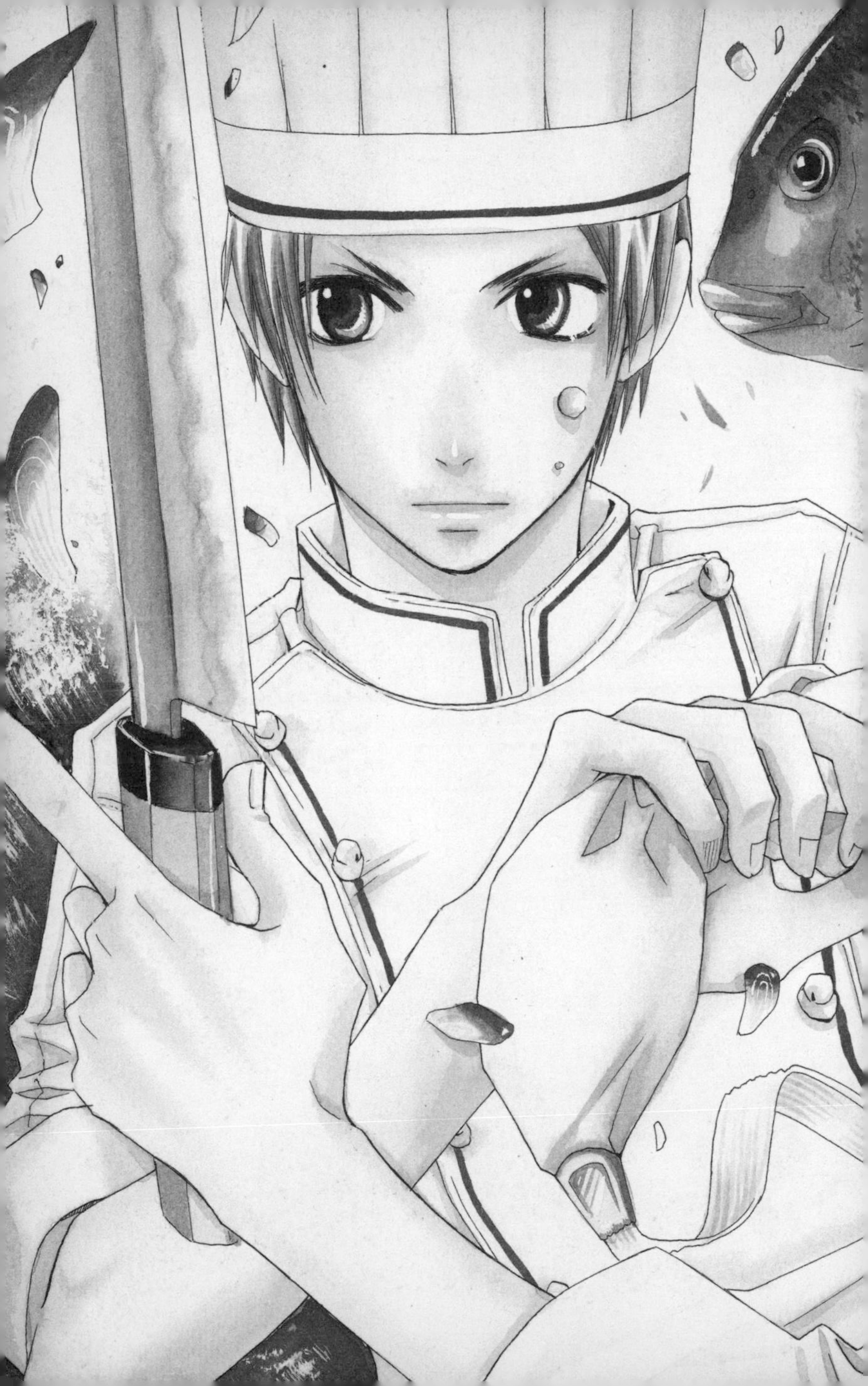

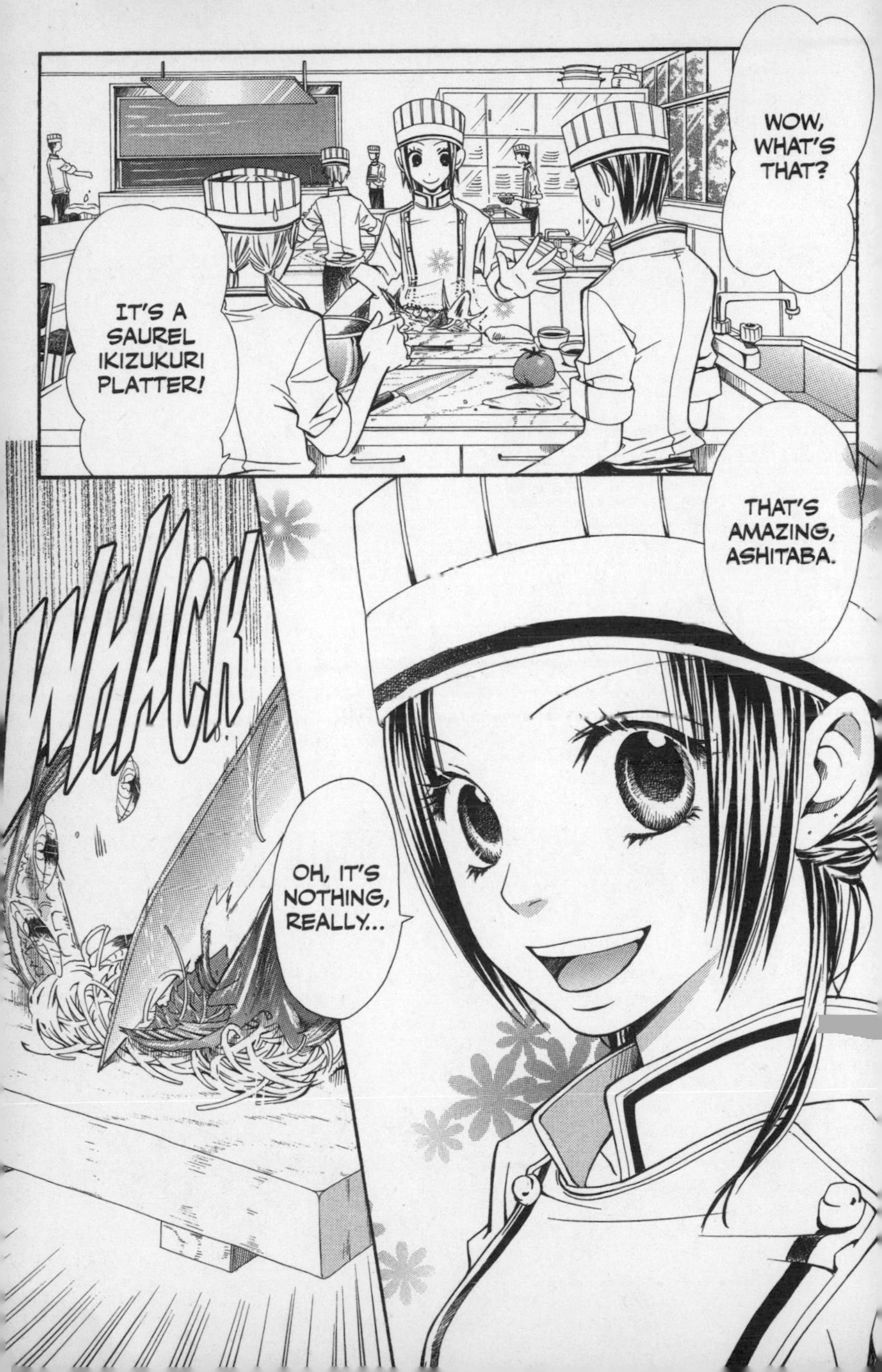
WOW, WHAT'S THAT?
IT'S A SAUREL IKIZUKURI PLATTER!
THAT'S AMAZING, ASHITABA.
OH, IT'S NOTHING, REALLY...
WHACK

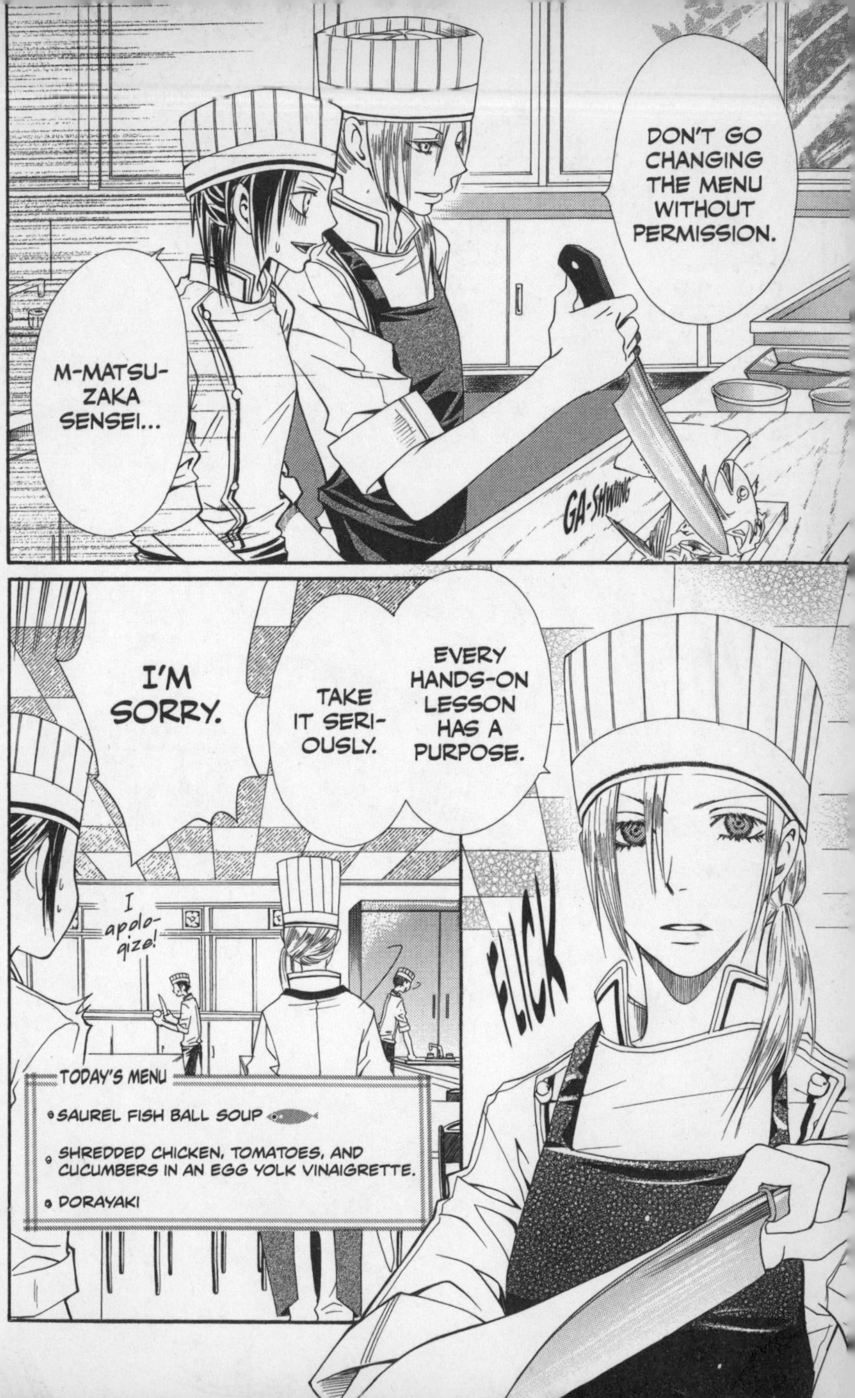
DON'T GO CHANGING THE MENU WITHOUT PERMISSION.
GA-SHWING
M-MATSU-ZAKA SENSEI...
EVERY HANDS-ON LESSON HAS A PURPOSE.
TAKE IT SERI-OUSLY.
I'M SORRY.
FLICK
I apolo-gize!
TODAY'S MENU
SAUREL FISH BALL SOUP
SHREDDED CHICKEN, TOMATOES, AND CUCUMBERS IN AN EGG YOLK VINAIGRETTE.
DORAYAKI

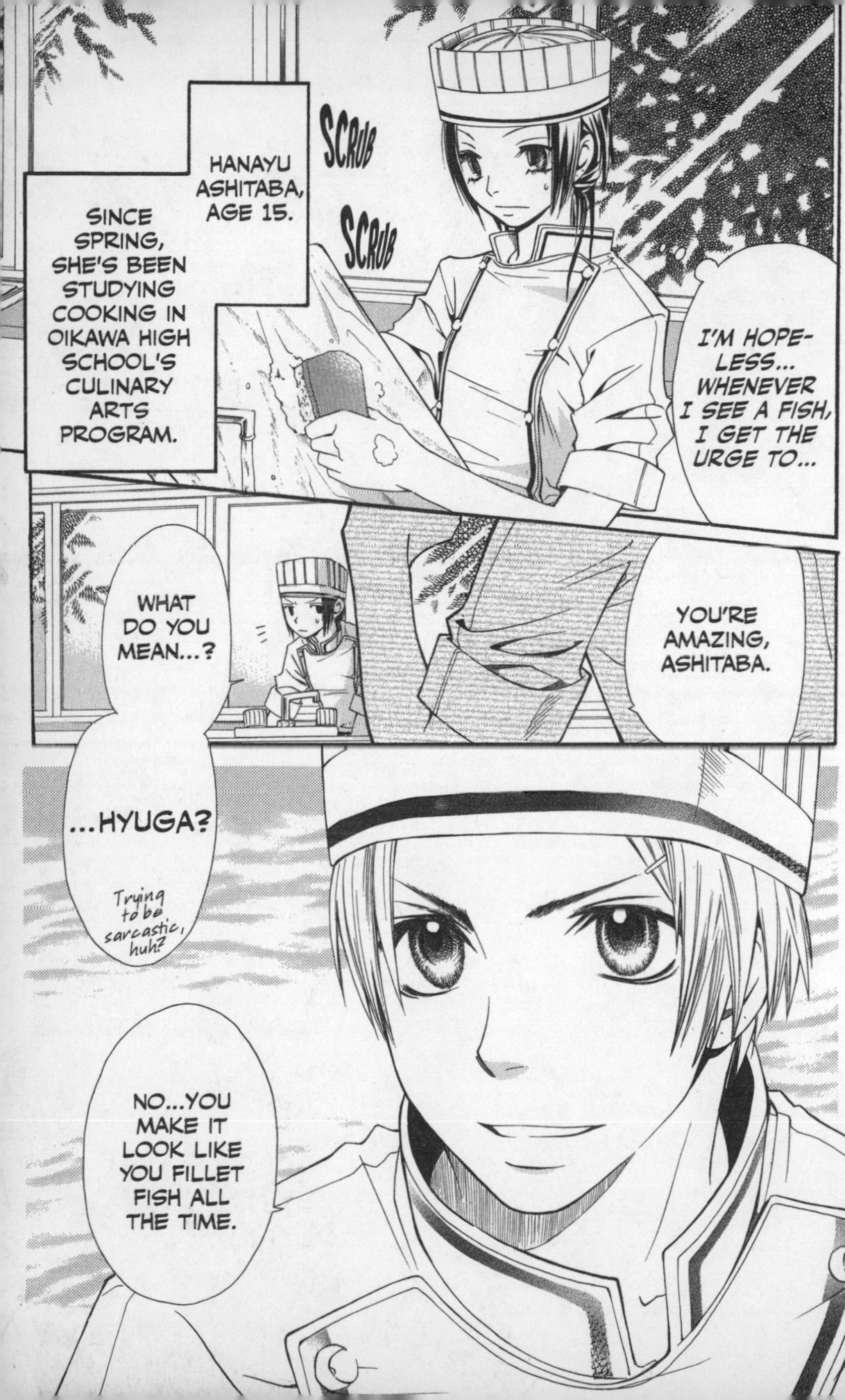
I'M HOPELESS... WHENEVER I SEE A FISH, I GET THE URGE TO...
SCRUB
SCRUB
HANAYU ASHITABA, AGE 15.
SINCE SPRING, SHE'S BEEN STUDYING COOKING IN OIKAWA HIGH SCHOOL'S CULINARY ARTS PROGRAM.
YOU'RE AMAZING, ASHITABA.
WHAT DO YOU MEAN...?
...HYUGA?
Trying to be sarcastic, huh?
NO...YOU MAKE IT LOOK LIKE YOU FILLET FISH ALL THE TIME.

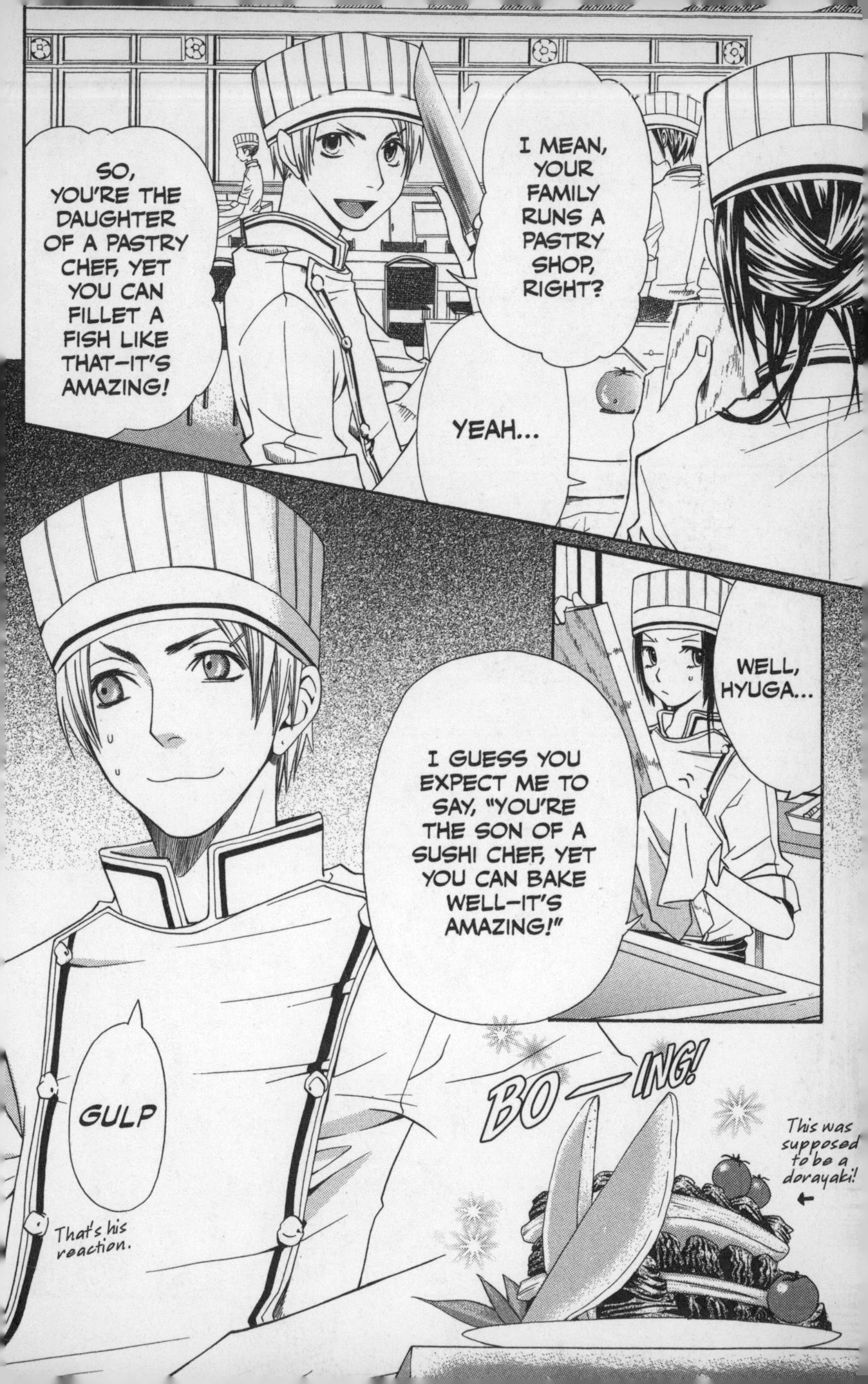
I MEAN, YOUR FAMILY RUNS A PASTRY SHOP, RIGHT?
SO, YOU'RE THE DAUGHTER OF A PASTRY CHEF, YET YOU CAN FILLET A FISH LIKE THAT—IT'S AMAZING!
YEAH...
WELL, HYUGA...
I GUESS YOU EXPECT ME TO SAY, "YOU'RE THE SON OF A SUSHI CHEF, YET YOU CAN BAKE WELL—IT'S AMAZING!"
This was supposed to be a dorayaki!
BO—ING!
GULP
That's his reaction.

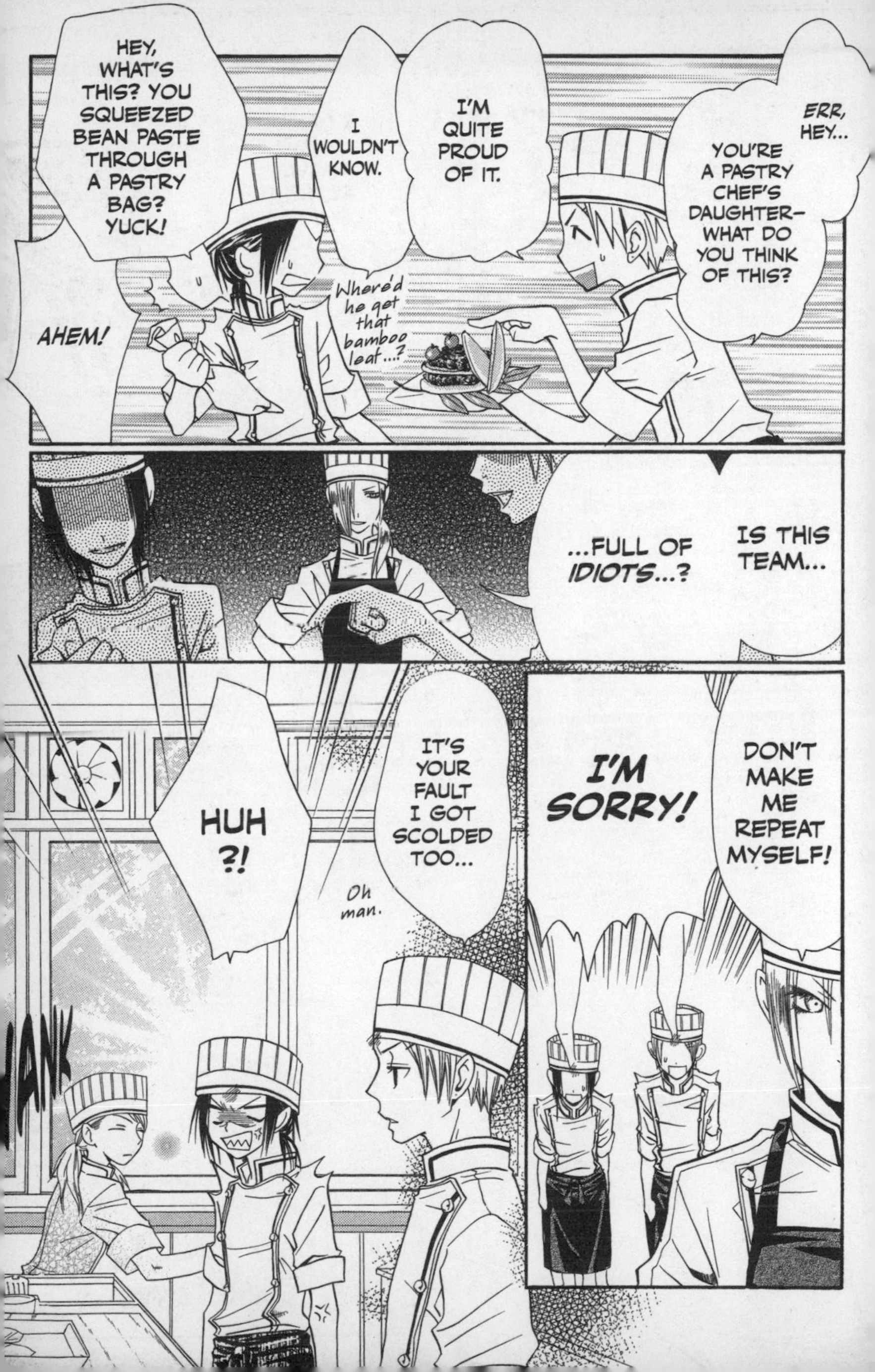
ERR, HEY...
YOU'RE A PASTRY CHEF'S DAUGHTER—WHAT DO YOU THINK OF THIS?
I'M QUITE PROUD OF IT.
I WOULDN'T KNOW.
Where'd he get that bamboo leaf...?
HEY, WHAT'S THIS? YOU SQUEEZED BEAN PASTE THROUGH A PASTRY BAG? YUCK!
AHEM!
IS THIS TEAM...
...FULL OF IDIOTS...?
DON'T MAKE ME REPEAT MYSELF!
I'M SORRY!
IT'S YOUR FAULT I GOT SCOLDED TOO...
Oh man.
HUH?!

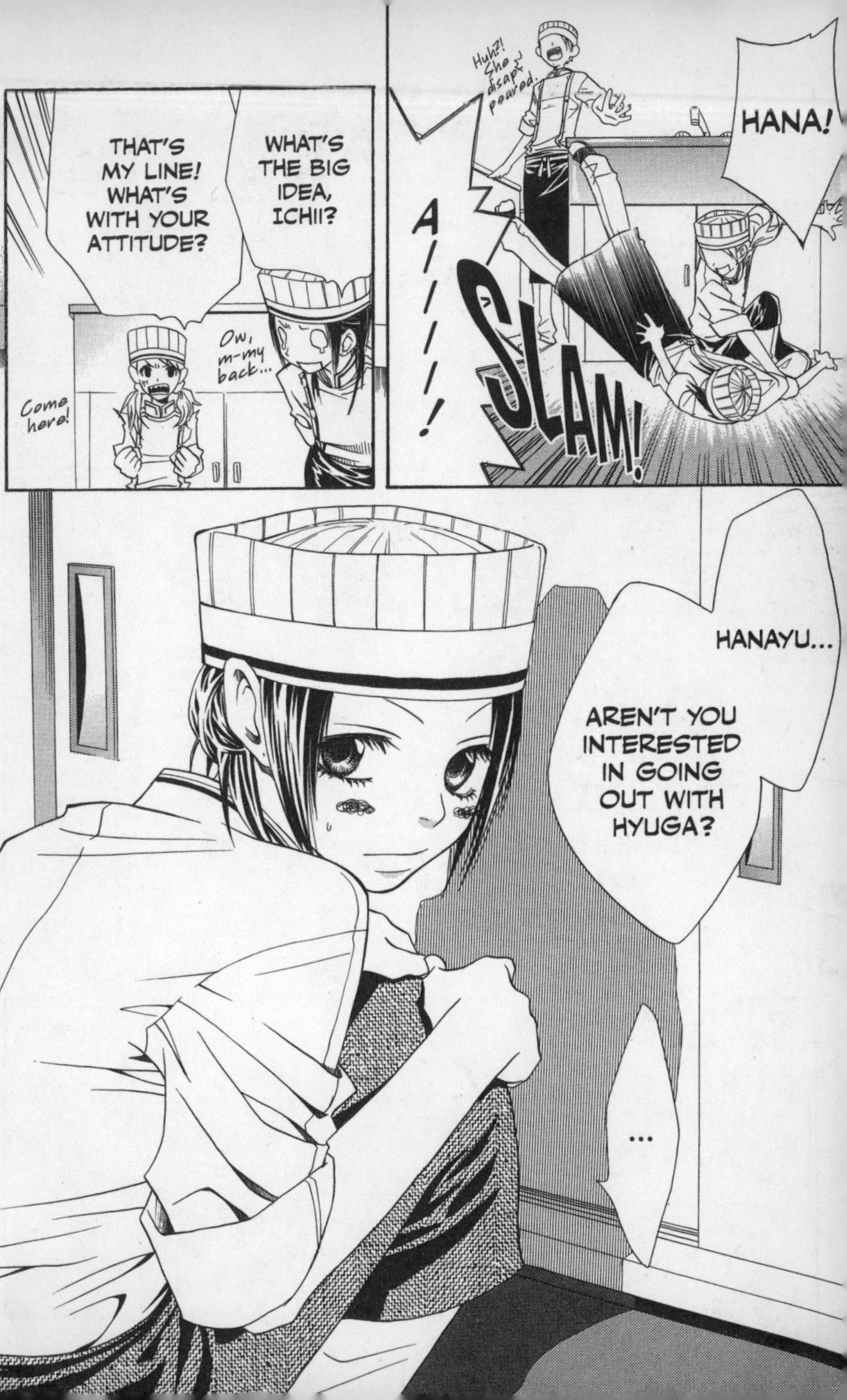
HANA!
Huh?! She disappeared.
A----!
SLAM!
WHAT'S THE BIG IDEA, ICHII?
THAT'S MY LINE! WHAT'S WITH YOUR ATTITUDE?
Ow, m-my back...
Come here!
HANAYU...
AREN'T YOU INTERESTED IN GOING OUT WITH HYUGA?
...

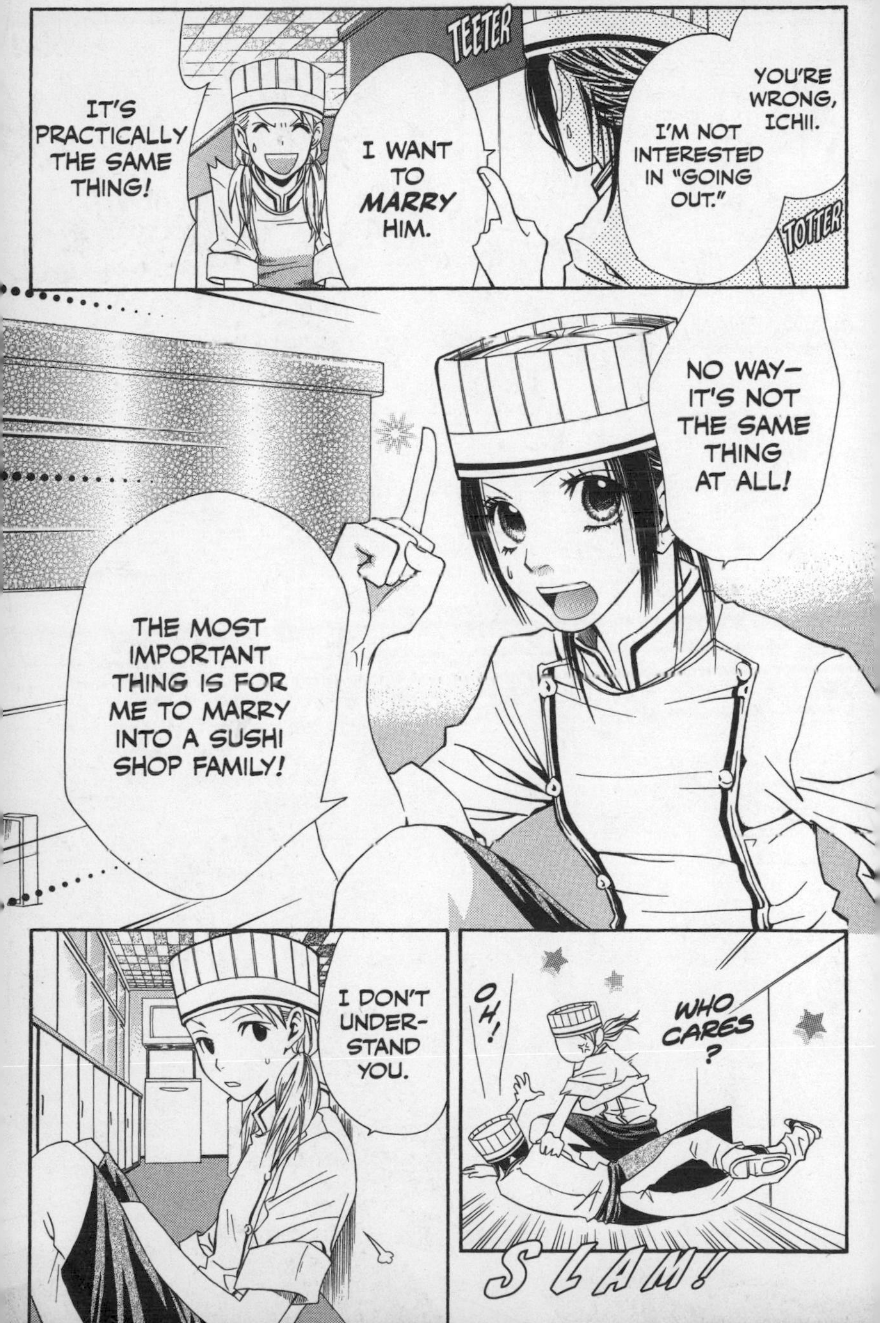
YOU'RE WRONG, ICHII. I'M NOT INTERESTED IN "GOING OUT."
TEETER
TOTTER
I WANT TO MARRY HIM.
IT'S PRACTICALLY THE SAME THING!
NO WAY— IT'S NOT THE SAME THING AT ALL!
THE MOST IMPORTANT THING IS FOR ME TO MARRY INTO A SUSHI SHOP FAMILY!
WHO CARES?
OH!
SLAM!
I DON'T UNDER-STAND YOU.

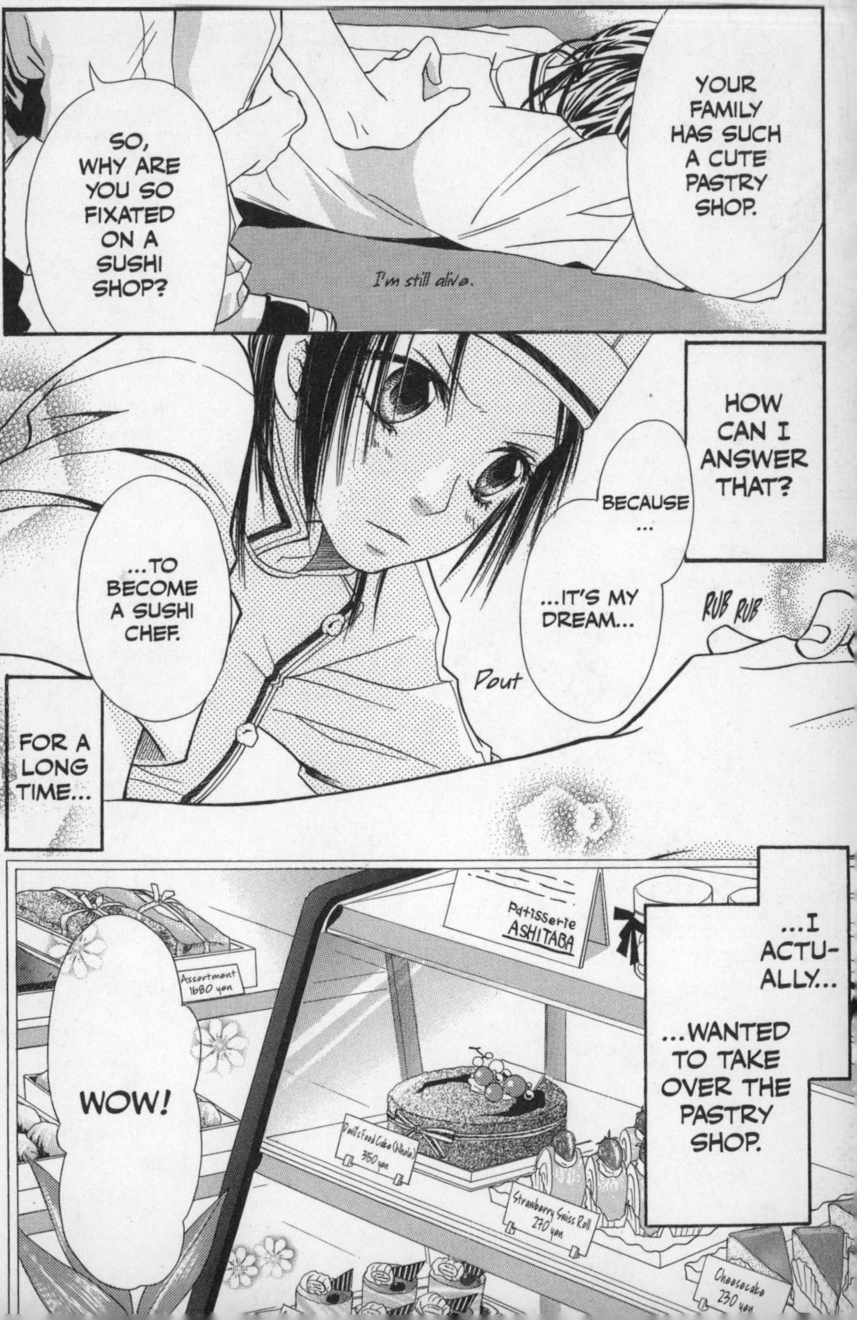
YOUR FAMILY HAS SUCH A CUTE PASTRY SHOP.
SO, WHY ARE YOU SO FIXATED ON A SUSHI SHOP?
I'm still alive.
HOW CAN I ANSWER THAT?
RUB RUB
BECAUSE ...
...IT'S MY DREAM...
Pout
...TO BECOME A SUSHI CHEF.
FOR A LONG TIME...
...I ACTU-ALLY...
...WANTED TO TAKE OVER THE PASTRY SHOP.
Patisserie ASHITABA
Strawberry Swiss Roll 270 yen
Cheesecake 230 yen
Devil's Food Cake (Whole) 3150 yen
Assortment 1680 yen
WOW!

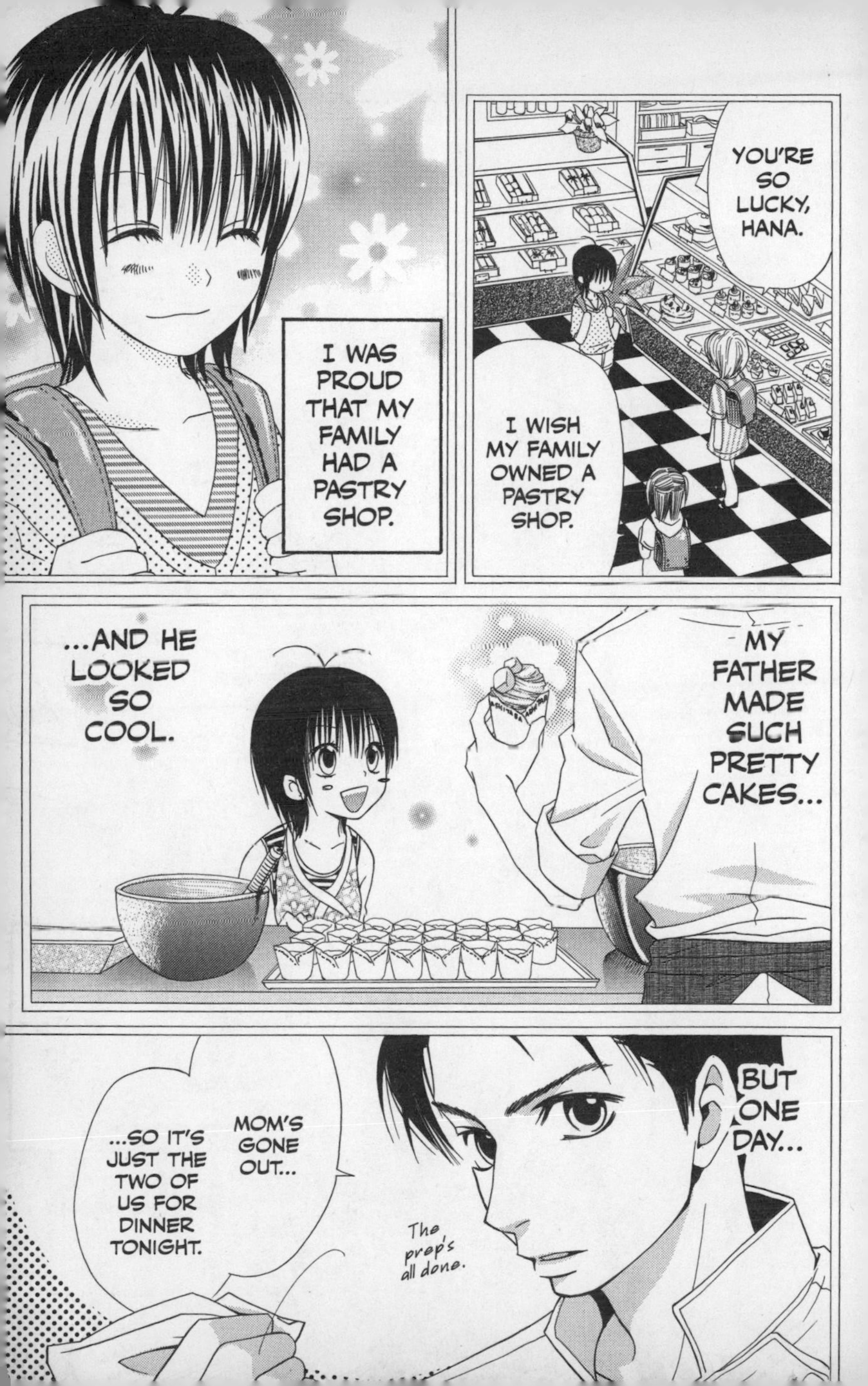
YOU'RE SO LUCKY, HANA.
I WISH MY FAMILY OWNED A PASTRY SHOP.
I WAS PROUD THAT MY FAMILY HAD A PASTRY SHOP.
MY FATHER MADE SUCH PRETTY CAKES...
...AND HE LOOKED SO COOL.
BUT ONE DAY...
MOM'S GONE OUT...
...SO IT'S JUST THE TWO OF US FOR DINNER TONIGHT.
The prep's all done.

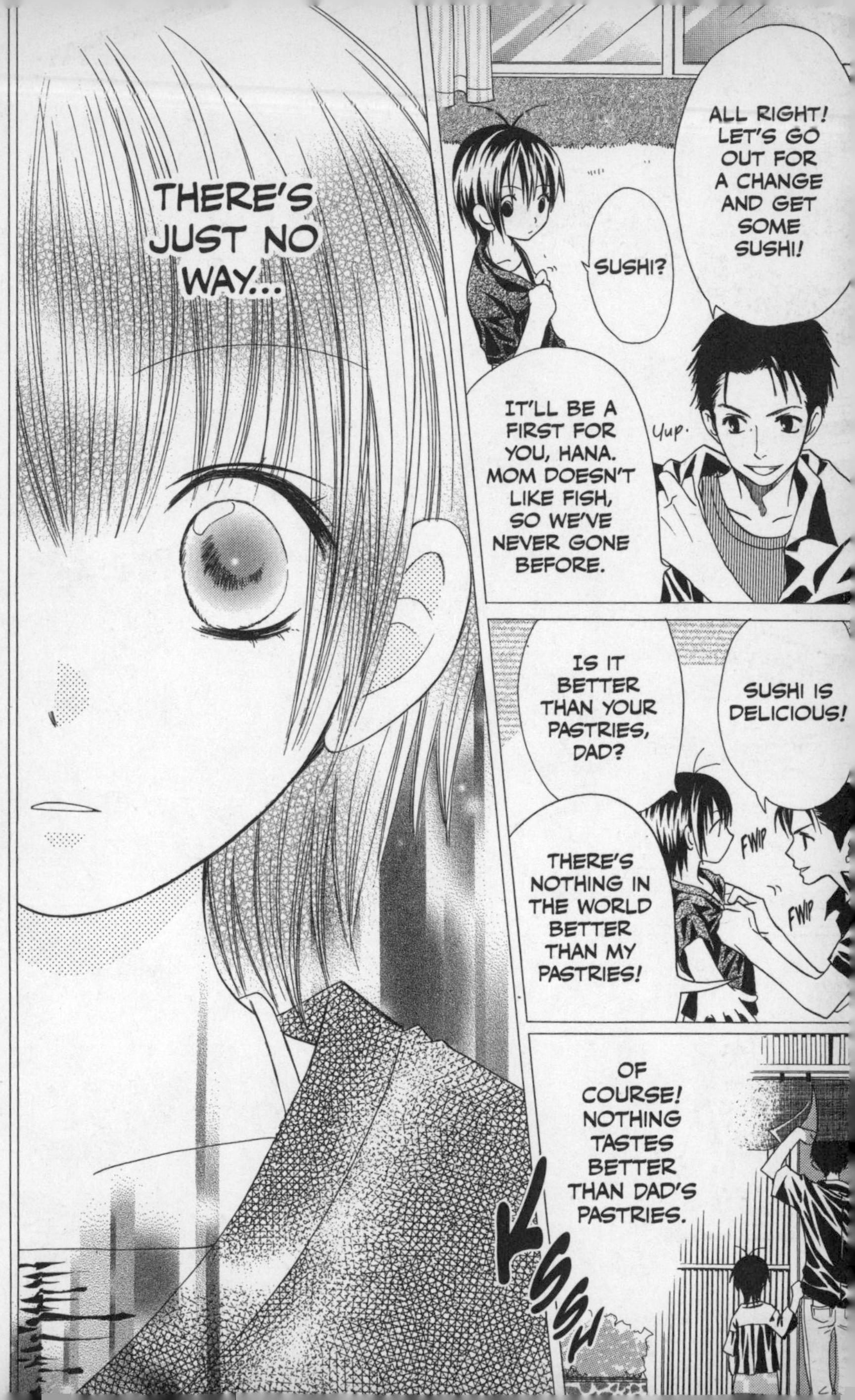
ALL RIGHT! LET'S GO OUT FOR A CHANGE AND GET SOME SUSHI!
SUSHI?
Yup.
IT'LL BE A FIRST FOR YOU, HANA. MOM DOESN'T LIKE FISH, SO WE'VE NEVER GONE BEFORE.
SUSHI IS DELICIOUS!
IS IT BETTER THAN YOUR PASTRIES, DAD?
FWIP
FWIP
THERE'S NOTHING IN THE WORLD BETTER THAN MY PASTRIES!
OF COURSE! NOTHING TASTES BETTER THAN DAD'S PASTRIES.
KSSSH
THERE'S JUST NO WAY...

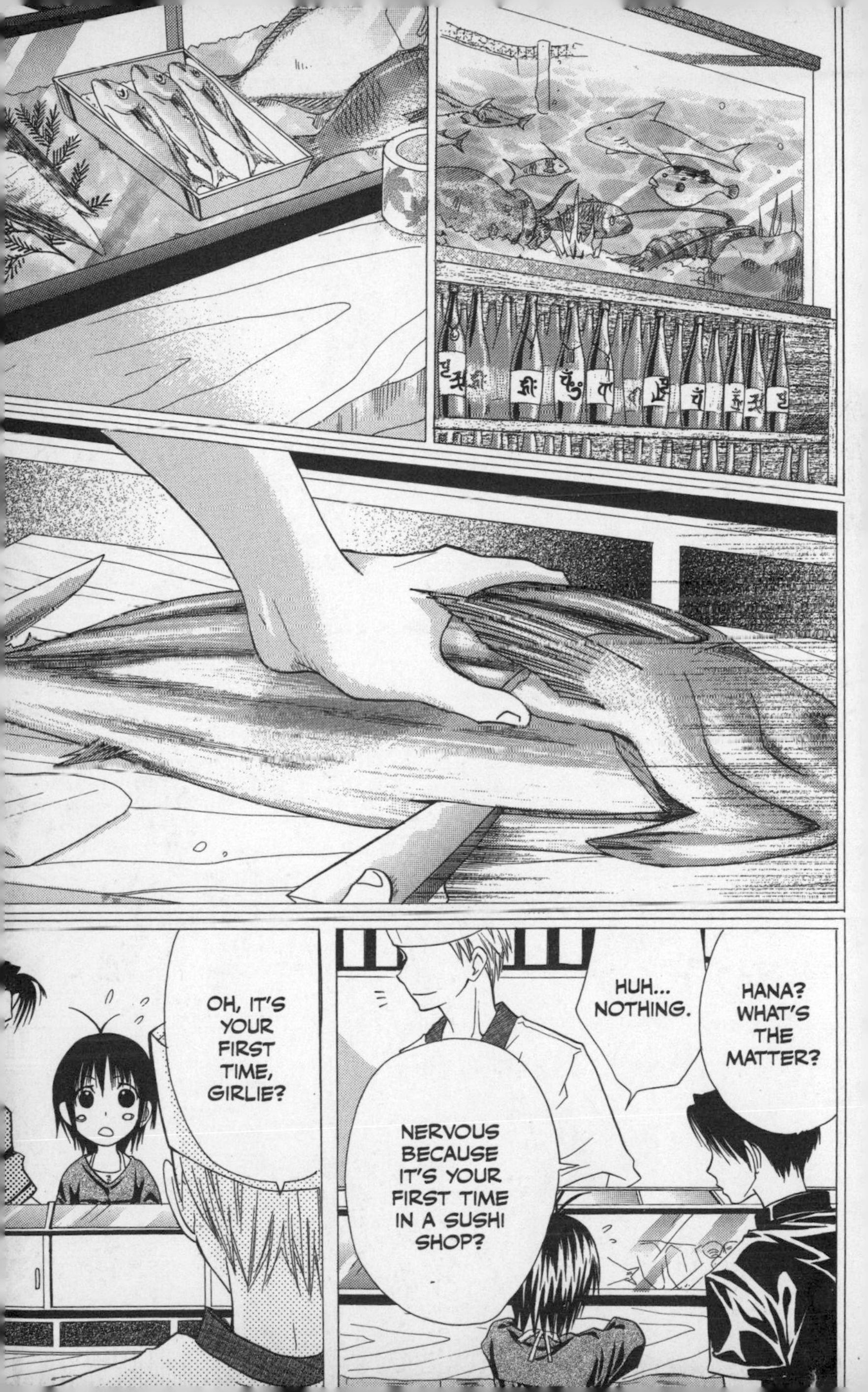
HANA? WHAT'S THE MATTER?
HUH... NOTHING.
NERVOUS BECAUSE IT'S YOUR FIRST TIME IN A SUSHI SHOP?
OH, IT'S YOUR FIRST TIME, GIRLIE?

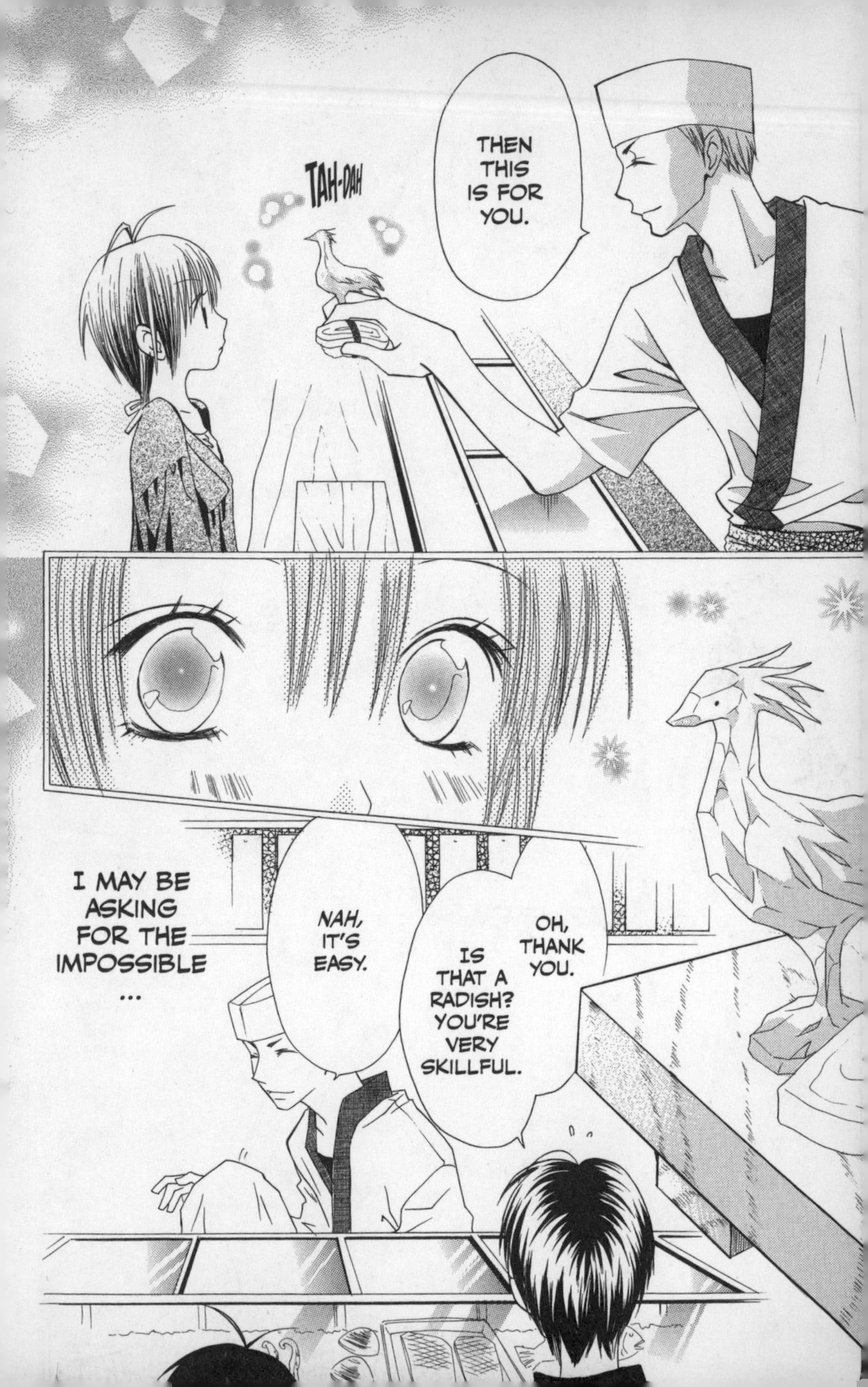
THEN THIS IS FOR YOU.
TAH-DAH
OH, THANK YOU.
IS THAT A RADISH? YOU'RE VERY SKILLFUL.
NAH, IT'S EASY.
I MAY BE ASKING FOR THE IMPOSSIBLE...

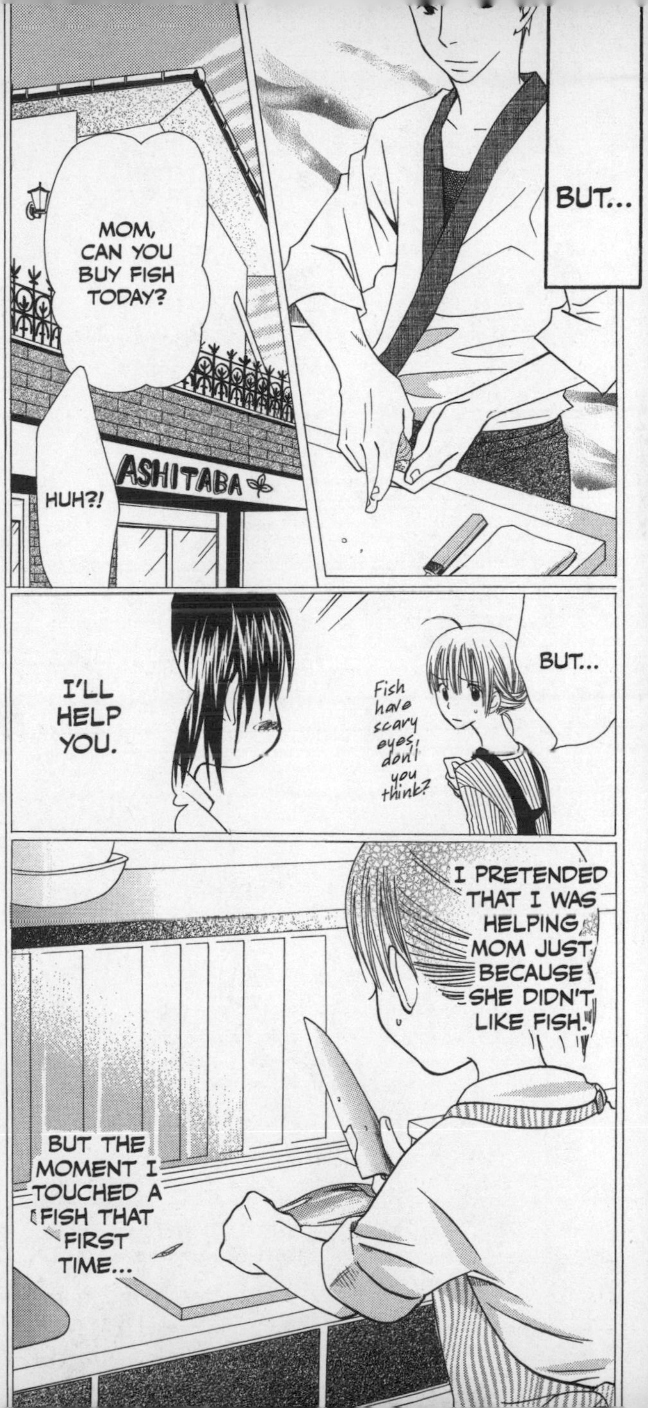
BUT...
MOM, CAN YOU BUY FISH TODAY?
HUH?!
BUT...
Fish have scary eyes, don't you think?
I'LL HELP YOU.
I PRETENDED THAT I WAS HELPING MOM JUST BECAUSE SHE DIDN'T LIKE FISH.
BUT THE MOMENT I TOUCHED A FISH THAT FIRST TIME...

Extra MV

Both father and daughter wear black to the sushi shop.

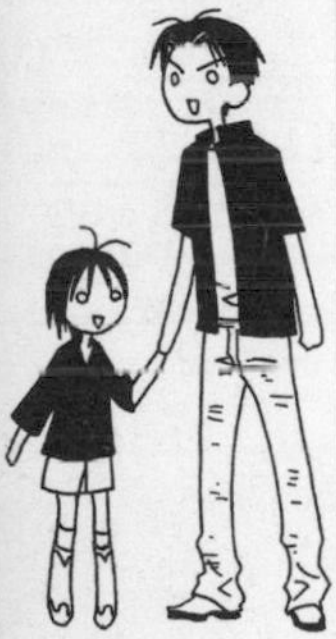
That's because you might get soy sauce on your shirt.

Please don't you spill on your shirt.

Huh?

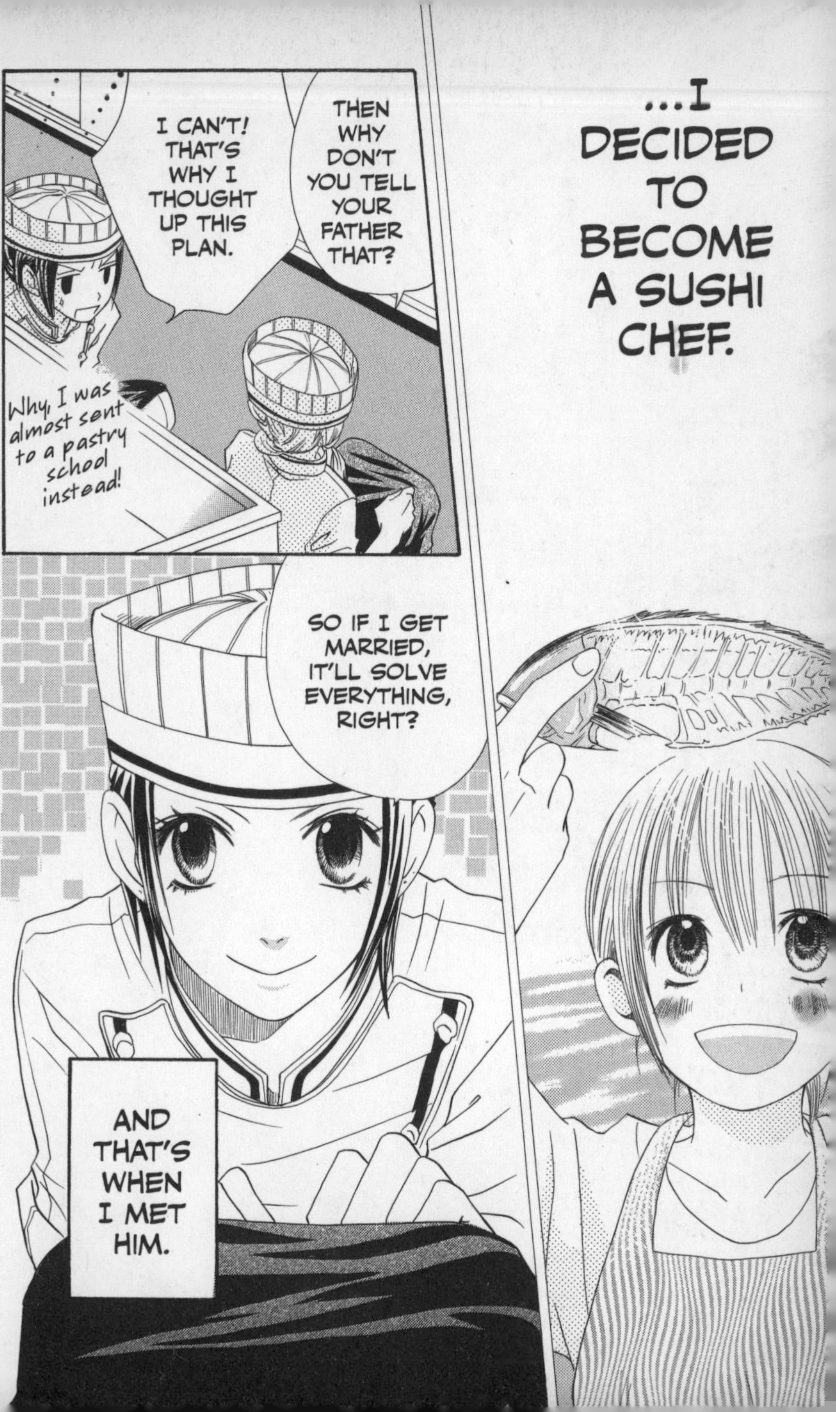
...I DECIDED TO BECOME A SUSHI CHEF.
THEN WHY DON'T YOU TELL YOUR FATHER THAT?
I CAN'T! THAT'S WHY I THOUGHT UP THIS PLAN.
Why, I was almost sent to a pastry school instead!
SO IF I GET MARRIED, IT'LL SOLVE EVERYTHING, RIGHT?
AND THAT'S WHEN I MET HIM.

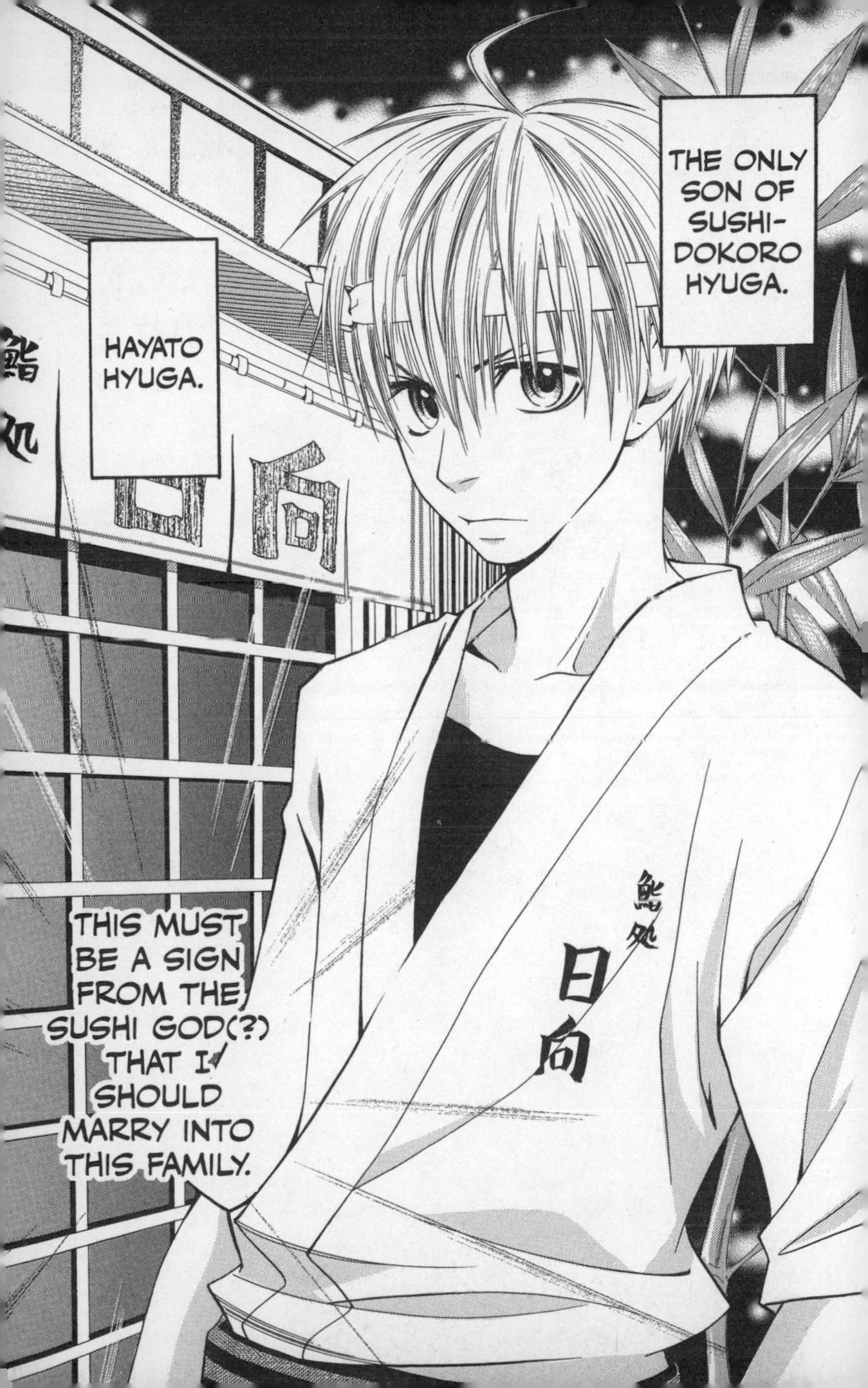
THE ONLY SON OF SUSHI-DOKORO HYUGA.
HAYATO HYUGA.
鮨処
日向
THIS MUST BE A SIGN FROM THE SUSHI GOD(?) THAT I SHOULD MARRY INTO THIS FAMILY.

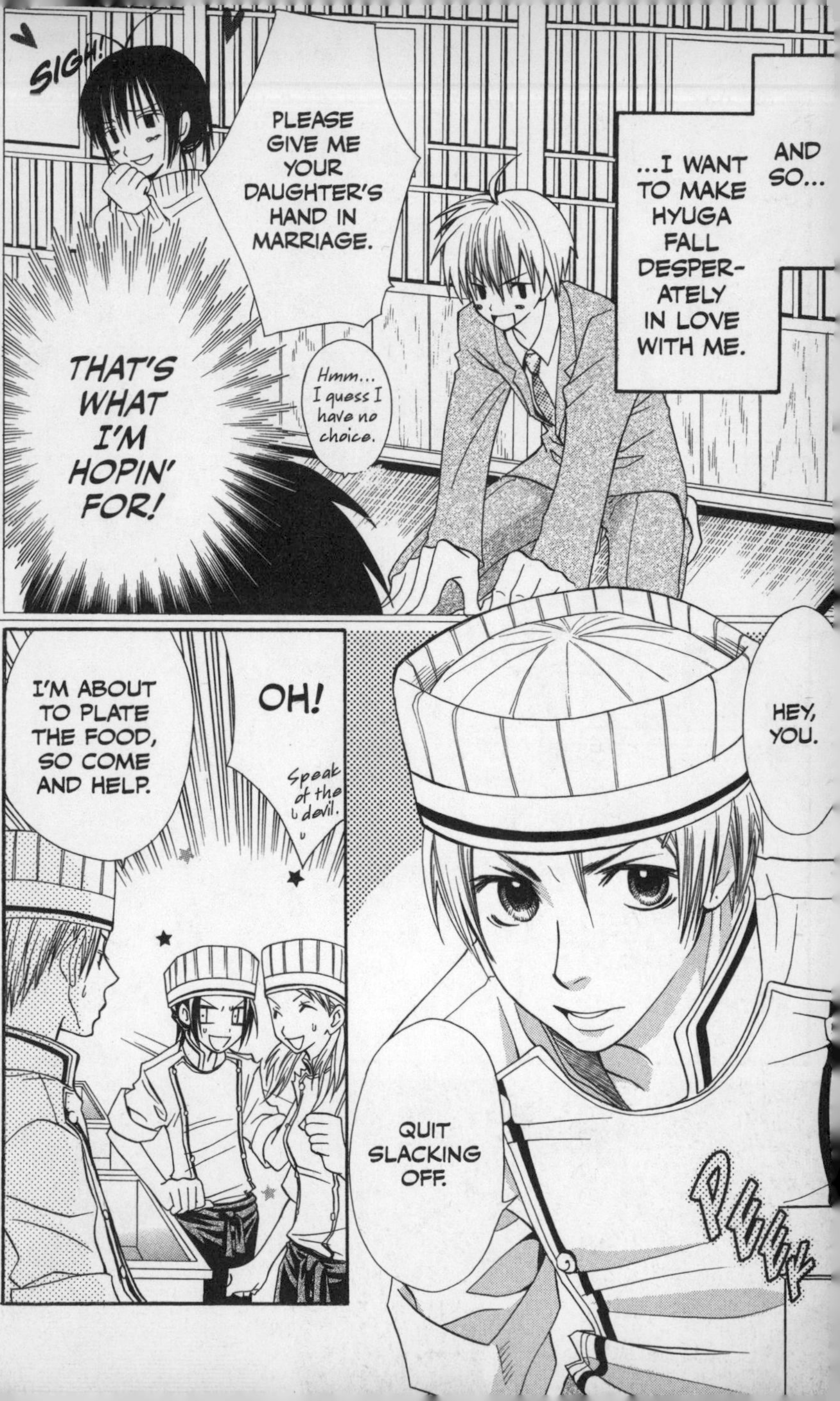
AND SO...
...I WANT TO MAKE HYUGA FALL DESPERATELY IN LOVE WITH ME.
PLEASE GIVE ME YOUR DAUGHTER'S HAND IN MARRIAGE.
SIGH!
Hmm... I guess I have no choice.
THAT'S WHAT I'M HOPIN' FOR!
HEY, YOU.
QUIT SLACKING OFF.
I'M ABOUT TO PLATE THE FOOD, SO COME AND HELP.
OH!
Speak of the devil.

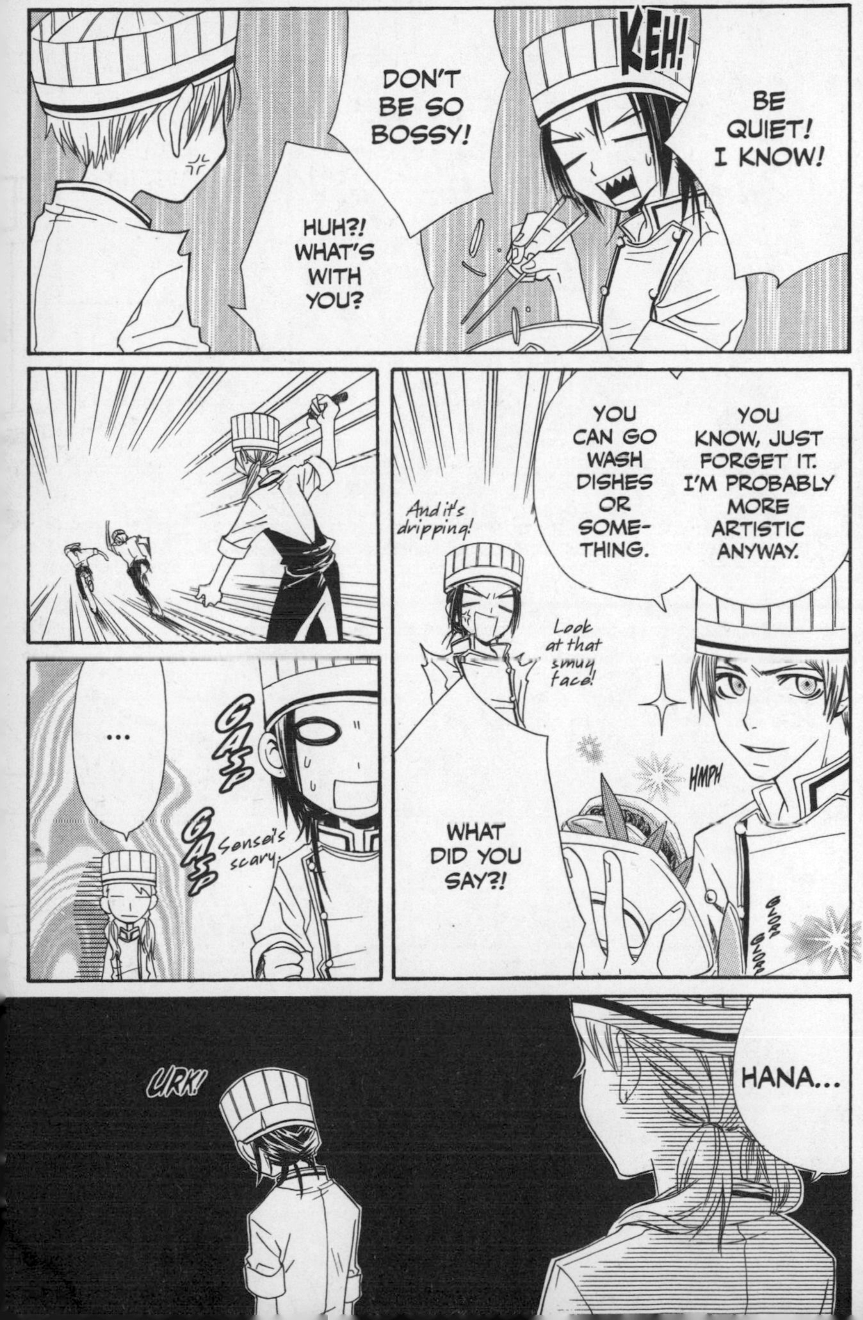
KEH!
BE QUIET! I KNOW!
DON'T BE SO BOSSY!
HUH?! WHAT'S WITH YOU?
YOU KNOW, JUST FORGET IT. I'M PROBABLY MORE ARTISTIC ANYWAY.
YOU CAN GO WASH DISHES OR SOME-THING.
And it's dripping!
Look at that smug face!
HMPH
WHAT DID YOU SAY?!
GLOM GLOM
GASP GASP
Sensei's scary.
...
HANA...
URK!

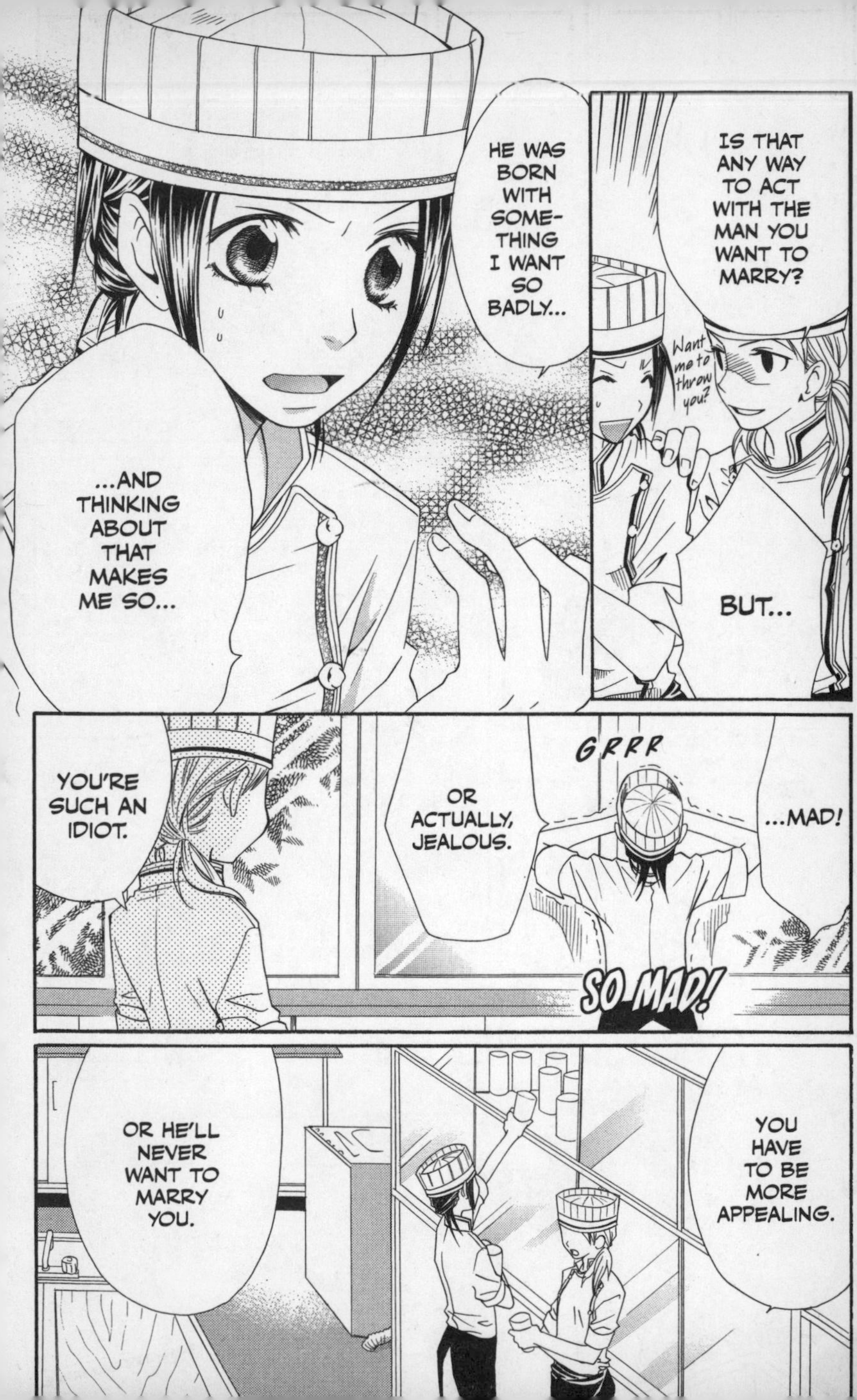
IS THAT ANY WAY TO ACT WITH THE MAN YOU WANT TO MARRY?
Want me to throw you?
BUT...
HE WAS BORN WITH SOME-THING I WANT SO BADLY...
...AND THINKING ABOUT THAT MAKES ME SO...
...MAD!
GRRR
SO MAD!
OR ACTUALLY, JEALOUS.
YOU'RE SUCH AN IDIOT.
YOU HAVE TO BE MORE APPEALING.
OR HE'LL NEVER WANT TO MARRY YOU.

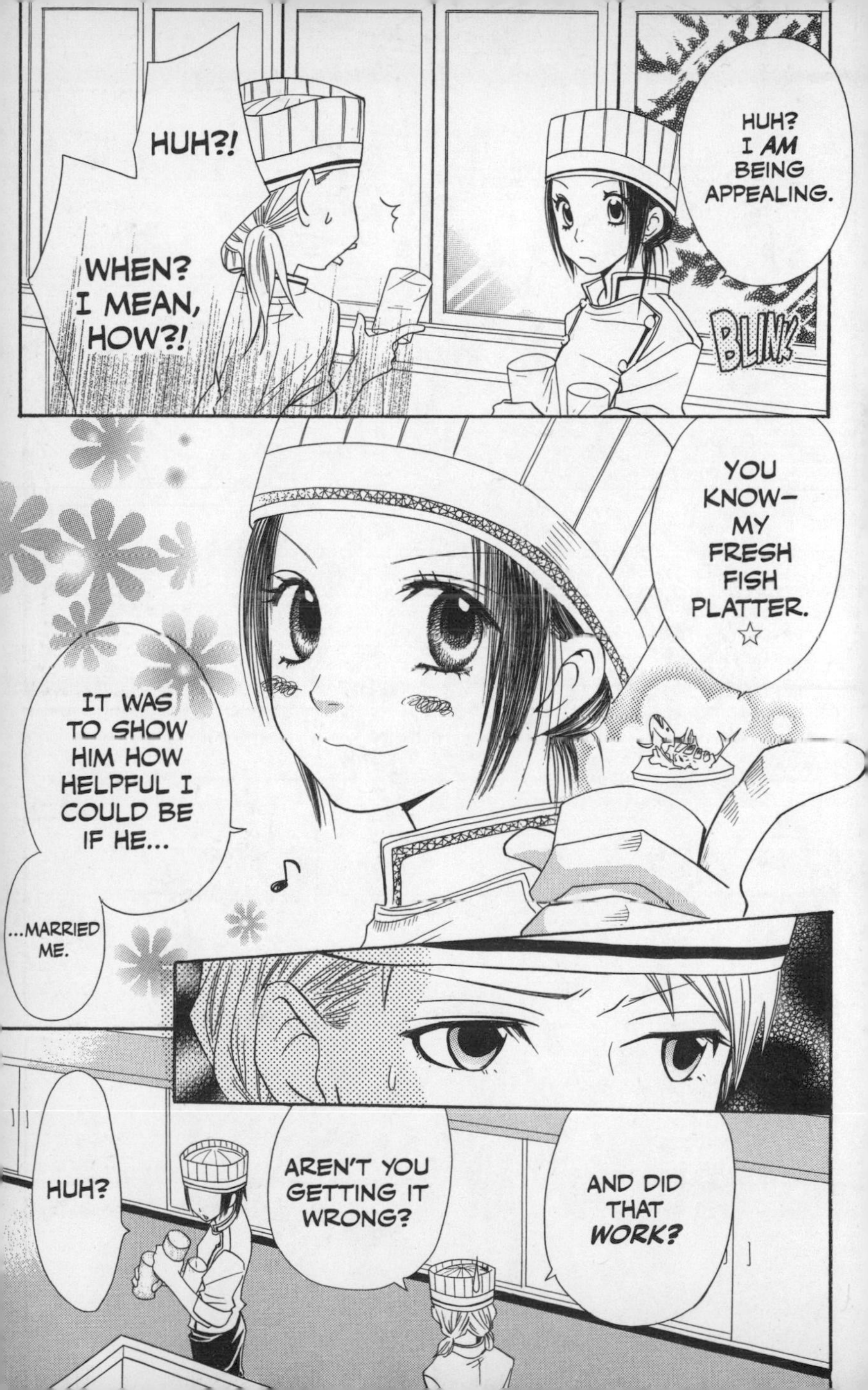
HUH? I *AM* BEING APPEALING.
BLINK
HUH?!
WHEN? I MEAN, HOW?!
YOU KNOW— MY FRESH FISH PLATTER. ☆
IT WAS TO SHOW HIM HOW HELPFUL I COULD BE IF HE...
...MARRIED ME.
AND DID THAT *WORK?*
AREN'T YOU GETTING IT WRONG?
HUH?

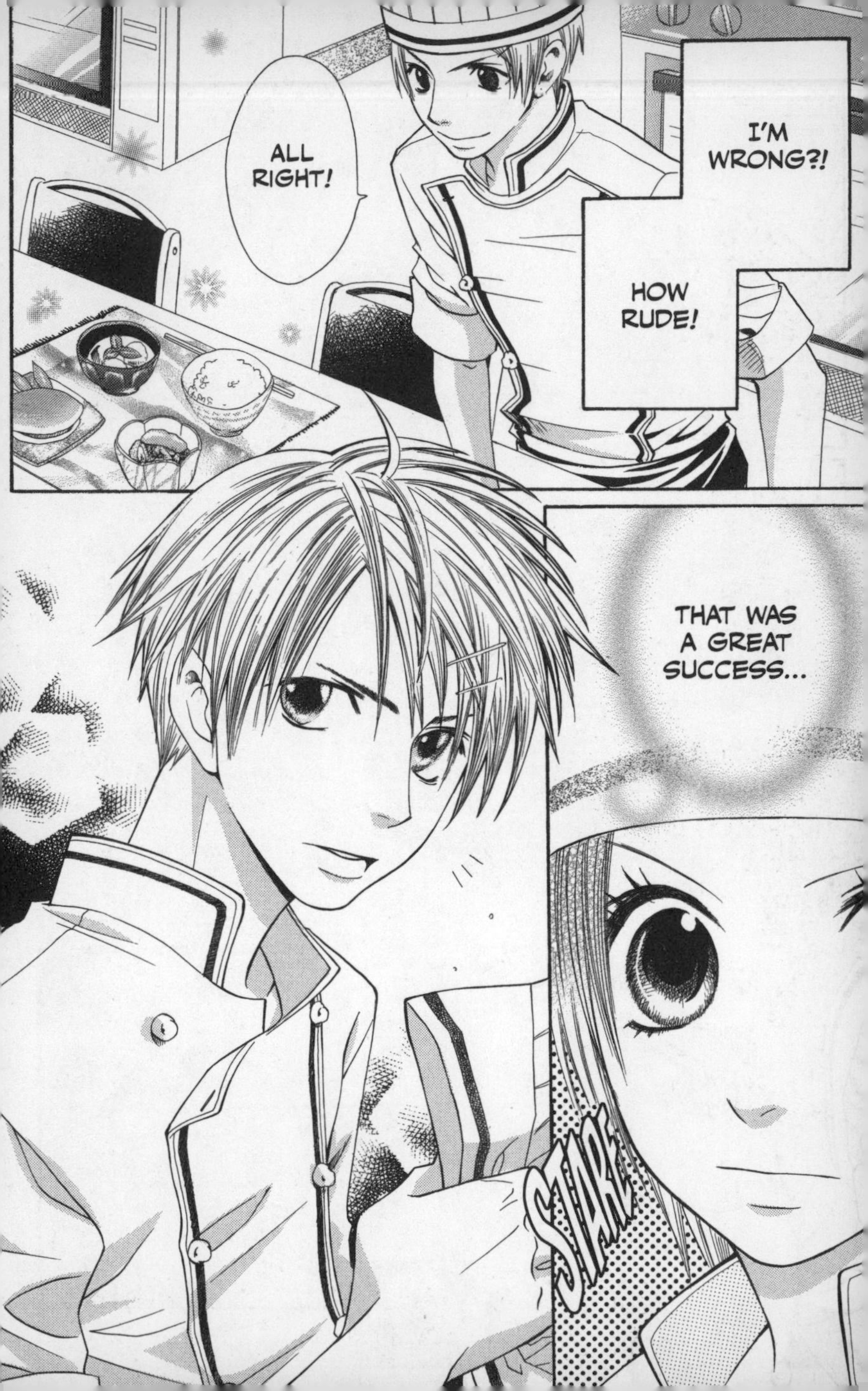
I'M WRONG?!
HOW RUDE!
ALL RIGHT!
THAT WAS A GREAT SUCCESS...
STARE

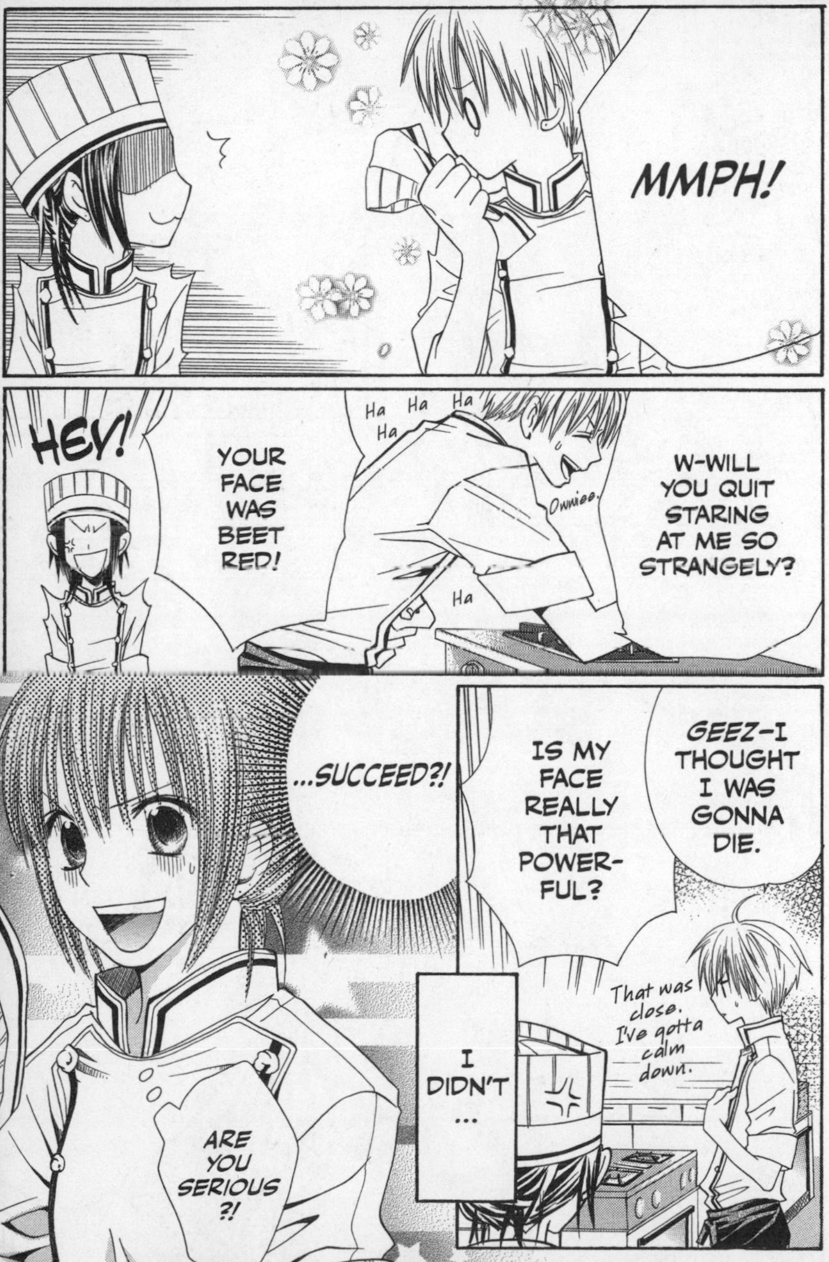
MMPH!
W-WILL YOU QUIT STARING AT ME SO STRANGELY?
Ha Ha Ha Ha
Owwiee.
Ha
HEY!
YOUR FACE WAS BEET RED!
GEEZ—I THOUGHT I WAS GONNA DIE.
IS MY FACE REALLY THAT POWERFUL?
That was close. I've gotta calm down.
I DIDN'T ...
...SUCCEED?!
ARE YOU SERIOUS ?!

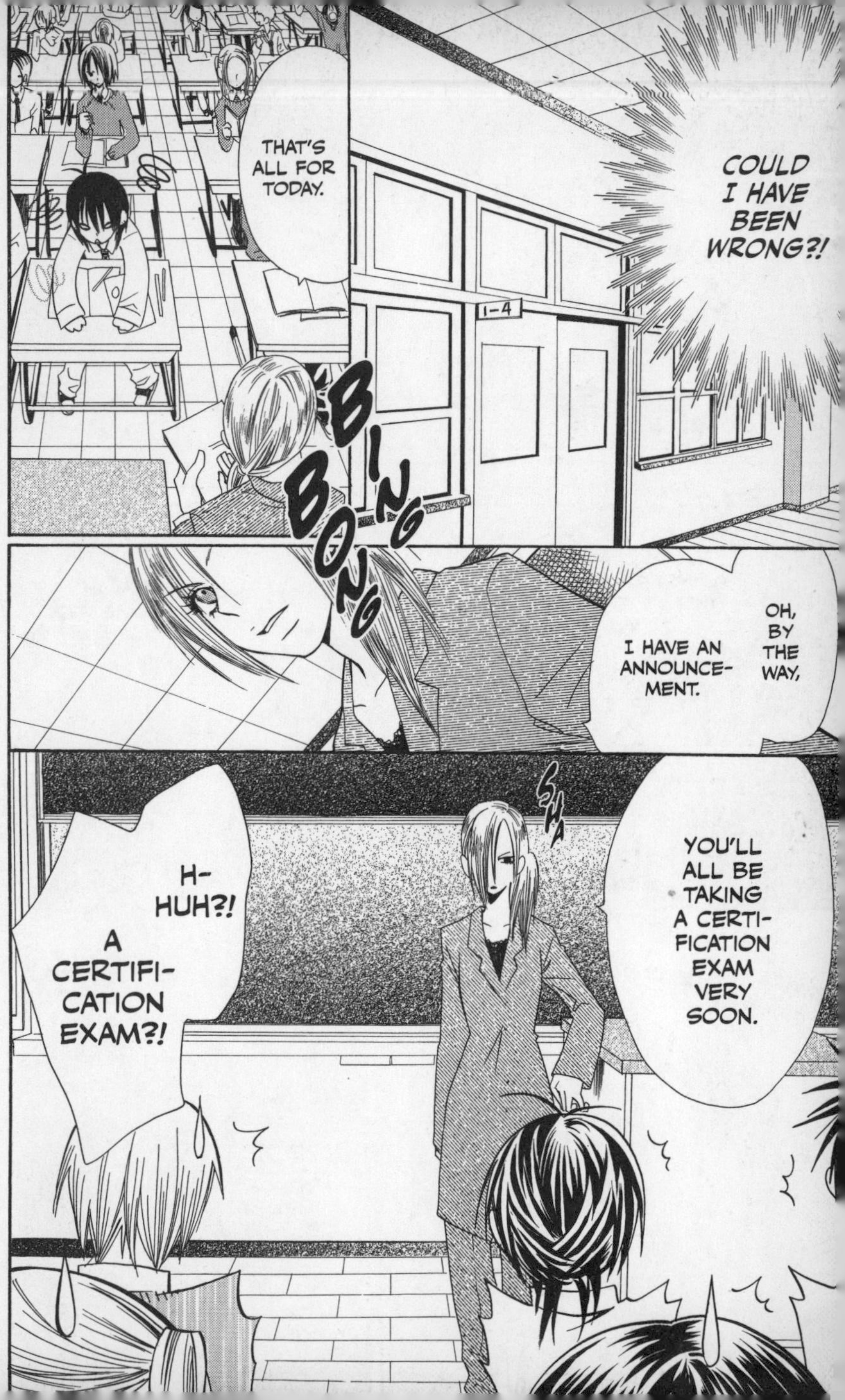
COULD I HAVE BEEN WRONG?!
THAT'S ALL FOR TODAY.
BING BONG
OH, BY THE WAY,
I HAVE AN ANNOUNCEMENT.
YOU'LL ALL BE TAKING A CERTIFICATION EXAM VERY SOON.
SHA
H-HUH?!
A CERTIFICATION EXAM?!

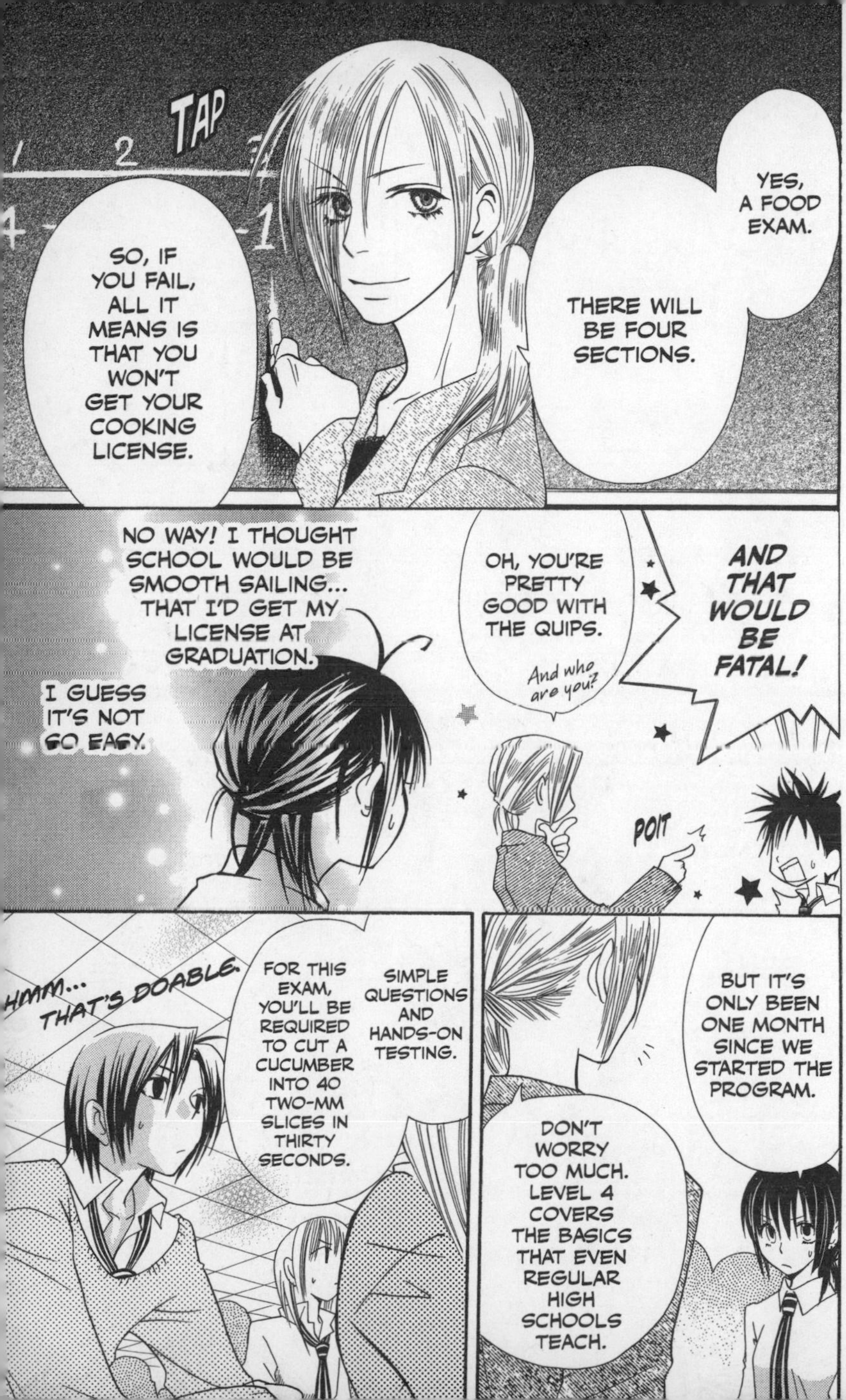
YES, A FOOD EXAM.
THERE WILL BE FOUR SECTIONS.
TAP
SO, IF YOU FAIL, ALL IT MEANS IS THAT YOU WON'T GET YOUR COOKING LICENSE.
AND THAT WOULD BE FATAL!
OH, YOU'RE PRETTY GOOD WITH THE QUIPS.
And who are you?
POIT
NO WAY! I THOUGHT SCHOOL WOULD BE SMOOTH SAILING... THAT I'D GET MY LICENSE AT GRADUATION.
I GUESS IT'S NOT SO EASY.
BUT IT'S ONLY BEEN ONE MONTH SINCE WE STARTED THE PROGRAM.
DON'T WORRY TOO MUCH. LEVEL 4 COVERS THE BASICS THAT EVEN REGULAR HIGH SCHOOLS TEACH.
SIMPLE QUESTIONS AND HANDS-ON TESTING.
FOR THIS EXAM, YOU'LL BE REQUIRED TO CUT A CUCUMBER INTO 40 TWO-MM SLICES IN THIRTY SECONDS.
HMM... THAT'S DOABLE.

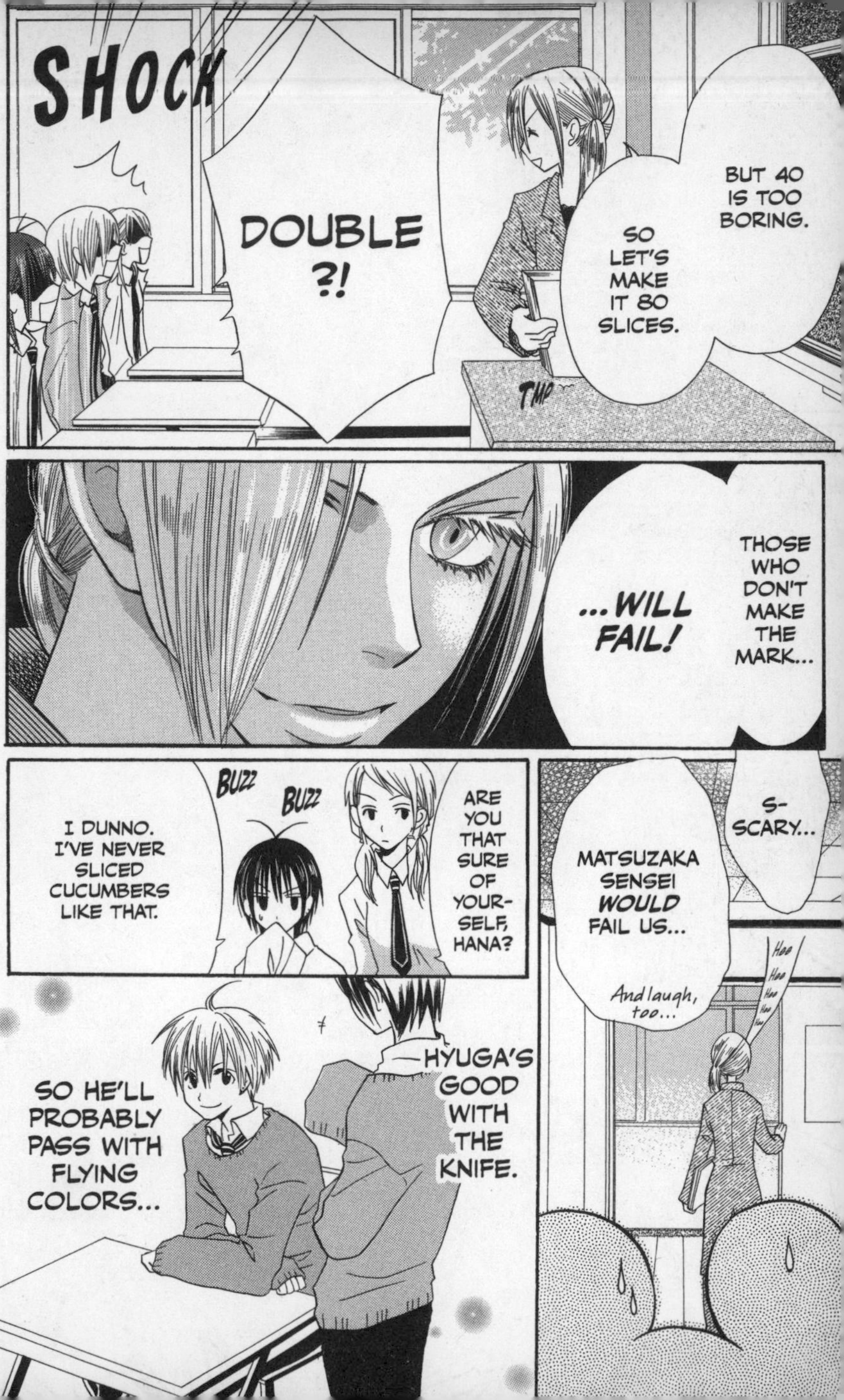
BUT 40 IS TOO BORING.
SO LET'S MAKE IT 80 SLICES.
TMP
SHOCK
DOUBLE ?!
THOSE WHO DON'T MAKE THE MARK...
...WILL FAIL!
S-SCARY...
MATSUZAKA SENSEI WOULD FAIL US...
And laugh, too...
BUZZ
BUZZ
ARE YOU THAT SURE OF YOURSELF, HANA?
I DUNNO. I'VE NEVER SLICED CUCUMBERS LIKE THAT.
HYUGA'S GOOD WITH THE KNIFE.
SO HE'LL PROBABLY PASS WITH FLYING COLORS...

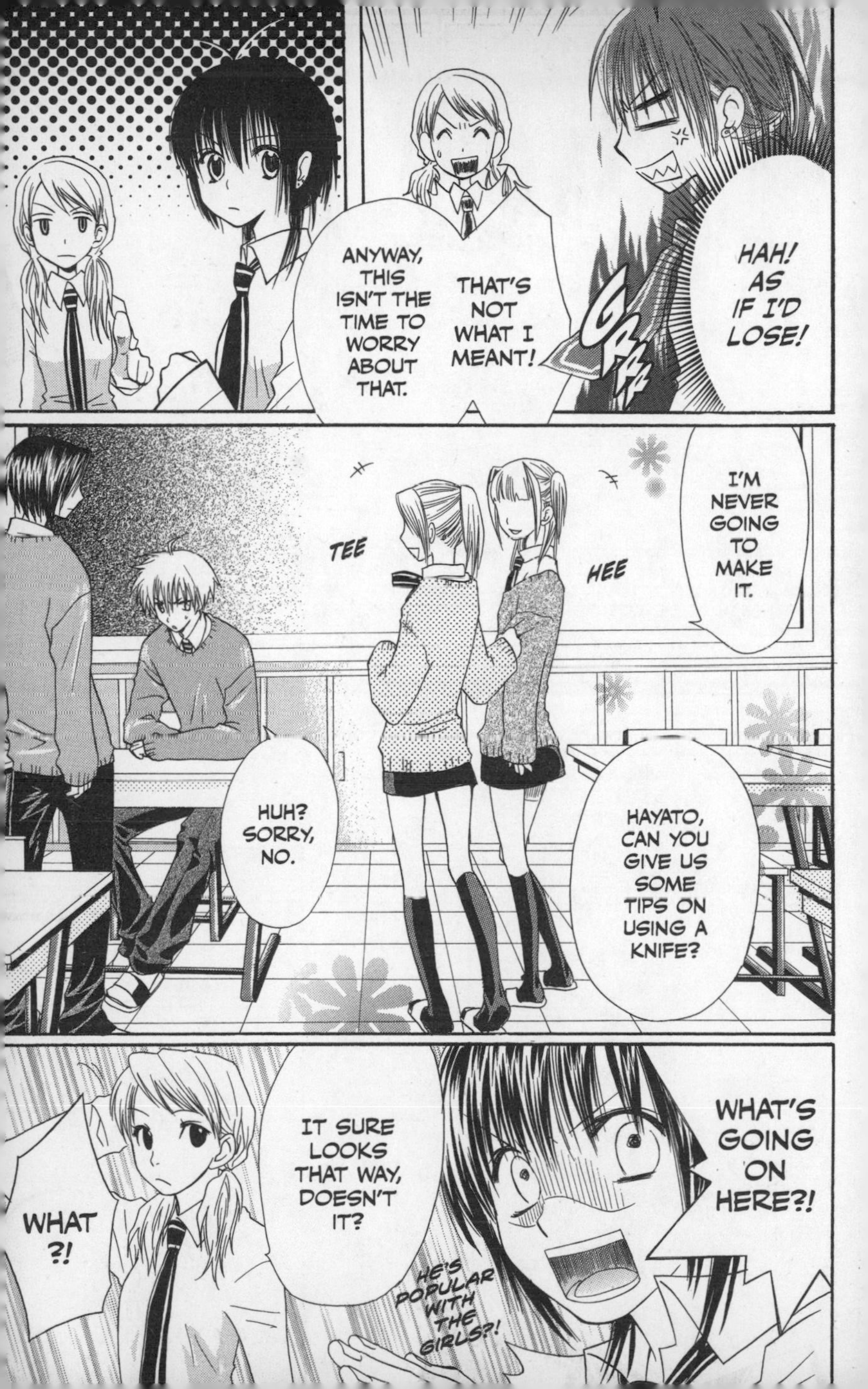
HAH! AS IF I'D LOSE!
THAT'S NOT WHAT I MEANT!
ANYWAY, THIS ISN'T THE TIME TO WORRY ABOUT THAT.
I'M NEVER GOING TO MAKE IT.
HEE
TEE
HAYATO, CAN YOU GIVE US SOME TIPS ON USING A KNIFE?
HUH? SORRY, NO.
WHAT'S GOING ON HERE?!
HE'S POPULAR WITH THE GIRLS?!
IT SURE LOOKS THAT WAY, DOESN'T IT?
WHAT ?!

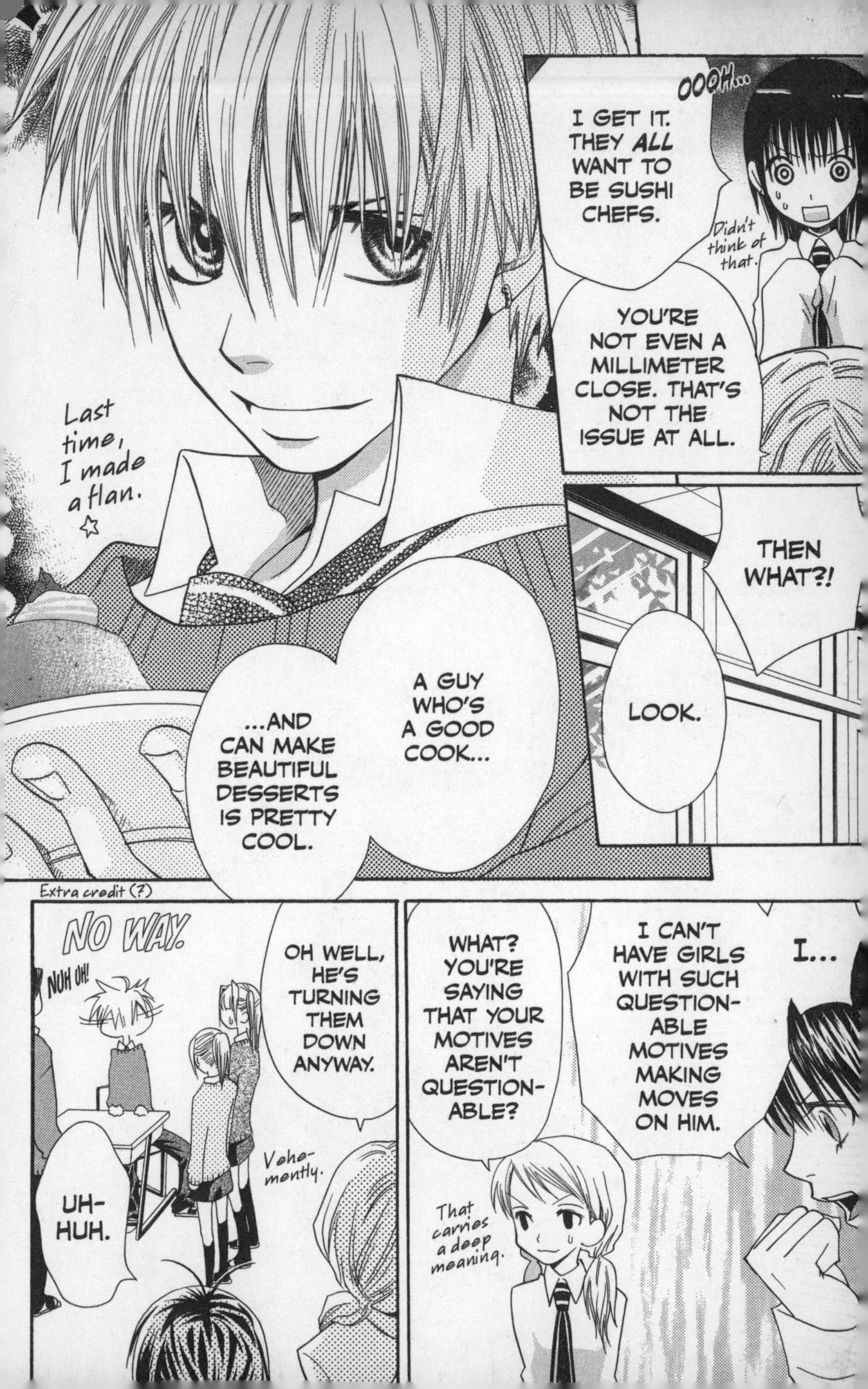
OOOH...
I GET IT. THEY ALL WANT TO BE SUSHI CHEFS.
Didn't think of that.
YOU'RE NOT EVEN A MILLIMETER CLOSE. THAT'S NOT THE ISSUE AT ALL.
THEN WHAT?!
LOOK.
A GUY WHO'S A GOOD COOK...
...AND CAN MAKE BEAUTIFUL DESSERTS IS PRETTY COOL.
Last time, I made a flan. ☆
Extra credit (?)
I...
I CAN'T HAVE GIRLS WITH SUCH QUESTION-ABLE MOTIVES MAKING MOVES ON HIM.
WHAT? YOU'RE SAYING THAT YOUR MOTIVES AREN'T QUESTION-ABLE?
That carries a deep meaning.
OH WELL, HE'S TURNING THEM DOWN ANYWAY.
Vehe-mently.
NO WAY.
NUH UH!
UH-HUH.

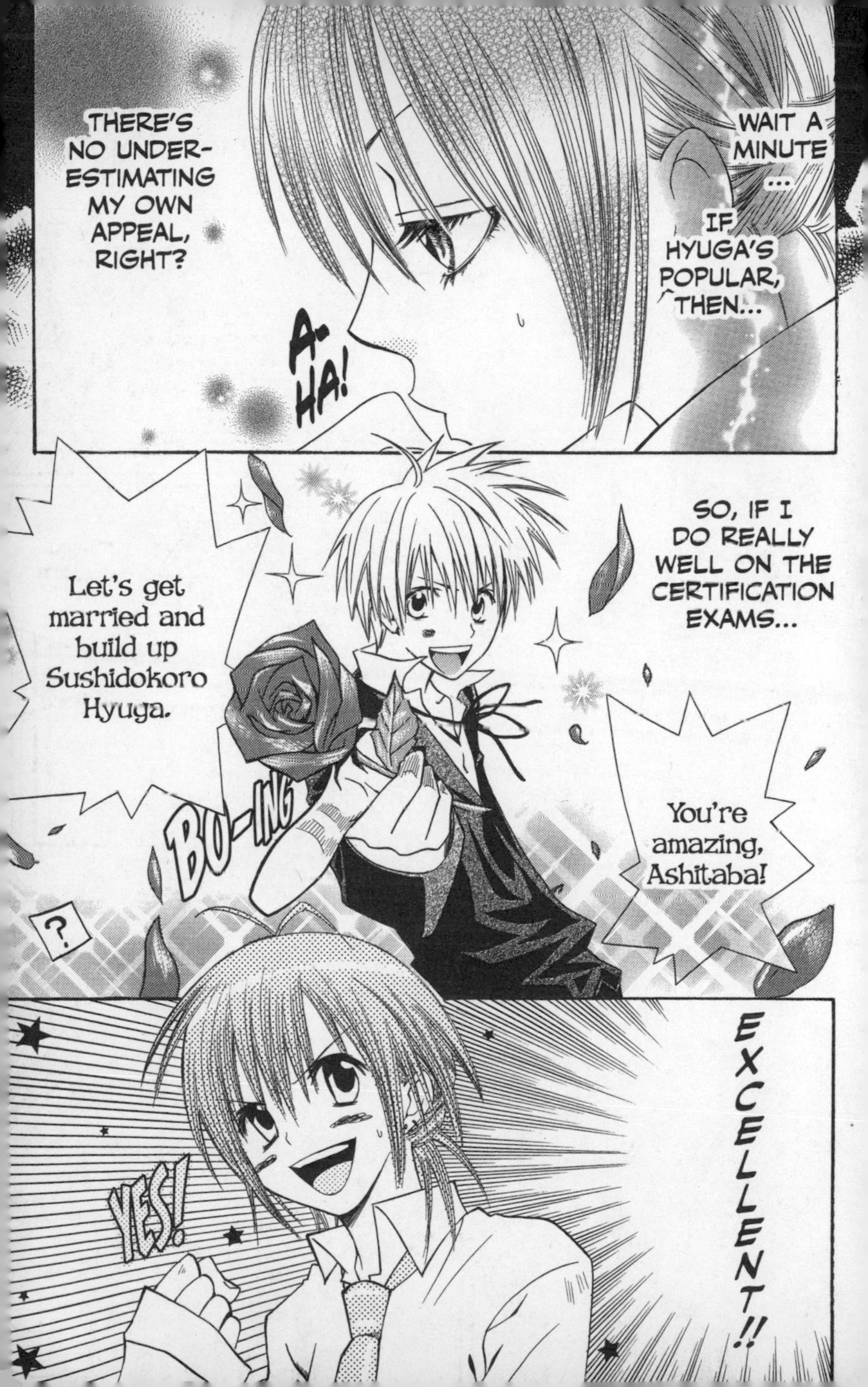
WAIT A MINUTE...
IF HYUGA'S POPULAR, THEN...
THERE'S NO UNDER-ESTIMATING MY OWN APPEAL, RIGHT?
A-HA!
SO, IF I DO REALLY WELL ON THE CERTIFICATION EXAMS...
You're amazing, Ashitaba!
Let's get married and build up Sushidokoro Hyuga.
BO-ING
?
EXCELLENT!!
YES!

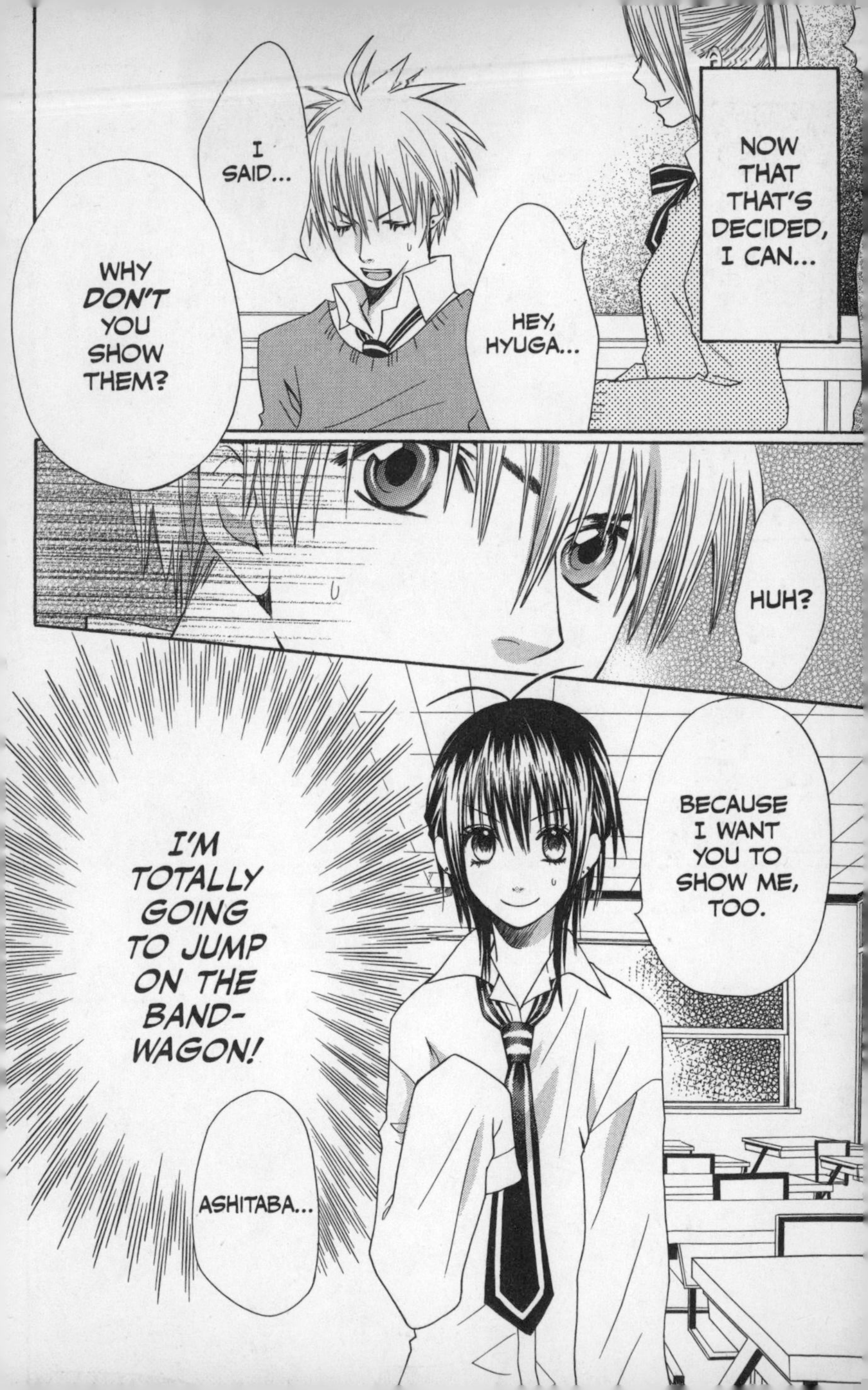
NOW THAT THAT'S DECIDED, I CAN...
HEY, HYUGA...
I SAID...
WHY DON'T YOU SHOW THEM?
HUH?
BECAUSE I WANT YOU TO SHOW ME, TOO.
I'M TOTALLY GOING TO JUMP ON THE BAND-WAGON!
ASHITABA...

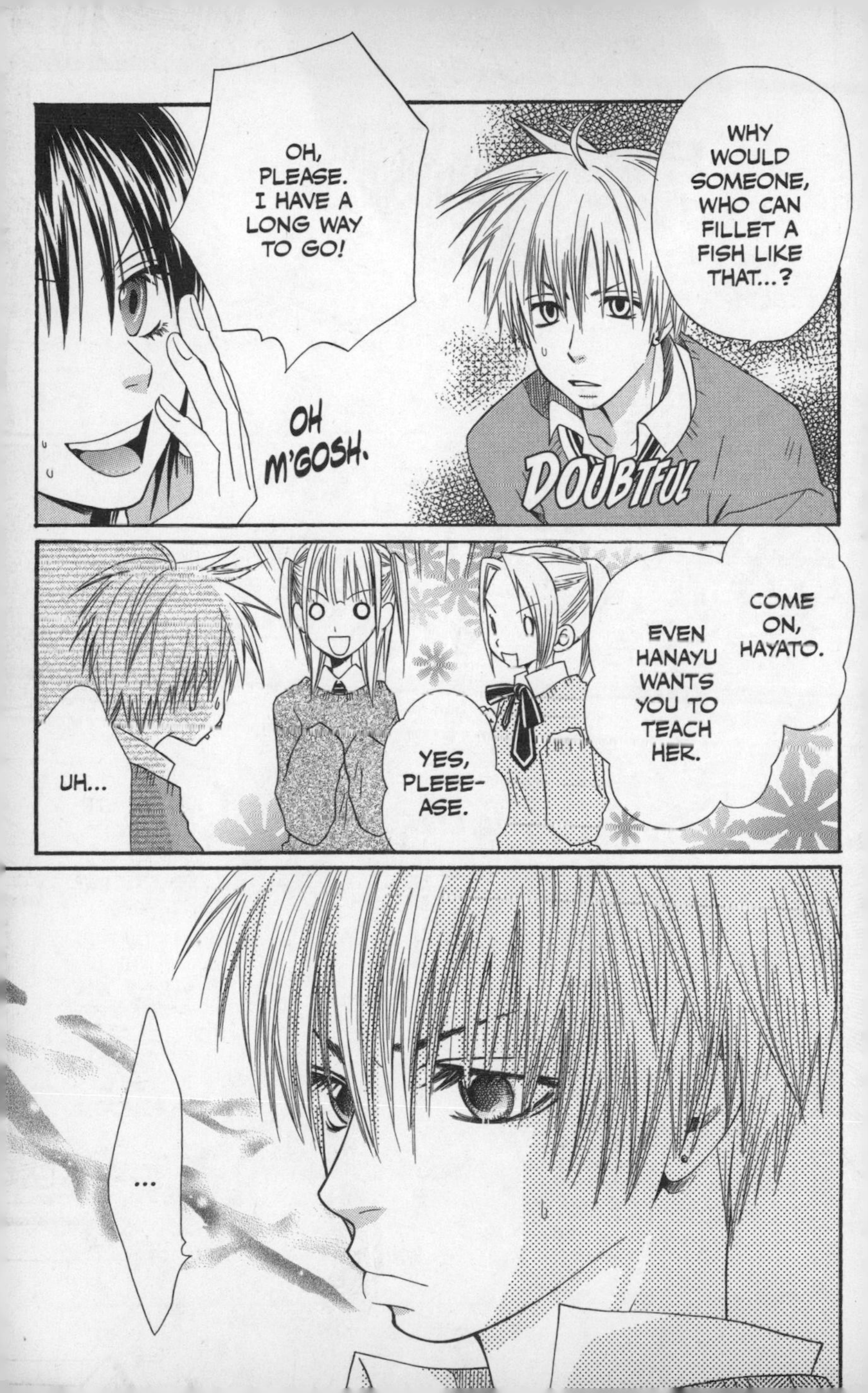
WHY WOULD SOMEONE, WHO CAN FILLET A FISH LIKE THAT...?
DOUBTFUL
OH, PLEASE. I HAVE A LONG WAY TO GO!
OH M'GOSH.
COME ON, HAYATO.
EVEN HANAYU WANTS YOU TO TEACH HER.
YES, PLEEE-ASE.
UH...
...

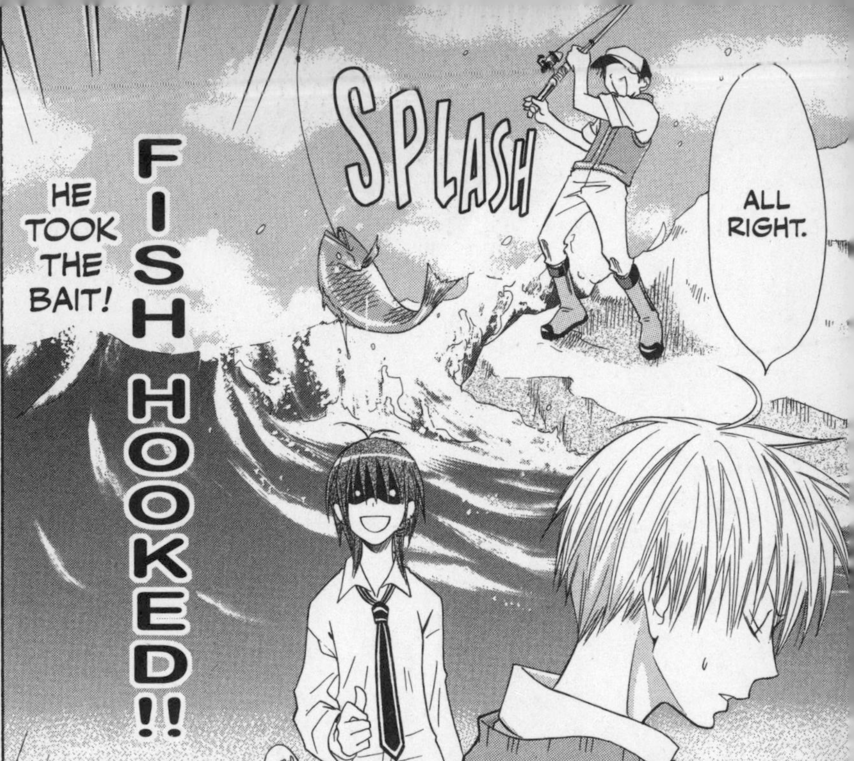
ALL RIGHT.
SPLASH
HE TOOK THE BAIT!
FISH HOOKED!!
SNIK
Yes!
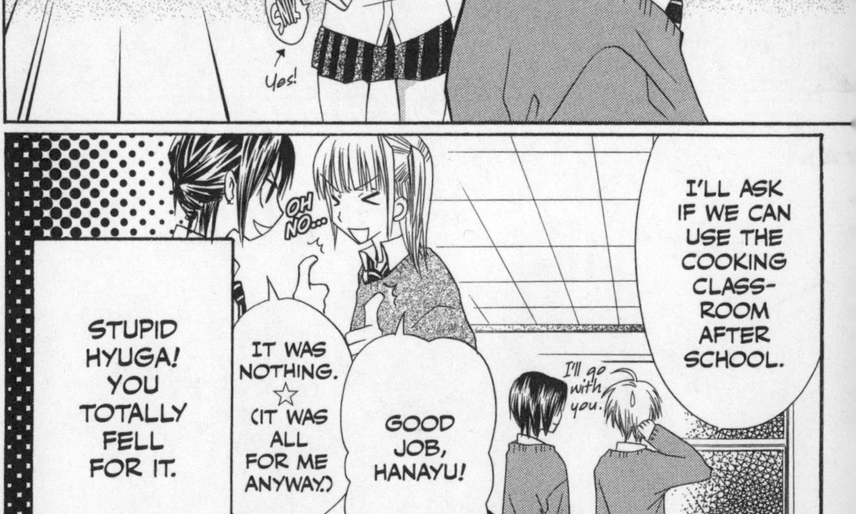
I'LL ASK IF WE CAN USE THE COOKING CLASS-ROOM AFTER SCHOOL.
I'll go with you.
GOOD JOB, HANAYU!
IT WAS NOTHING. ☆ (IT WAS ALL FOR ME ANYWAY.)
OH NO...
STUPID HYUGA! YOU TOTALLY FELL FOR IT.

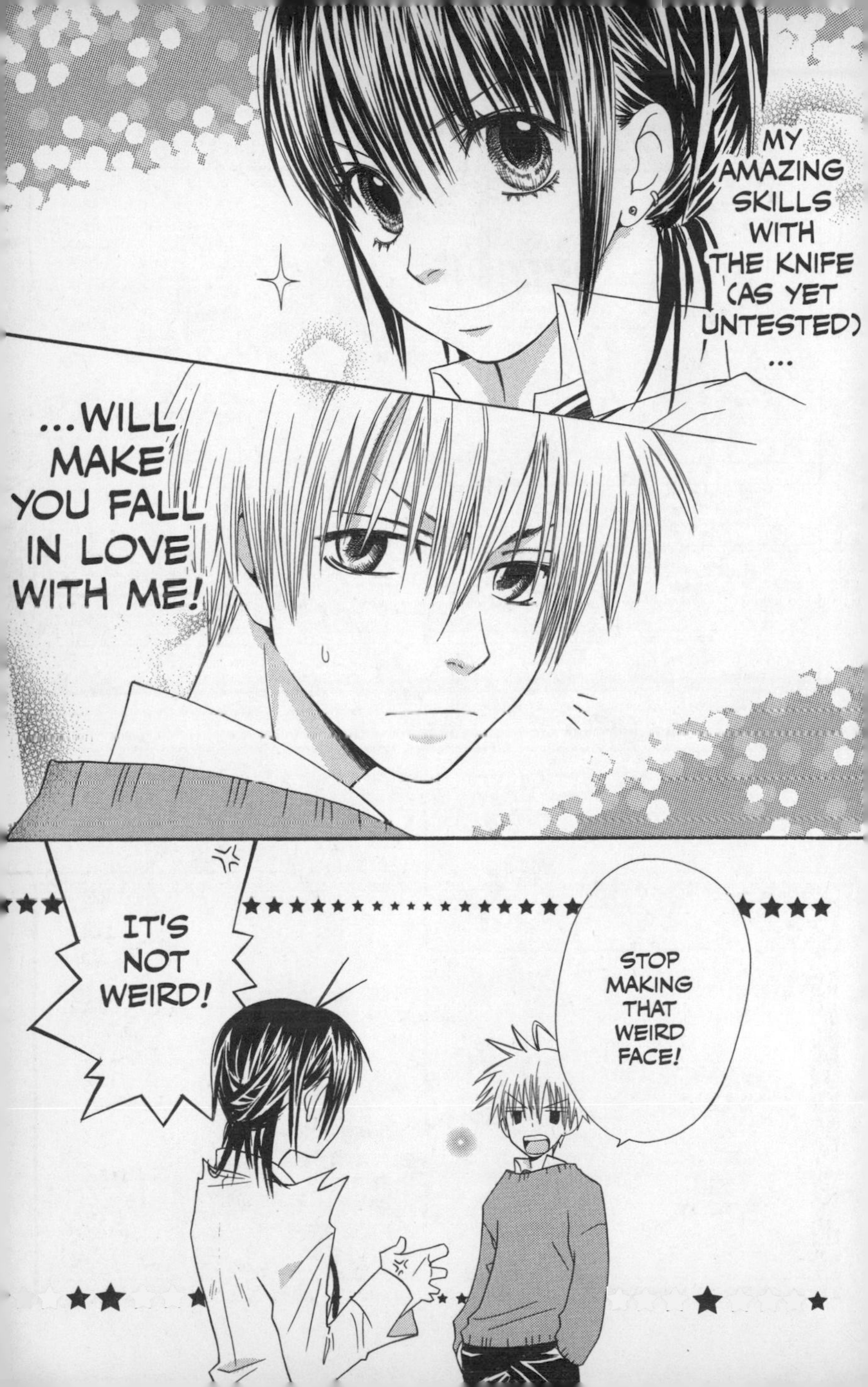
MY AMAZING SKILLS WITH THE KNIFE (AS YET UNTESTED)...
...WILL MAKE YOU FALL IN LOVE WITH ME!
STOP MAKING THAT WEIRD FACE!
IT'S NOT WEIRD!

SIDE DISH Mixed Vegetables 1

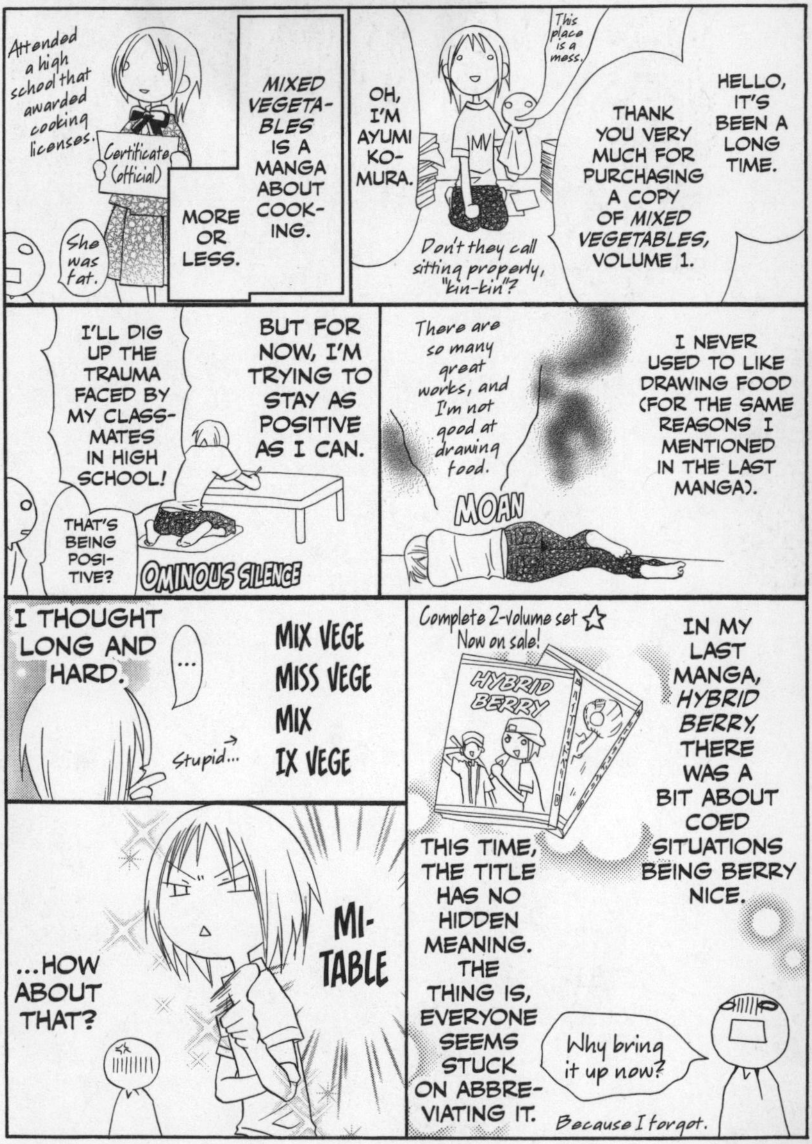
HELLO, IT'S BEEN A LONG TIME.
THANK YOU VERY MUCH FOR PURCHASING A COPY OF MIXED VEGETABLES, VOLUME 1.
This place is a mess.
OH, I'M AYUMI KOMURA.
Don't they call sitting properly, "kin-kin"?
MIXED VEGETABLES IS A MANGA ABOUT COOKING.
MORE OR LESS.
Attended a high school that awarded cooking licenses.
Certificate (official)
She was fat.
I NEVER USED TO LIKE DRAWING FOOD (FOR THE SAME REASONS I MENTIONED IN THE LAST MANGA).
There are so many great works, and I'm not good at drawing food.
MOAN
BUT FOR NOW, I'M TRYING TO STAY AS POSITIVE AS I CAN.
I'LL DIG UP THE TRAUMA FACED BY MY CLASSMATES IN HIGH SCHOOL!
THAT'S BEING POSITIVE?
OMINOUS SILENCE
IN MY LAST MANGA, HYBRID BERRY, THERE WAS A BIT ABOUT COED SITUATIONS BEING BERRY NICE.
Complete 2-volume set ☆ Now on sale!
HYBRID BERRY
THIS TIME, THE TITLE HAS NO HIDDEN MEANING. THE THING IS, EVERYONE SEEMS STUCK ON ABBREVIATING IT.
Why bring it up now?
Because I forgot.
MIX VEGE
MISS VEGE
MIX
IX VEGE
I THOUGHT LONG AND HARD.
...
Stupid...
MI-TABLE
...HOW ABOUT THAT?

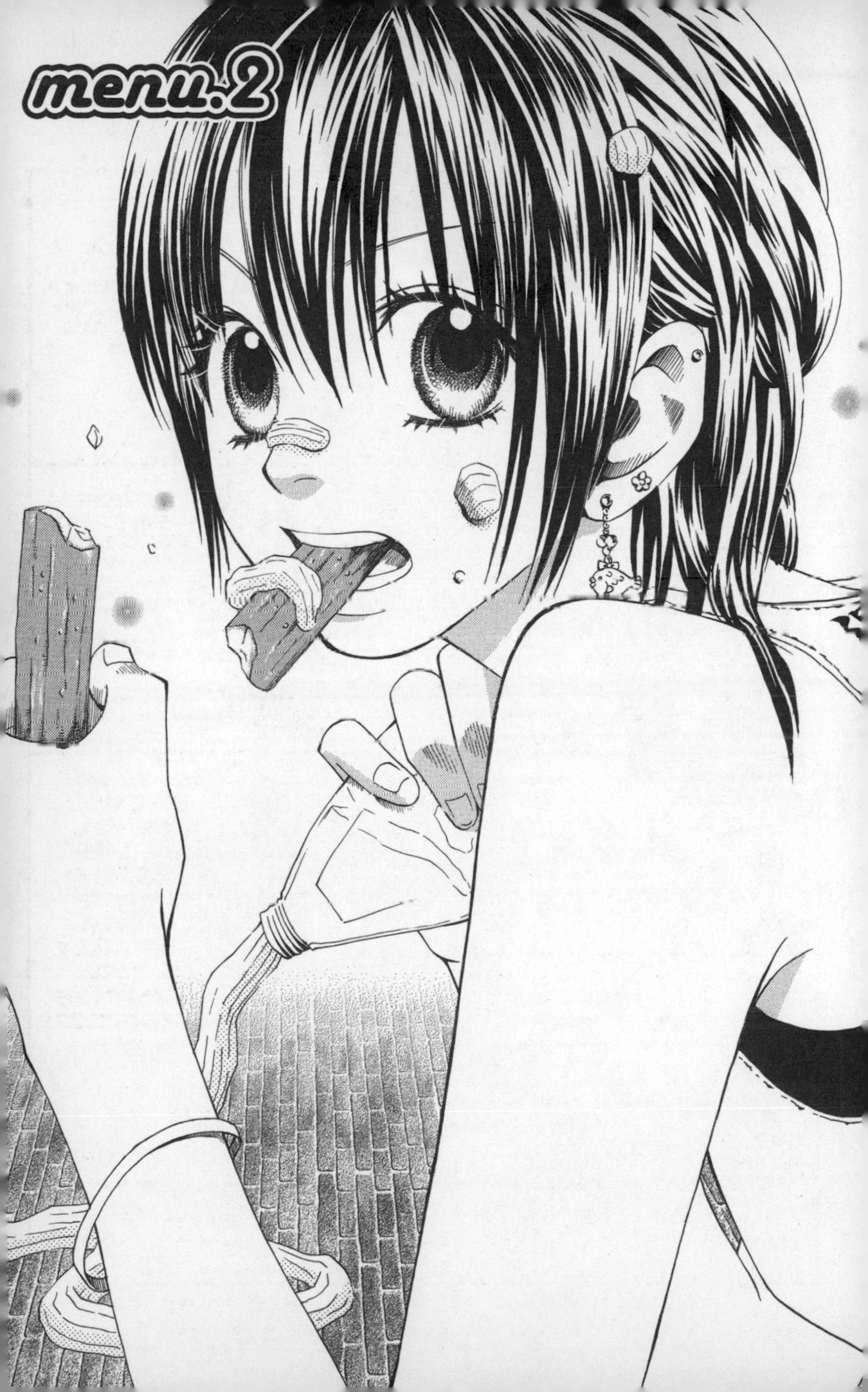
menu.2

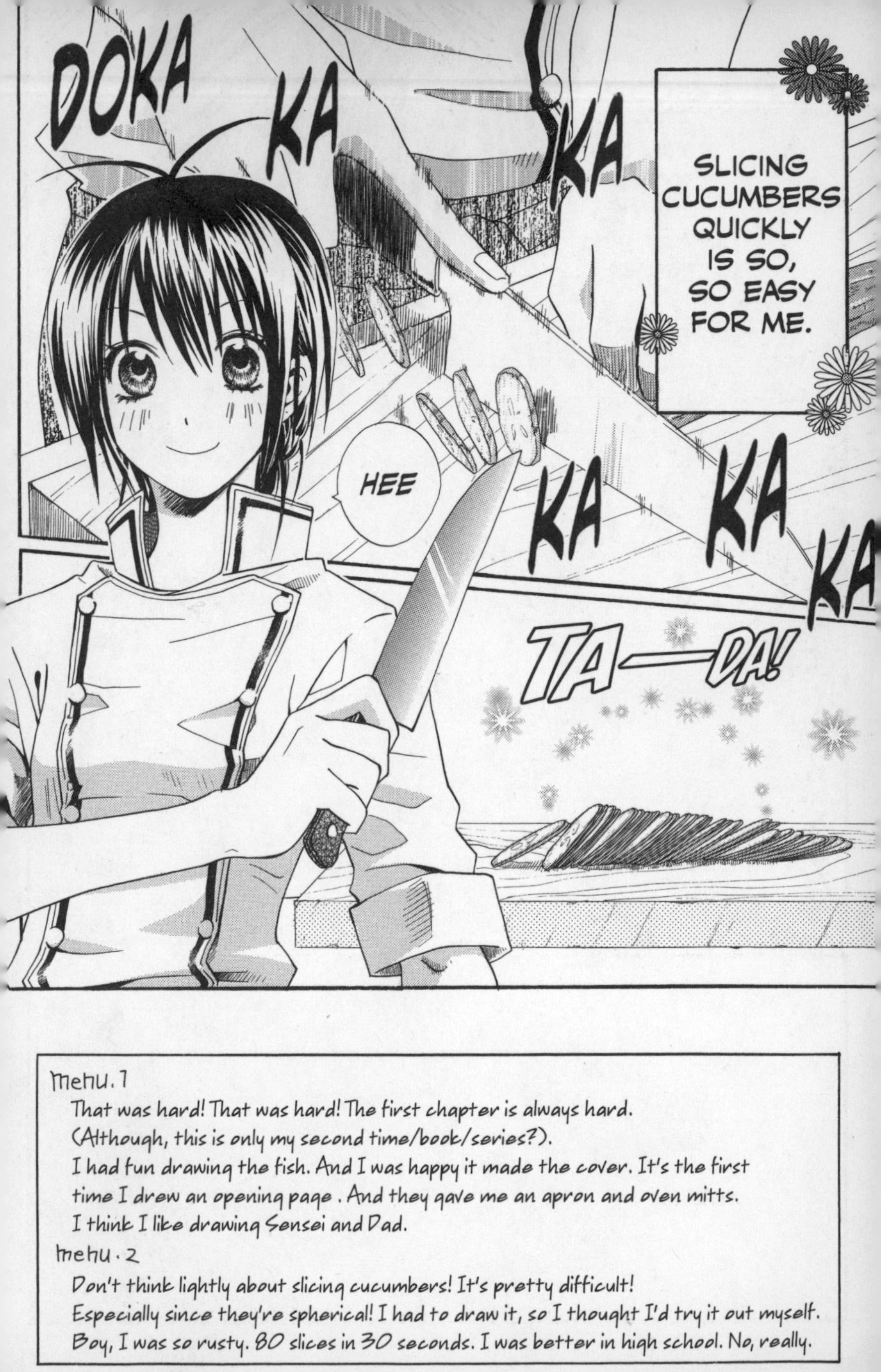
SLICING CUCUMBERS QUICKLY IS SO, SO EASY FOR ME.
DOKA
KA
KA
HEE
KA
KA
KA
TA—DA!

menu. 1

That was hard! That was hard! The first chapter is always hard.
(Although, this is only my second time/book/series?).
I had fun drawing the fish. And I was happy it made the cover. It's the first time I drew an opening page . And they gave me an apron and oven mitts.
I think I like drawing Sensei and Dad.

menu . 2

Don't think lightly about slicing cucumbers! It's pretty difficult!
Especially since they're spherical! I had to draw it, so I thought I'd try it out myself.
Boy, I was so rusty. 80 slices in 30 seconds. I was better in high school. No, really.

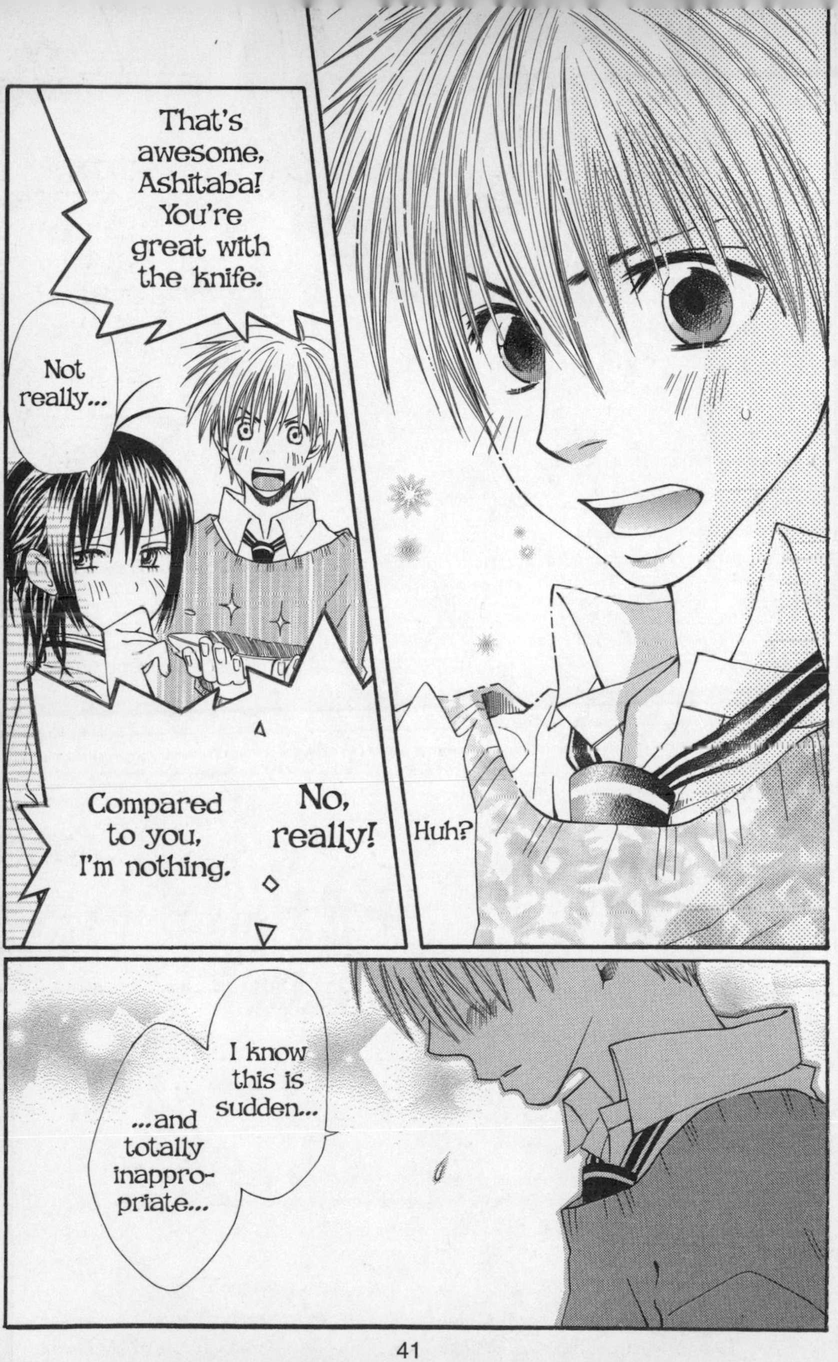
That's awesome, Ashitaba! You're great with the knife.
Not really...
No, really!
Compared to you, I'm nothing.
Huh?
I know this is sudden...
...and totally inappropriate...

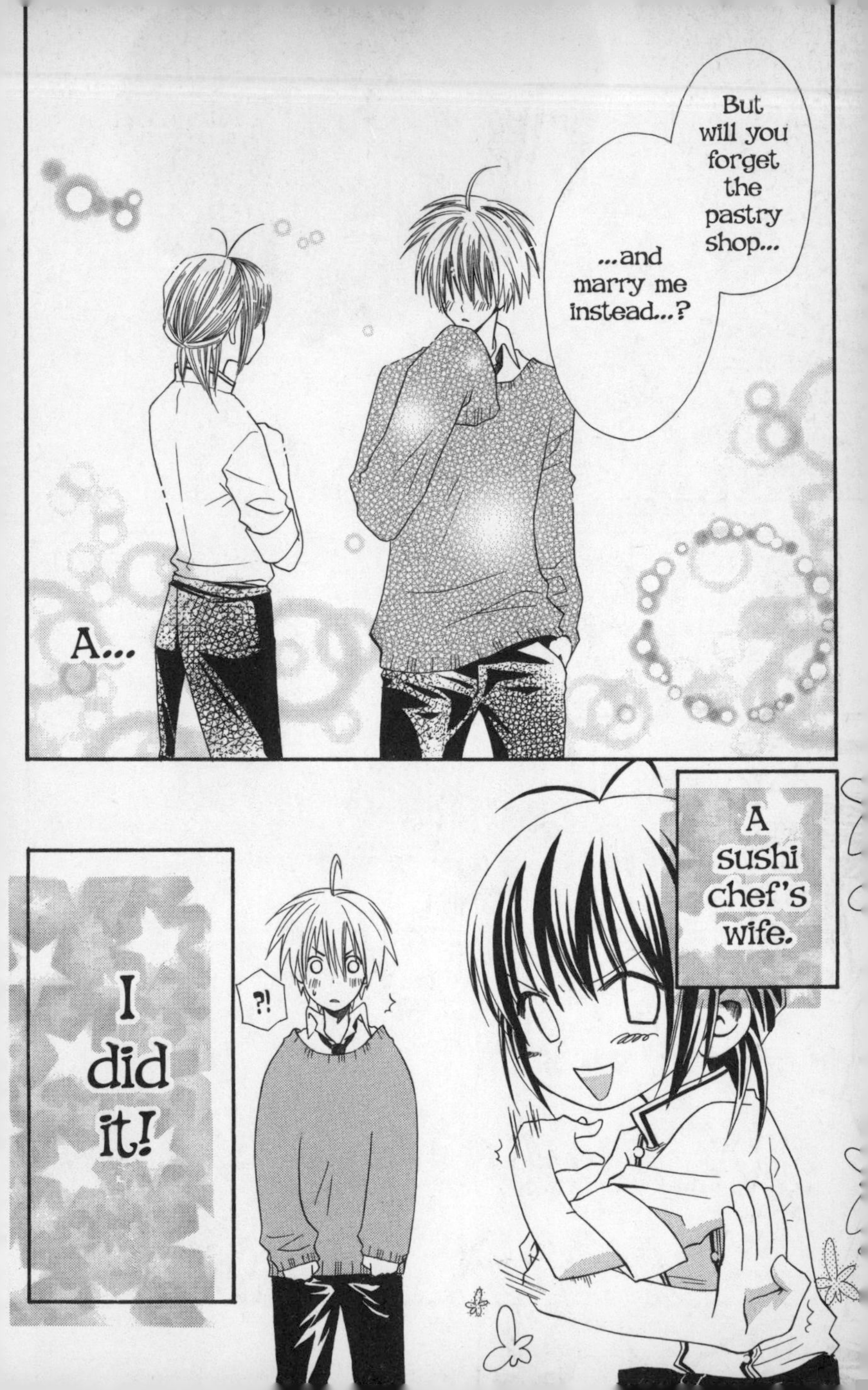
But will you forget the pastry shop...
...and marry me instead...?
A...
A sushi chef's wife.
?!
I did it!

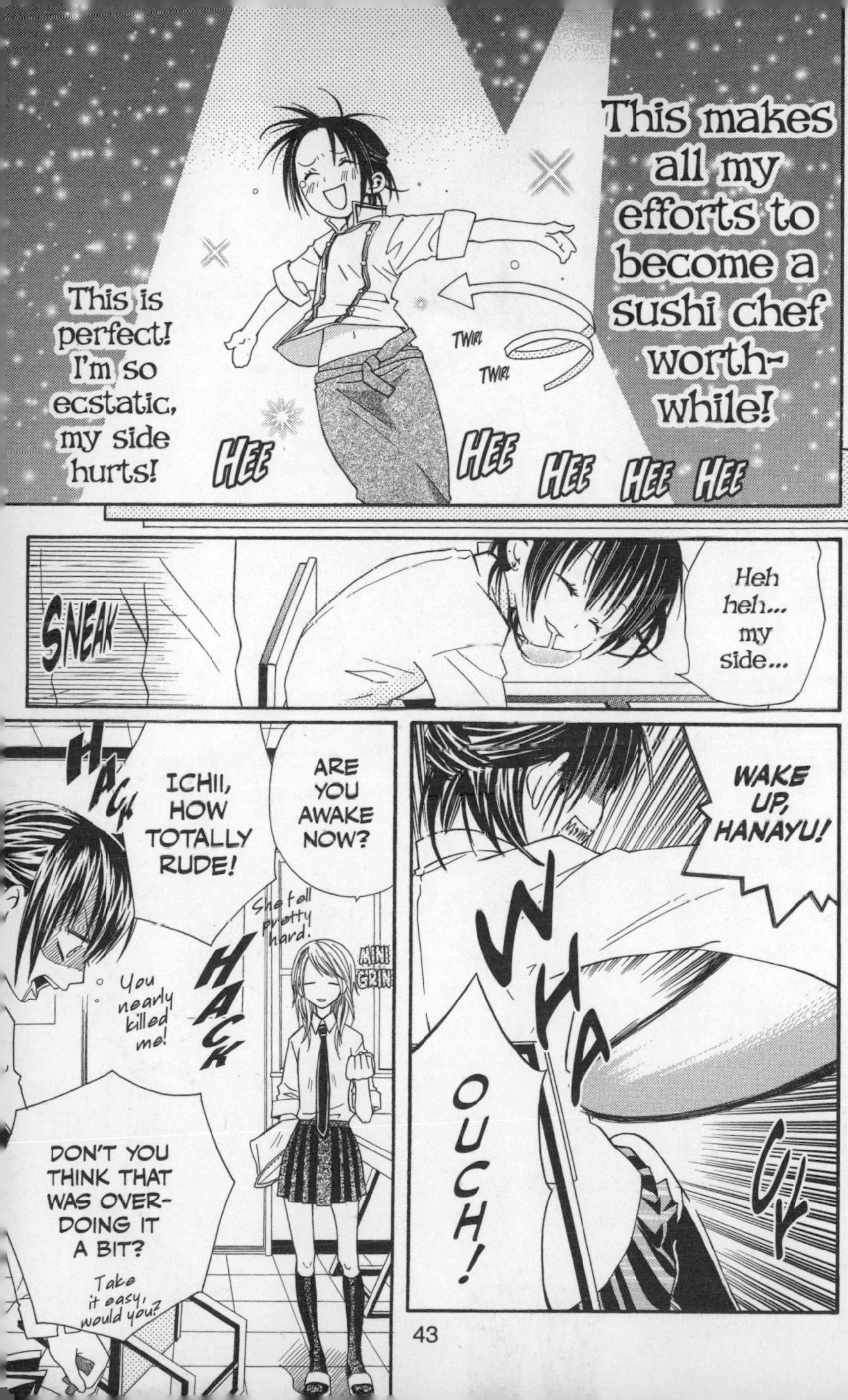
This makes all my efforts to become a sushi chef worthwhile!
TWIRL TWIRL
This is perfect! I'm so ecstatic, my side hurts!
HEE HEE HEE HEE HEE
Heh heh... my side...
SNEAK
WAKE UP, HANAYU!
WHA
OUCH!
ARE YOU AWAKE NOW?
ICHII, HOW TOTALLY RUDE!
She fell pretty hard.
MINI GRIN
HACK
HACK
You nearly killed me!
DON'T YOU THINK THAT WAS OVER-DOING IT A BIT?
Take it easy, would you?

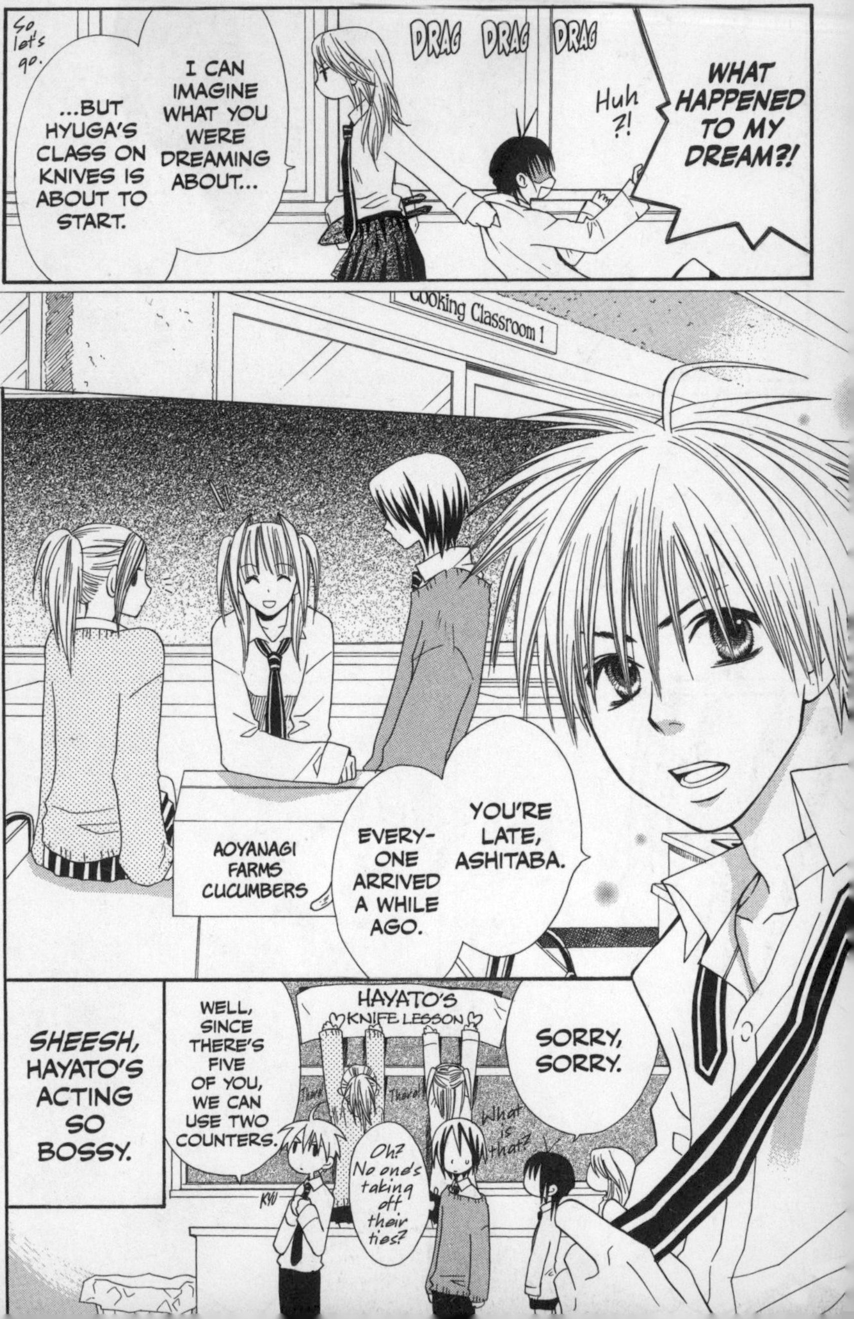
WHAT HAPPENED TO MY DREAM?!
Huh ?!
DRAG DRAG DRAG
I CAN IMAGINE WHAT YOU WERE DREAMING ABOUT...
...BUT HYUGA'S CLASS ON KNIVES IS ABOUT TO START.
So let's go.
Cooking Classroom 1
YOU'RE LATE, ASHITABA.
EVERY-ONE ARRIVED A WHILE AGO.
AOYANAGI FARMS CUCUMBERS
SORRY, SORRY.
HAYATO'S KNIFE LESSON
What is that?
There!
There
WELL, SINCE THERE'S FIVE OF YOU, WE CAN USE TWO COUNTERS.
Oh? No one's taking off their ties?
KYU
SHEESH, HAYATO'S ACTING SO BOSSY.

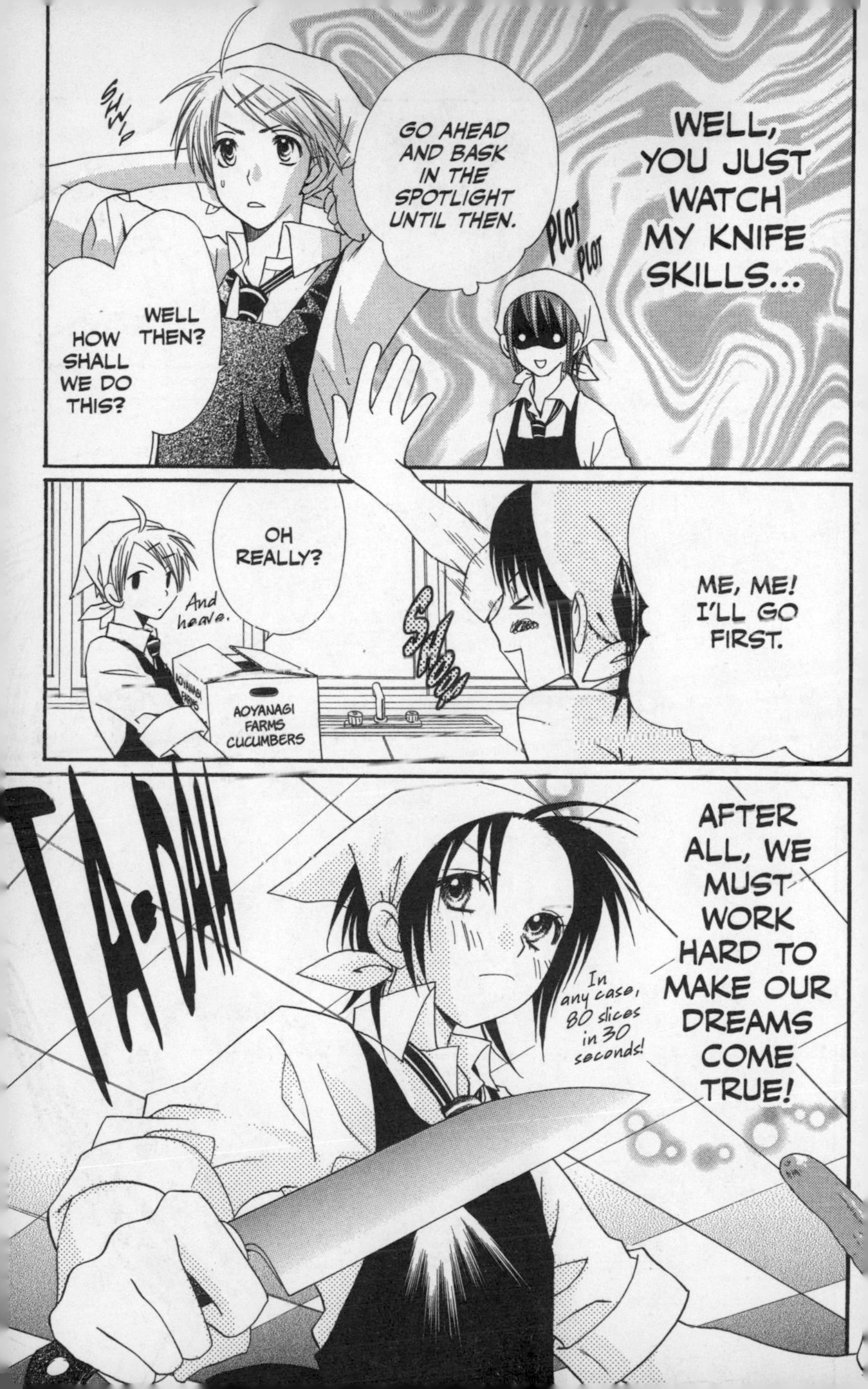
WELL, YOU JUST WATCH MY KNIFE SKILLS...
PLOT PLOT
GO AHEAD AND BASK IN THE SPOTLIGHT UNTIL THEN.
SHWIP
WELL THEN?
HOW SHALL WE DO THIS?
ME, ME! I'LL GO FIRST.
OH REALLY?
And heave.
AOYANAGI FARMS
AOYANAGI FARMS CUCUMBERS
AFTER ALL, WE MUST WORK HARD TO MAKE OUR DREAMS COME TRUE!
In any case, 80 slices in 30 seconds!
TA-DAH

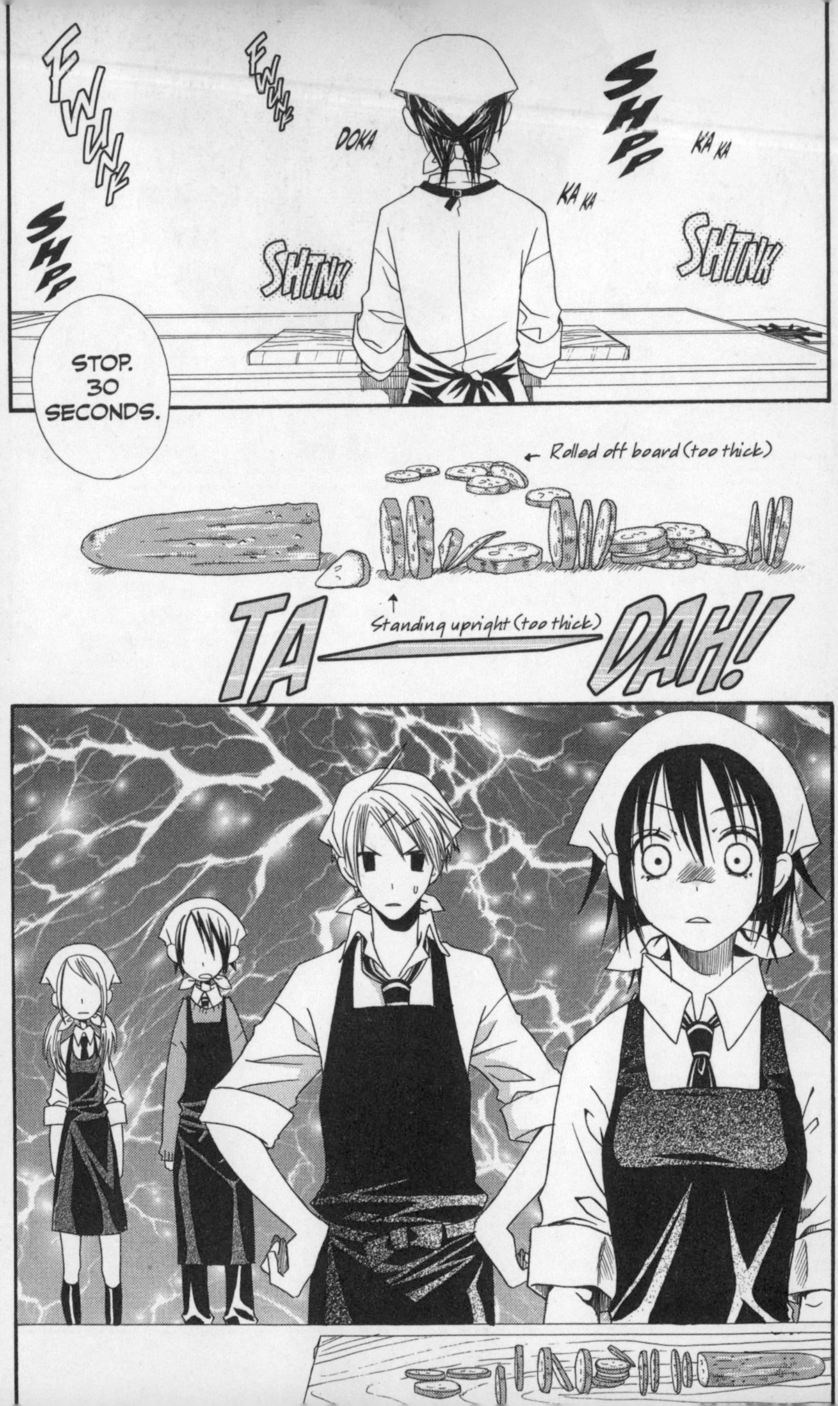
SHPP
KA KA
SHTNK
KA KA
SHPP
DOKA
FWUNK
SHTNK
SHPP
FWUNK
STOP. 30 SECONDS.
← Rolled off board (too thick)
↑ Standing upright (too thick)
TA—DAH!

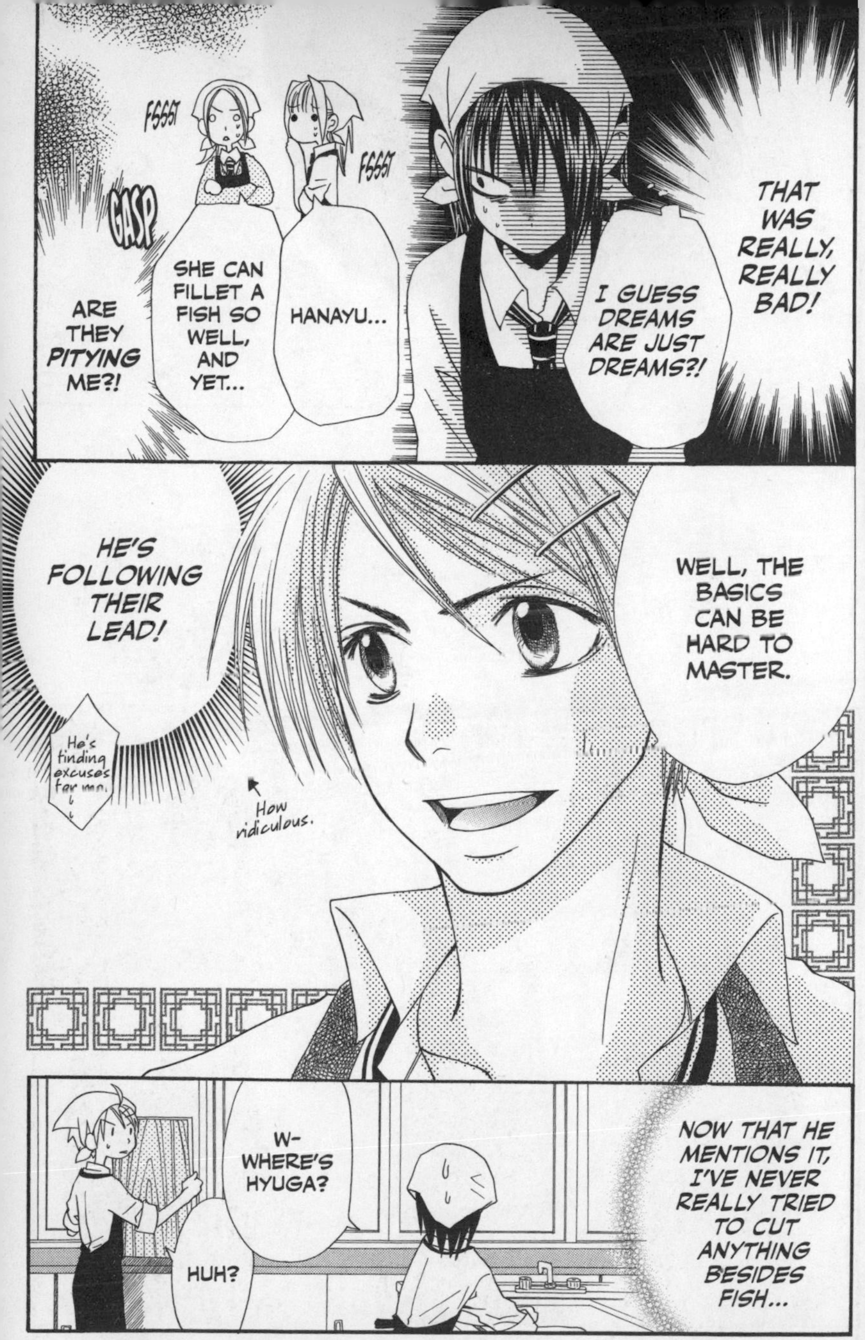
THAT WAS REALLY, REALLY BAD!
I GUESS DREAMS ARE JUST DREAMS?!
FSSST
HANAYU...
FSSST
SHE CAN FILLET A FISH SO WELL, AND YET...
GASP
ARE THEY *PITYING* ME?!
WELL, THE BASICS CAN BE HARD TO MASTER.
HE'S FOLLOWING THEIR LEAD!
He's finding excuses
How ridiculous.
NOW THAT HE MENTIONS IT, I'VE NEVER REALLY TRIED TO CUT ANYTHING BESIDES FISH...
W-WHERE'S HYUGA?
HUH?

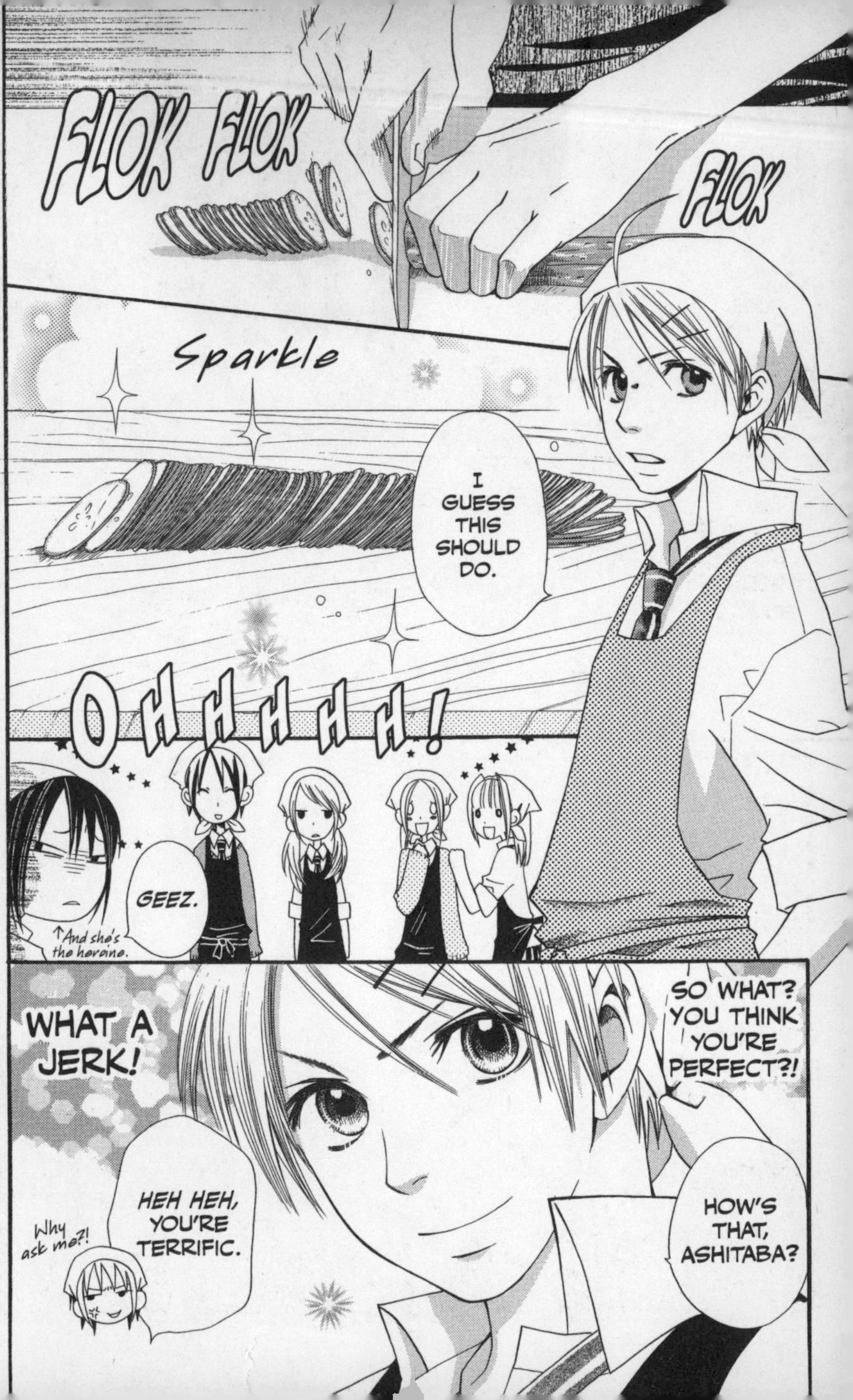
FLOK FLOK
FLOK
Sparkle
I GUESS THIS SHOULD DO.
OHHHHHH!
GEEZ.
↑And she's the heroine.
SO WHAT? YOU THINK YOU'RE PERFECT?!
WHAT A JERK!
HOW'S THAT, ASHITABA?
HEH HEH, YOU'RE TERRIFIC.
Why ask me?!

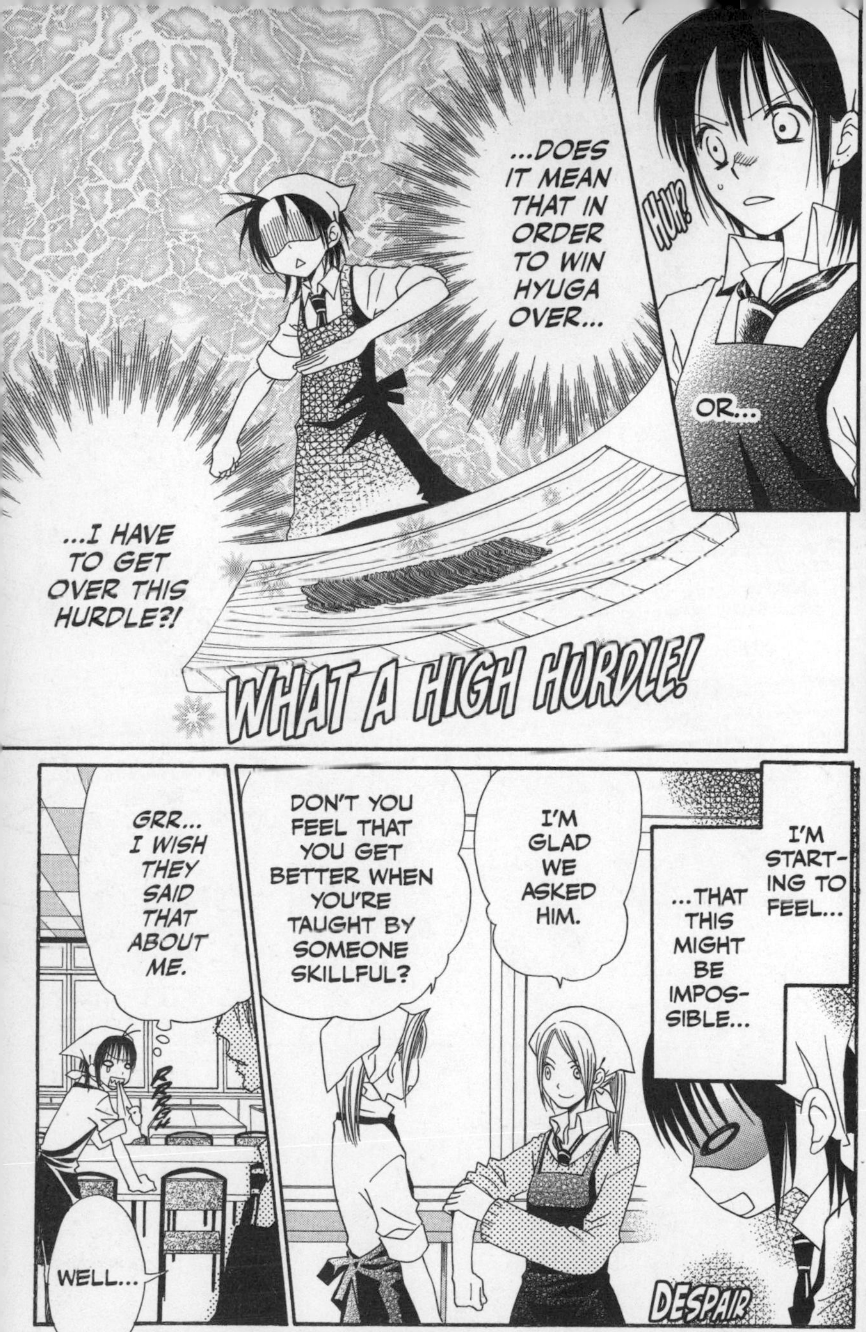
HUH?
OR...
...DOES IT MEAN THAT IN ORDER TO WIN HYUGA OVER...
...I HAVE TO GET OVER THIS HURDLE?!
WHAT A HIGH HURDLE!
I'M STARTING TO FEEL...
...THAT THIS MIGHT BE IMPOSSIBLE...
DESPAIR
I'M GLAD WE ASKED HIM.
DON'T YOU FEEL THAT YOU GET BETTER WHEN YOU'RE TAUGHT BY SOMEONE SKILLFUL?
GRR... I WISH THEY SAID THAT ABOUT ME.
WELL...

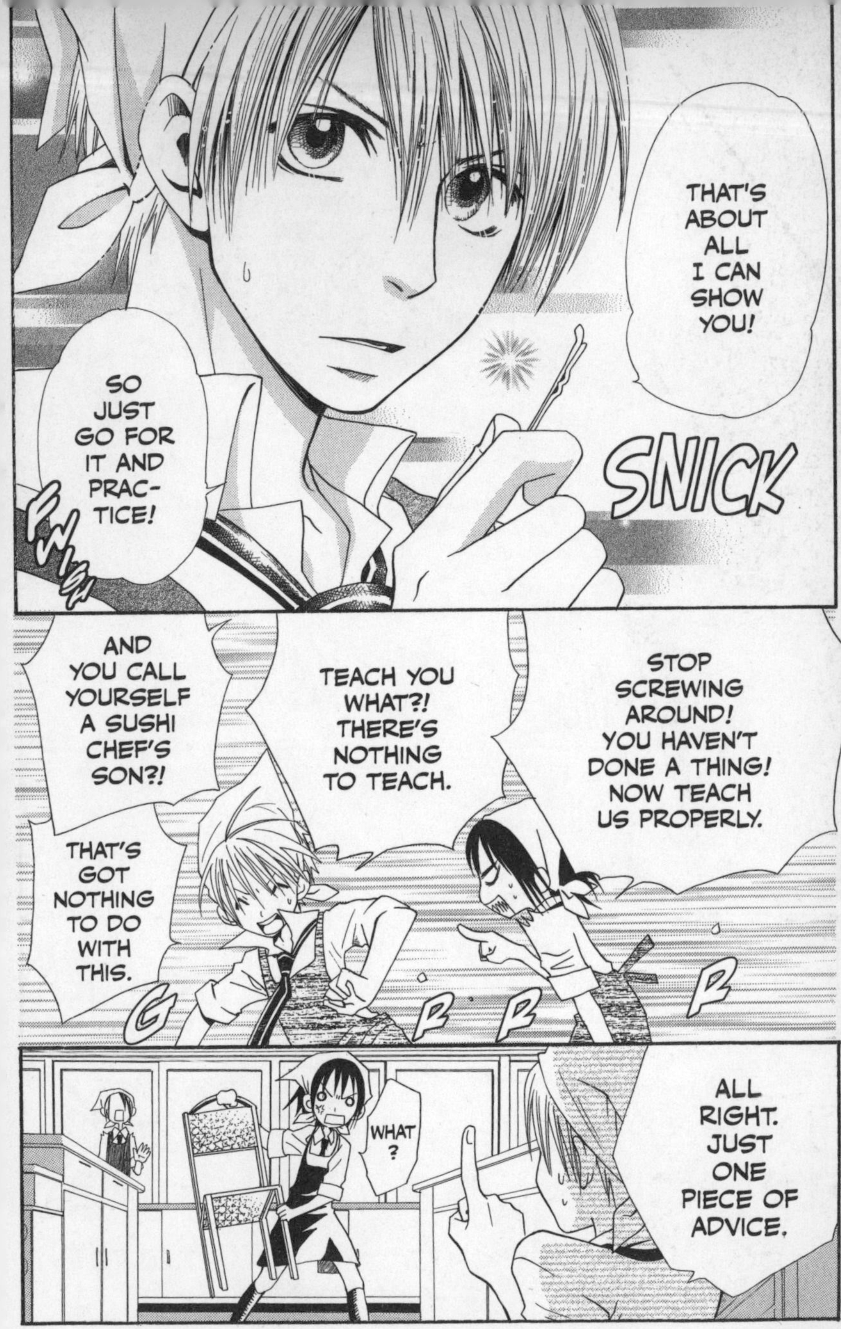
THAT'S ABOUT ALL I CAN SHOW YOU!
SNICK
SO JUST GO FOR IT AND PRAC-TICE!
STOP SCREWING AROUND! YOU HAVEN'T DONE A THING! NOW TEACH US PROPERLY.
TEACH YOU WHAT?! THERE'S NOTHING TO TEACH.
AND YOU CALL YOURSELF A SUSHI CHEF'S SON?!
THAT'S GOT NOTHING TO DO WITH THIS.
GRRR
ALL RIGHT. JUST ONE PIECE OF ADVICE.
WHAT?

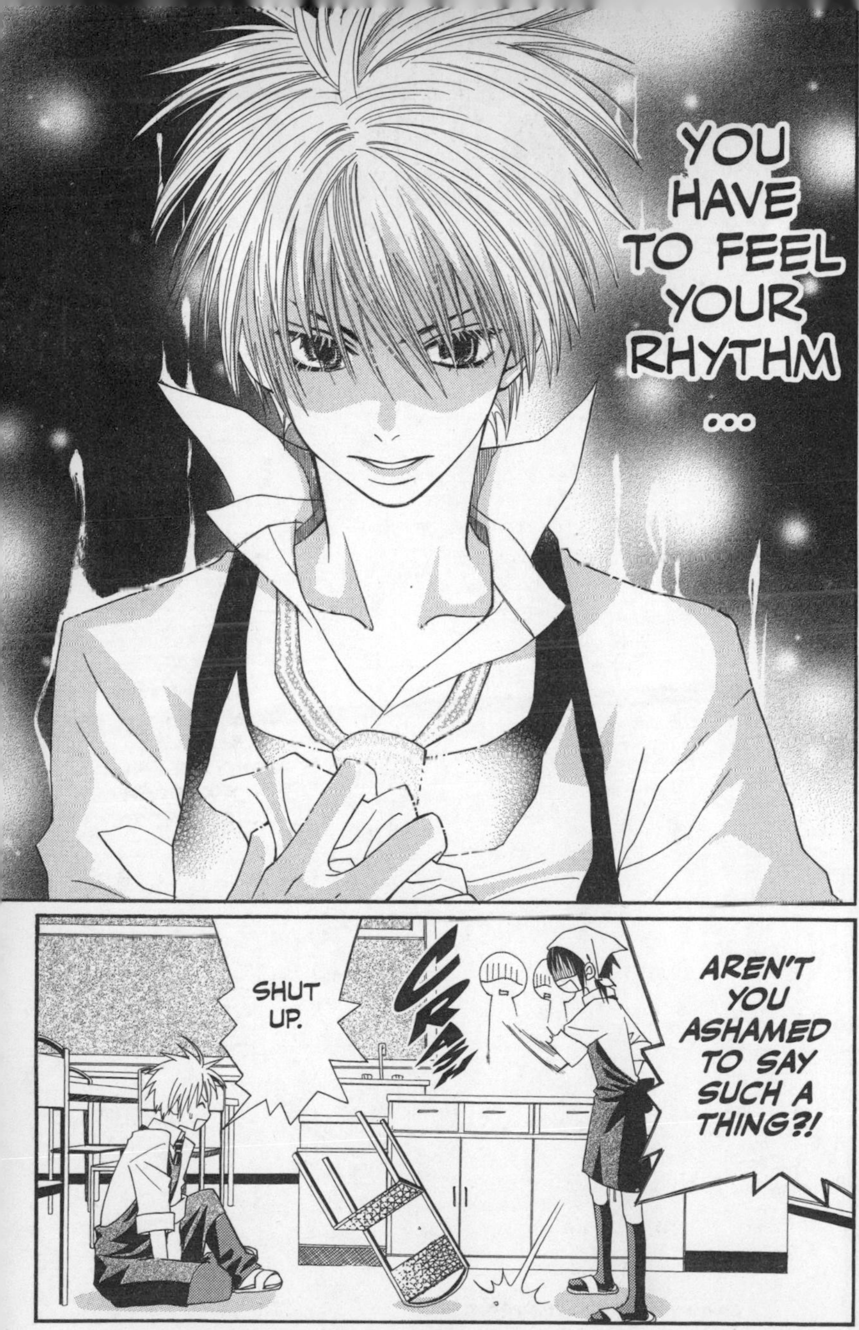
YOU HAVE TO FEEL YOUR RHYTHM ...
AREN'T YOU ASHAMED TO SAY SUCH A THING?!
CRASH
SHUT UP.

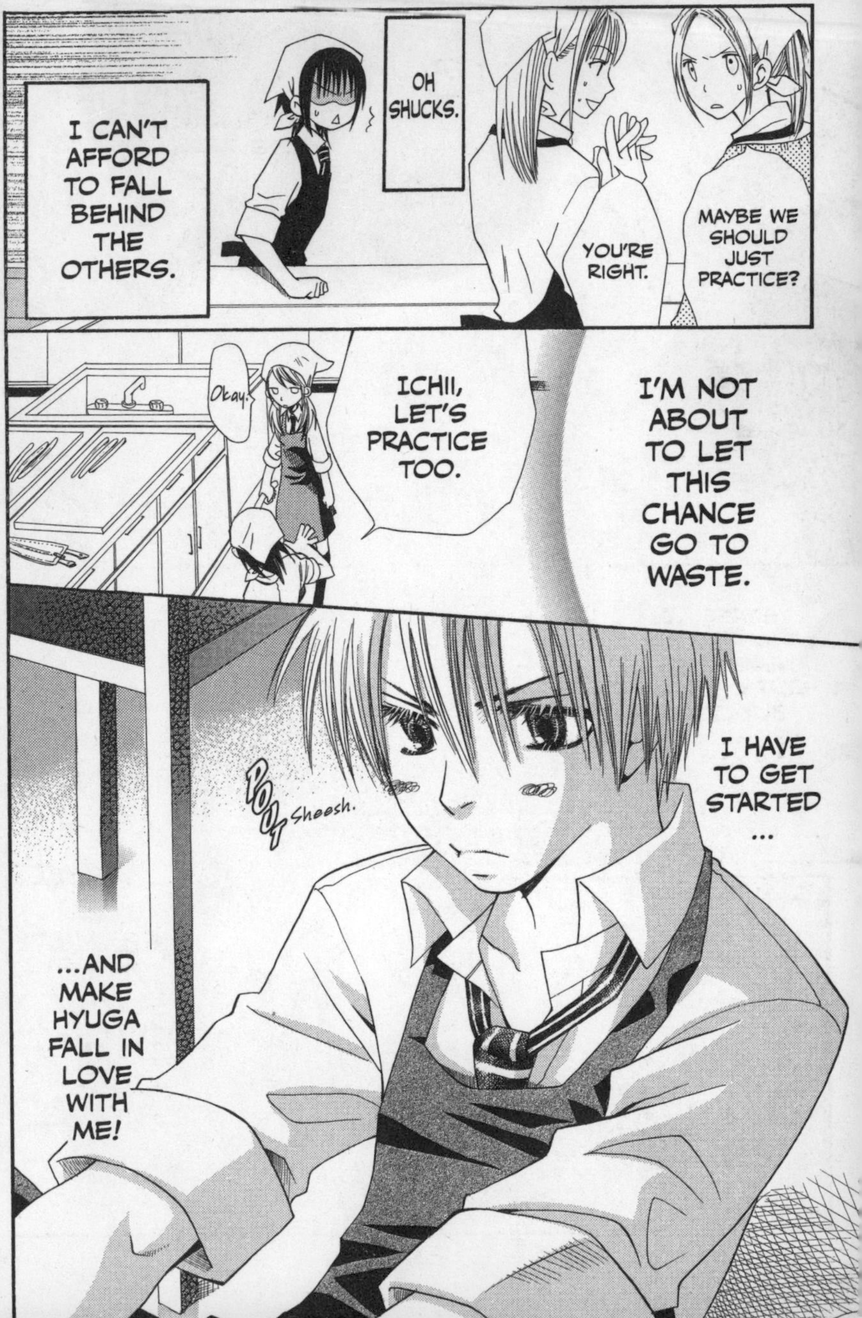
MAYBE WE SHOULD JUST PRACTICE?
YOU'RE RIGHT.
OH SHUCKS.
I CAN'T AFFORD TO FALL BEHIND THE OTHERS.
I'M NOT ABOUT TO LET THIS CHANCE GO TO WASTE.
ICHII, LET'S PRACTICE TOO.
Okay.
I HAVE TO GET STARTED ...
POUT
Sheesh.
...AND MAKE HYUGA FALL IN LOVE WITH ME!

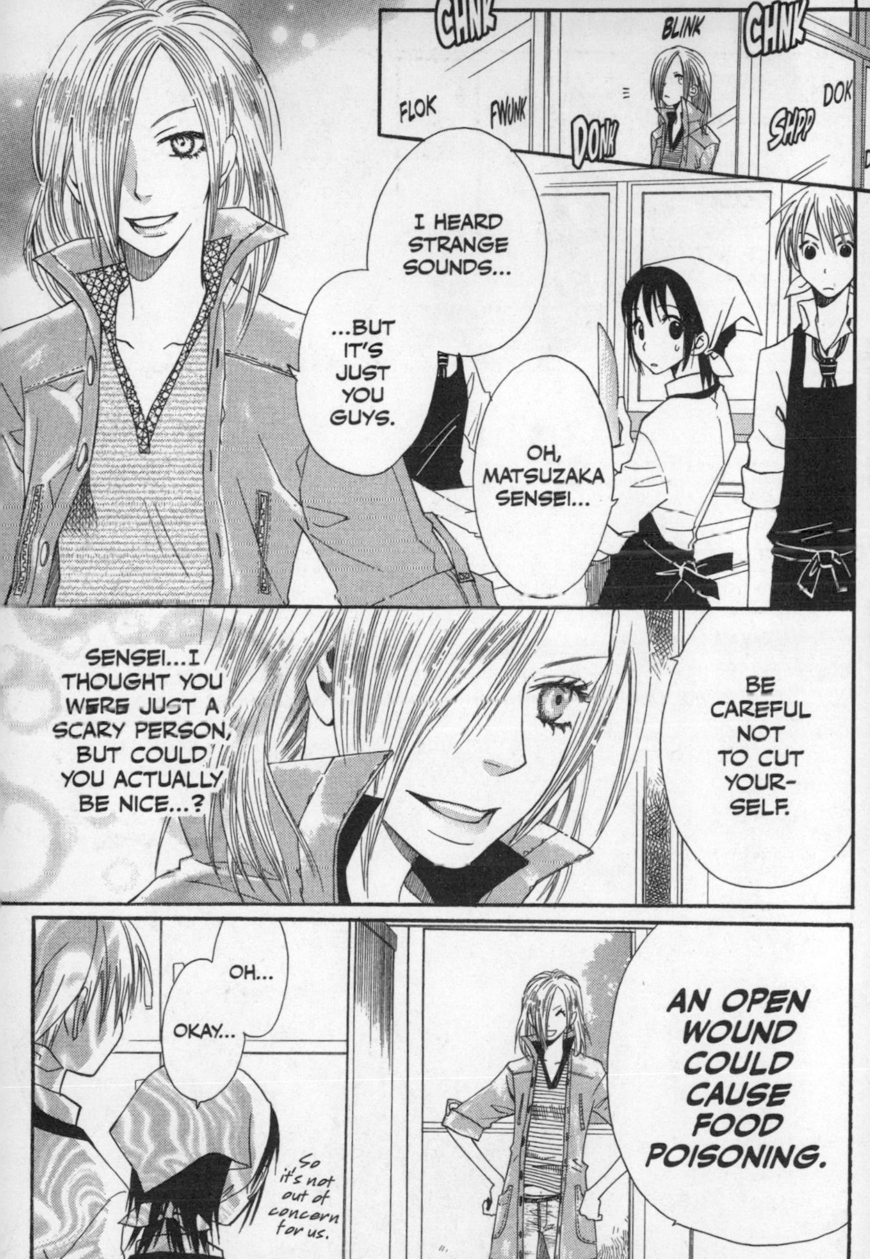
DOK
CHNK
SHPP
BLINK
DONK
FWUNK
CHNK
FLOK
OH, MATSUZAKA SENSEI...
I HEARD STRANGE SOUNDS...
...BUT IT'S JUST YOU GUYS.
BE CAREFUL NOT TO CUT YOUR-SELF.
SENSEI...I THOUGHT YOU WERE JUST A SCARY PERSON, BUT COULD YOU ACTUALLY BE NICE...?
AN OPEN WOUND COULD CAUSE FOOD POISONING.
OH...
OKAY...
So it's not out of concern for us.

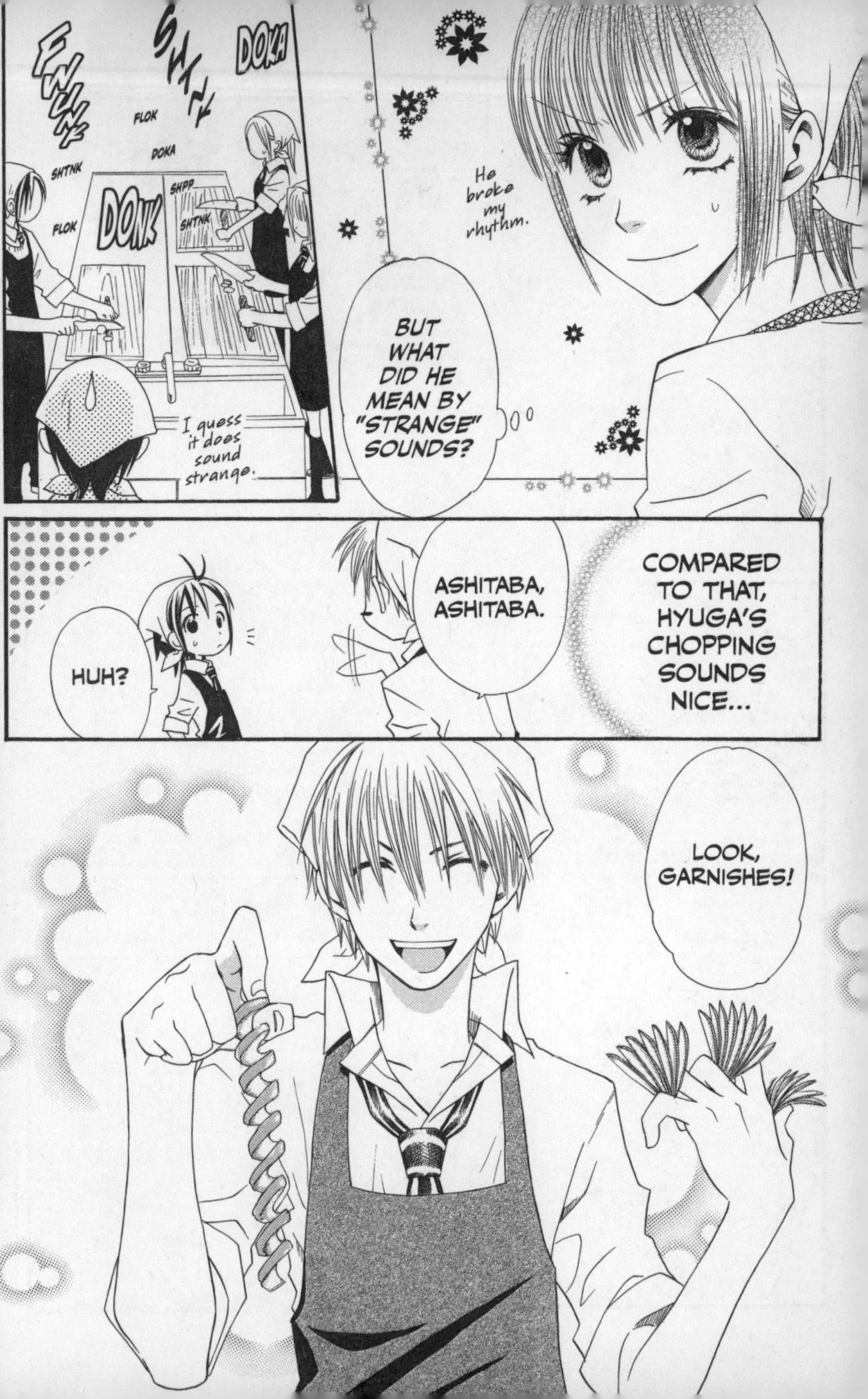
He broke my rhythm.
BUT WHAT DID HE MEAN BY "STRANGE" SOUNDS?
DOKA
SHANK
FWUMP
FLOK
DOKA
SHTNK
SHPP
DONK
SHTNK
FLOK
I guess it does sound strange.
COMPARED TO THAT, HYUGA'S CHOPPING SOUNDS NICE...
ASHITABA, ASHITABA.
HUH?
LOOK, GARNISHES!

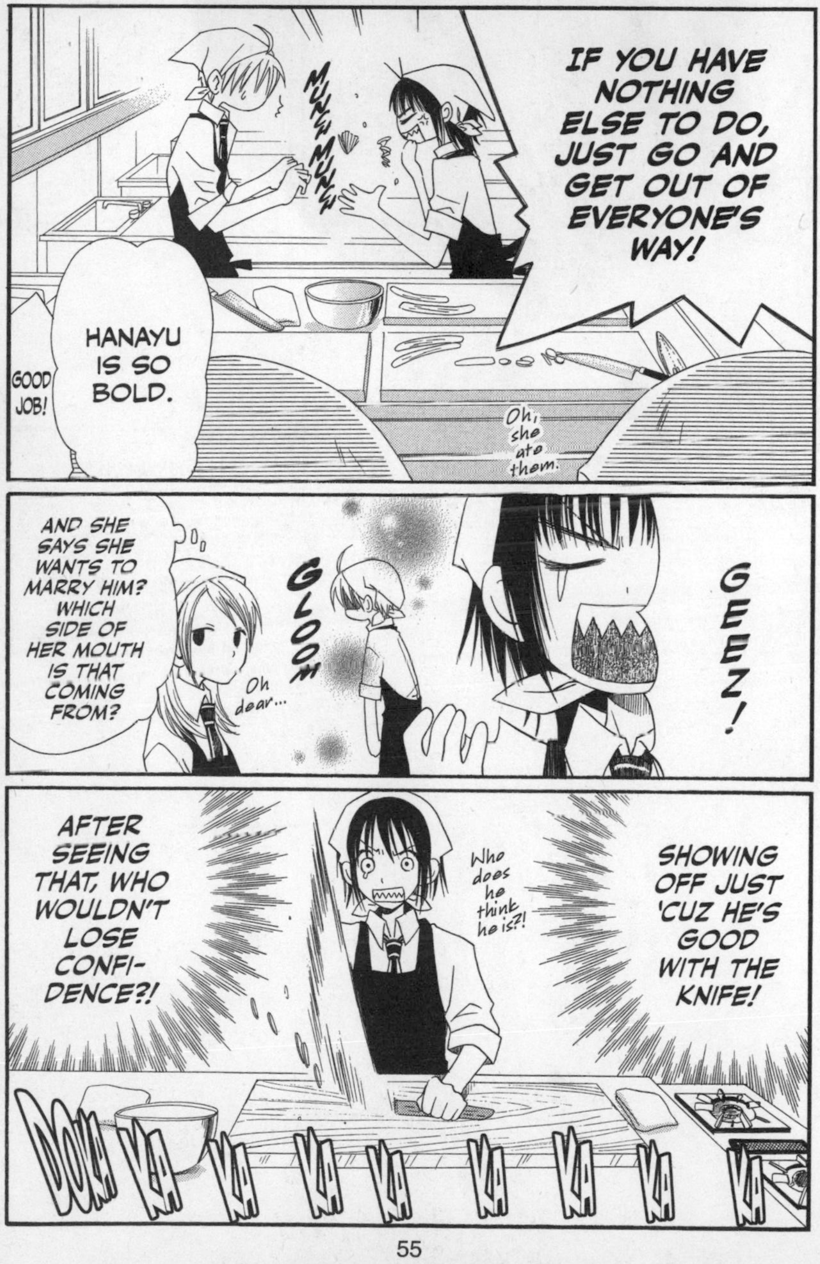
IF YOU HAVE NOTHING ELSE TO DO, JUST GO AND GET OUT OF EVERYONE'S WAY!
MUNCH MUNCH
Oh, she ate them.
HANAYU IS SO BOLD.
GOOD JOB!
GEEZ!
GLOOM
Oh dear...
AND SHE SAYS SHE WANTS TO MARRY HIM? WHICH SIDE OF HER MOUTH IS THAT COMING FROM?
SHOWING OFF JUST 'CUZ HE'S GOOD WITH THE KNIFE!
Who does he think he is?!
AFTER SEEING THAT, WHO WOULDN'T LOSE CONFI-DENCE?!
DOKA KA KA KA KA KA KA KA KA

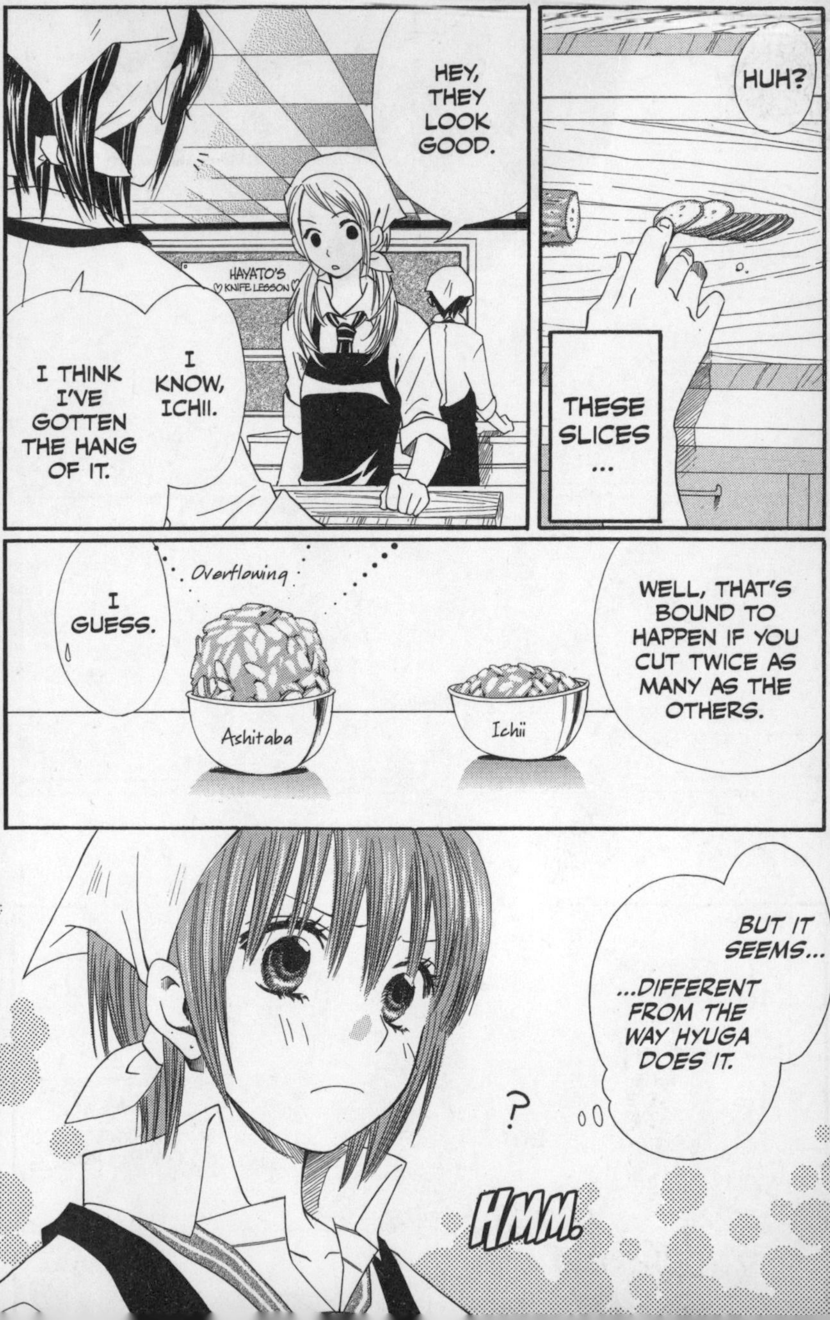
HUH?
THESE SLICES ...
HEY, THEY LOOK GOOD.
HAYATO'S KNIFE LESSON
I KNOW, ICHII.
I THINK I'VE GOTTEN THE HANG OF IT.
WELL, THAT'S BOUND TO HAPPEN IF YOU CUT TWICE AS MANY AS THE OTHERS.
Ichii
Ashitaba
Overflowing
I GUESS.
BUT IT SEEMS...
...DIFFERENT FROM THE WAY HYUGA DOES IT.
?
HMM.

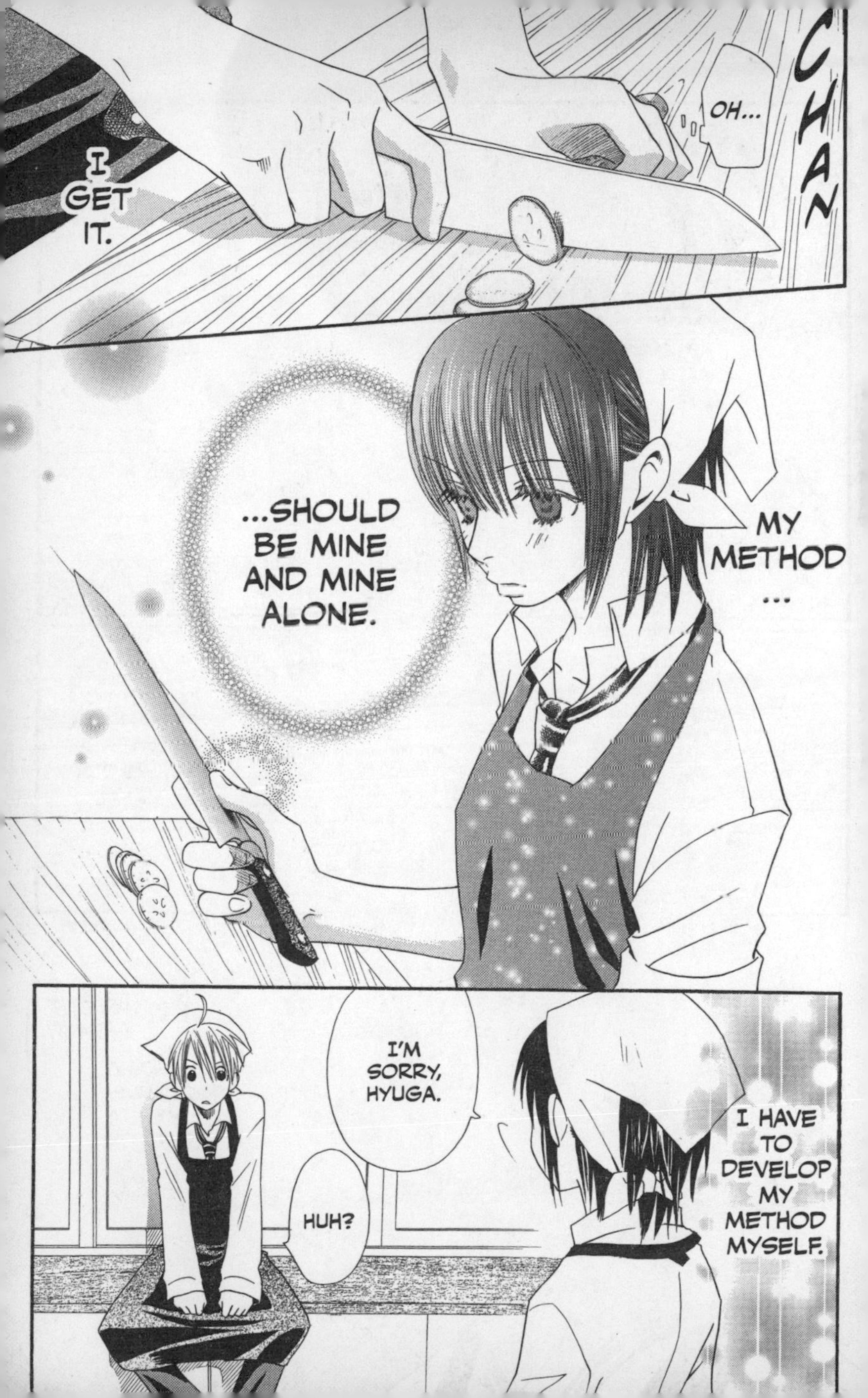
CHAN
OH...
I GET IT.
MY METHOD...
...SHOULD BE MINE AND MINE ALONE.
I HAVE TO DEVELOP MY METHOD MYSELF.
I'M SORRY, HYUGA.
HUH?

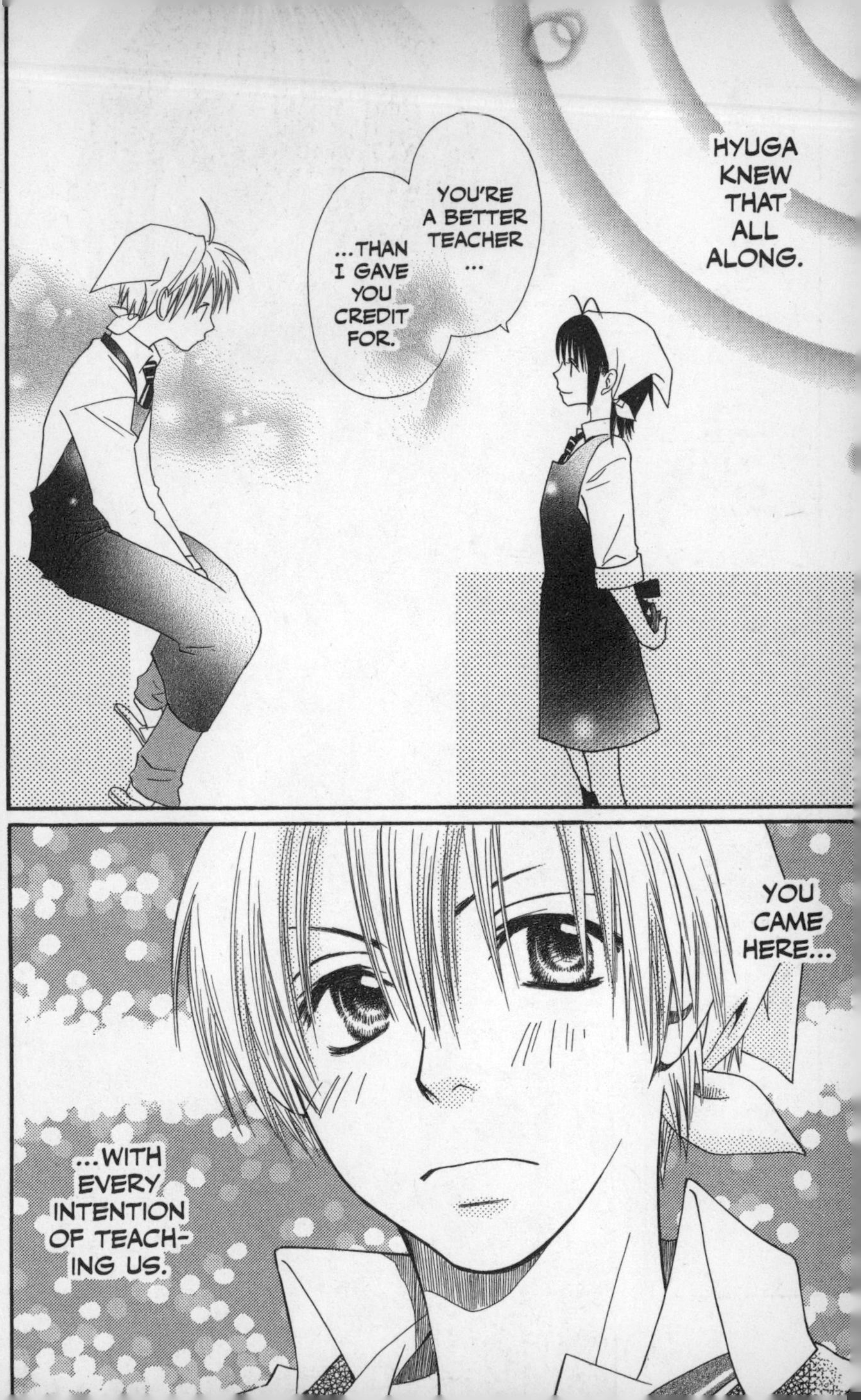
HYUGA KNEW THAT ALL ALONG.
YOU'RE A BETTER TEACHER ...
...THAN I GAVE YOU CREDIT FOR.
YOU CAME HERE...
...WITH EVERY INTENTION OF TEACHING US.

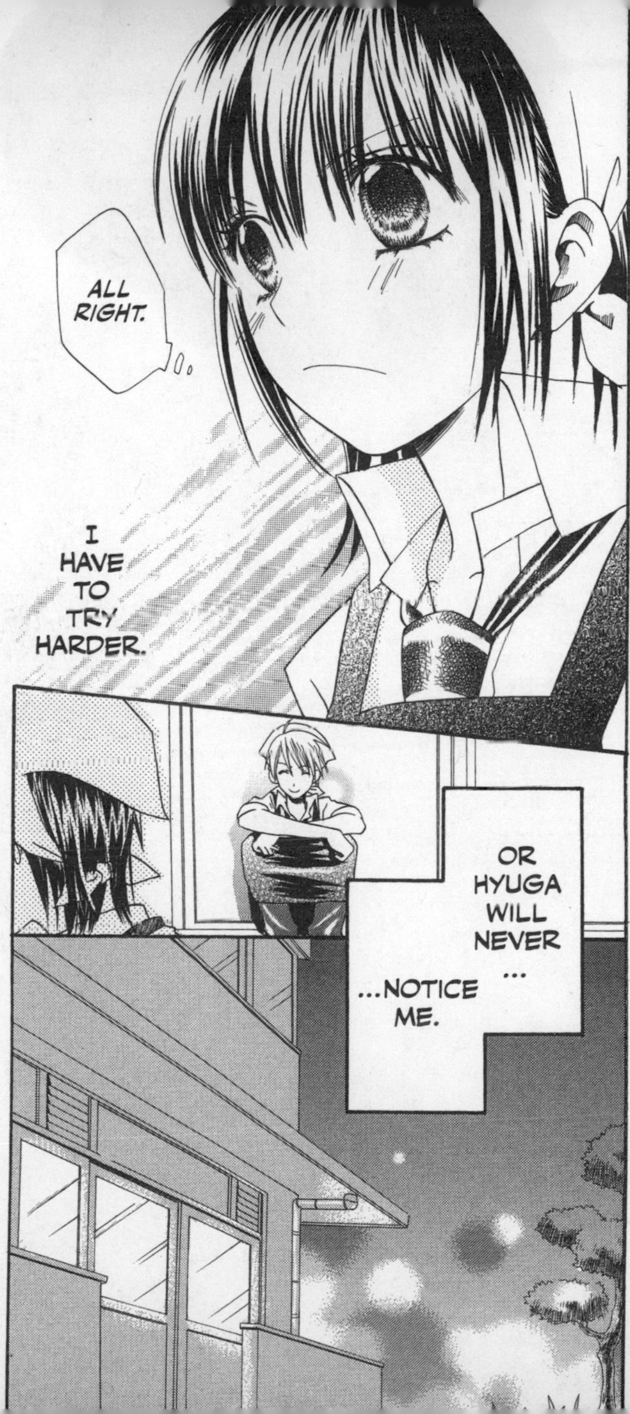
ALL RIGHT.
I HAVE TO TRY HARDER.
OR HYUGA WILL NEVER ...
...NOTICE ME.

Extra MV

I began a vegetable garden. Aoyanagi Farms

Umm... even my friend Fujii said he's impressed!

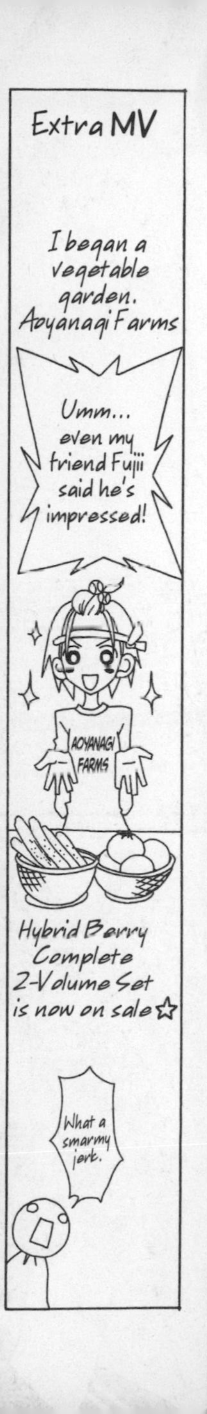
AOYANAGI FARMS

Hybrid Berry Complete 2-Volume Set is now on sale☆

What a smarmy jerk.

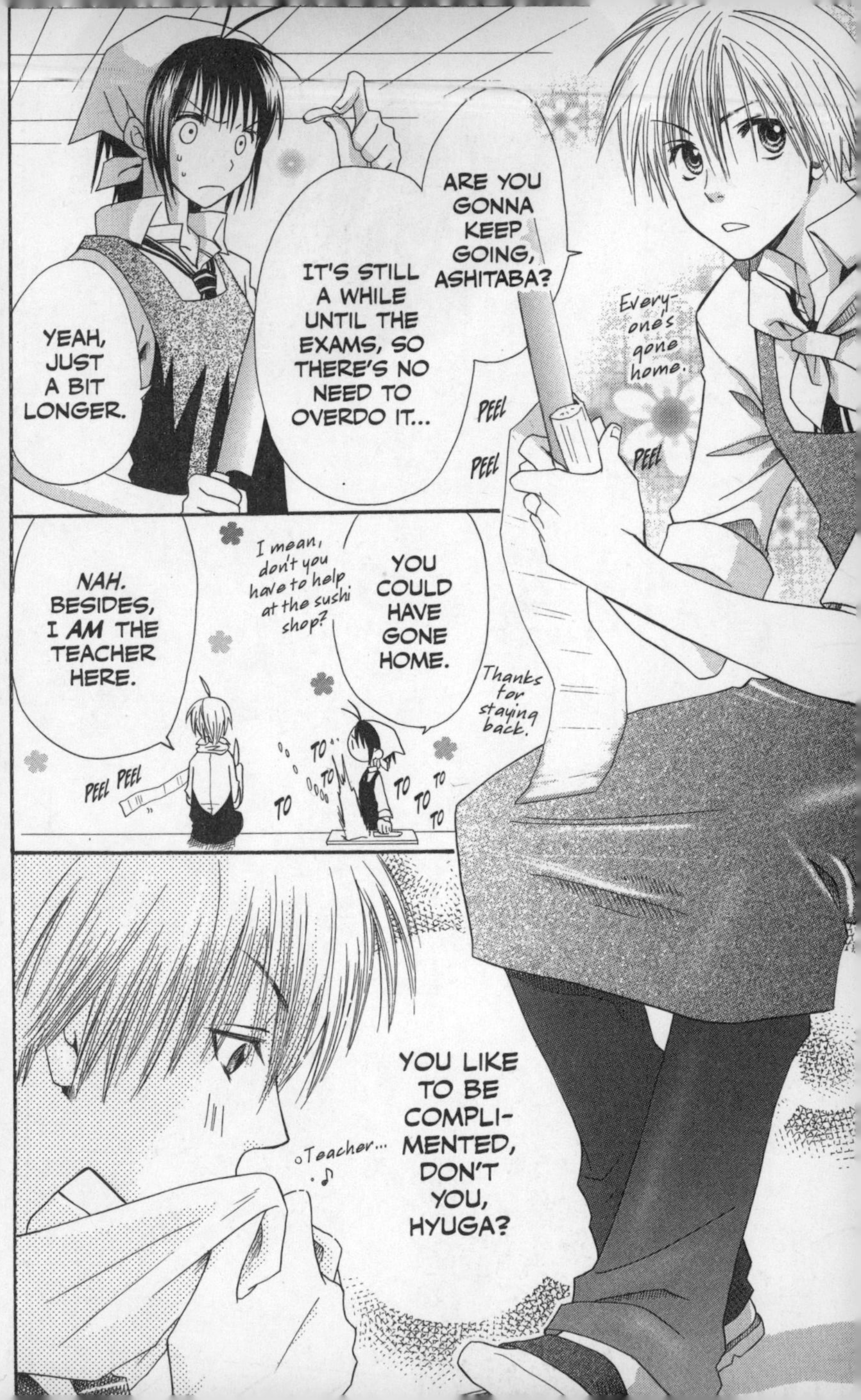
ARE YOU GONNA KEEP GOING, ASHITABA?
Every-one's gone home.
PEEL
YEAH, JUST A BIT LONGER.
IT'S STILL A WHILE UNTIL THE EXAMS, SO THERE'S NO NEED TO OVERDO IT...
PEEL
PEEL
YOU COULD HAVE GONE HOME.
I mean, don't you have to help at the sushi shop?
NAH. BESIDES, I AM THE TEACHER HERE.
TO TO TO TO TO TO TO
PEEL PEEL
Thanks for staying back.
YOU LIKE TO BE COMPLI-MENTED, DON'T YOU, HYUGA?
Teacher...

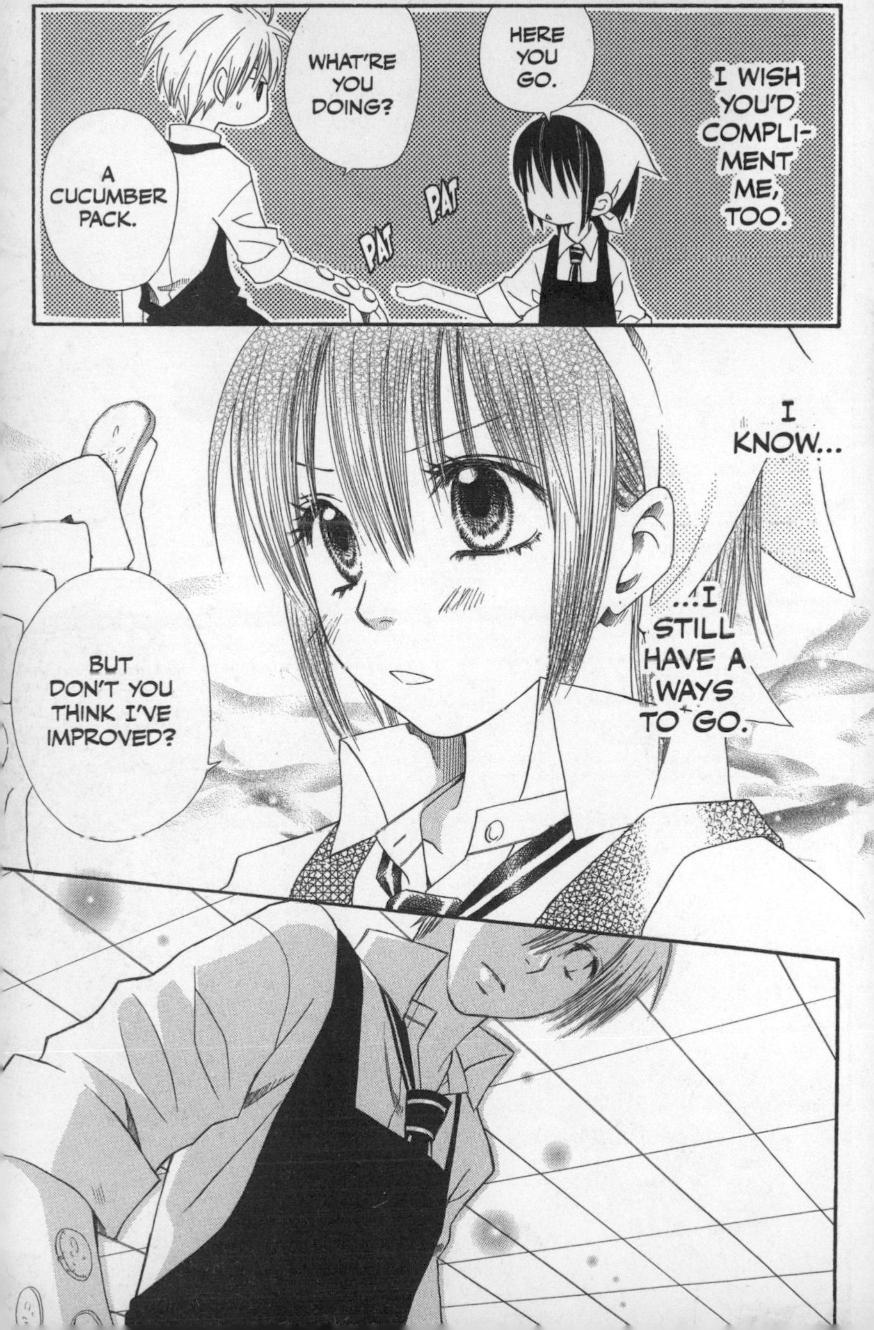
I WISH YOU'D COMPLI-MENT ME, TOO.
HERE YOU GO.
WHAT'RE YOU DOING?
PAT
PAT
A CUCUMBER PACK.
...I KNOW...
...I STILL HAVE A WAYS TO GO.
BUT DON'T YOU THINK I'VE IMPROVED?

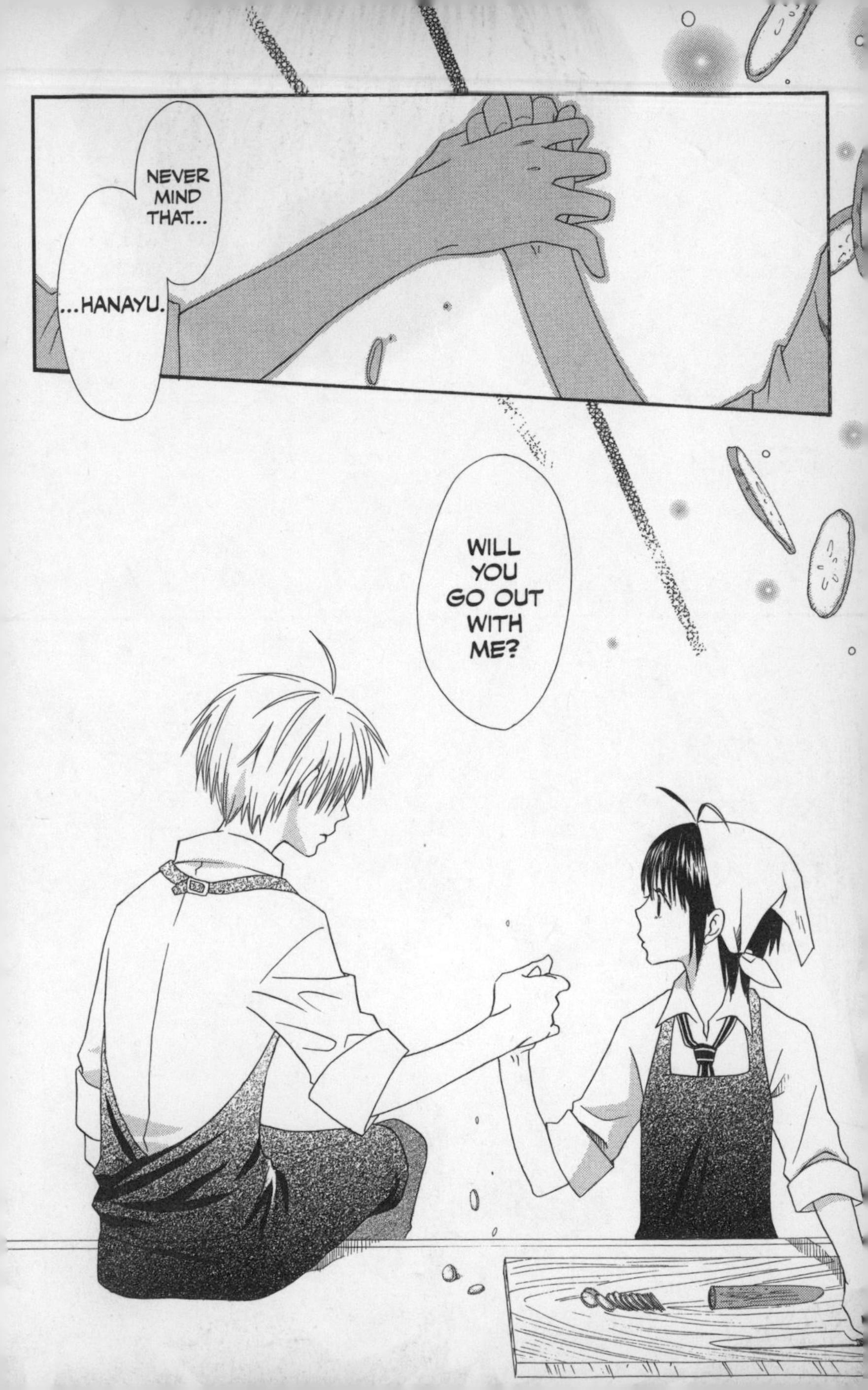
NEVER MIND THAT...
...HANAYU.
WILL YOU GO OUT WITH ME?

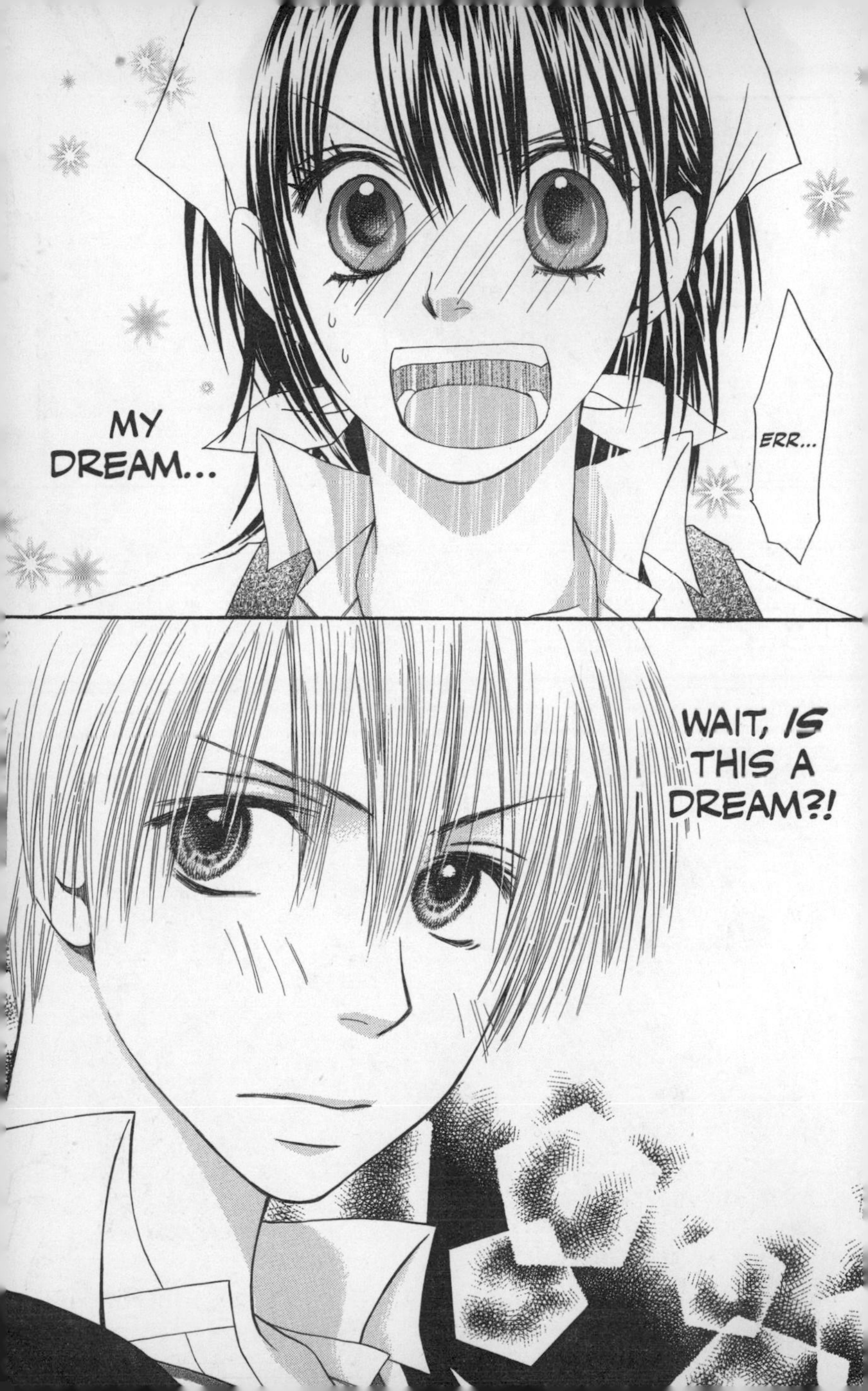
ERR...
MY DREAM...
WAIT, *IS* THIS A DREAM?!

SIDE DISH Mixed Vegetables 2

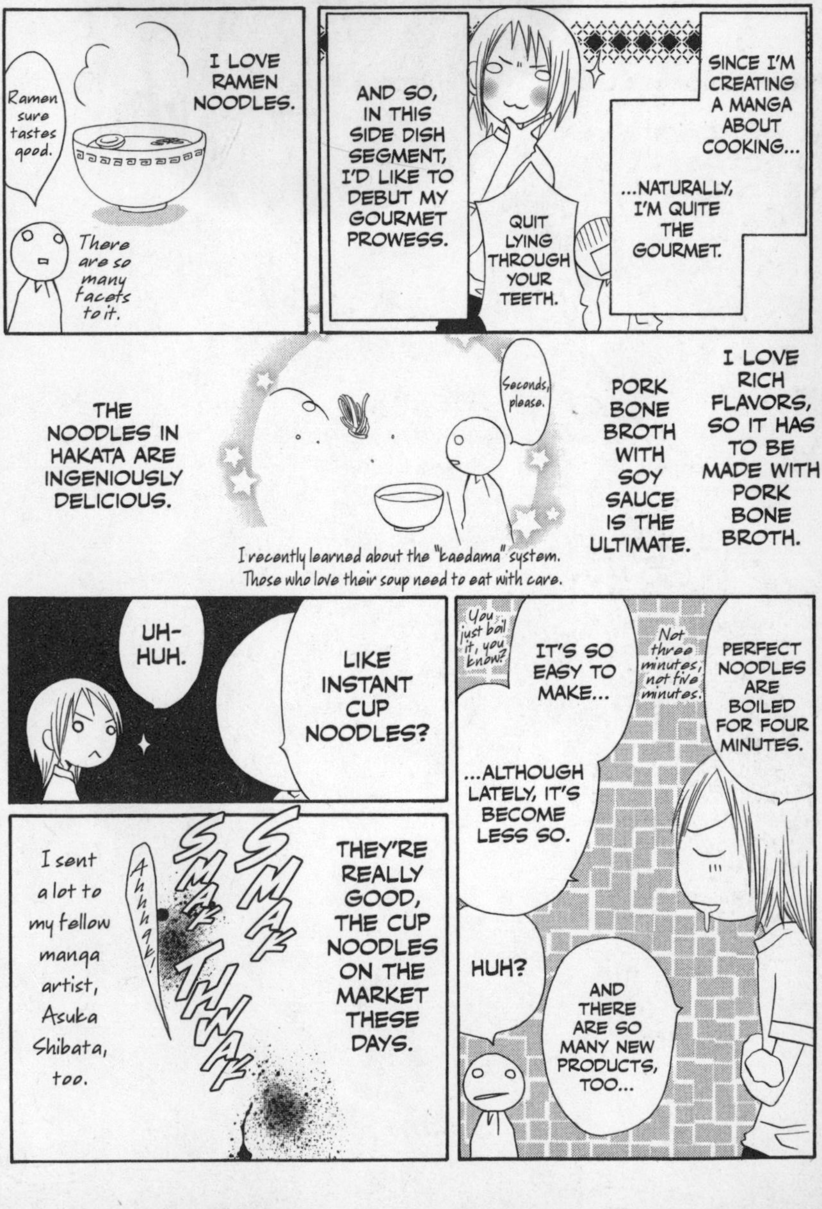
SINCE I'M CREATING A MANGA ABOUT COOKING...
...NATURALLY, I'M QUITE THE GOURMET.
AND SO, IN THIS SIDE DISH SEGMENT, I'D LIKE TO DEBUT MY GOURMET PROWESS.
QUIT LYING THROUGH YOUR TEETH.
I LOVE RAMEN NOODLES.
Ramen sure tastes good.
There are so many facets to it.
I LOVE RICH FLAVORS, SO IT HAS TO BE MADE WITH PORK BONE BROTH.
PORK BONE BROTH WITH SOY SAUCE IS THE ULTIMATE.
Seconds, please.
THE NOODLES IN HAKATA ARE INGENIOUSLY DELICIOUS.
I recently learned about the "kaedama" system. Those who love their soup need to eat with care.
PERFECT NOODLES ARE BOILED FOR FOUR MINUTES.
Not three minutes, not five minutes.
IT'S SO EASY TO MAKE...
You just boil it, you know?
...ALTHOUGH LATELY, IT'S BECOME LESS SO.
HUH?
AND THERE ARE SO MANY NEW PRODUCTS, TOO...
LIKE INSTANT CUP NOODLES?
UH-HUH.
THEY'RE REALLY GOOD, THE CUP NOODLES ON THE MARKET THESE DAYS.
SMAK
SMAK THWAK
I sent a lot to my fellow manga artist, Asuka Shibata, too.

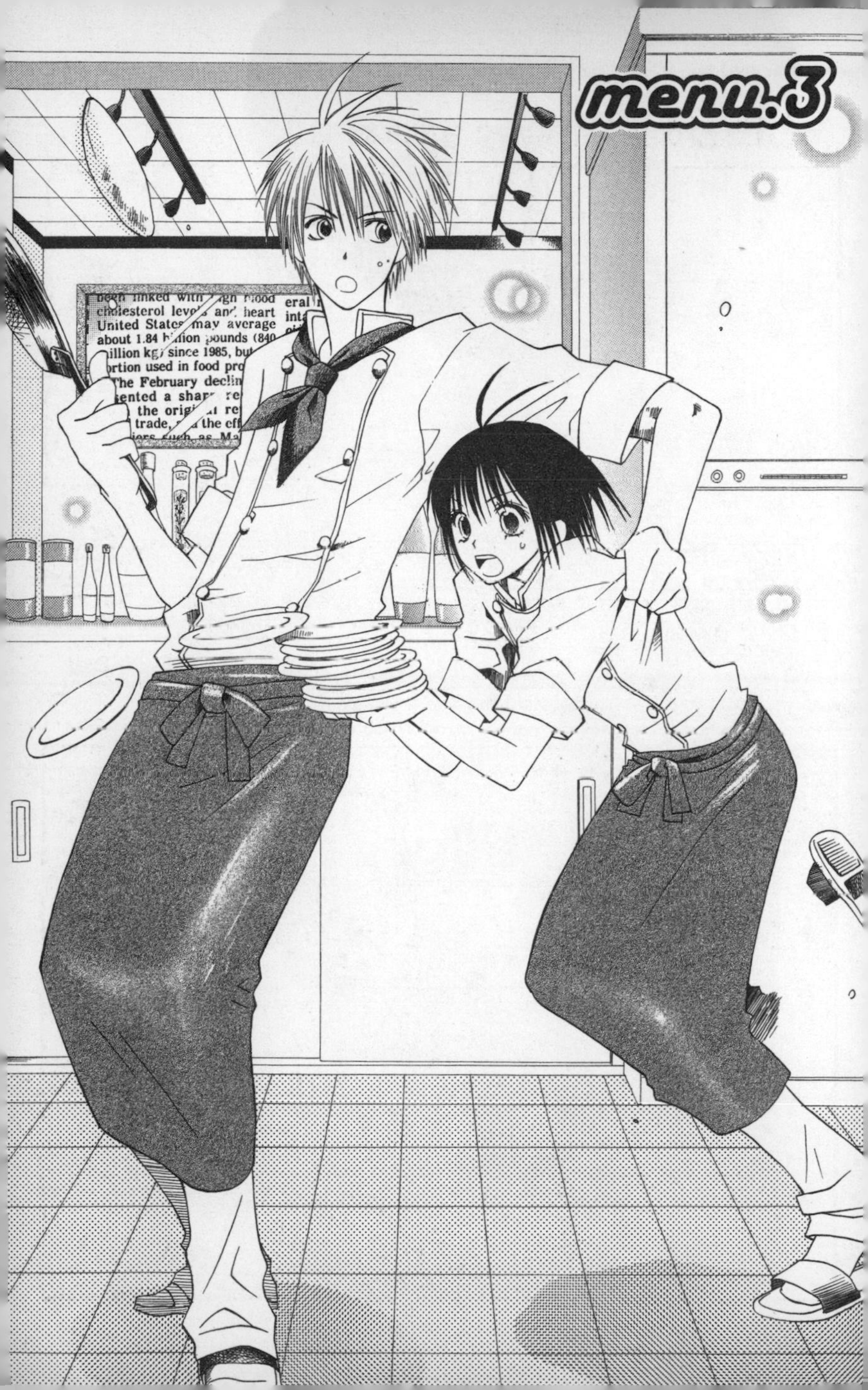
menu.3

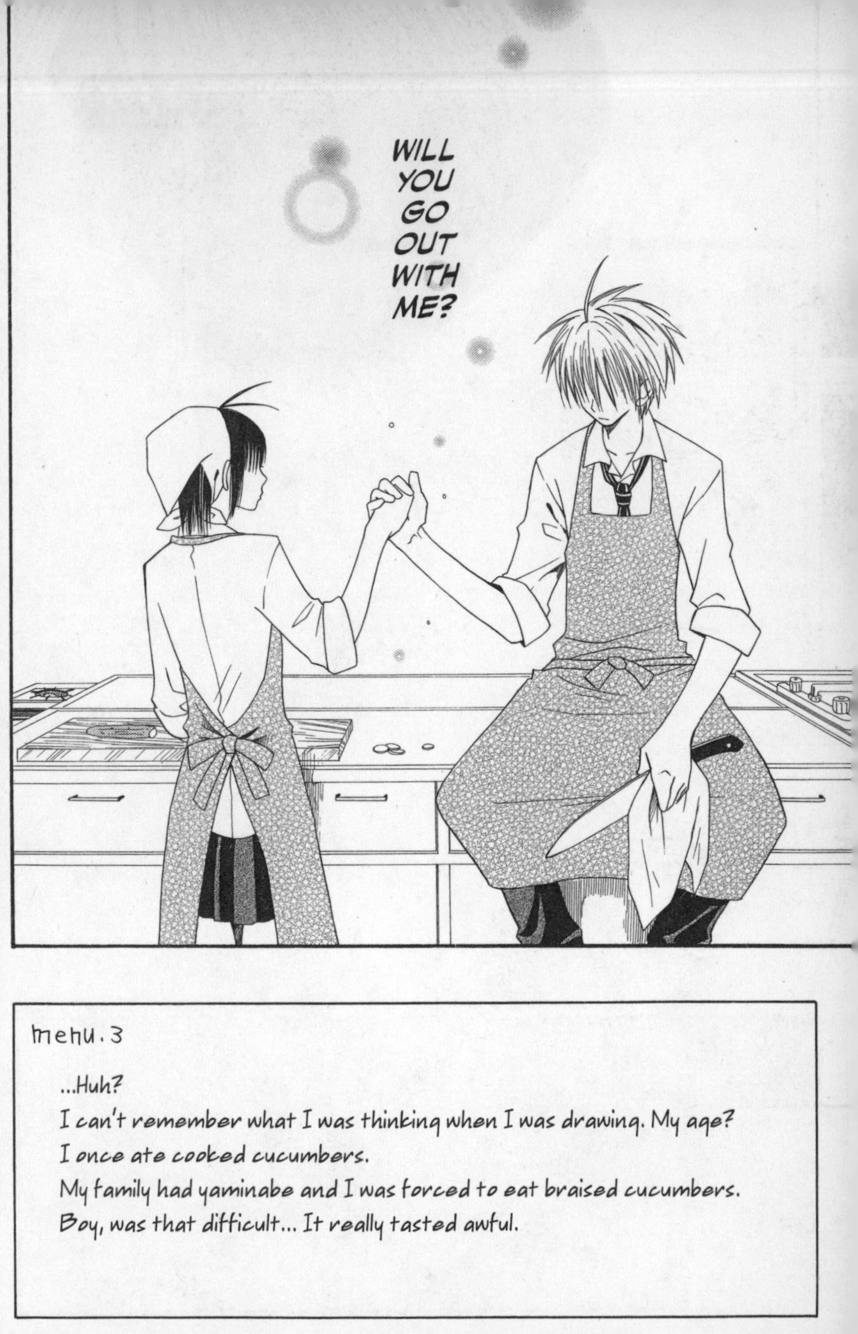
WILL YOU GO OUT WITH ME?

menu.3

...Huh?

I can't remember what I was thinking when I was drawing. My age?

I once ate cooked cucumbers.

My family had yaminabe and I was forced to eat braised cucumbers.

Boy, was that difficult... It really tasted awful.

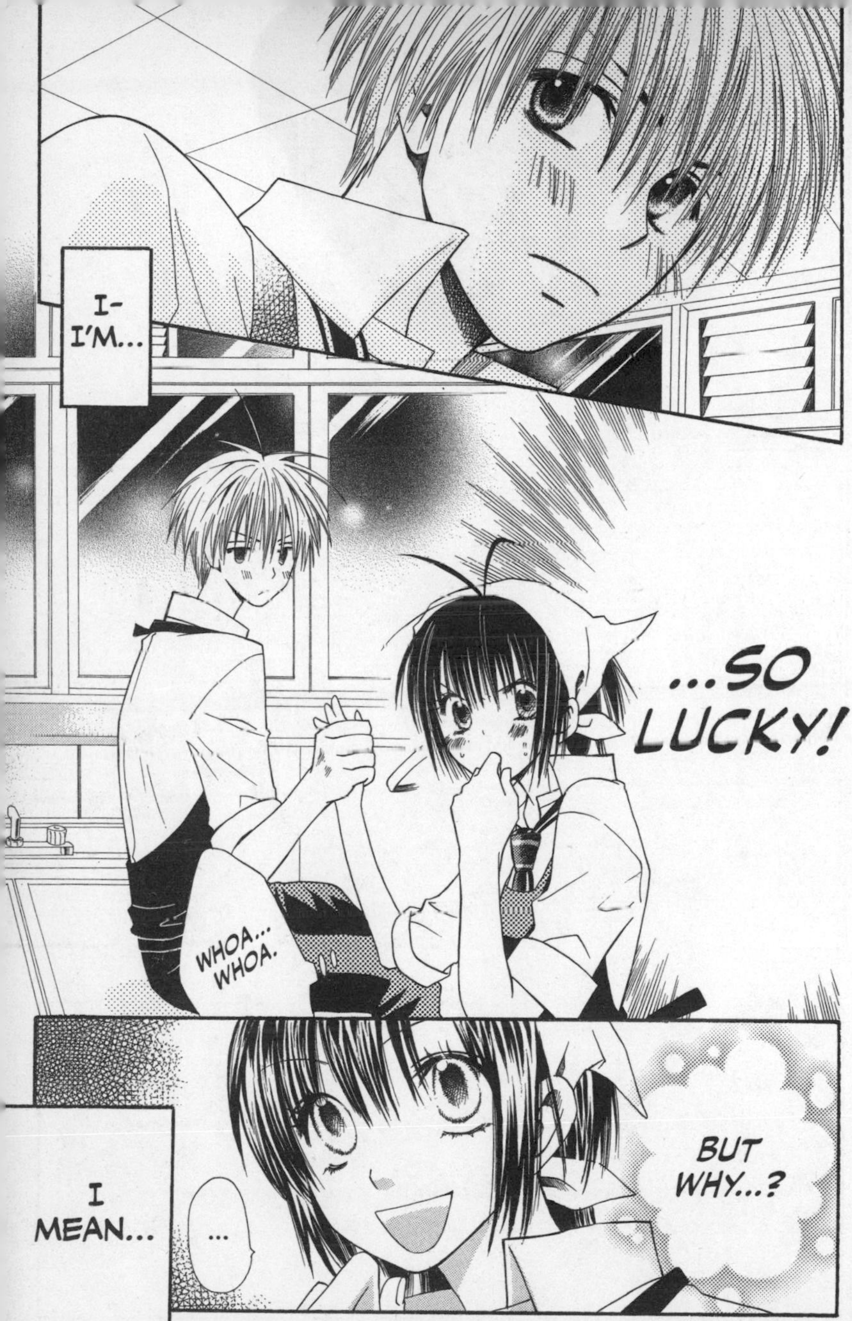
I- I'M...
...SO LUCKY!
WHOA... WHOA.
BUT WHY...?
...
I MEAN...

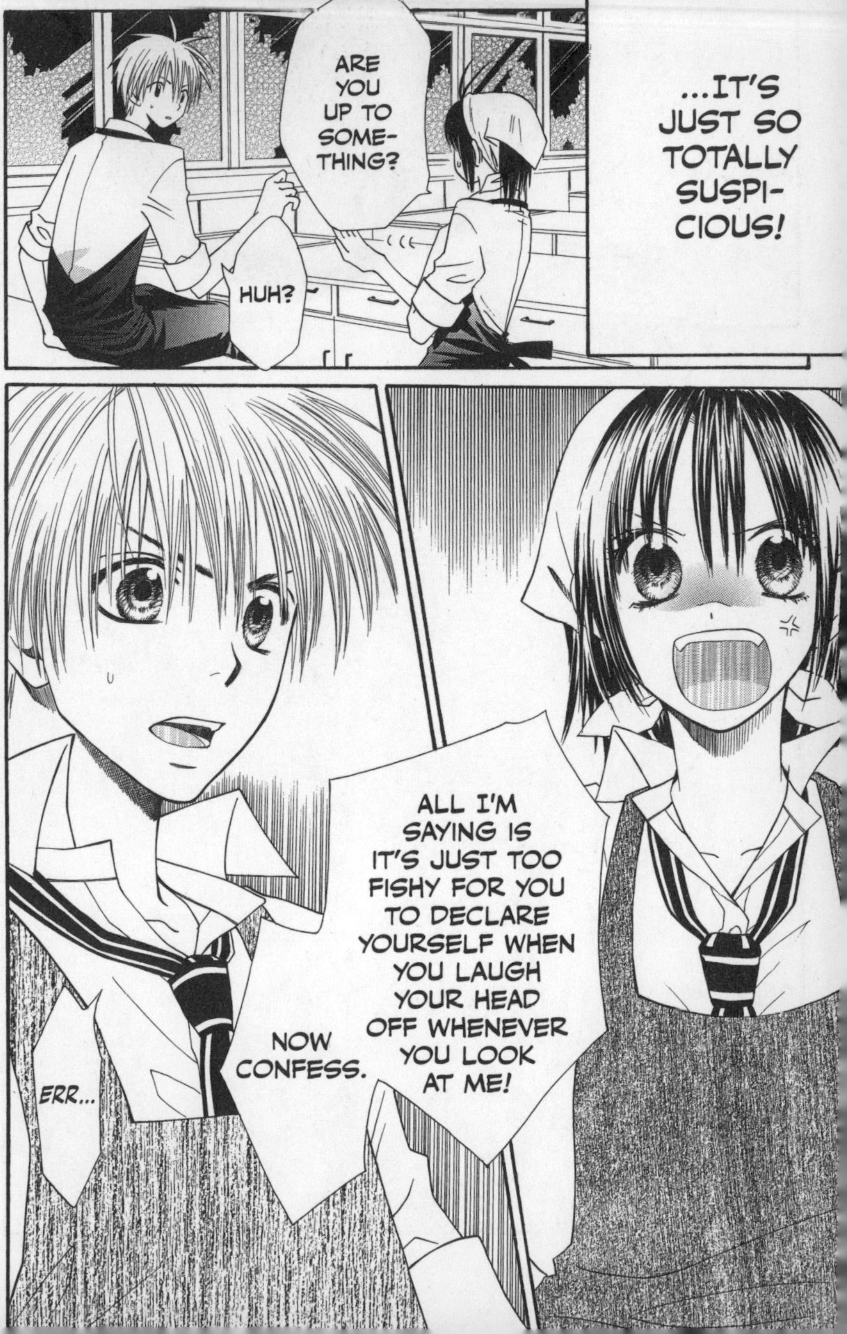
...IT'S JUST SO TOTALLY SUSPICIOUS!
ARE YOU UP TO SOMETHING?
HUH?
ALL I'M SAYING IS IT'S JUST TOO FISHY FOR YOU TO DECLARE YOURSELF WHEN YOU LAUGH YOUR HEAD OFF WHENEVER YOU LOOK AT ME!
NOW CONFESS.
ERR...

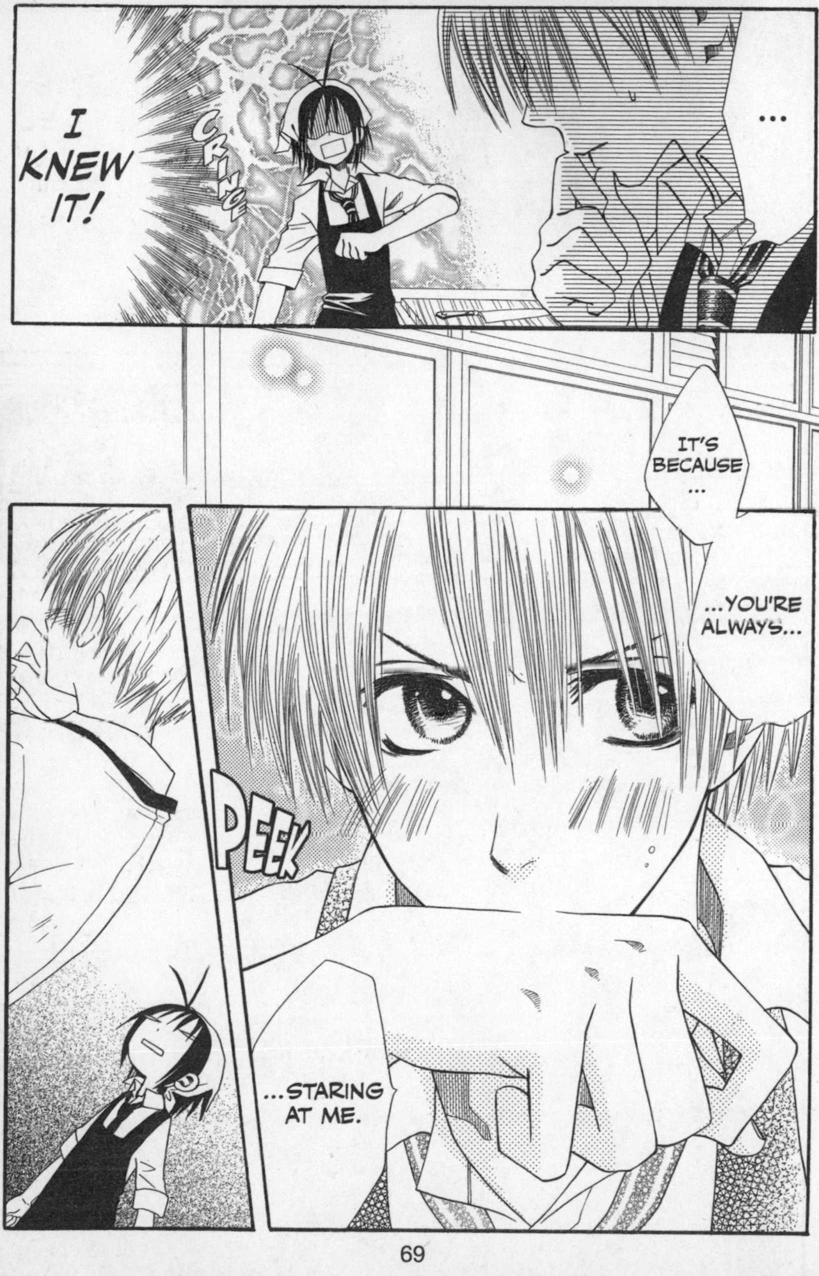
...
I KNEW IT!
CRINGE
IT'S BECAUSE ...
...YOU'RE ALWAYS...
PEEK
...STARING AT ME.

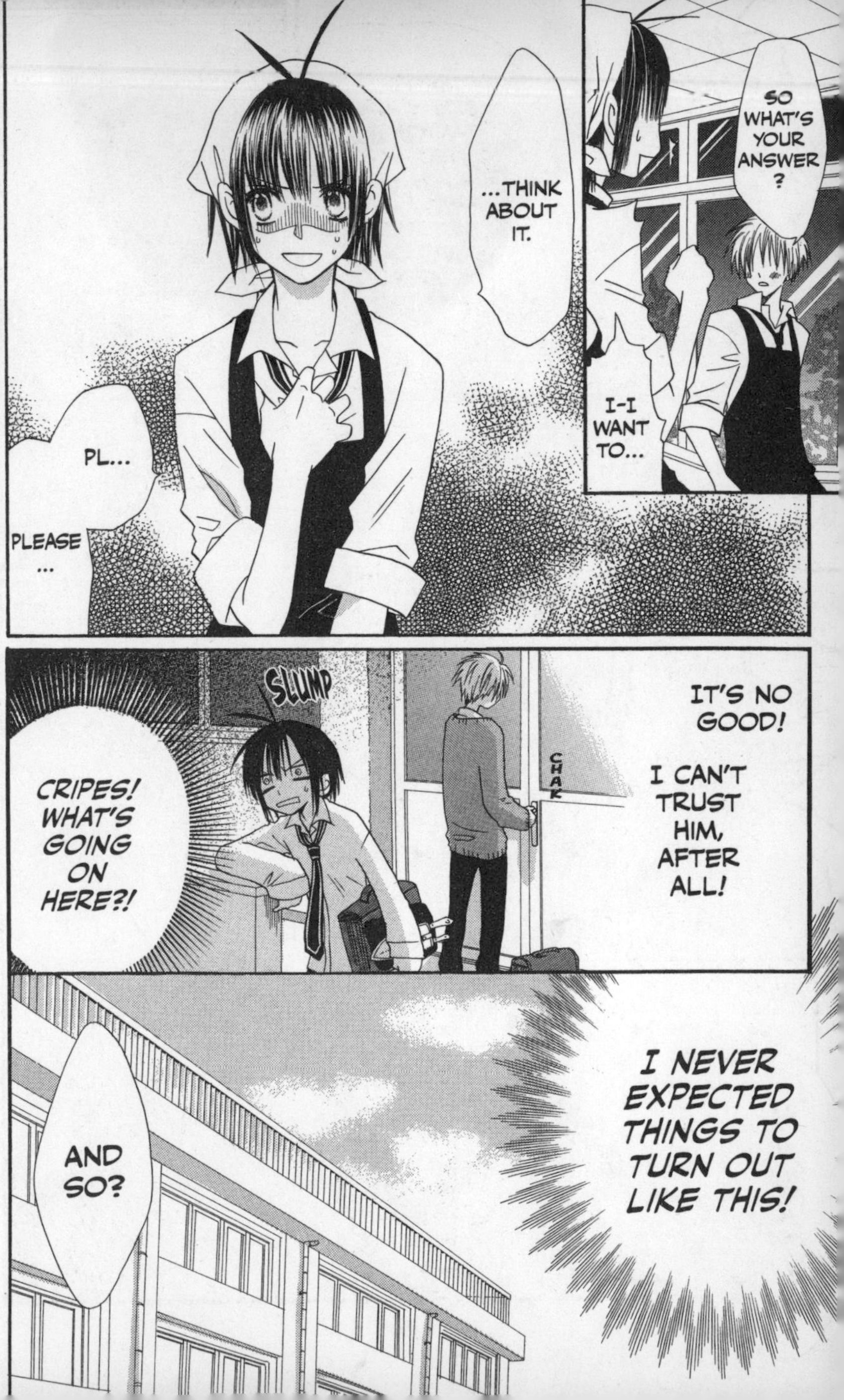
SO WHAT'S YOUR ANSWER?
I-I WANT TO...
...THINK ABOUT IT.
PL...
PLEASE...
IT'S NO GOOD!
I CAN'T TRUST HIM, AFTER ALL!
SLUMP
CHAK
CRIPES! WHAT'S GOING ON HERE?!
I NEVER EXPECTED THINGS TO TURN OUT LIKE THIS!
AND SO?

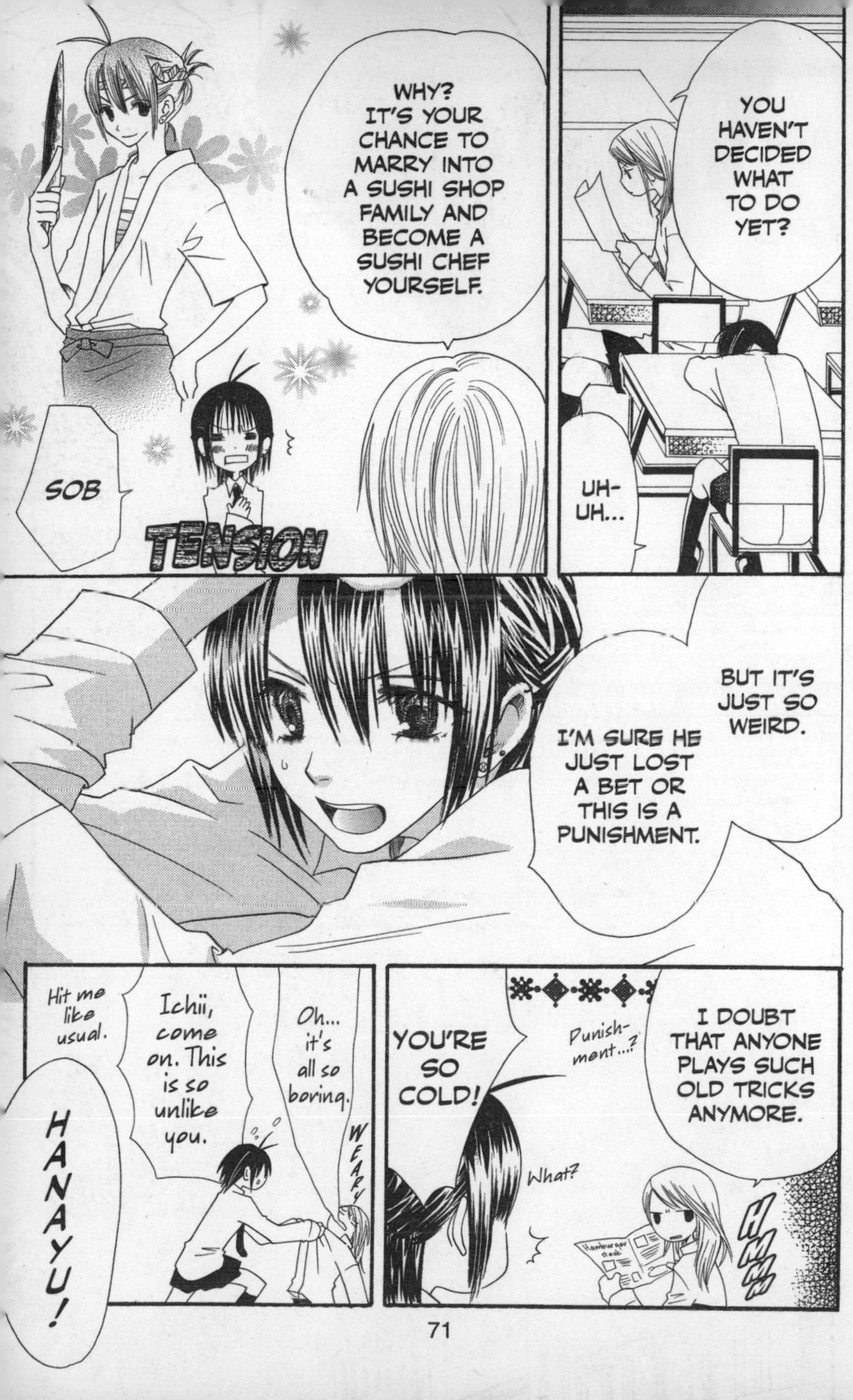
YOU HAVEN'T DECIDED WHAT TO DO YET?
UH-UH...
WHY? IT'S YOUR CHANCE TO MARRY INTO A SUSHI SHOP FAMILY AND BECOME A SUSHI CHEF YOURSELF.
SOB
TENSION
BUT IT'S JUST SO WEIRD.
I'M SURE HE JUST LOST A BET OR THIS IS A PUNISHMENT.
I DOUBT THAT ANYONE PLAYS SUCH OLD TRICKS ANYMORE.
HMMM
Punish-ment...?
YOU'RE SO COLD!
What?
Oh... it's all so boring.
WEARY
Ichii, come on. This is so unlike you.
Hit me like usual.
HANAYU!

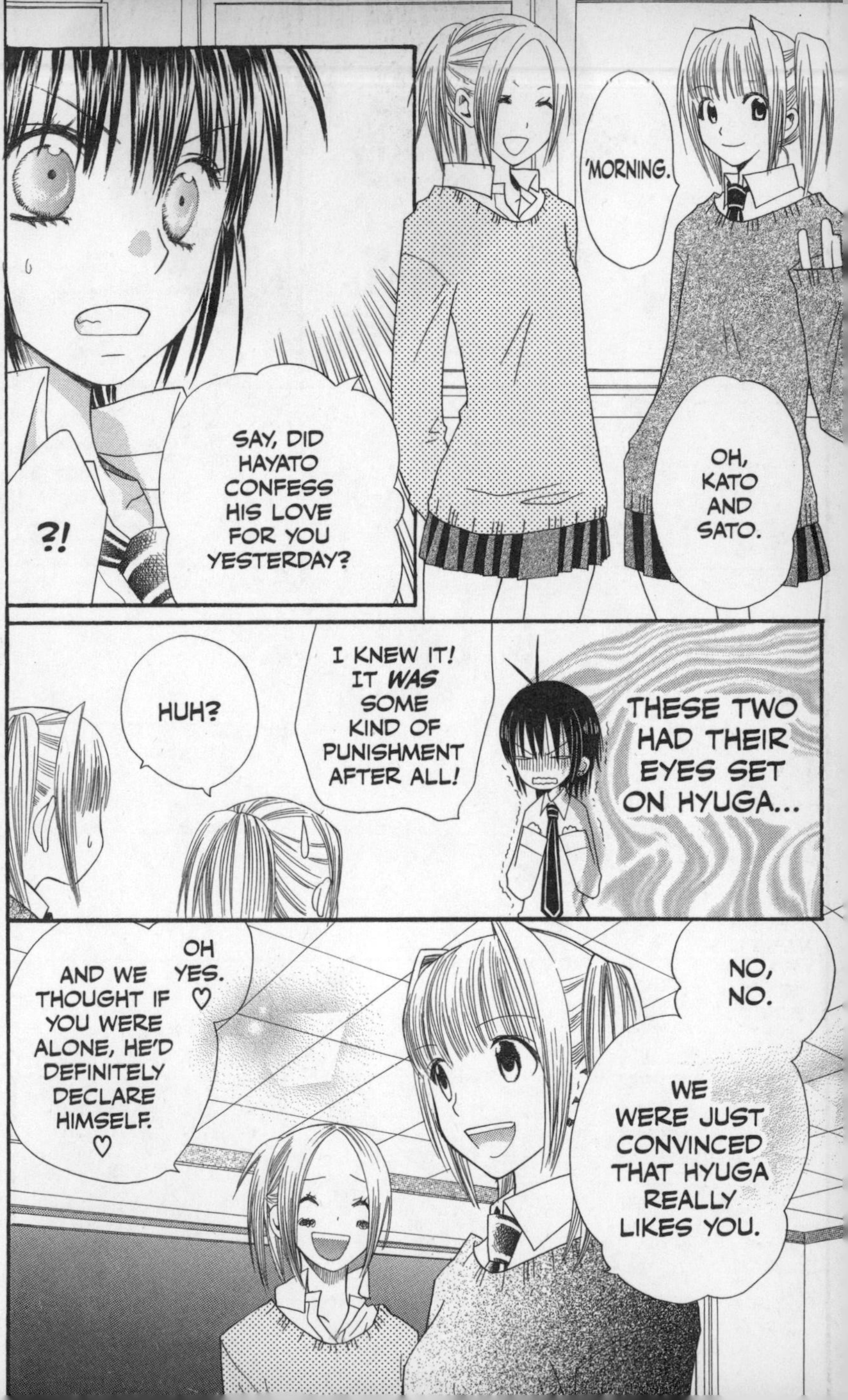
'MORNING.
OH, KATO AND SATO.
SAY, DID HAYATO CONFESS HIS LOVE FOR YOU YESTERDAY?
?!
THESE TWO HAD THEIR EYES SET ON HYUGA...
I KNEW IT! IT *WAS* SOME KIND OF PUNISHMENT AFTER ALL!
HUH?
NO, NO.
WE WERE JUST CONVINCED THAT HYUGA REALLY LIKES YOU.
OH YES. ♡
AND WE THOUGHT IF YOU WERE ALONE, HE'D DEFINITELY DECLARE HIMSELF. ♡

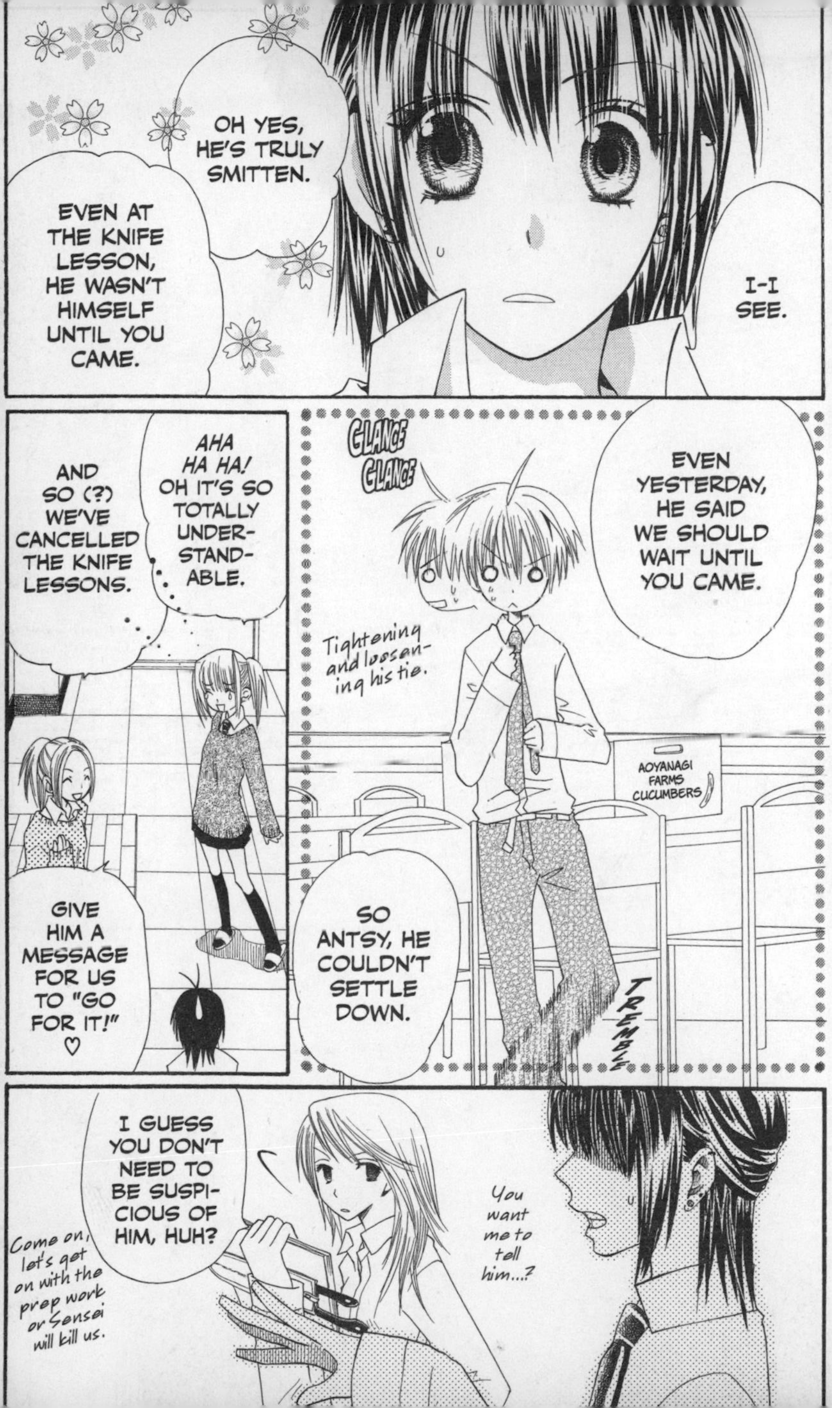
I-I SEE.
OH YES, HE'S TRULY SMITTEN.
EVEN AT THE KNIFE LESSON, HE WASN'T HIMSELF UNTIL YOU CAME.
EVEN YESTERDAY, HE SAID WE SHOULD WAIT UNTIL YOU CAME.
GLANCE GLANCE
Tightening and loosening his tie.
AOYANAGI FARMS CUCUMBERS
SO ANTSY, HE COULDN'T SETTLE DOWN.
TREMBLE
AHA HA HA! OH IT'S SO TOTALLY UNDER-STAND-ABLE.
AND SO (?) WE'VE CANCELLED THE KNIFE LESSONS.
GIVE HIM A MESSAGE FOR US TO "GO FOR IT!" ♡
You want me to tell him...?
I GUESS YOU DON'T NEED TO BE SUSPI-CIOUS OF HIM, HUH?
Come on, let's get on with the prep work or Sensei will kill us.

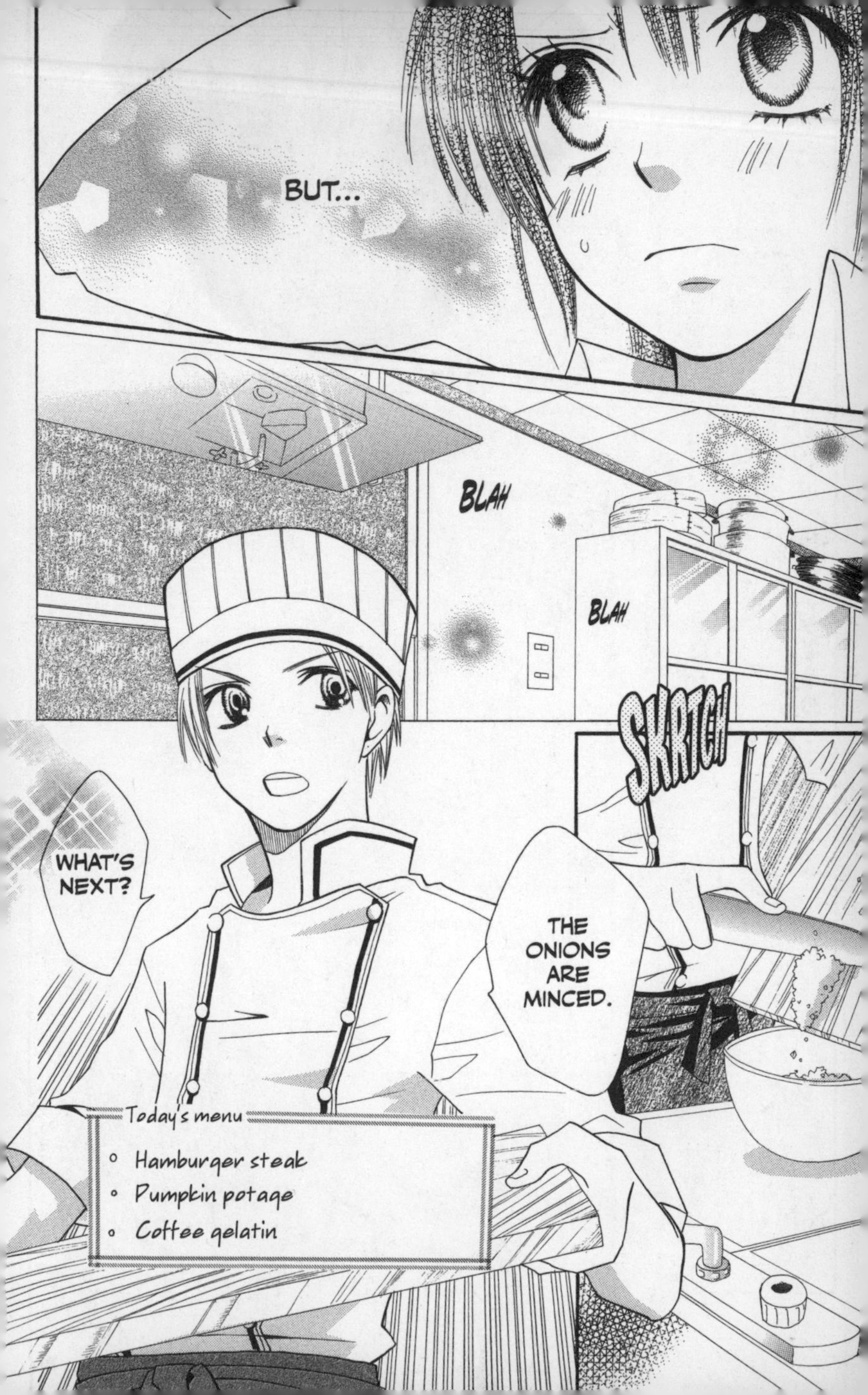
BUT...
BLAH
BLAH
SKRTCH
THE ONIONS ARE MINCED.
WHAT'S NEXT?
Today's menu
∘ Hamburger steak
∘ Pumpkin potage
∘ Coffee gelatin

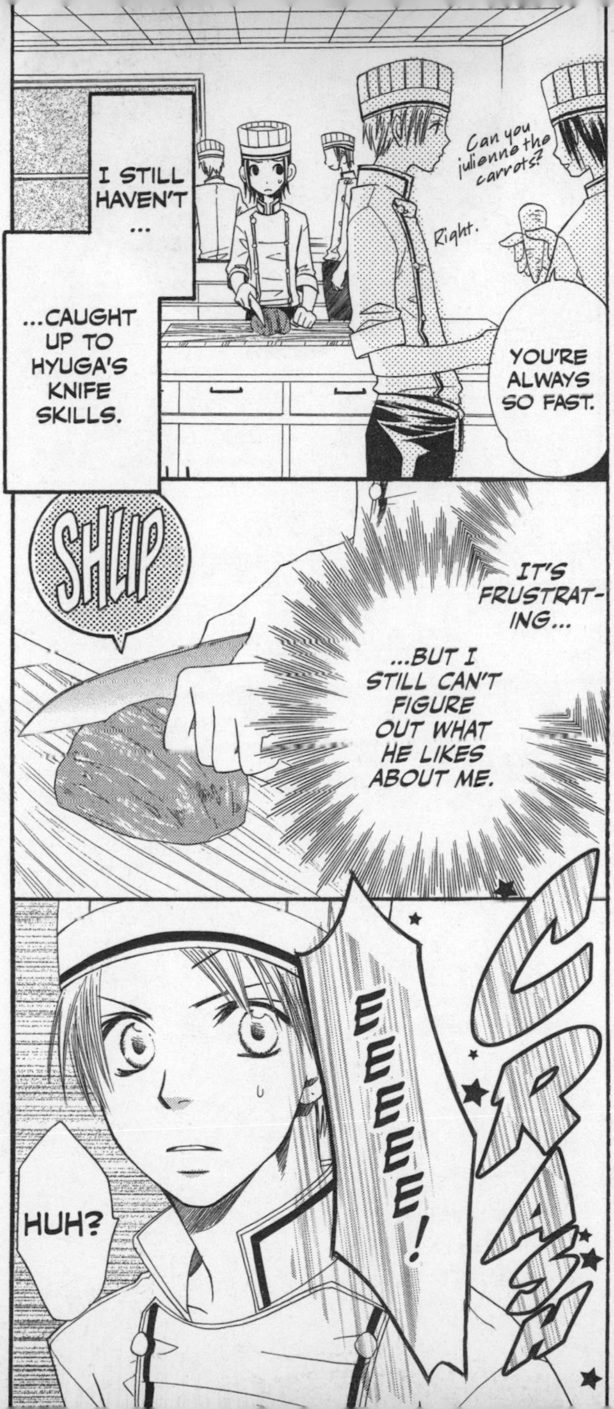
Can you julienne the carrots?
Right.
YOU'RE ALWAYS SO FAST.
I STILL HAVEN'T ...
...CAUGHT UP TO HYUGA'S KNIFE SKILLS.
IT'S FRUSTRATING...
...BUT I STILL CAN'T FIGURE OUT WHAT HE LIKES ABOUT ME.
SHLIP
CRASH
EEEEEE!
HUH?

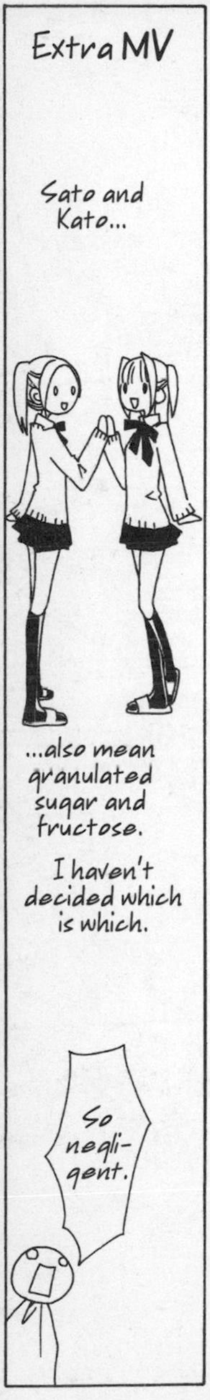
Extra MV
Sato and Kato...
...also mean granulated sugar and fructose.
I haven't decided which is which.
So negligent.

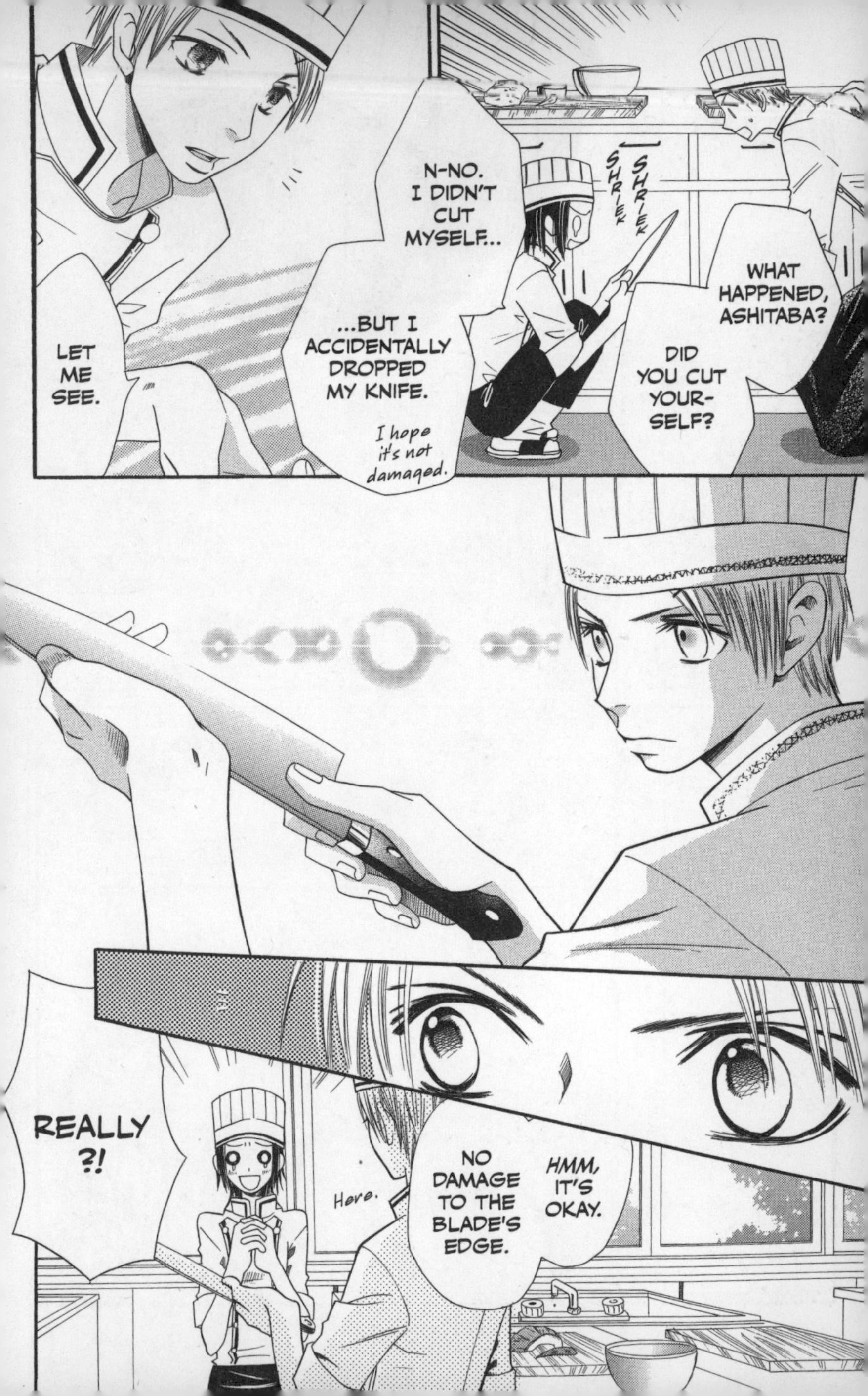
WHAT HAPPENED, ASHITABA?
DID YOU CUT YOURSELF?
SHRIEK
SHRIEK
N-NO. I DIDN'T CUT MYSELF...
...BUT I ACCIDENTALLY DROPPED MY KNIFE.
I hope it's not damaged.
LET ME SEE.
HMM, IT'S OKAY.
NO DAMAGE TO THE BLADE'S EDGE.
Here.
REALLY ?!

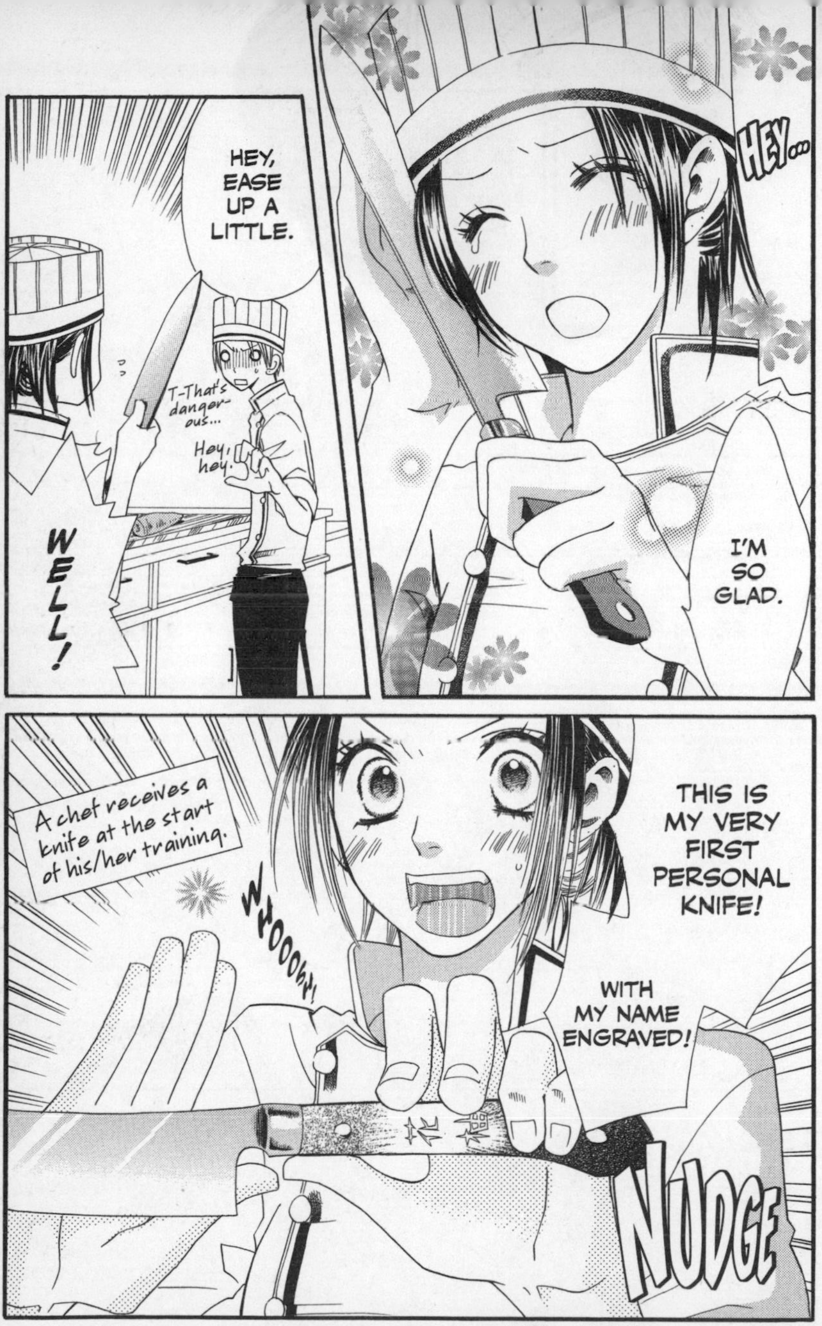
HEY...
I'M SO GLAD.
HEY, EASE UP A LITTLE.
T-That's danger-ous...
Hey, hey.
WELL!
THIS IS MY VERY FIRST PERSONAL KNIFE!
A chef receives a knife at the start of his/her training.
WITH MY NAME ENGRAVED!
WHOOOAH!
NUDGE

*KNIFE: HANAYU

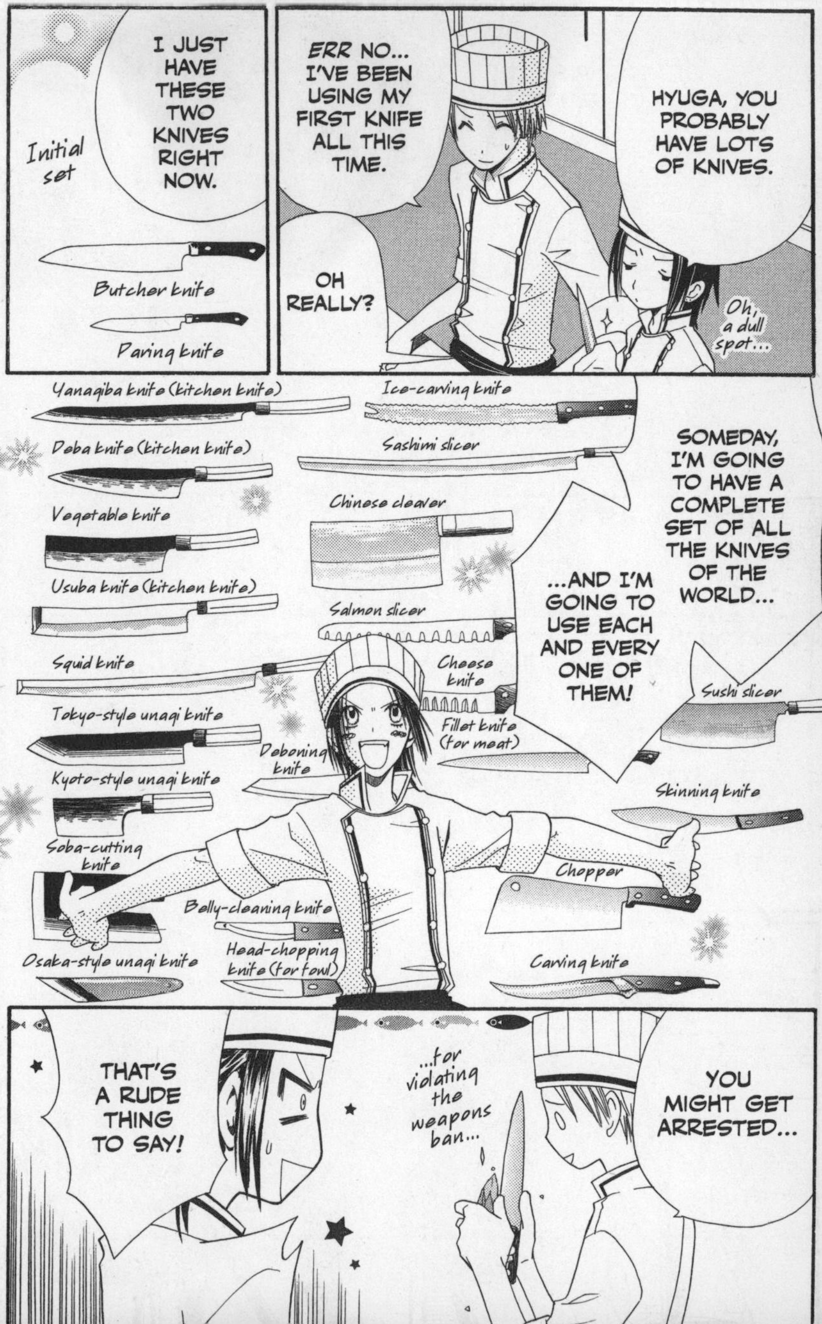
HYUGA, YOU PROBABLY HAVE LOTS OF KNIVES.
Oh, a dull spot...
ERR NO... I'VE BEEN USING MY FIRST KNIFE ALL THIS TIME.
OH REALLY?
I JUST HAVE THESE TWO KNIVES RIGHT NOW.
Initial set
Butcher knife
Paring knife
SOMEDAY, I'M GOING TO HAVE A COMPLETE SET OF ALL THE KNIVES OF THE WORLD...
...AND I'M GOING TO USE EACH AND EVERY ONE OF THEM!
Ice-carving knife
Sashimi slicer
Chinese cleaver
Salmon slicer
Cheese knife
Sushi slicer
Fillet knife (for meat)
Skinning knife
Chopper
Carving knife
Yanagiba knife (kitchen knife)
Deba knife (kitchen knife)
Vegetable knife
Usuba knife (kitchen knife)
Squid knife
Tokyo-style unagi knife
Deboning knife
Kyoto-style unagi knife
Soba-cutting knife
Belly-cleaning knife
Head-chopping knife (for fowl)
Osaka-style unagi knife
YOU MIGHT GET ARRESTED...
...for violating the weapons ban...
THAT'S A RUDE THING TO SAY!

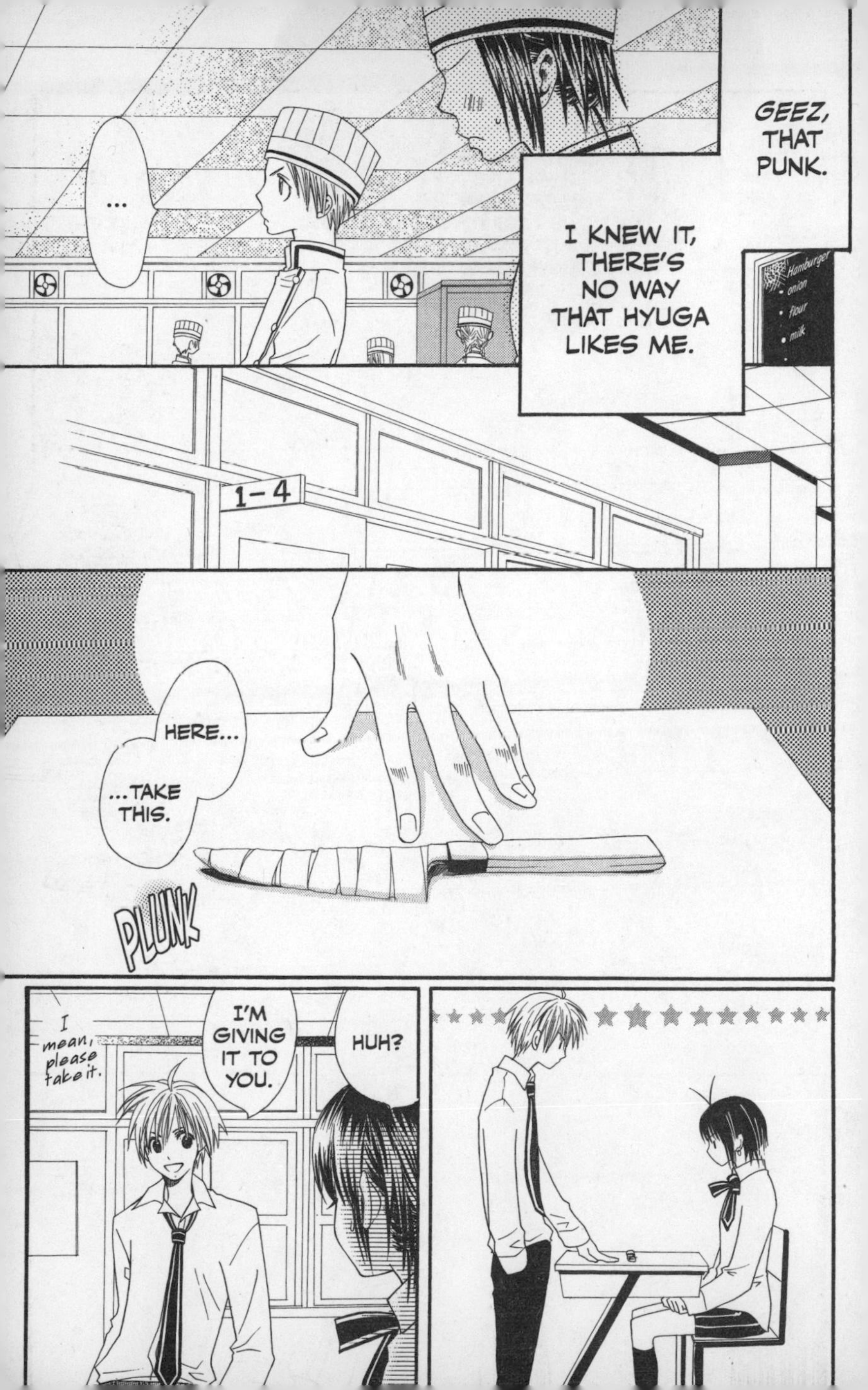
GEEZ, THAT PUNK.
I KNEW IT, THERE'S NO WAY THAT HYUGA LIKES ME.
Hamburger
onion
flour
milk
...
1-4
HERE...
...TAKE THIS.
PLUNK
HUH?
I'M GIVING IT TO YOU.
I mean, please take it.

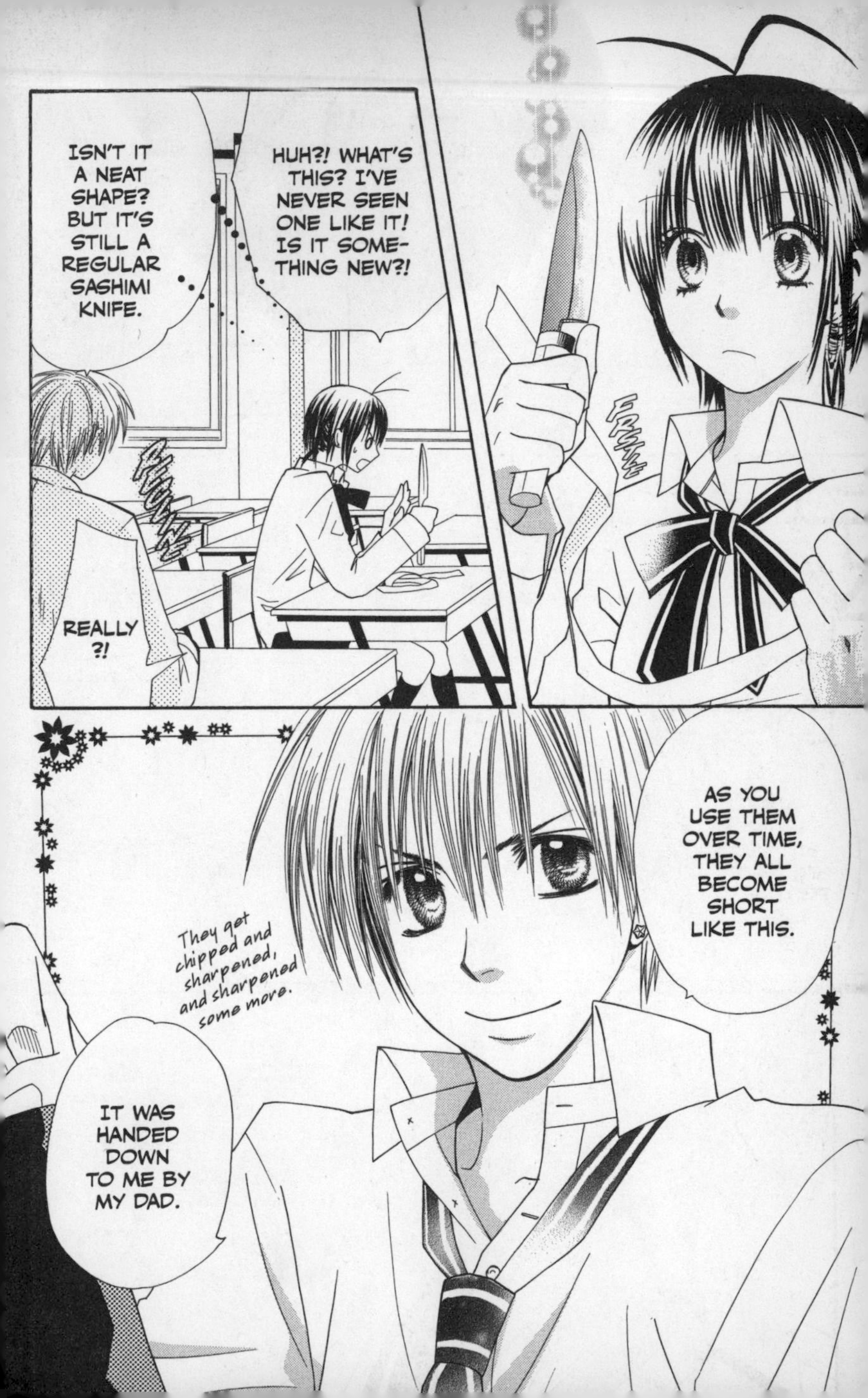
HUH?! WHAT'S THIS? I'VE NEVER SEEN ONE LIKE IT! IS IT SOME-THING NEW?!
ISN'T IT A NEAT SHAPE? BUT IT'S STILL A REGULAR SASHIMI KNIFE.
REALLY ?!
AS YOU USE THEM OVER TIME, THEY ALL BECOME SHORT LIKE THIS.
They get chipped and sharpened, and sharpened some more.
IT WAS HANDED DOWN TO ME BY MY DAD.

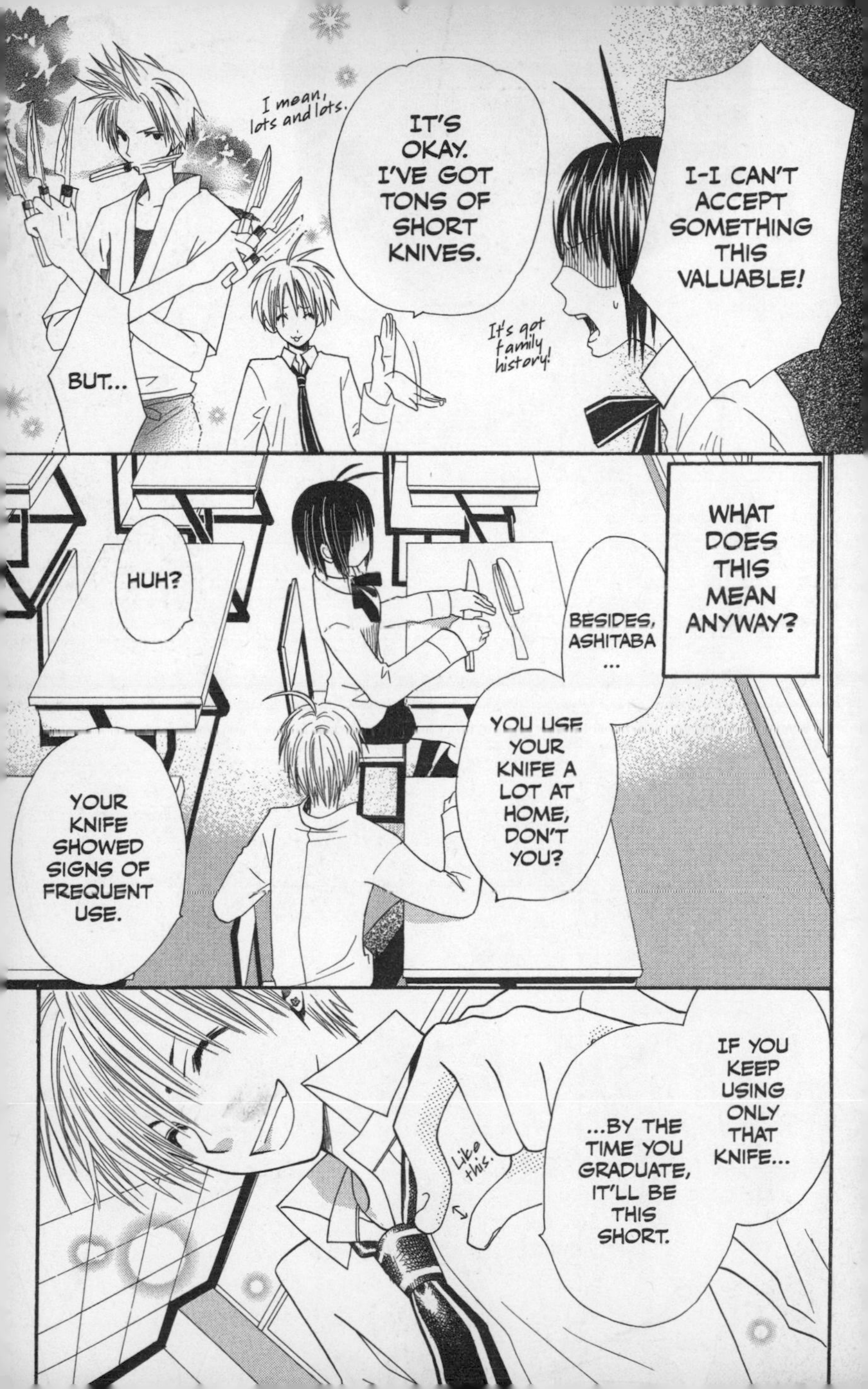
I-I CAN'T ACCEPT SOMETHING THIS VALUABLE!
It's got family history!
IT'S OKAY. I'VE GOT TONS OF SHORT KNIVES.
I mean, lots and lots.
BUT...
WHAT DOES THIS MEAN ANYWAY?
BESIDES, ASHITABA...
YOU USE YOUR KNIFE A LOT AT HOME, DON'T YOU?
HUH?
YOUR KNIFE SHOWED SIGNS OF FREQUENT USE.
IF YOU KEEP USING ONLY THAT KNIFE...
...BY THE TIME YOU GRADUATE, IT'LL BE THIS SHORT.
Like this.

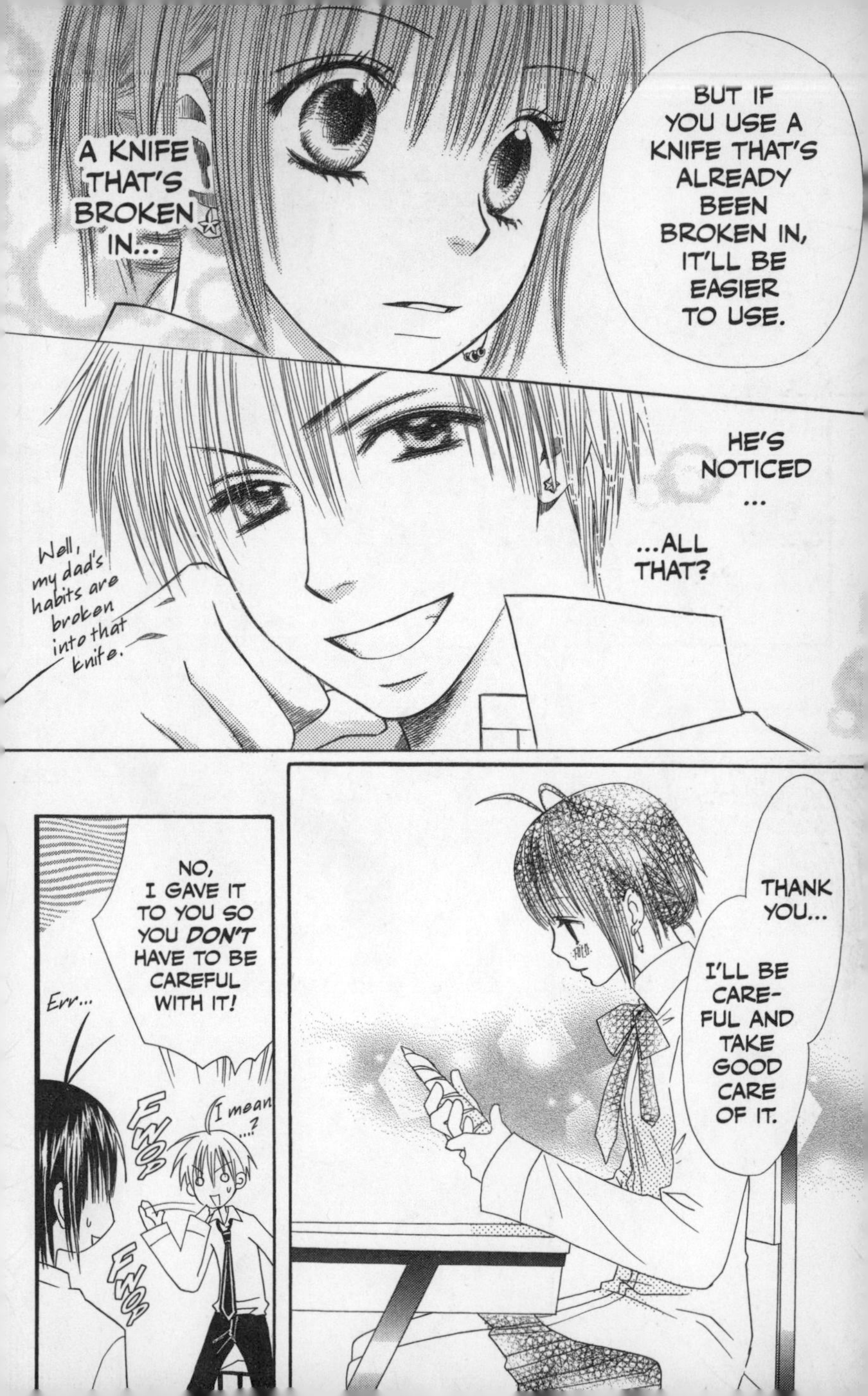
BUT IF YOU USE A KNIFE THAT'S ALREADY BEEN BROKEN IN, IT'LL BE EASIER TO USE.
A KNIFE THAT'S BROKEN IN...
HE'S NOTICED ...
...ALL THAT?
Well, my dad's habits are broken into that knife.
THANK YOU...
I'LL BE CARE-FUL AND TAKE GOOD CARE OF IT.
NO, I GAVE IT TO YOU SO YOU *DON'T* HAVE TO BE CAREFUL WITH IT!
Err...
FWOP
I mean ...?
FWOP

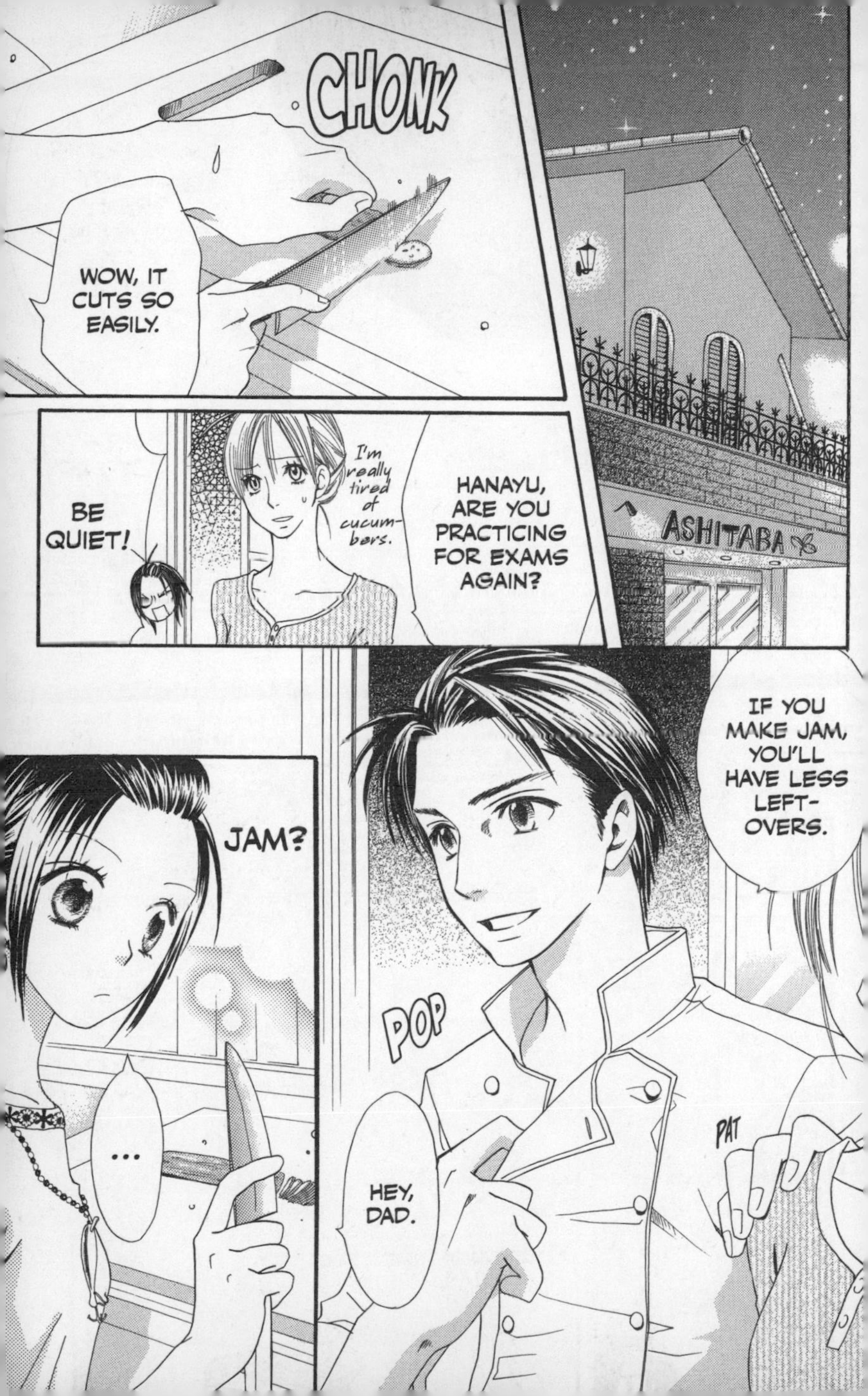
CHONK
WOW, IT CUTS SO EASILY.
HANAYU, ARE YOU PRACTICING FOR EXAMS AGAIN?
I'm really tired of cucumbers.
BE QUIET!
ASHITABA
IF YOU MAKE JAM, YOU'LL HAVE LESS LEFTOVERS.
POP
PAT
HEY, DAD.
JAM?
...

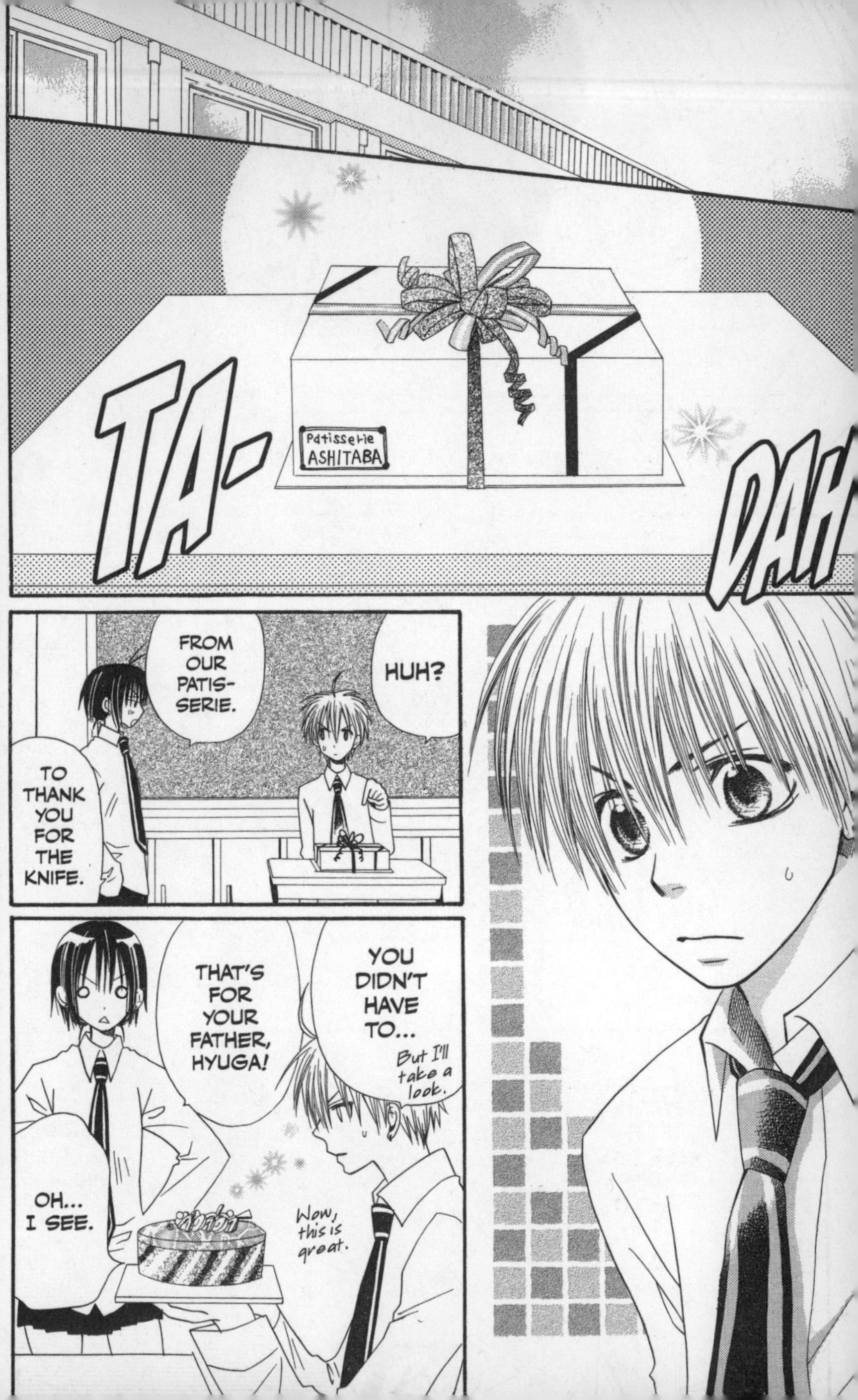

TA-DAH
Patisserie ASHITABA
HUH?
FROM OUR PATIS-SERIE.
TO THANK YOU FOR THE KNIFE.
YOU DIDN'T HAVE TO...
But I'll take a look.
THAT'S FOR YOUR FATHER, HYUGA!
Wow, this is great.
OH... I SEE.

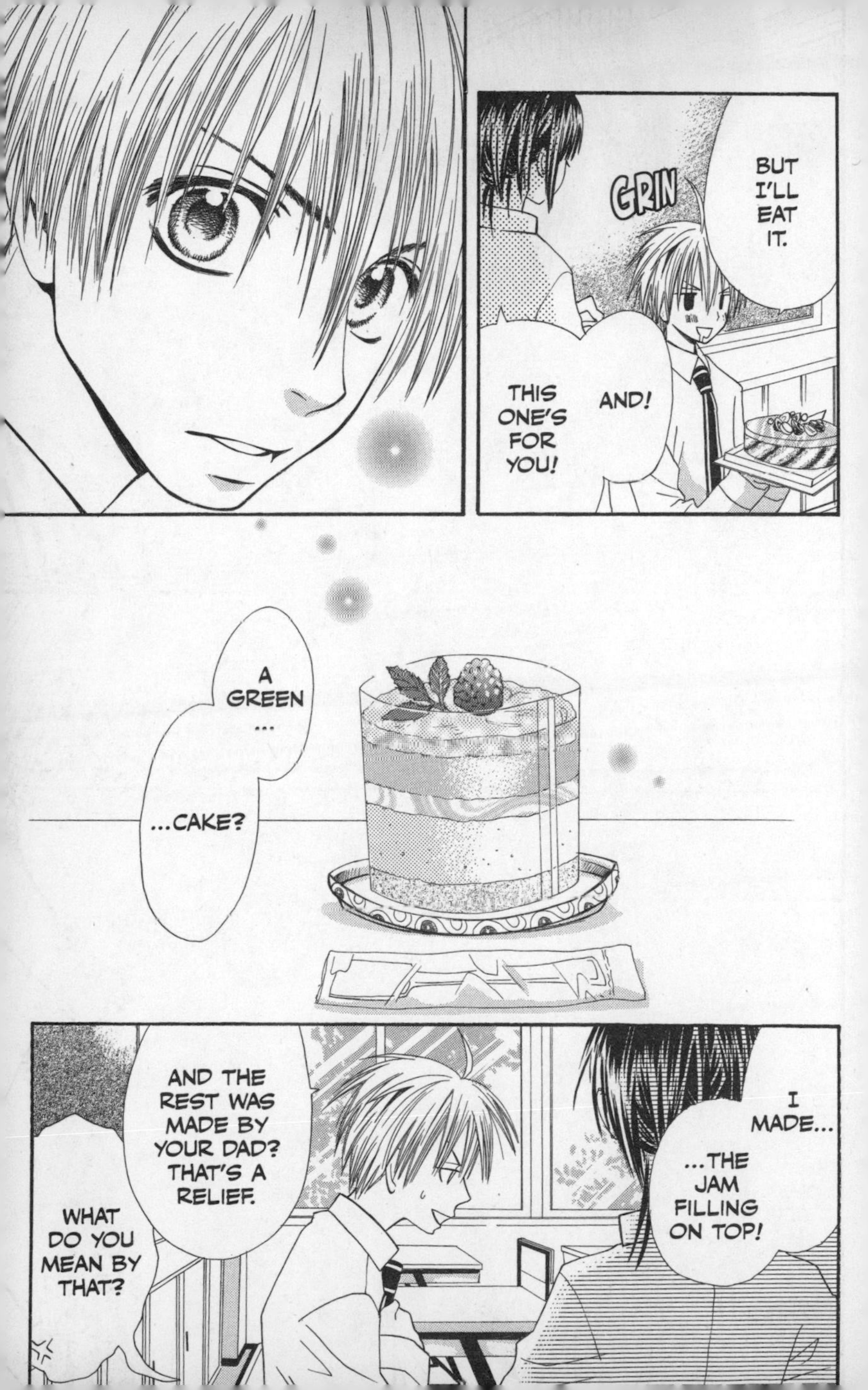
BUT I'LL EAT IT.
GRIN
AND!
THIS ONE'S FOR YOU!
A GREEN...
...CAKE?
I MADE...
...THE JAM FILLING ON TOP!
AND THE REST WAS MADE BY YOUR DAD? THAT'S A RELIEF.
WHAT DO YOU MEAN BY THAT?

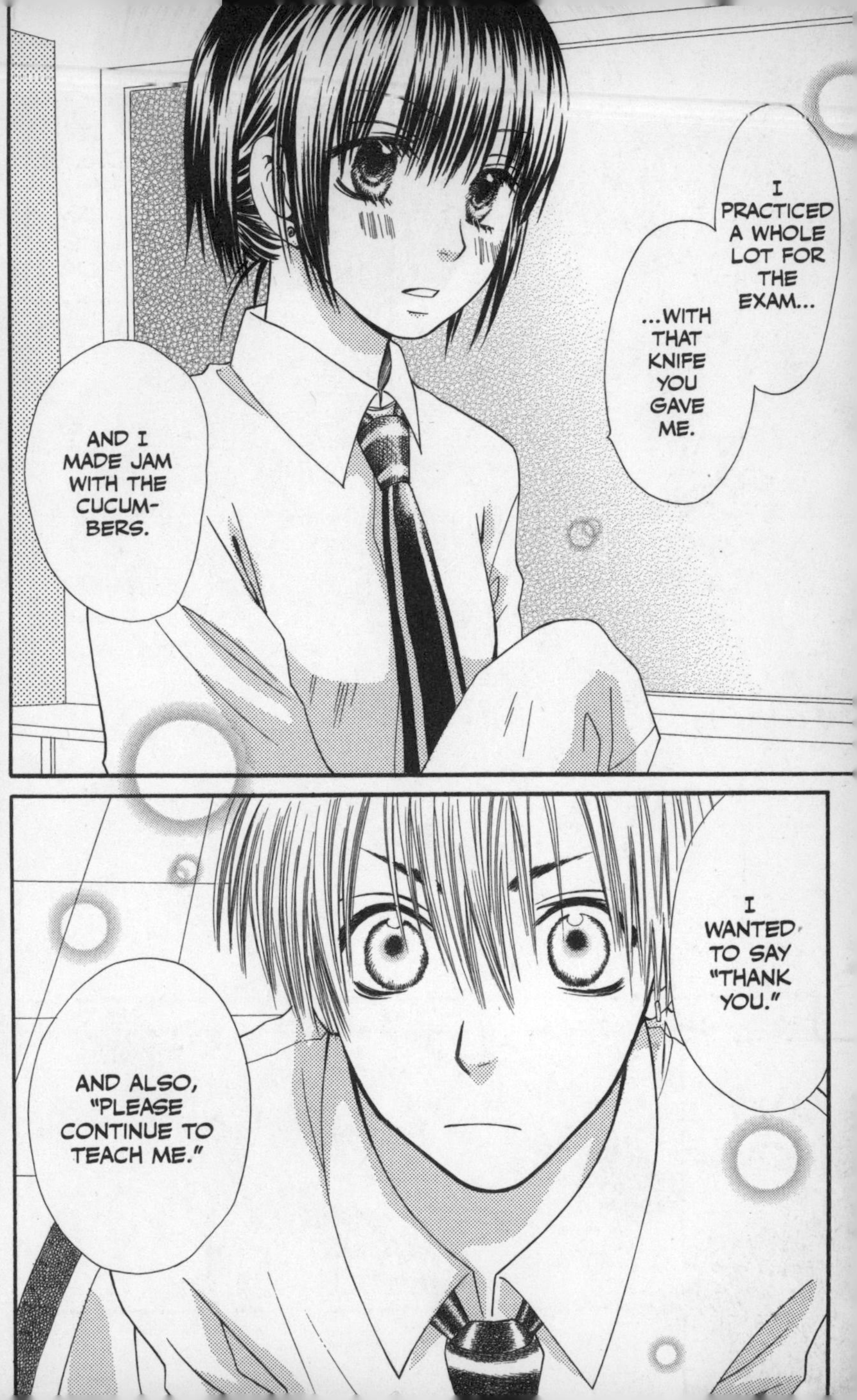
I PRACTICED A WHOLE LOT FOR THE EXAM...
...WITH THAT KNIFE YOU GAVE ME.
AND I MADE JAM WITH THE CUCUM-BERS.
I WANTED TO SAY "THANK YOU."
AND ALSO, "PLEASE CONTINUE TO TEACH ME."

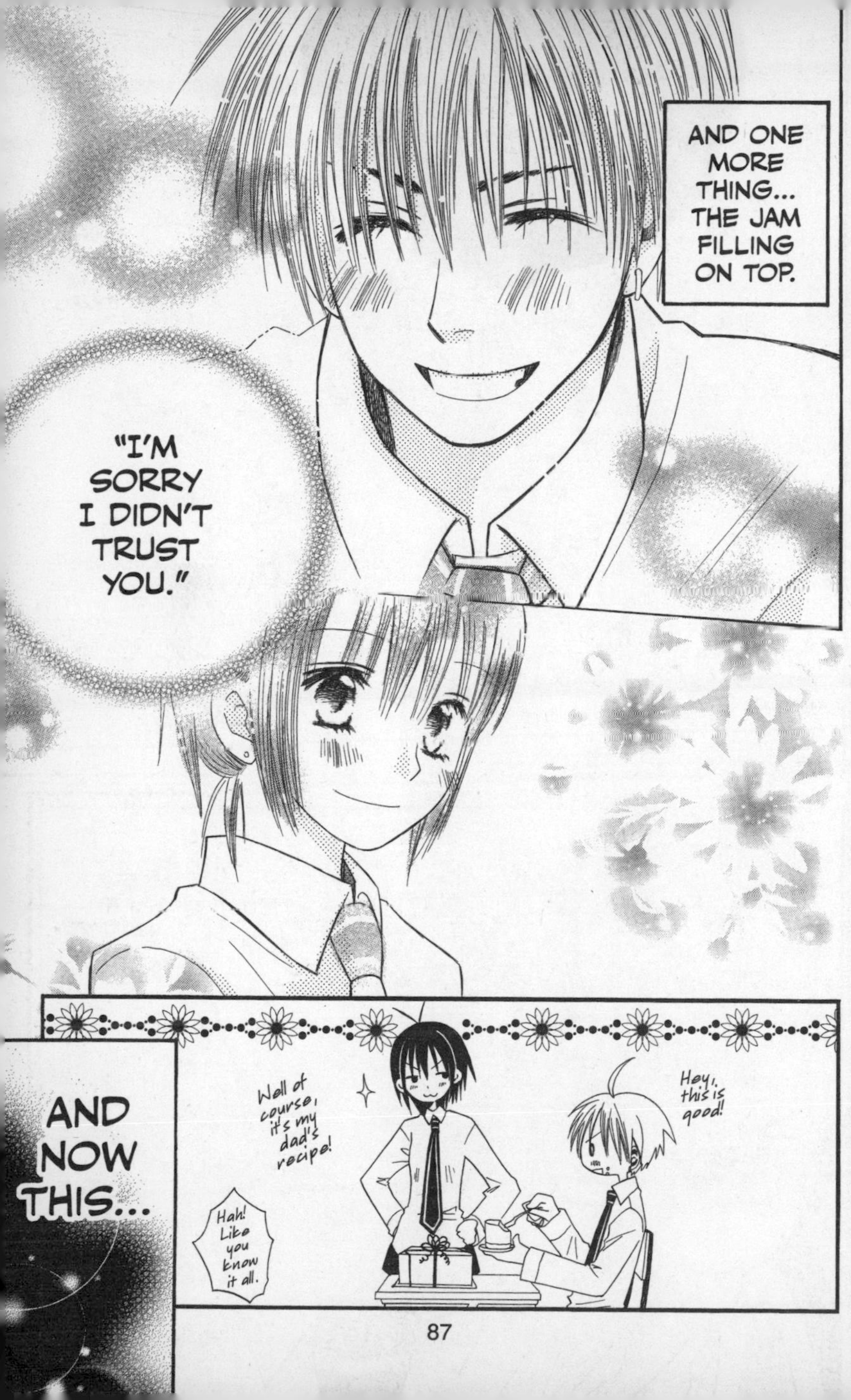
AND ONE MORE THING... THE JAM FILLING ON TOP.
"I'M SORRY I DIDN'T TRUST YOU."
Hey, this is good!
Well of course, it's my dad's recipe!
Hah! Like you know it all.
AND NOW THIS...

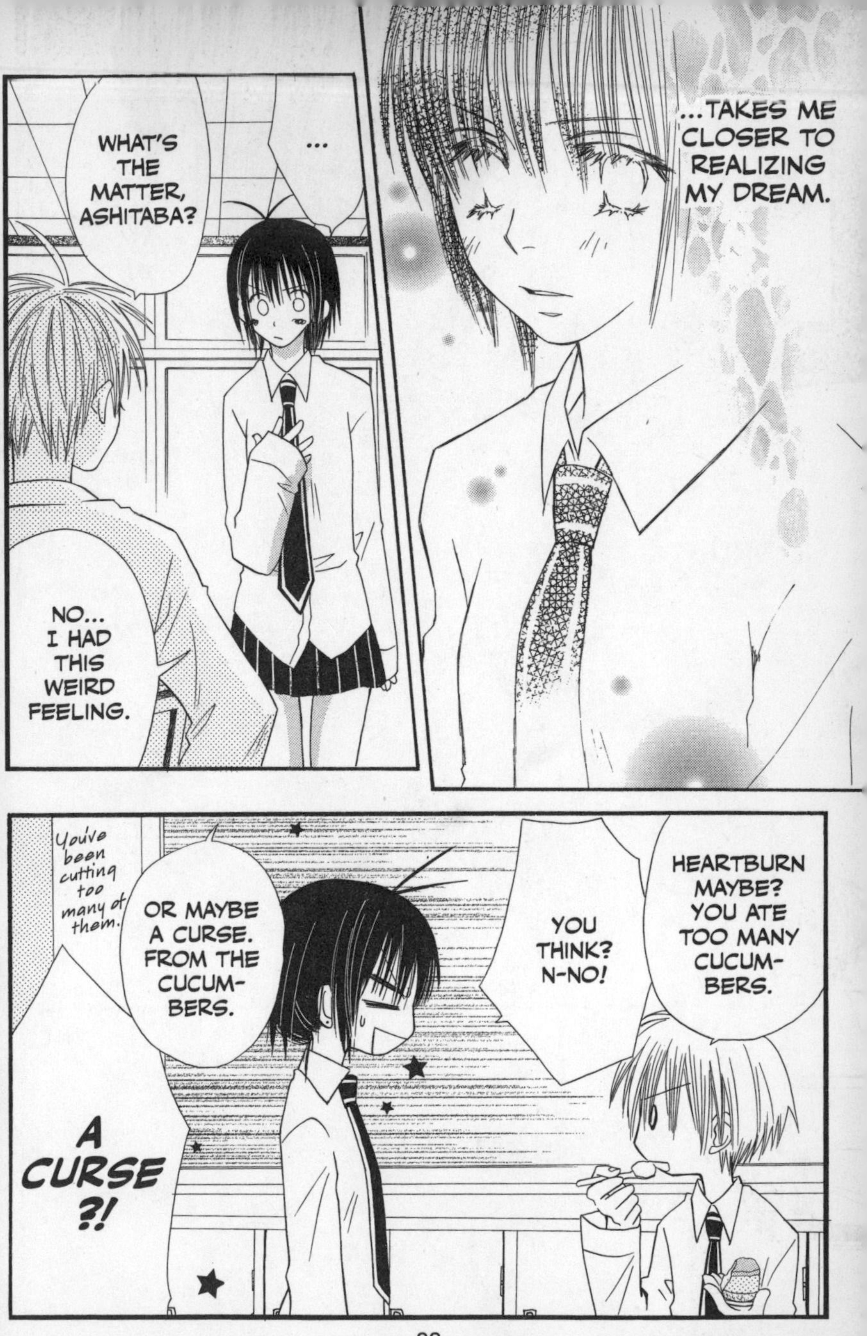
...TAKES ME CLOSER TO REALIZING MY DREAM.
...
WHAT'S THE MATTER, ASHITABA?
NO... I HAD THIS WEIRD FEELING.
HEARTBURN MAYBE? YOU ATE TOO MANY CUCUM-BERS.
YOU THINK? N-NO!
OR MAYBE A CURSE. FROM THE CUCUM-BERS.
You've been cutting too many of them.
A CURSE?!

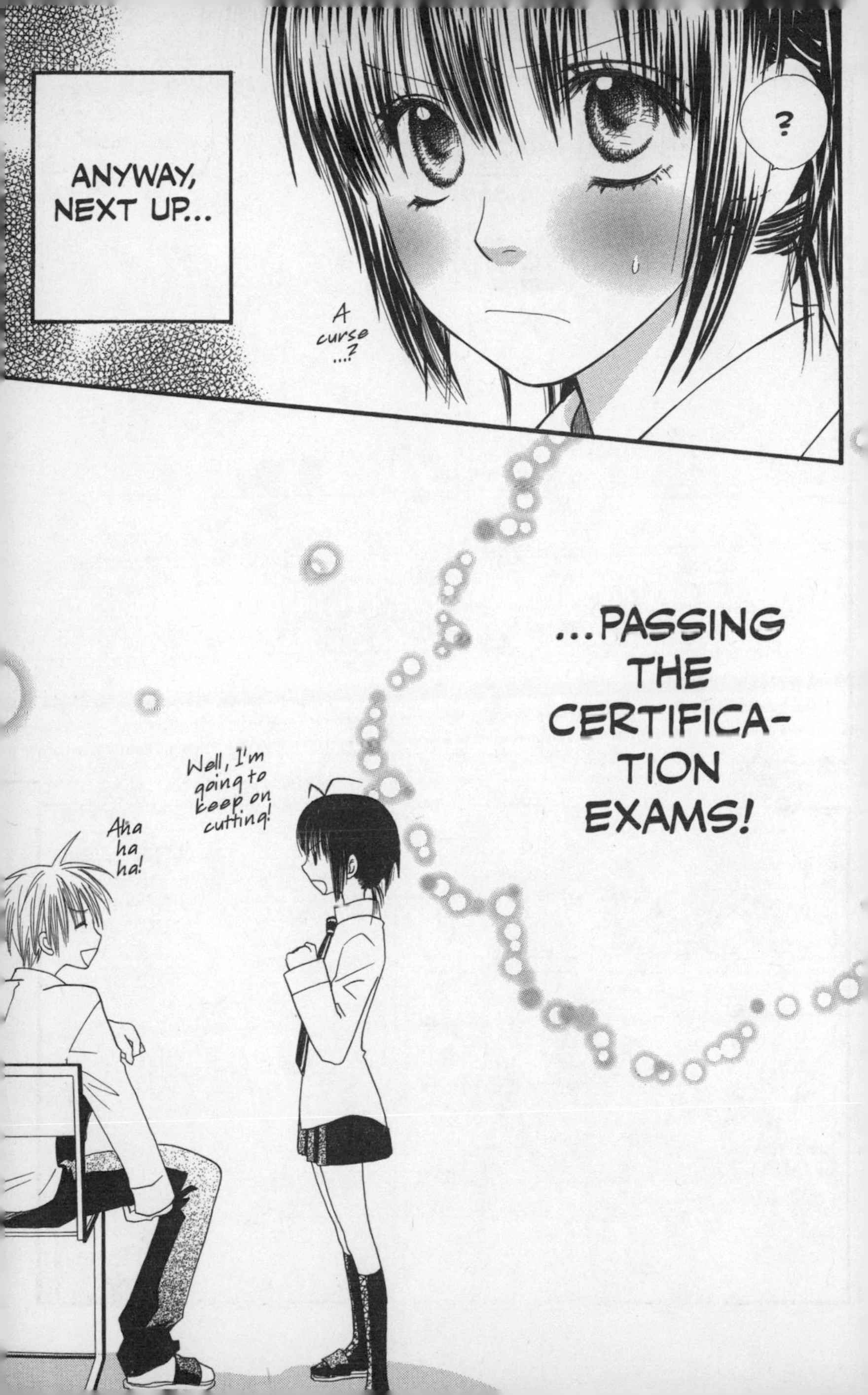
?
ANYWAY, NEXT UP...
A curse...?
...PASSING THE CERTIFICATION EXAMS!
Well, I'm going to keep on cutting!
Aha ha ha!

SIDE DISH Mixed Vegetables 3

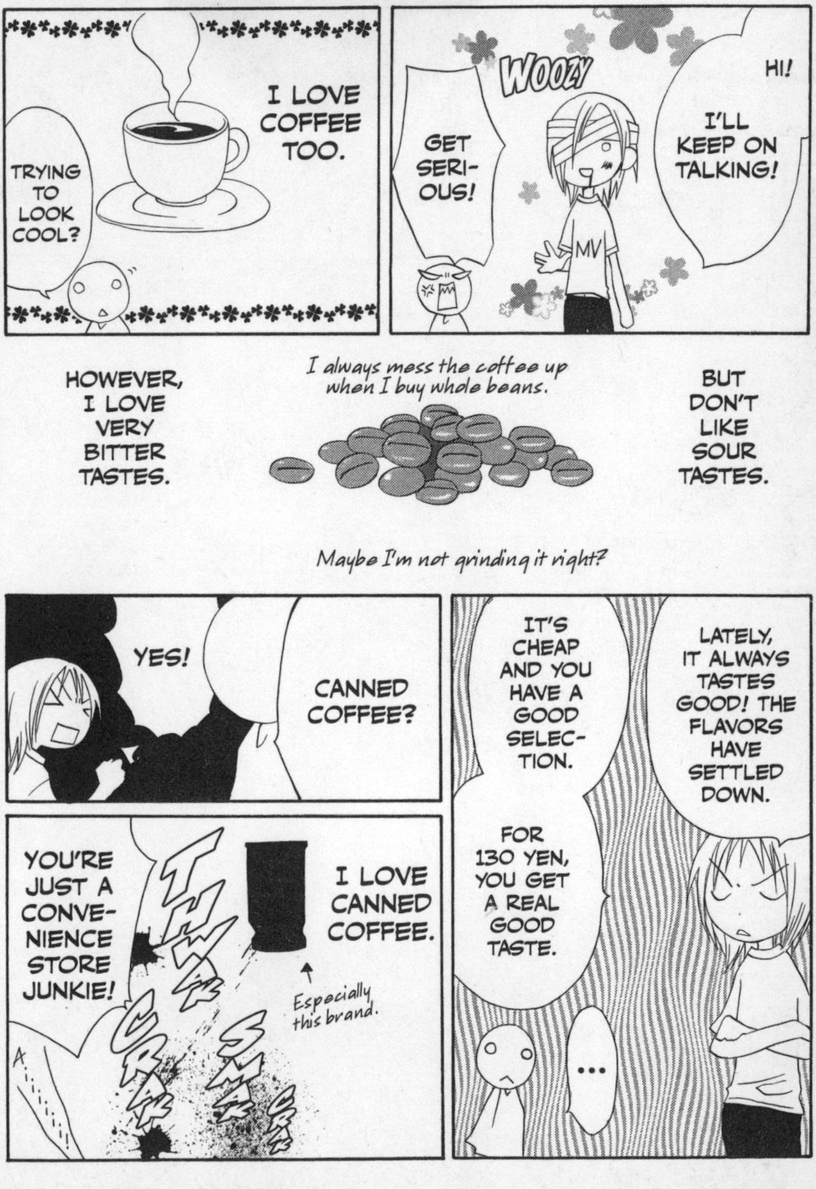
HI!
I'LL KEEP ON TALKING!
WOOZY
GET SERI-OUS!
I LOVE COFFEE TOO.
TRYING TO LOOK COOL?
BUT DON'T LIKE SOUR TASTES.
I always mess the coffee up when I buy whole beans.
HOWEVER, I LOVE VERY BITTER TASTES.
Maybe I'm not grinding it right?
LATELY, IT ALWAYS TASTES GOOD! THE FLAVORS HAVE SETTLED DOWN.
IT'S CHEAP AND YOU HAVE A GOOD SELEC-TION.
FOR 130 YEN, YOU GET A REAL GOOD TASTE.
...
CANNED COFFEE?
YES!
I LOVE CANNED COFFEE.
Especially this brand.
YOU'RE JUST A CONVE-NIENCE STORE JUNKIE!

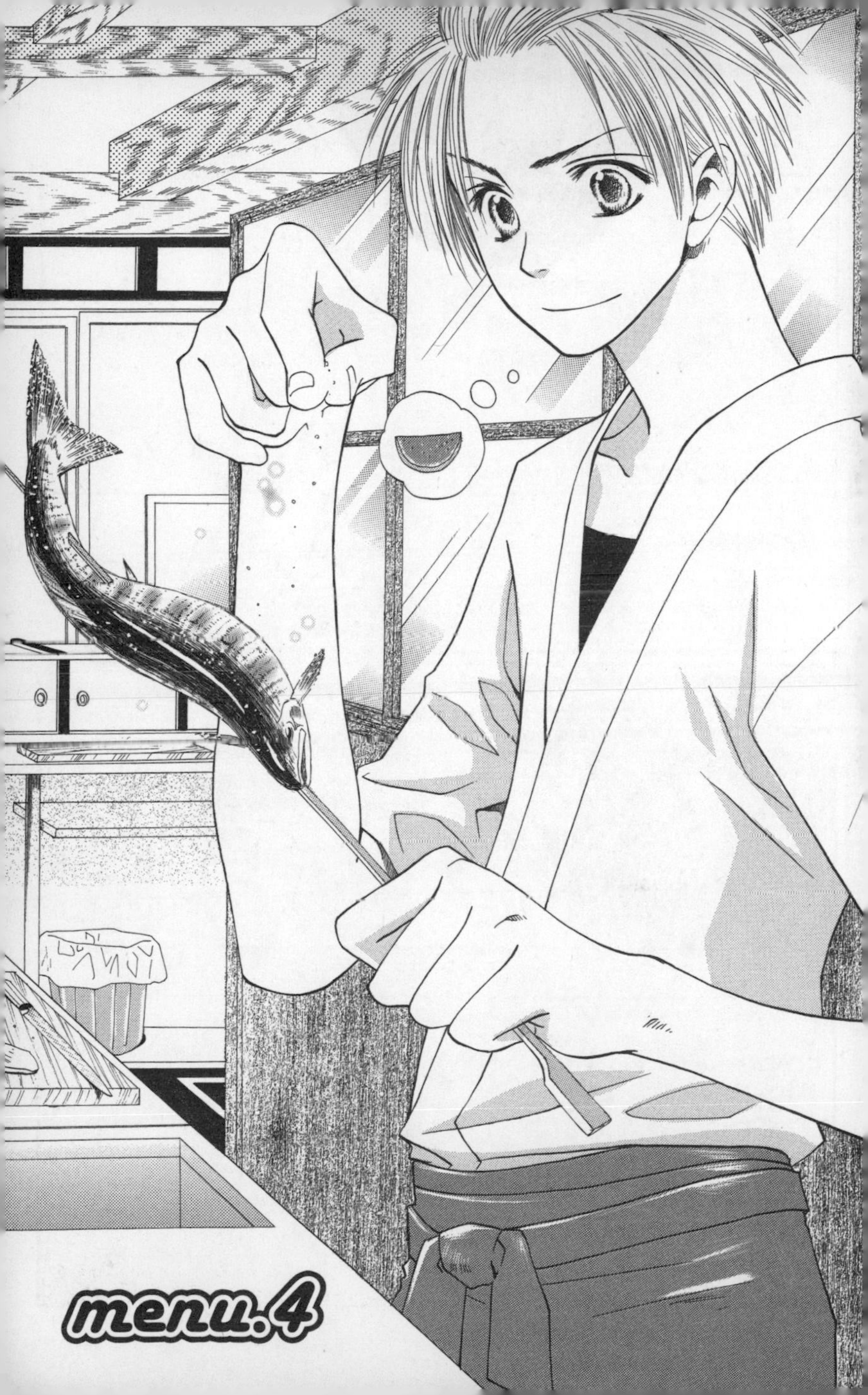
menu.4

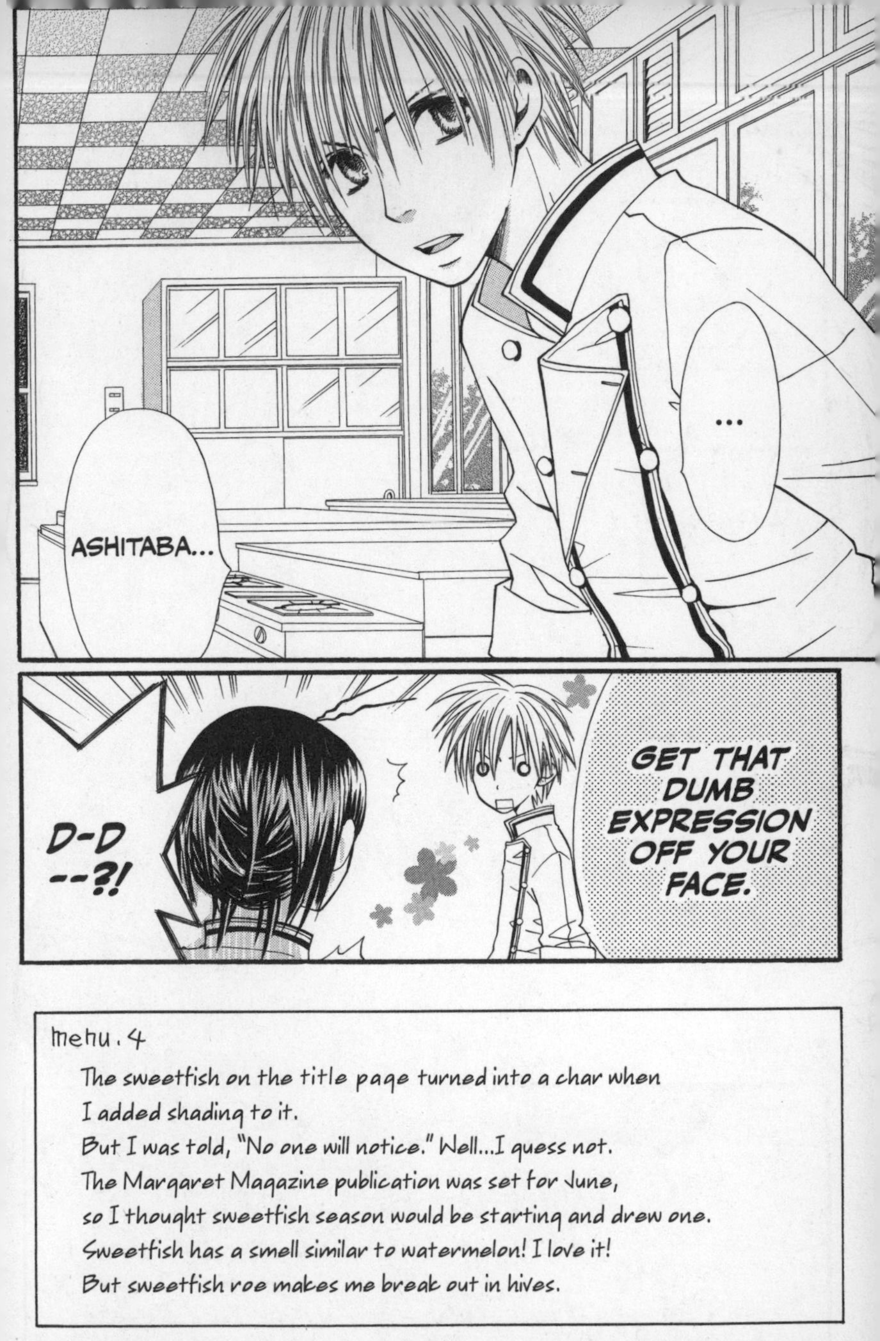
...
ASHITABA...
GET THAT DUMB EXPRESSION OFF YOUR FACE.
D-D --?!

menu. 4

The sweetfish on the title page turned into a char when I added shading to it.
But I was told, "No one will notice." Well...I guess not.
The Margaret Magazine publication was set for June, so I thought sweetfish season would be starting and drew one.
Sweetfish has a smell similar to watermelon! I love it!
But sweetfish roe makes me break out in hives.

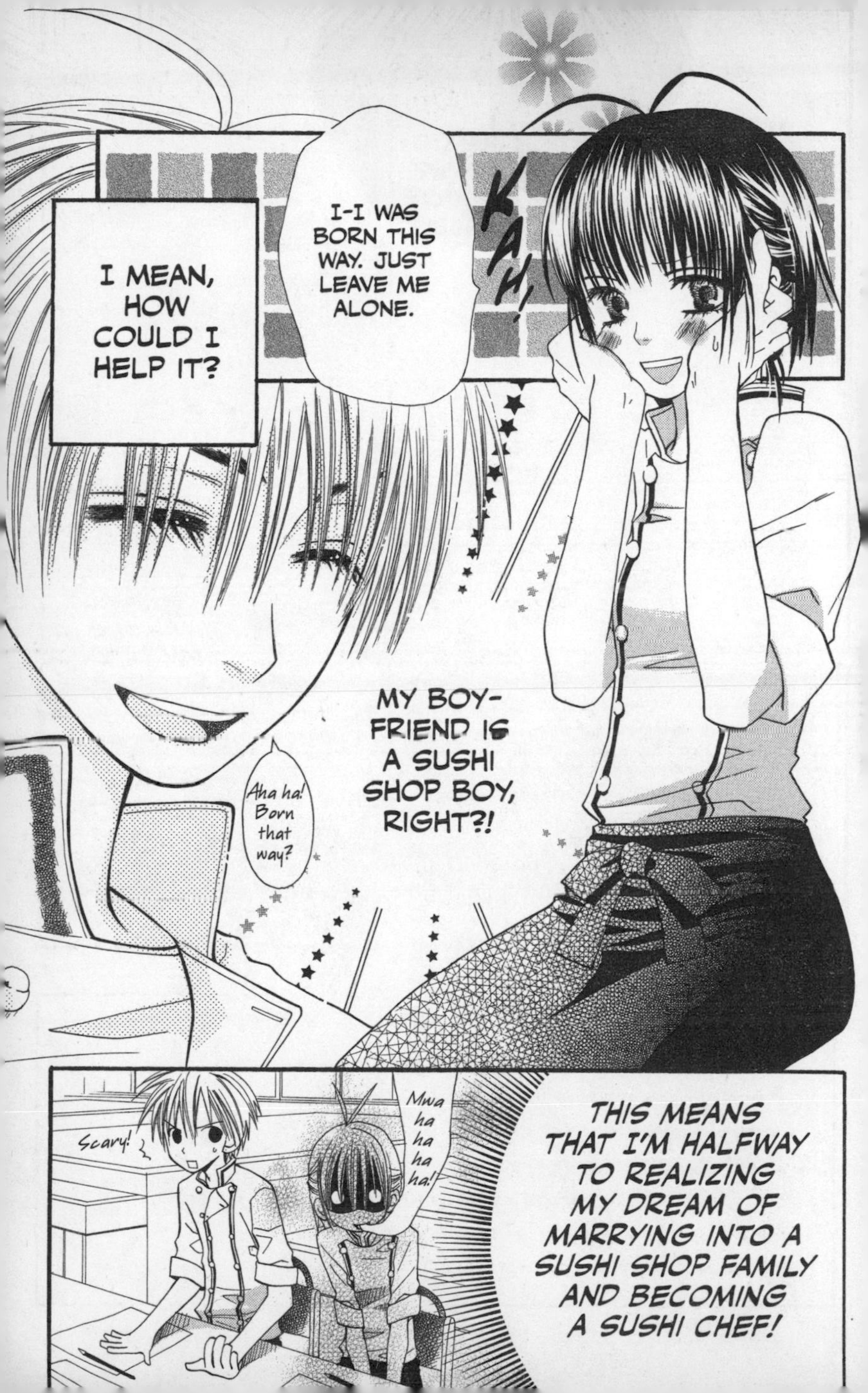
KAH!
I-I WAS BORN THIS WAY. JUST LEAVE ME ALONE.
I MEAN, HOW COULD I HELP IT?
MY BOY-FRIEND IS A SUSHI SHOP BOY, RIGHT?!
Aha ha! Born that way?
THIS MEANS THAT I'M HALFWAY TO REALIZING MY DREAM OF MARRYING INTO A SUSHI SHOP FAMILY AND BECOMING A SUSHI CHEF!
Mwa ha ha ha ha!
Scary!

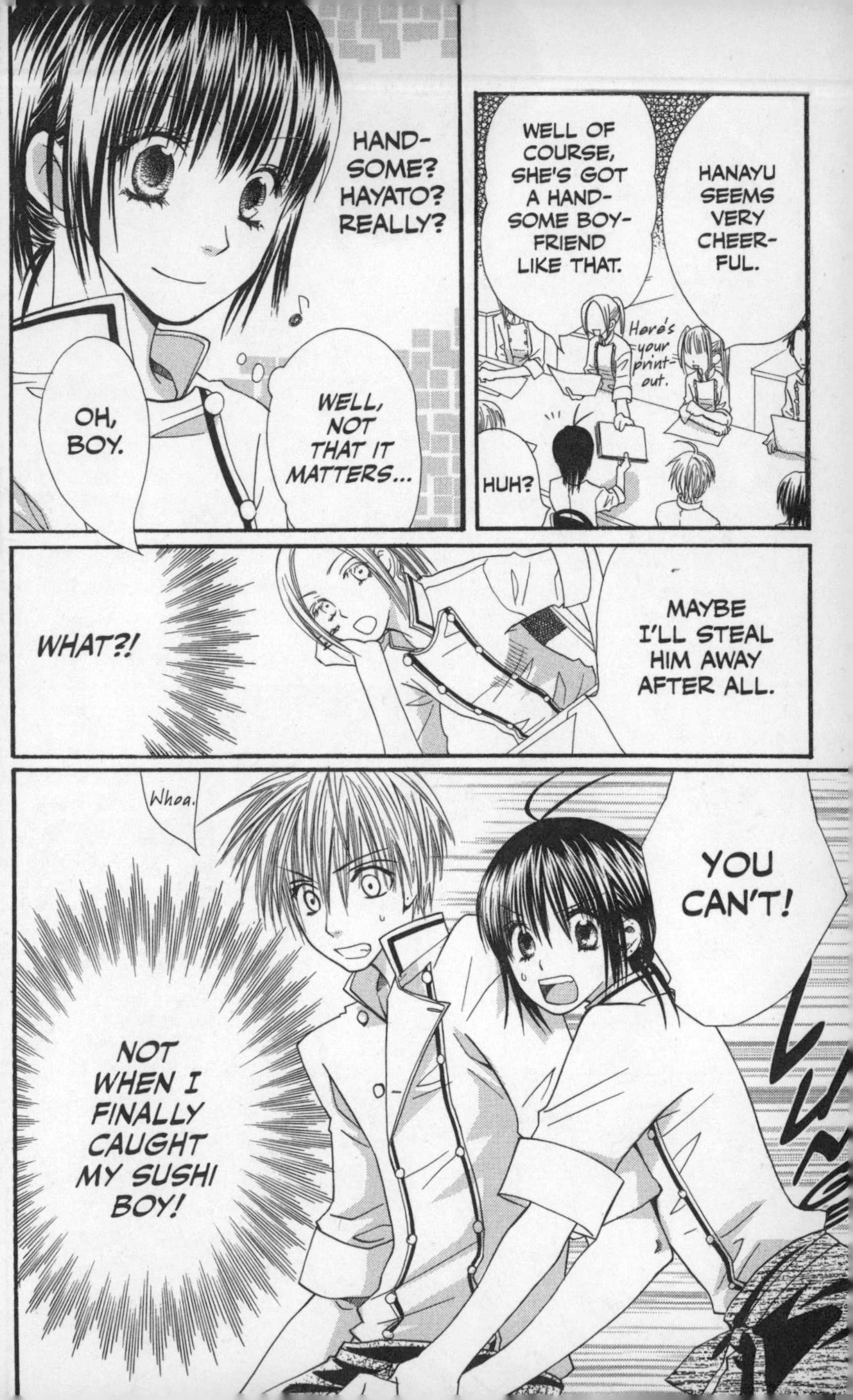
HANAYU SEEMS VERY CHEERFUL.
WELL OF COURSE, SHE'S GOT A HANDSOME BOYFRIEND LIKE THAT.
Here's your print-out.
HUH?
HANDSOME? HAYATO? REALLY?
WELL, NOT THAT IT MATTERS...
OH, BOY.
MAYBE I'LL STEAL HIM AWAY AFTER ALL.
WHAT?!
YOU CAN'T!
Whoa.
NOT WHEN I FINALLY CAUGHT MY SUSHI BOY!

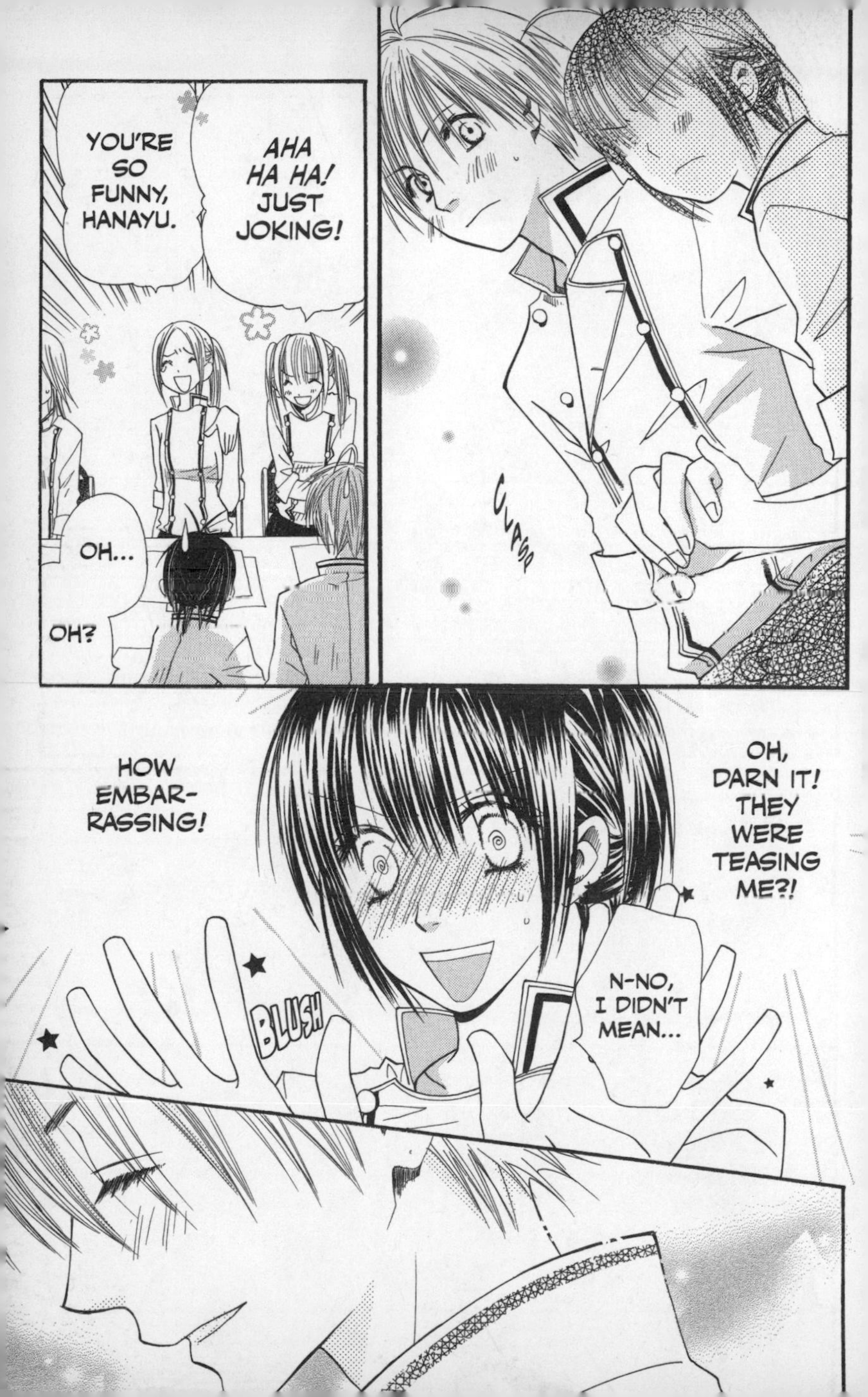
CLASP
AHA HA HA! JUST JOKING!
YOU'RE SO FUNNY, HANAYU.
OH...
OH?
OH, DARN IT! THEY WERE TEASING ME?!
HOW EMBARRASSING!
N-NO, I DIDN'T MEAN...
BLUSH

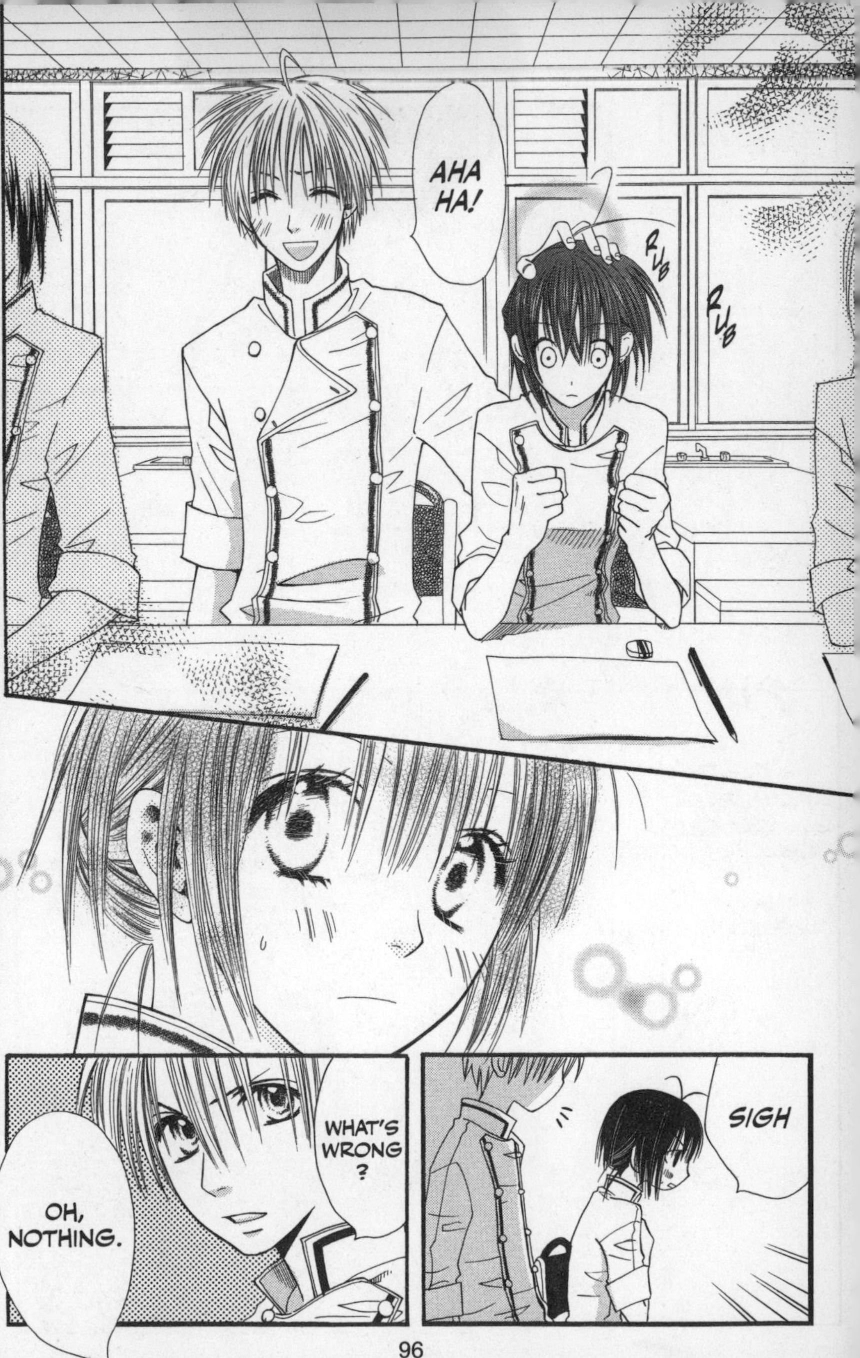
AHA HA!
RUB
RUB
SIGH
WHAT'S WRONG?
OH, NOTHING.

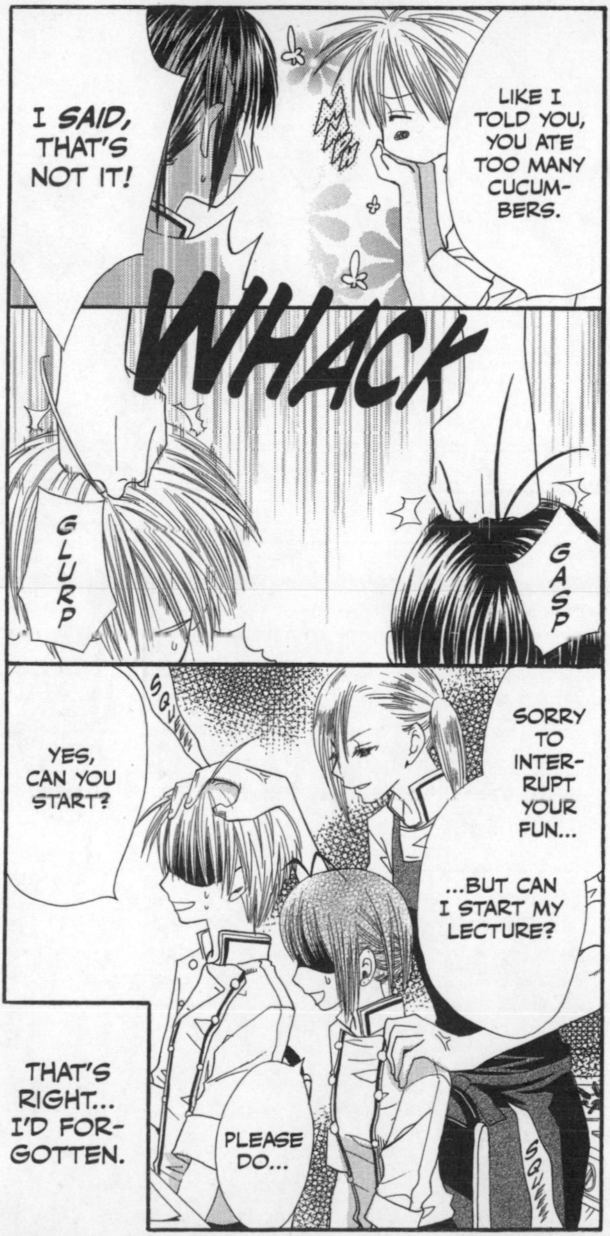
LIKE I TOLD YOU, YOU ATE TOO MANY CUCUMBERS.
I SAID, THAT'S NOT IT!
WHACK
GASP
GLURP
SORRY TO INTERRUPT YOUR FUN...
...BUT CAN I START MY LECTURE?
YES, CAN YOU START?
PLEASE DO...
THAT'S RIGHT... I'D FORGOTTEN.

Extra MV

Find these!

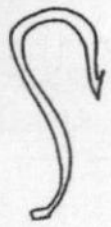

Fish hook

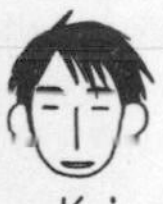

Kei
(A character my kid brother thought up)

He appears in Menu 4!

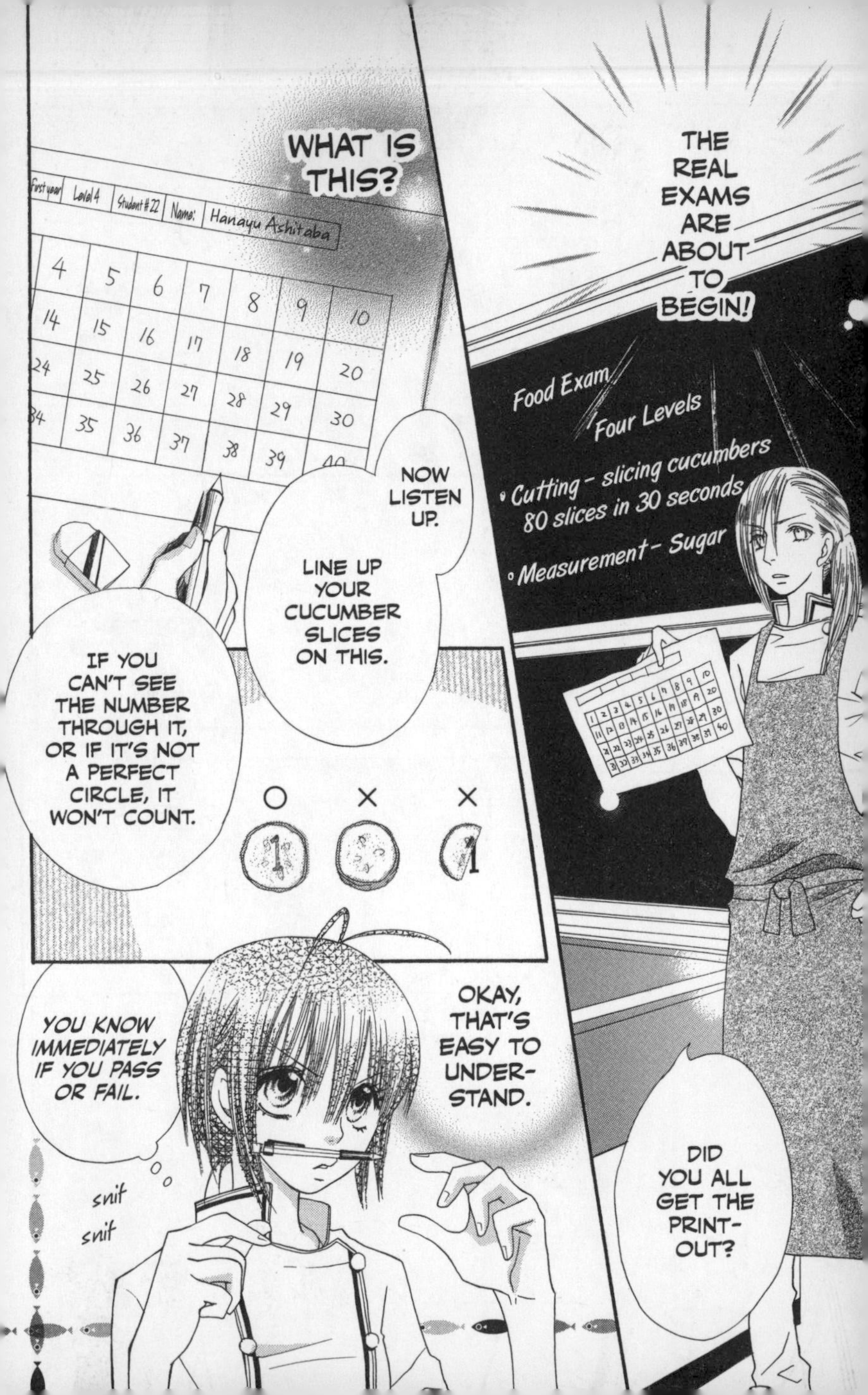
THE REAL EXAMS ARE ABOUT TO BEGIN!
Food Exam
Four Levels
• Cutting - slicing cucumbers 80 slices in 30 seconds
• Measurement - Sugar
DID YOU ALL GET THE PRINT-OUT?
WHAT IS THIS?
First year | Level 4 | Student #22 | Name: Hanayu Ashitaba
NOW LISTEN UP.
LINE UP YOUR CUCUMBER SLICES ON THIS.
IF YOU CAN'T SEE THE NUMBER THROUGH IT, OR IF IT'S NOT A PERFECT CIRCLE, IT WON'T COUNT.
○ × ×
OKAY, THAT'S EASY TO UNDERSTAND.
YOU KNOW IMMEDIATELY IF YOU PASS OR FAIL.
snif snif

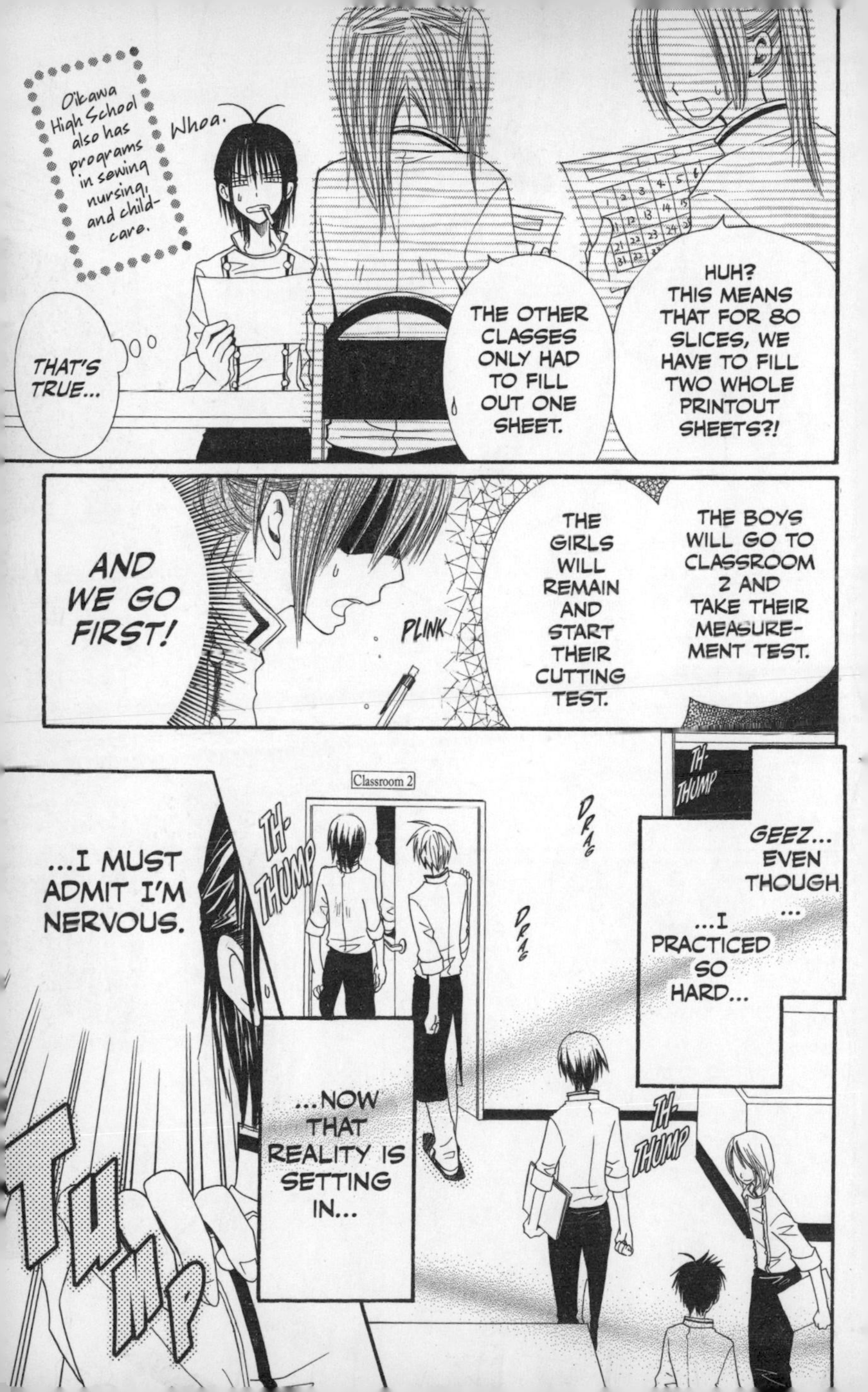
HUH? THIS MEANS THAT FOR 80 SLICES, WE HAVE TO FILL TWO WHOLE PRINTOUT SHEETS?!
THE OTHER CLASSES ONLY HAD TO FILL OUT ONE SHEET.
Whoa.
Oikawa High School also has programs in sewing, nursing, and child-care.
THAT'S TRUE...
THE BOYS WILL GO TO CLASSROOM 2 AND TAKE THEIR MEASUREMENT TEST.
THE GIRLS WILL REMAIN AND START THEIR CUTTING TEST.
PLINK
AND WE GO FIRST!
TH-THUMP
GEEZ... EVEN THOUGH...
...I PRACTICED SO HARD...
TH-THUMP
DRAG
DRAG
Classroom 2
TH-THUMP
...I MUST ADMIT I'M NERVOUS.
...NOW THAT REALITY IS SETTING IN...
THUMP

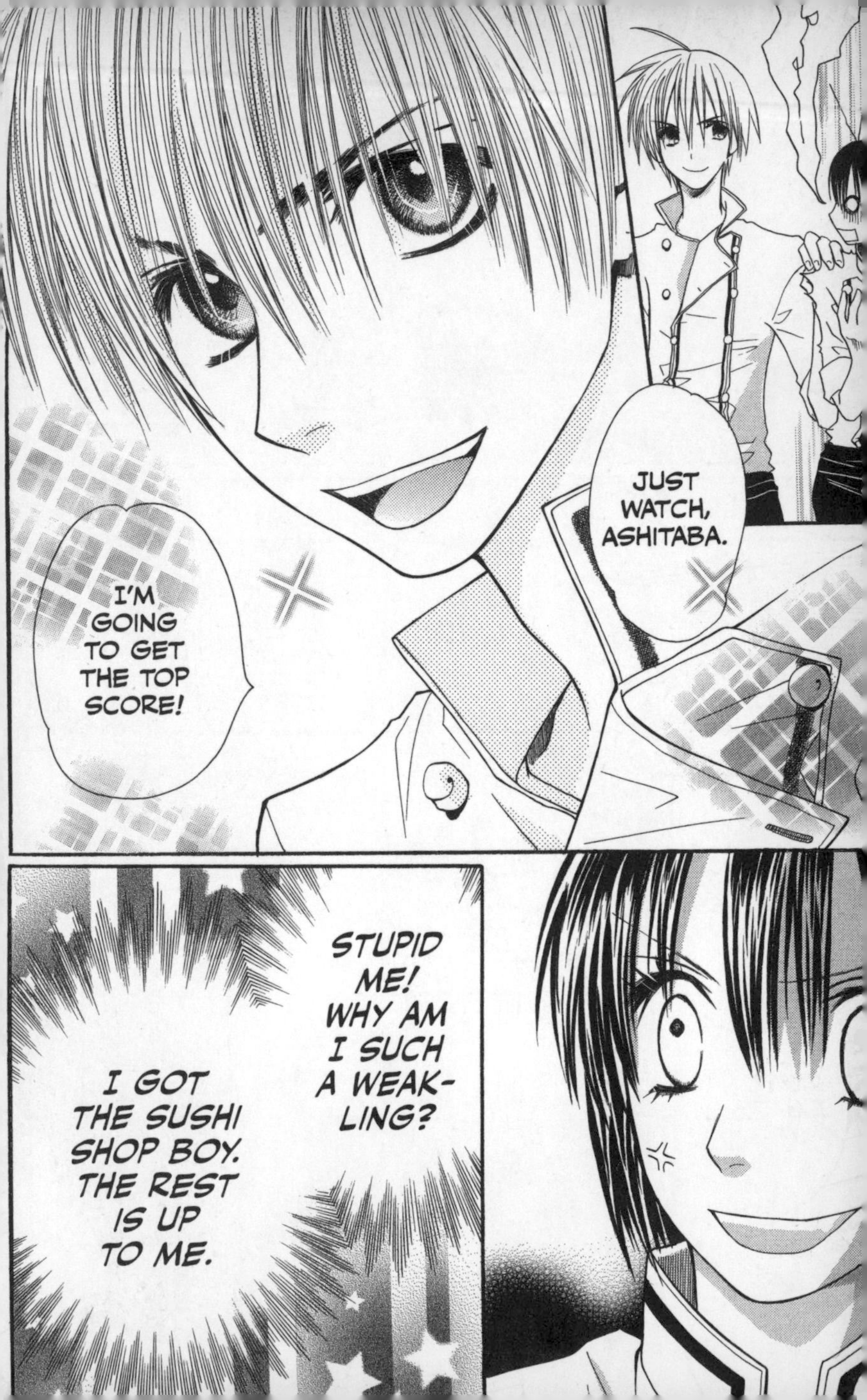
JUST WATCH, ASHITABA.
I'M GOING TO GET THE TOP SCORE!
STUPID ME! WHY AM I SUCH A WEAK-LING?
I GOT THE SUSHI SHOP BOY. THE REST IS UP TO ME.

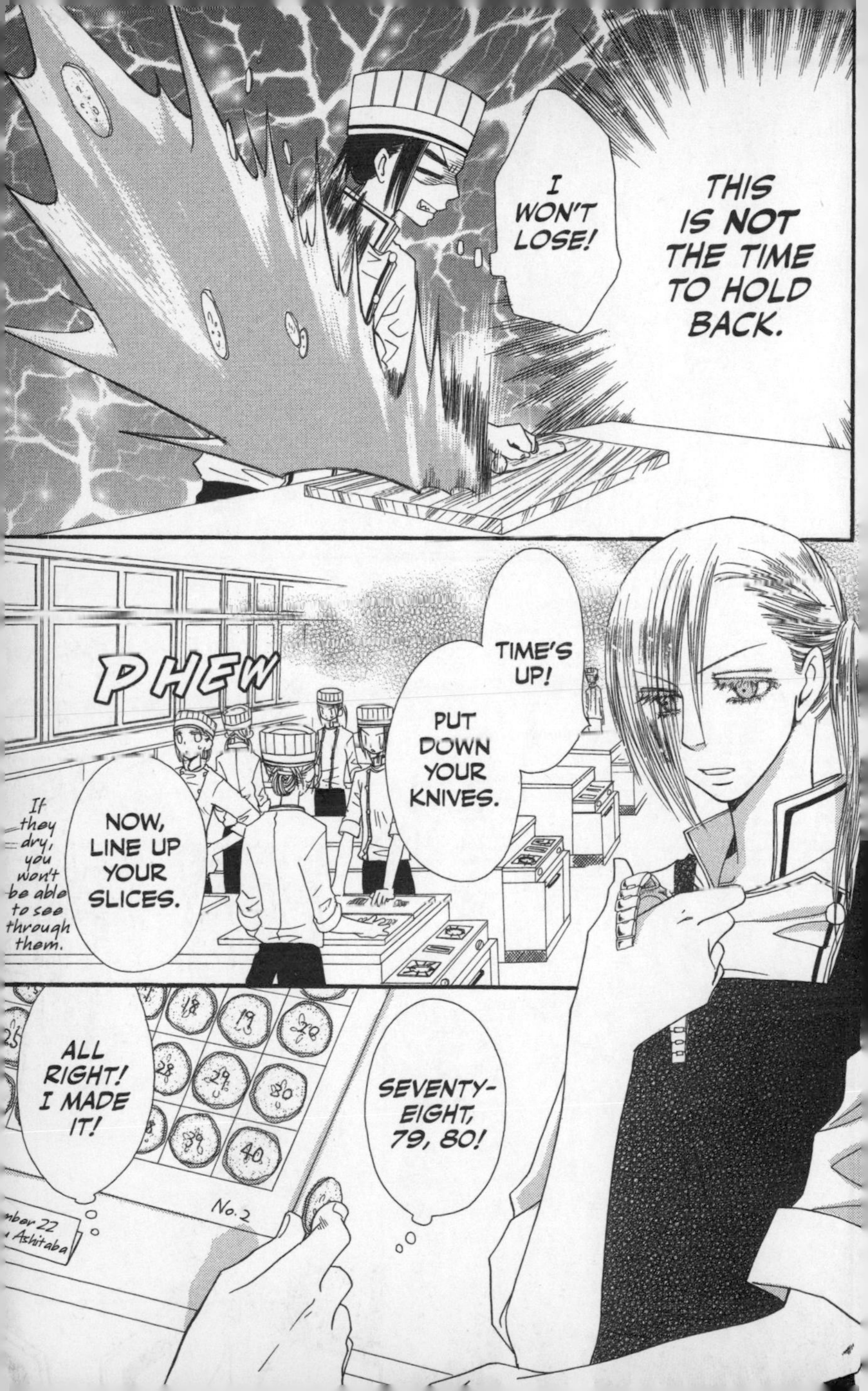
THIS IS NOT THE TIME TO HOLD BACK.
I WON'T LOSE!
TIME'S UP!
PUT DOWN YOUR KNIVES.
PHEW
NOW, LINE UP YOUR SLICES.
If they dry, you won't be able to see through them.
SEVENTY-EIGHT, 79, 80!
ALL RIGHT! I MADE IT!
No. 2

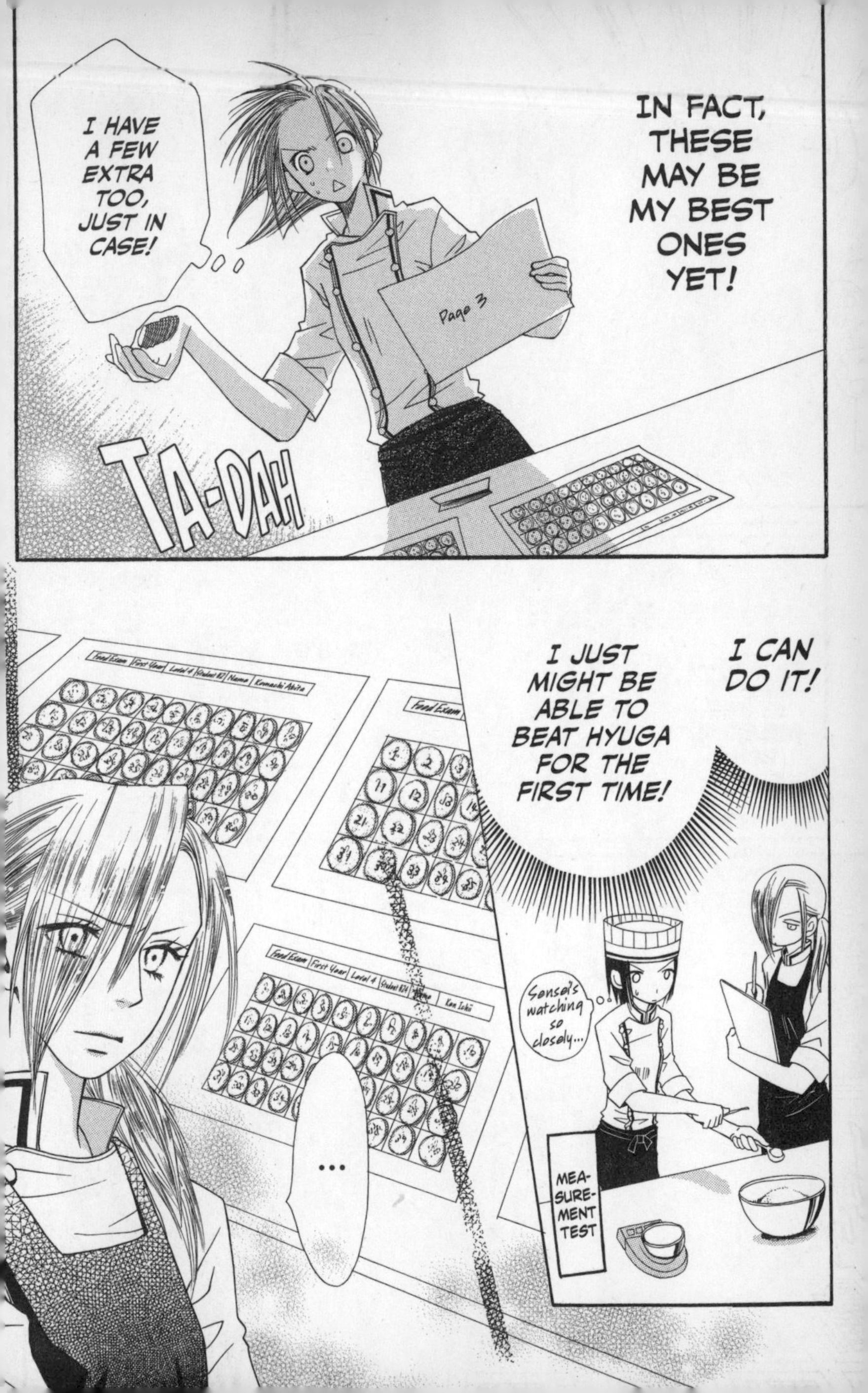
IN FACT, THESE MAY BE MY BEST ONES YET!
I HAVE A FEW EXTRA TOO, JUST IN CASE!
Page 3
TA-DAH
I CAN DO IT!
I JUST MIGHT BE ABLE TO BEAT HYUGA FOR THE FIRST TIME!
Sensei's watching so closely...
MEASUREMENT TEST
Food Exam
First Year
Level 4
Name
Komachi Akita
Food Exam
...

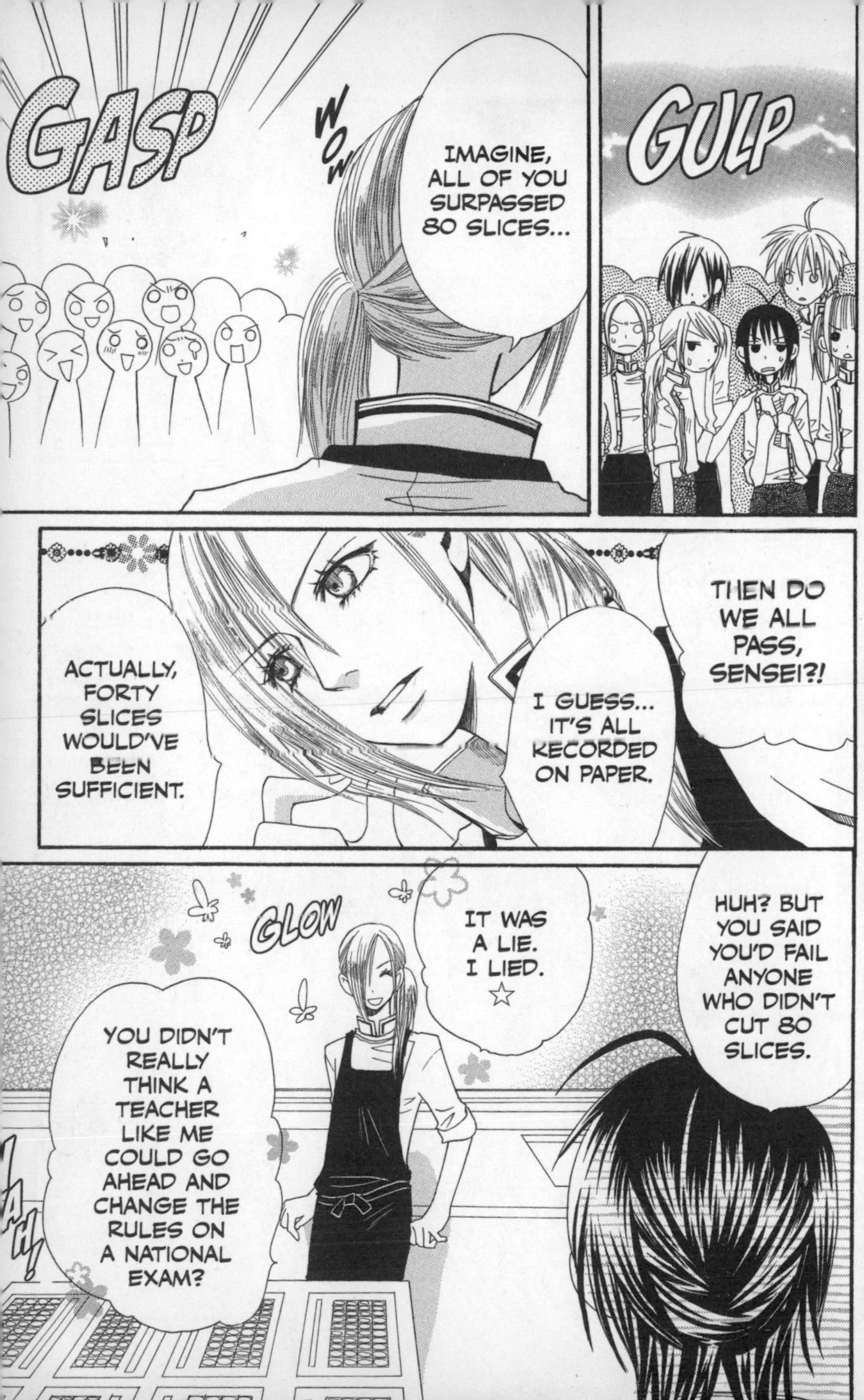
GULP
WOW
IMAGINE, ALL OF YOU SURPASSED 80 SLICES...
GASP
THEN DO WE ALL PASS, SENSEI?!
I GUESS... IT'S ALL RECORDED ON PAPER.
ACTUALLY, FORTY SLICES WOULD'VE BEEN SUFFICIENT.
HUH? BUT YOU SAID YOU'D FAIL ANYONE WHO DIDN'T CUT 80 SLICES.
IT WAS A LIE. I LIED. ☆
GLOW
YOU DIDN'T REALLY THINK A TEACHER LIKE ME COULD GO AHEAD AND CHANGE THE RULES ON A NATIONAL EXAM?

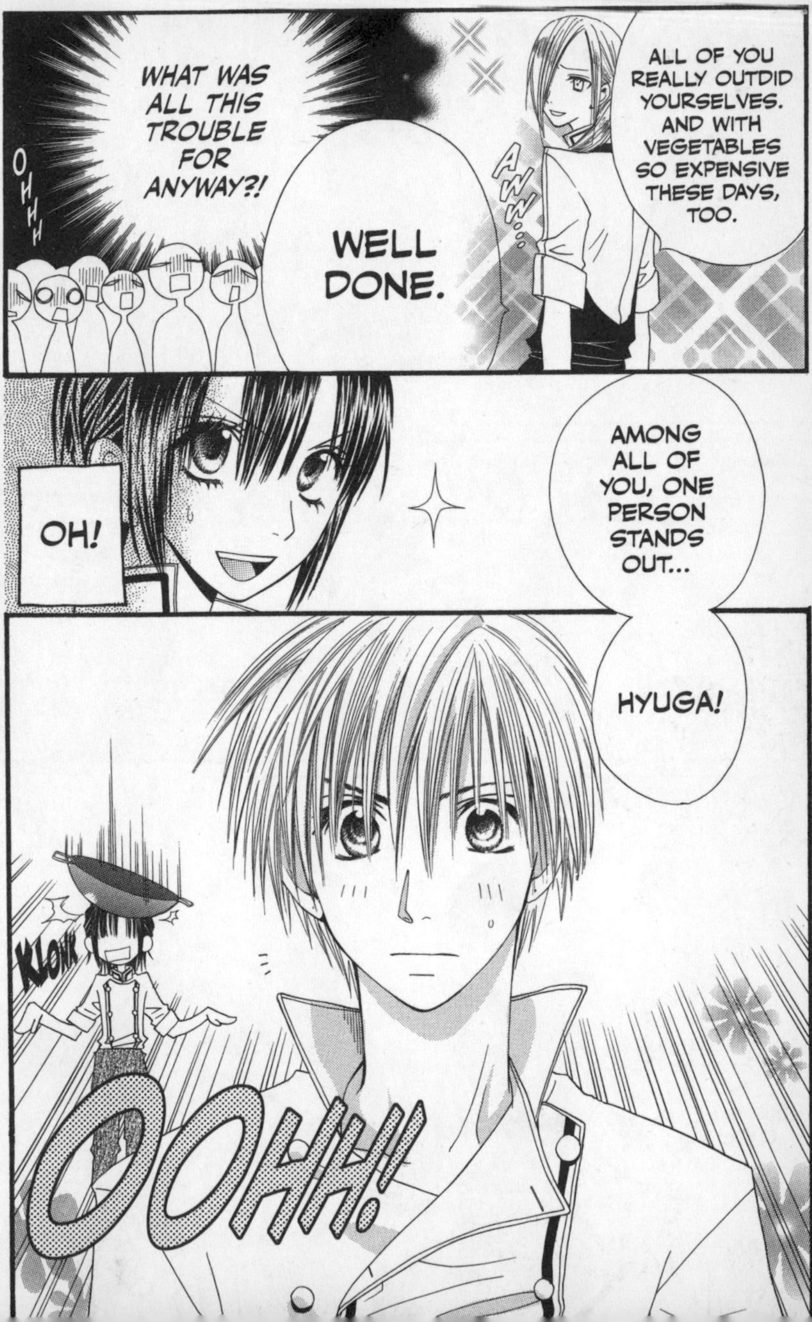
ALL OF YOU REALLY OUTDID YOURSELVES. AND WITH VEGETABLES SO EXPENSIVE THESE DAYS, TOO.
AWW...
WELL DONE.
WHAT WAS ALL THIS TROUBLE FOR ANYWAY?!
OHHH
AMONG ALL OF YOU, ONE PERSON STANDS OUT...
OH!
HYUGA!
KLONK
OOHH!

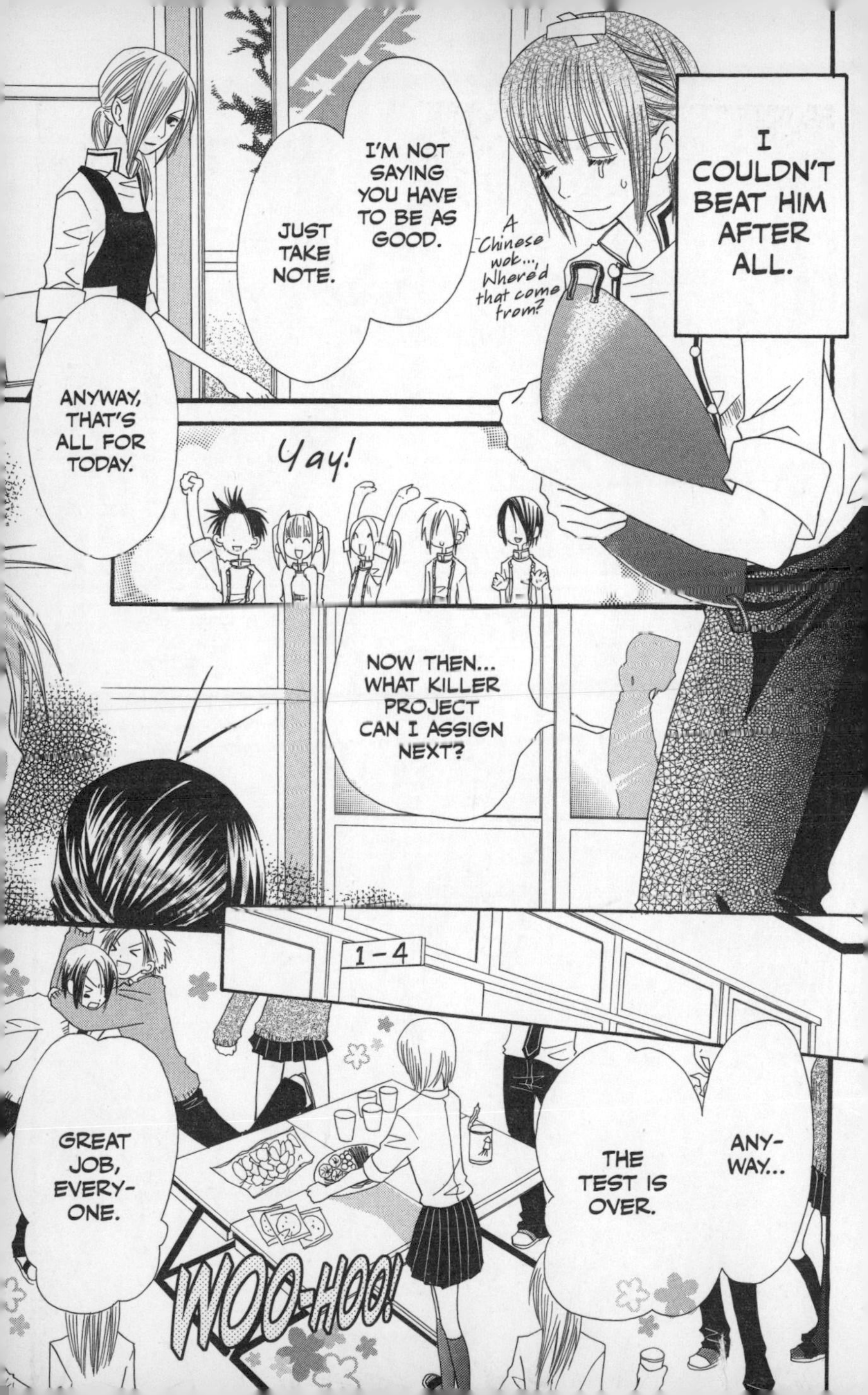
I COULDN'T BEAT HIM AFTER ALL.
A Chinese wok... Where'd that come from?
I'M NOT SAYING YOU HAVE TO BE AS GOOD.
JUST TAKE NOTE.
ANYWAY, THAT'S ALL FOR TODAY.
Yay!
NOW THEN... WHAT KILLER PROJECT CAN I ASSIGN NEXT?
1-4
ANYWAY...
THE TEST IS OVER.
GREAT JOB, EVERYONE.
WOO-HOO!

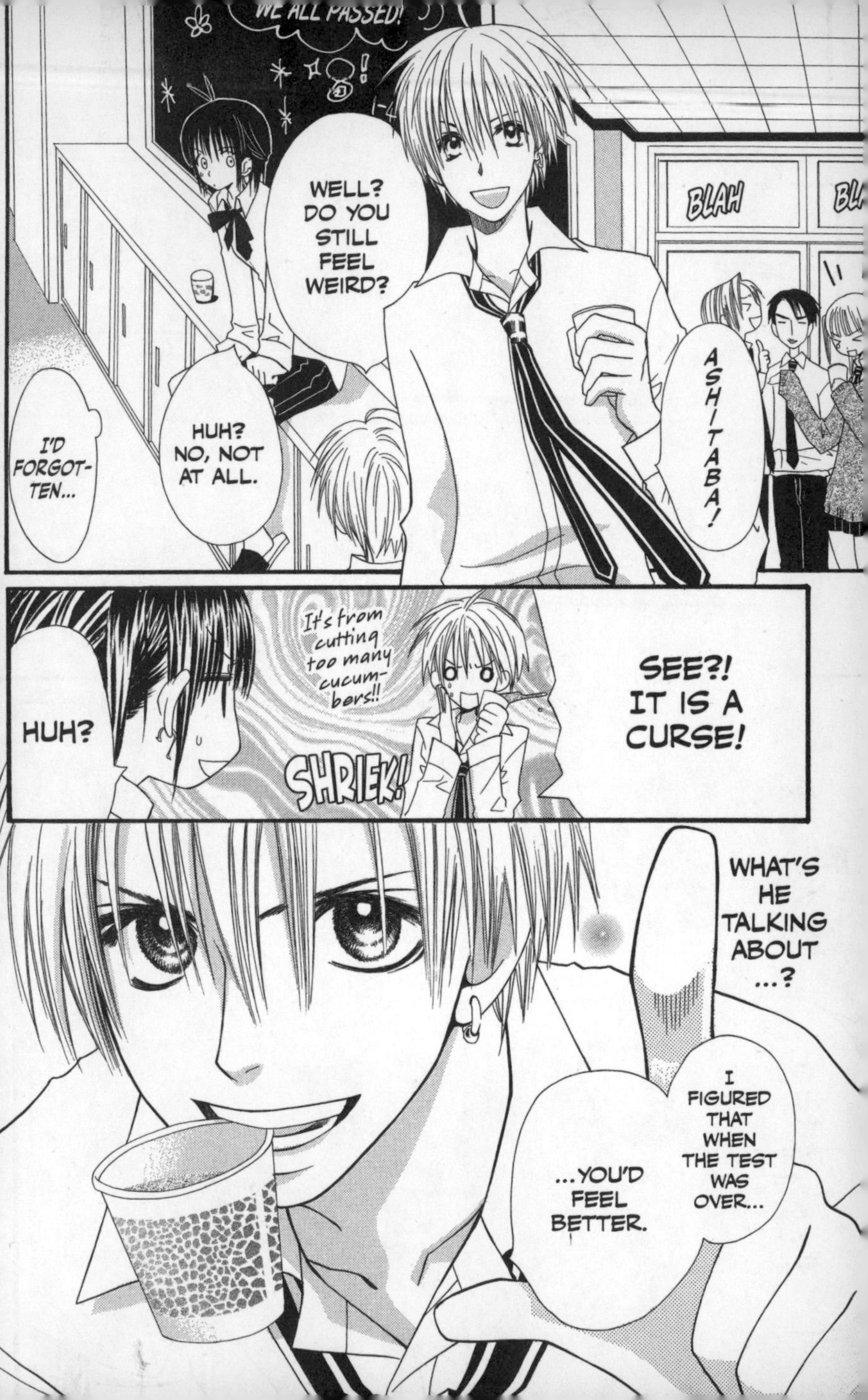
WE ALL PASSED!
BLAH
ASHITABA!
WELL? DO YOU STILL FEEL WEIRD?
HUH? NO, NOT AT ALL.
I'D FORGOT-TEN...
SEE?! IT IS A CURSE!
It's from cutting too many cucum-bers!!
SHRIEK!
HUH?
WHAT'S HE TALKING ABOUT ...?
I FIGURED THAT WHEN THE TEST WAS OVER...
...YOU'D FEEL BETTER.

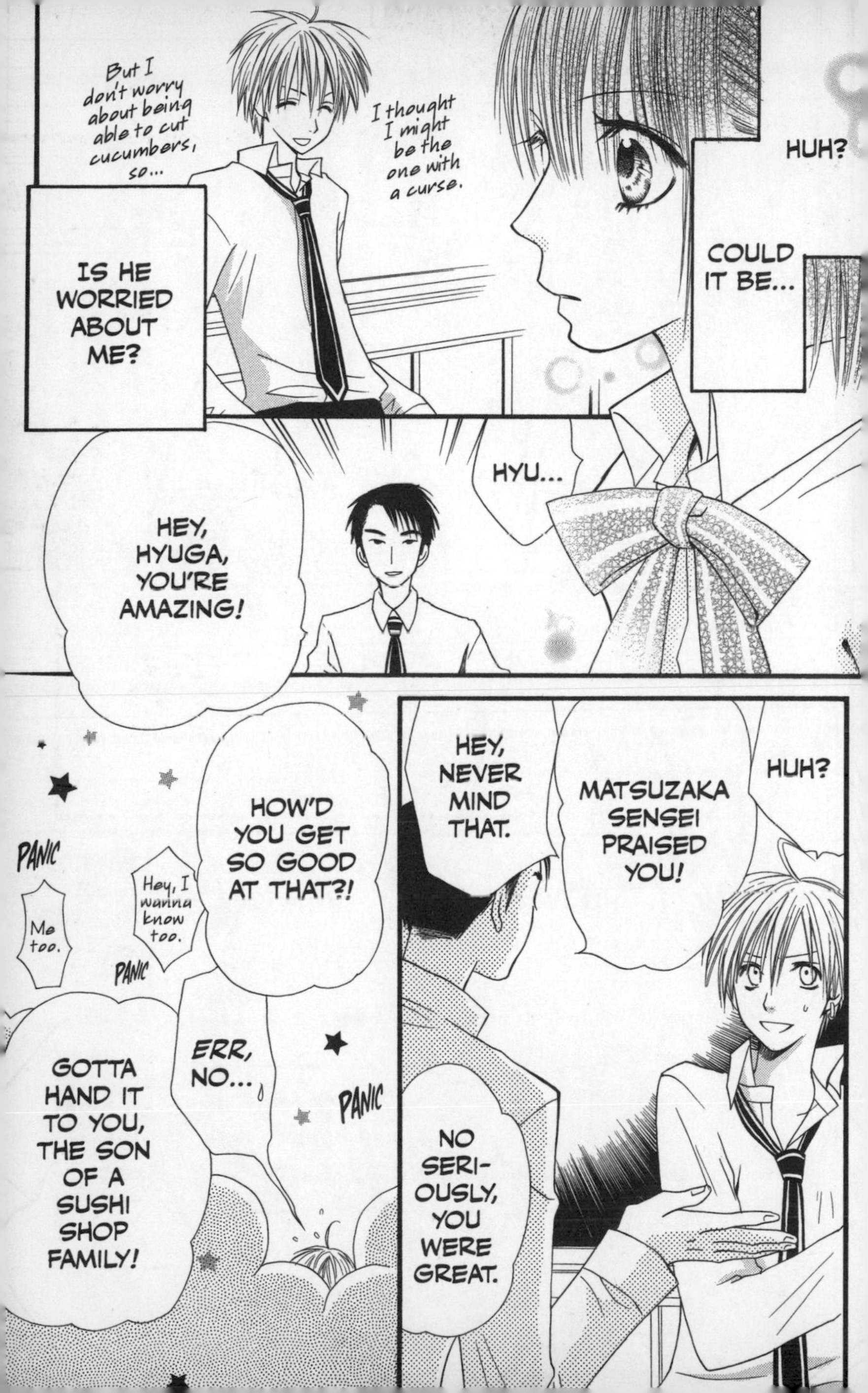
HUH?
COULD IT BE...
But I don't worry about being able to cut cucumbers, so...
I thought I might be the one with a curse.
IS HE WORRIED ABOUT ME?
HYU...
HEY, HYUGA, YOU'RE AMAZING!
HUH?
MATSUZAKA SENSEI PRAISED YOU!
HEY, NEVER MIND THAT.
NO SERIOUSLY, YOU WERE GREAT.
HOW'D YOU GET SO GOOD AT THAT?!
Hey, I wanna know too.
PANIC
Me too.
PANIC
ERR, NO...
PANIC
GOTTA HAND IT TO YOU, THE SON OF A SUSHI SHOP FAMILY!

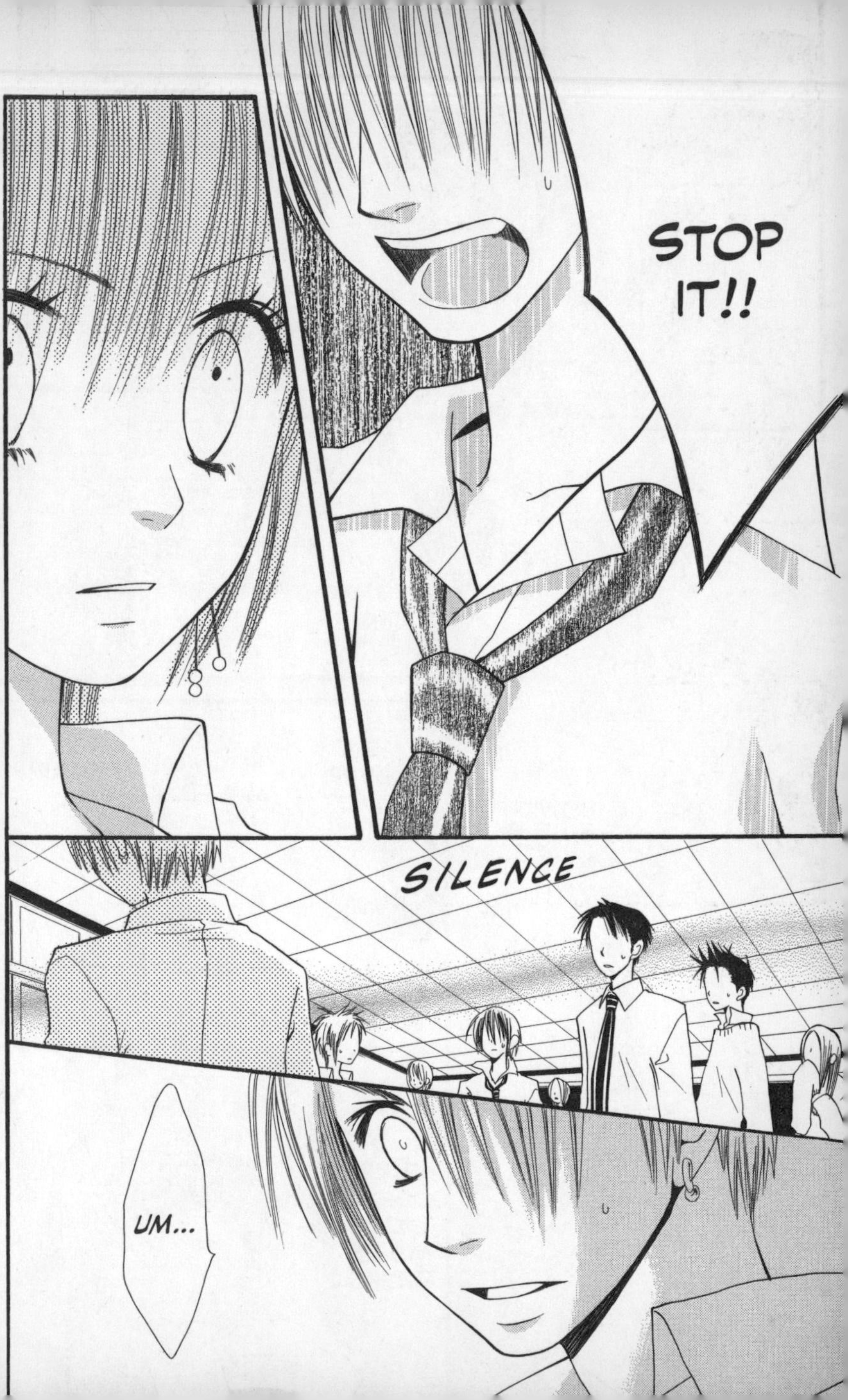
STOP IT!!
SILENCE
UM...

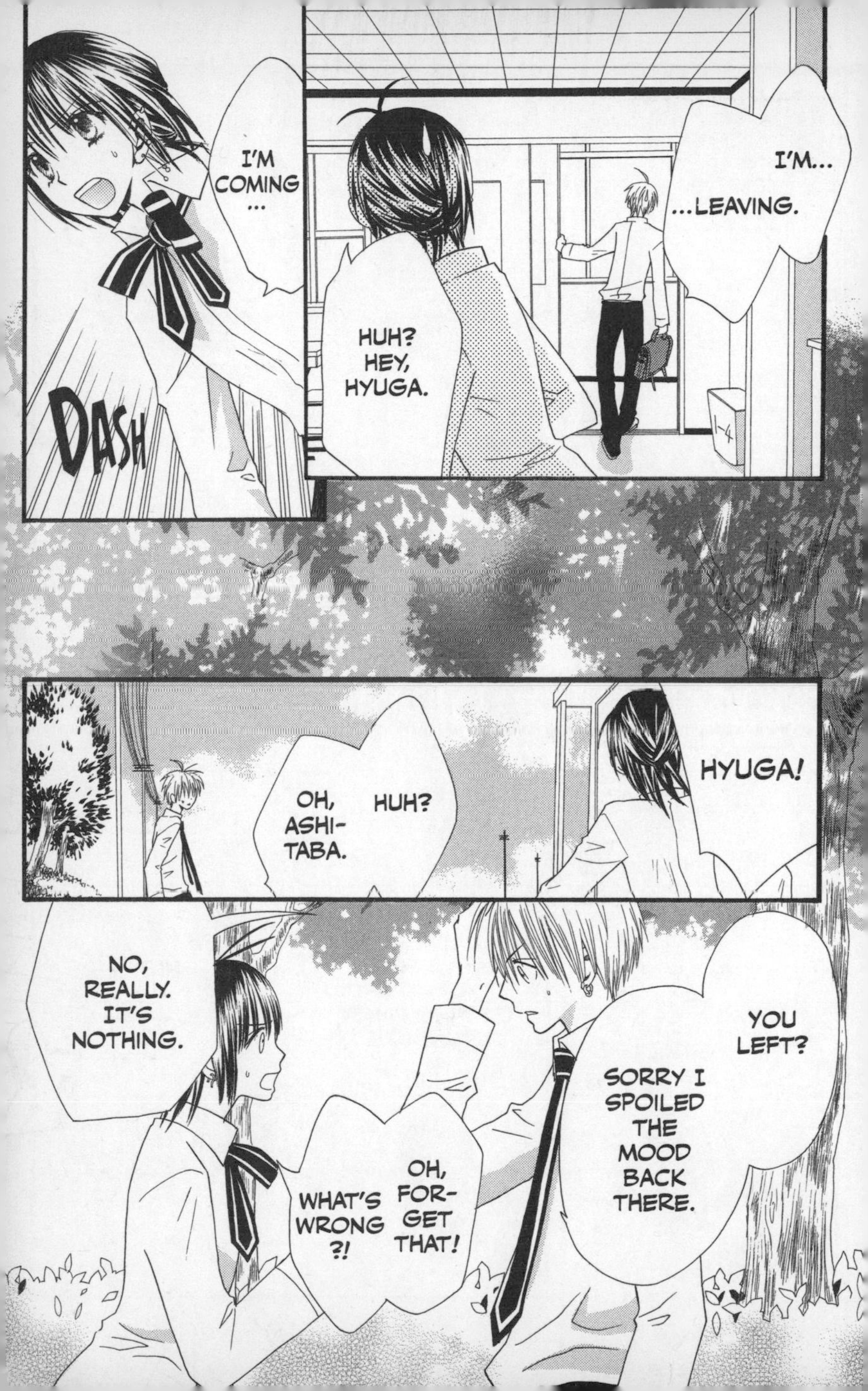
I'M...
...LEAVING.
HUH? HEY, HYUGA.
I'M COMING...
DASH
HYUGA!
HUH?
OH, ASHI-TABA.
YOU LEFT?
SORRY I SPOILED THE MOOD BACK THERE.
OH, FOR-GET THAT!
WHAT'S WRONG?!
NO, REALLY. IT'S NOTHING.

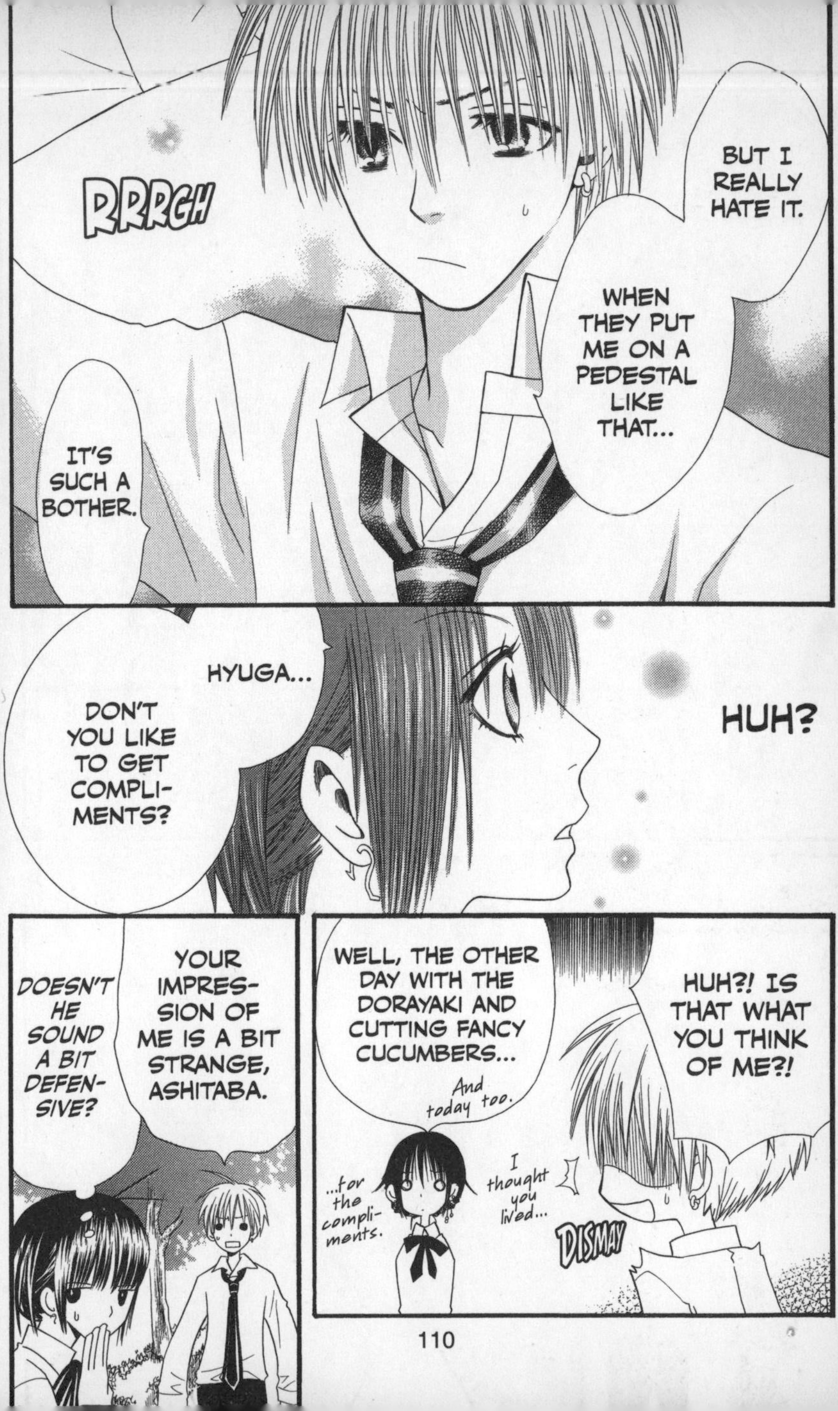
RRRGH
BUT I REALLY HATE IT.
WHEN THEY PUT ME ON A PEDESTAL LIKE THAT...
IT'S SUCH A BOTHER.
HUH?
HYUGA...
DON'T YOU LIKE TO GET COMPLIMENTS?
HUH?! IS THAT WHAT YOU THINK OF ME?!
WELL, THE OTHER DAY WITH THE DORAYAKI AND CUTTING FANCY CUCUMBERS...
And today too.
I thought you lived...
...for the compliments.
DISMAY
YOUR IMPRESSION OF ME IS A BIT STRANGE, ASHITABA.
DOESN'T HE SOUND A BIT DEFENSIVE?

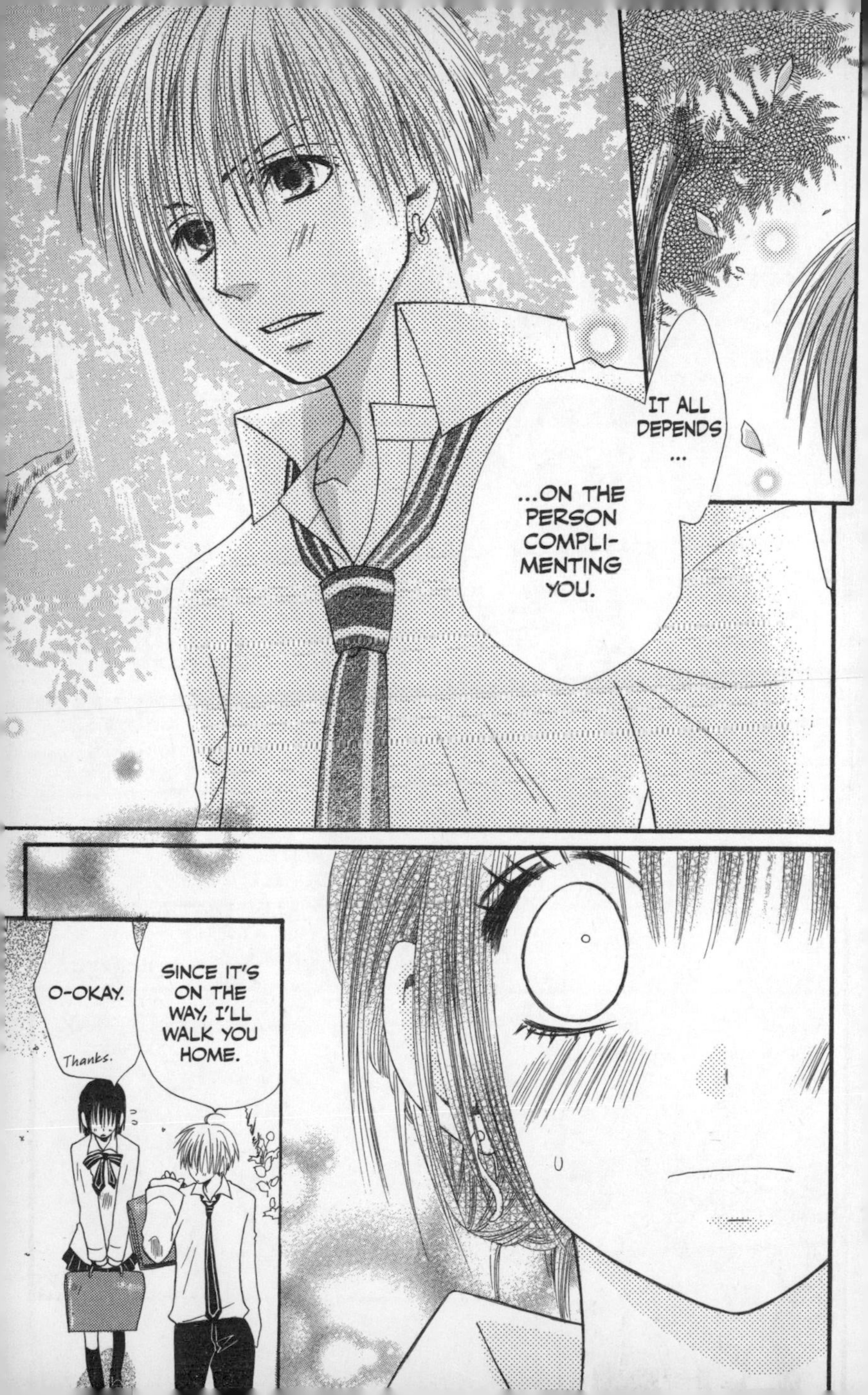
IT ALL DEPENDS...
...ON THE PERSON COMPLI-MENTING YOU.
SINCE IT'S ON THE WAY, I'LL WALK YOU HOME.
O-OKAY.
Thanks.

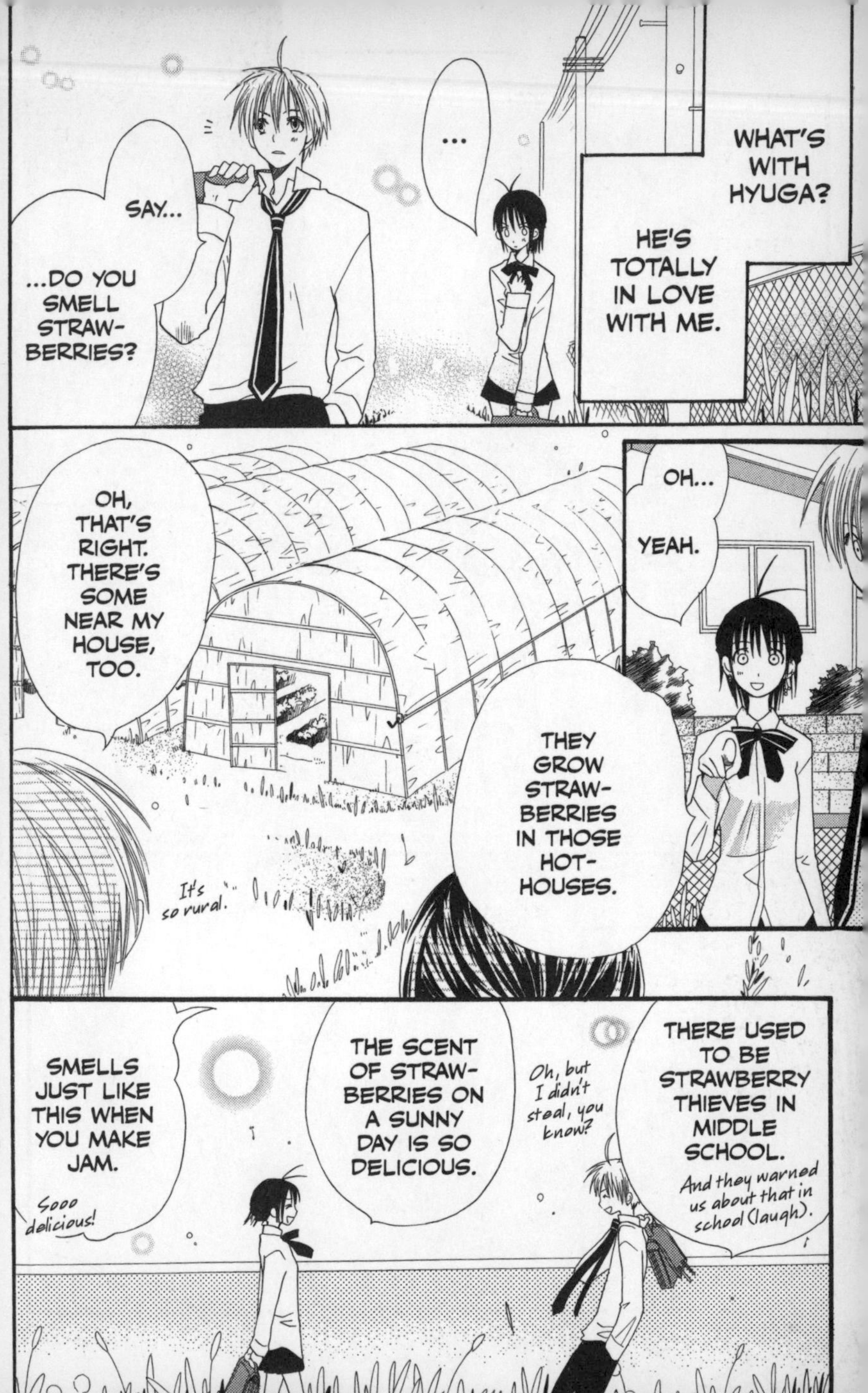
WHAT'S WITH HYUGA?
HE'S TOTALLY IN LOVE WITH ME.
...
SAY...
...DO YOU SMELL STRAW-BERRIES?
OH... YEAH.
THEY GROW STRAW-BERRIES IN THOSE HOT-HOUSES.
OH, THAT'S RIGHT. THERE'S SOME NEAR MY HOUSE, TOO.
It's so rural.
THERE USED TO BE STRAWBERRY THIEVES IN MIDDLE SCHOOL.
And they warned us about that in school (laugh).
Oh, but I didn't steal, you know?
THE SCENT OF STRAW-BERRIES ON A SUNNY DAY IS SO DELICIOUS.
SMELLS JUST LIKE THIS WHEN YOU MAKE JAM.
Sooo delicious!

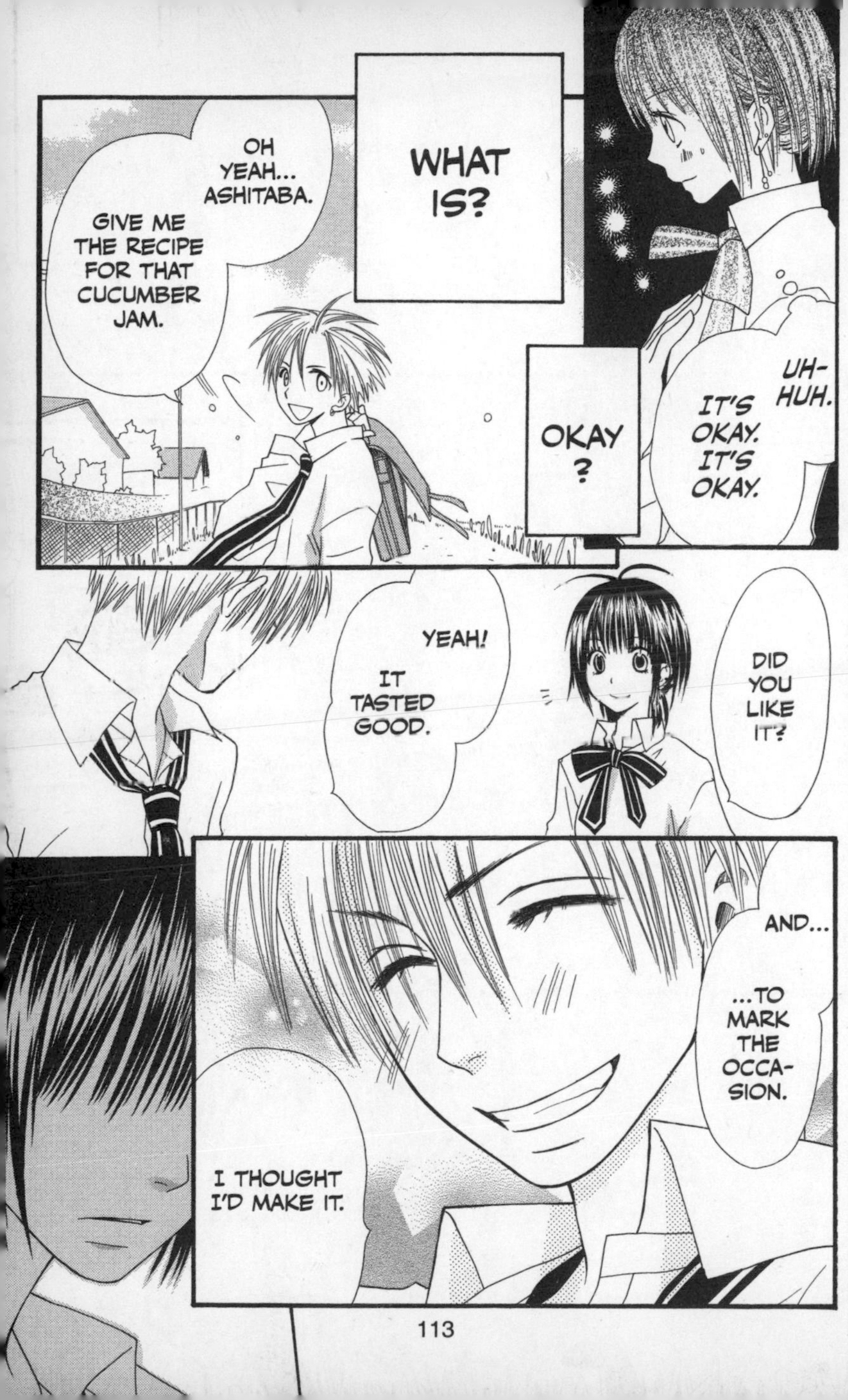
UH-HUH.
IT'S OKAY. IT'S OKAY.
OKAY?
WHAT IS?
OH YEAH... ASHITABA.
GIVE ME THE RECIPE FOR THAT CUCUMBER JAM.
DID YOU LIKE IT?
YEAH!
IT TASTED GOOD.
AND...
...TO MARK THE OCCASION.
I THOUGHT I'D MAKE IT.

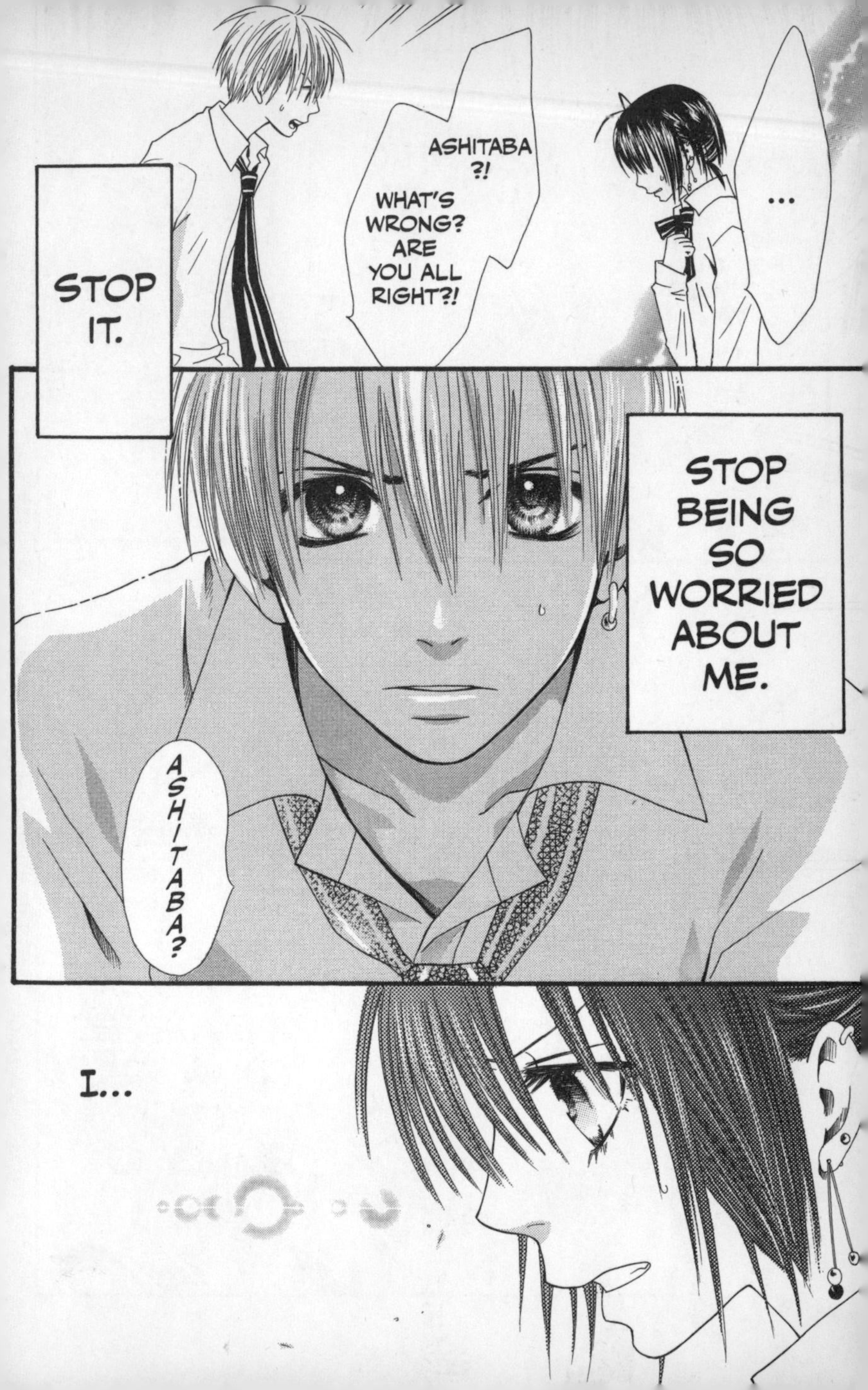
...
ASHITABA?! WHAT'S WRONG? ARE YOU ALL RIGHT?!
STOP IT.
STOP BEING SO WORRIED ABOUT ME.
ASHITABA?
I...

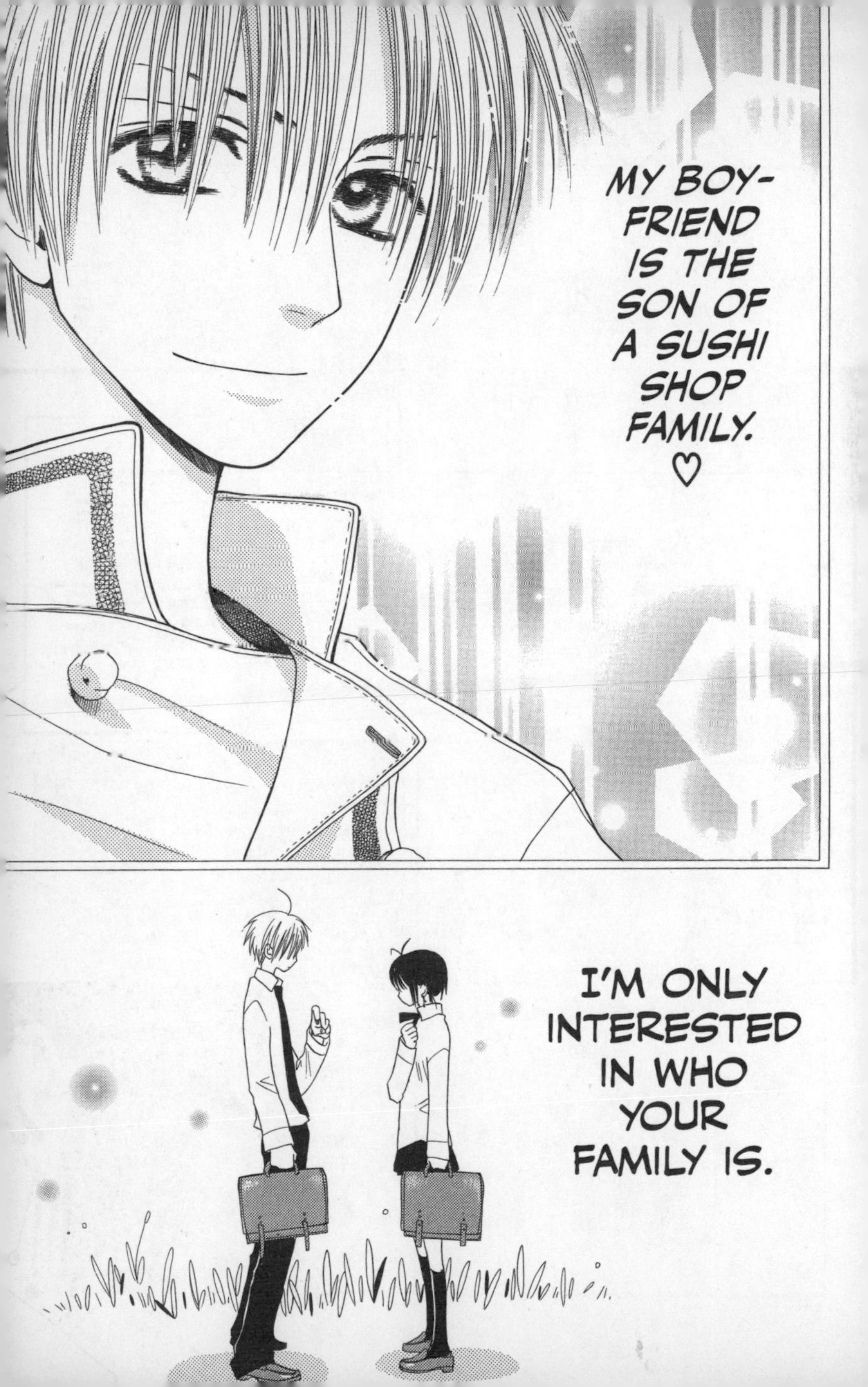
MY BOY-
FRIEND
IS THE
SON OF
A SUSHI
SHOP
FAMILY.
♡
I'M ONLY
INTERESTED
IN WHO
YOUR
FAMILY IS.

SIDE DISH Mixed Vegetables 4

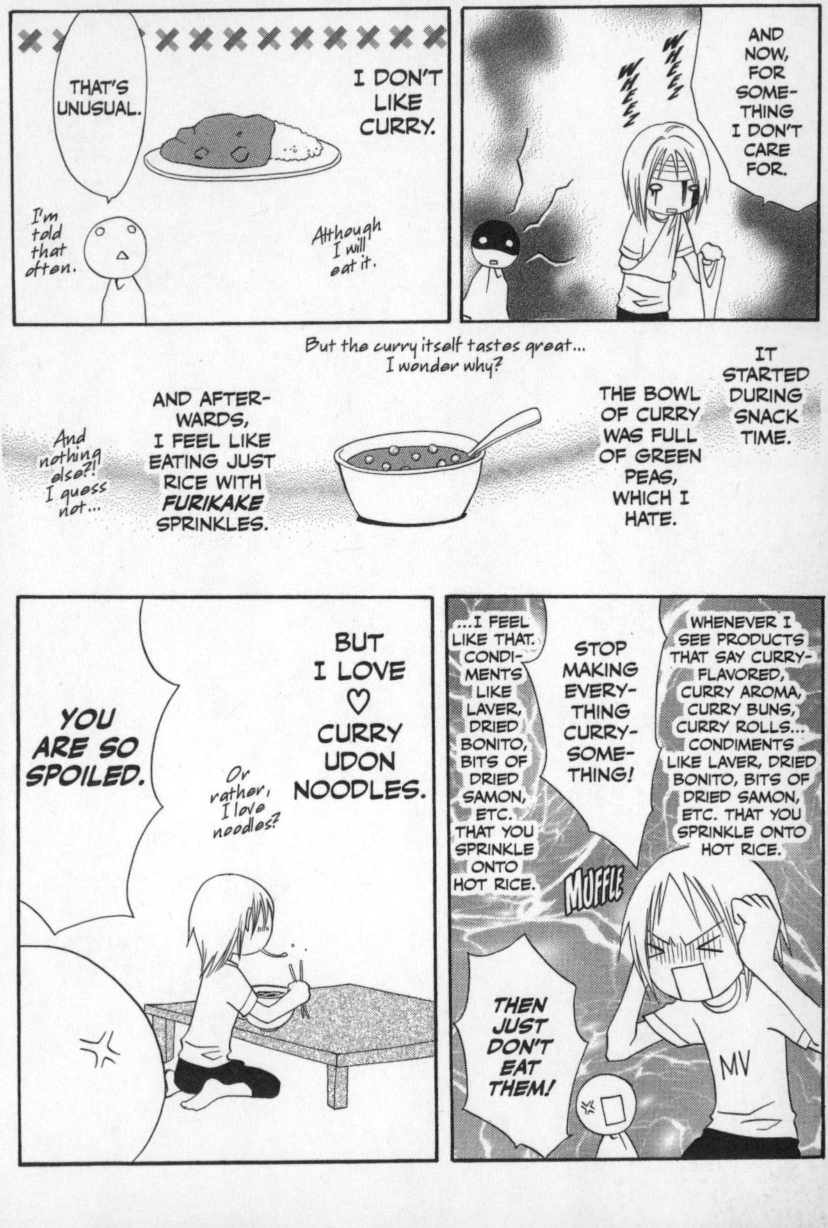
WHEEZE
WHEEZE
AND NOW, FOR SOMETHING I DON'T CARE FOR.
I DON'T LIKE CURRY.
Although I will eat it.
THAT'S UNUSUAL.
I'm told that often.
IT STARTED DURING SNACK TIME.
THE BOWL OF CURRY WAS FULL OF GREEN PEAS, WHICH I HATE.
But the curry itself tastes great... I wonder why?
AND AFTERWARDS, I FEEL LIKE EATING JUST RICE WITH FURIKAKE SPRINKLES.
And nothing else?! I guess not...
WHENEVER I SEE PRODUCTS THAT SAY CURRY-FLAVORED, CURRY AROMA, CURRY BUNS, CURRY ROLLS... CONDIMENTS LIKE LAVER, DRIED BONITO, BITS OF DRIED SAMON, ETC. THAT YOU SPRINKLE ONTO HOT RICE.
STOP MAKING EVERYTHING CURRY-SOMETHING!
...I FEEL LIKE THAT. CONDIMENTS LIKE LAVER, DRIED BONITO, BITS OF DRIED SAMON, ETC. THAT YOU SPRINKLE ONTO HOT RICE.
MUFFLE
MV
THEN JUST DON'T EAT THEM!
BUT I LOVE ♡ CURRY UDON NOODLES.
Or rather, I love noodles?
YOU ARE SO SPOILED.

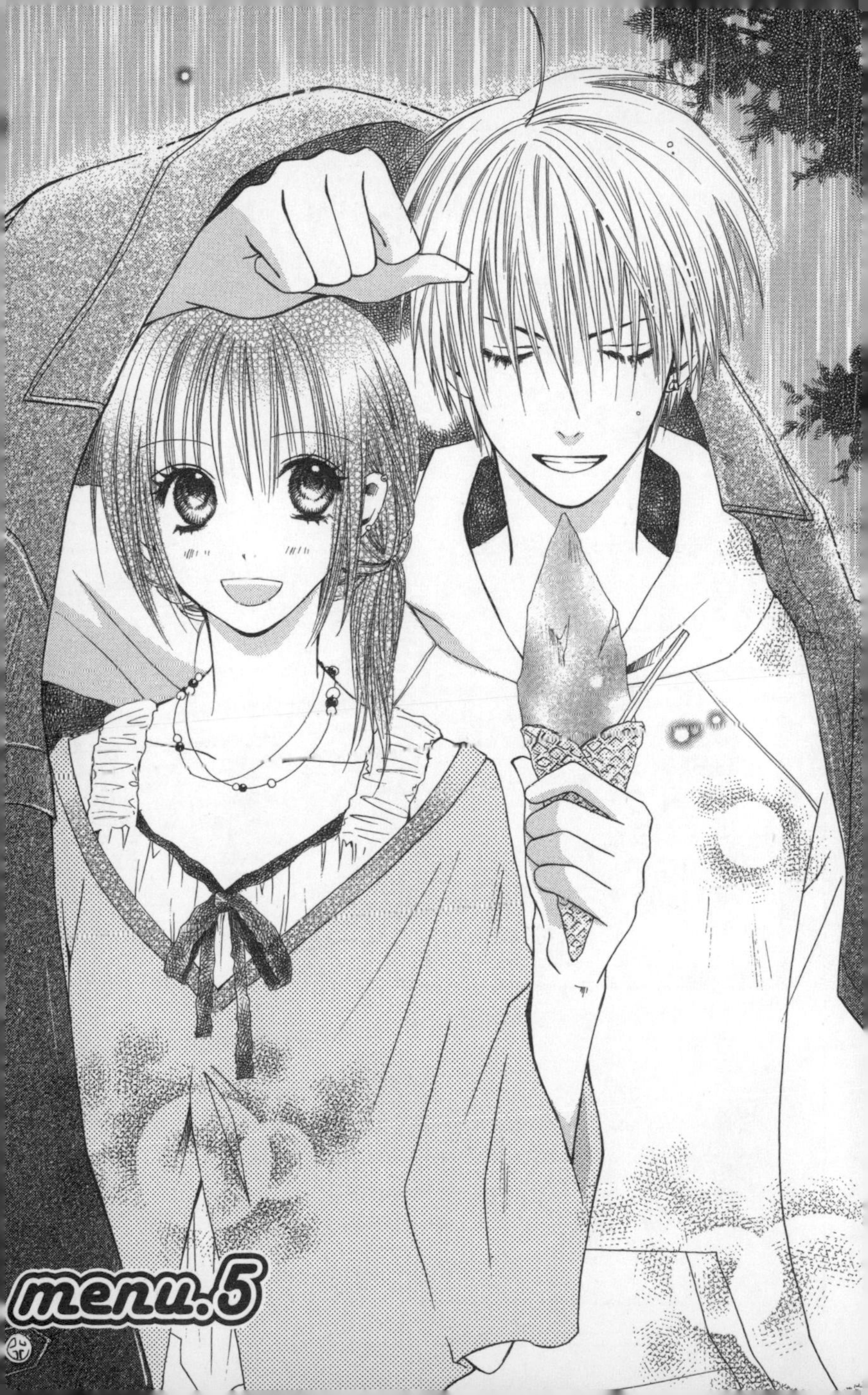
menu.5

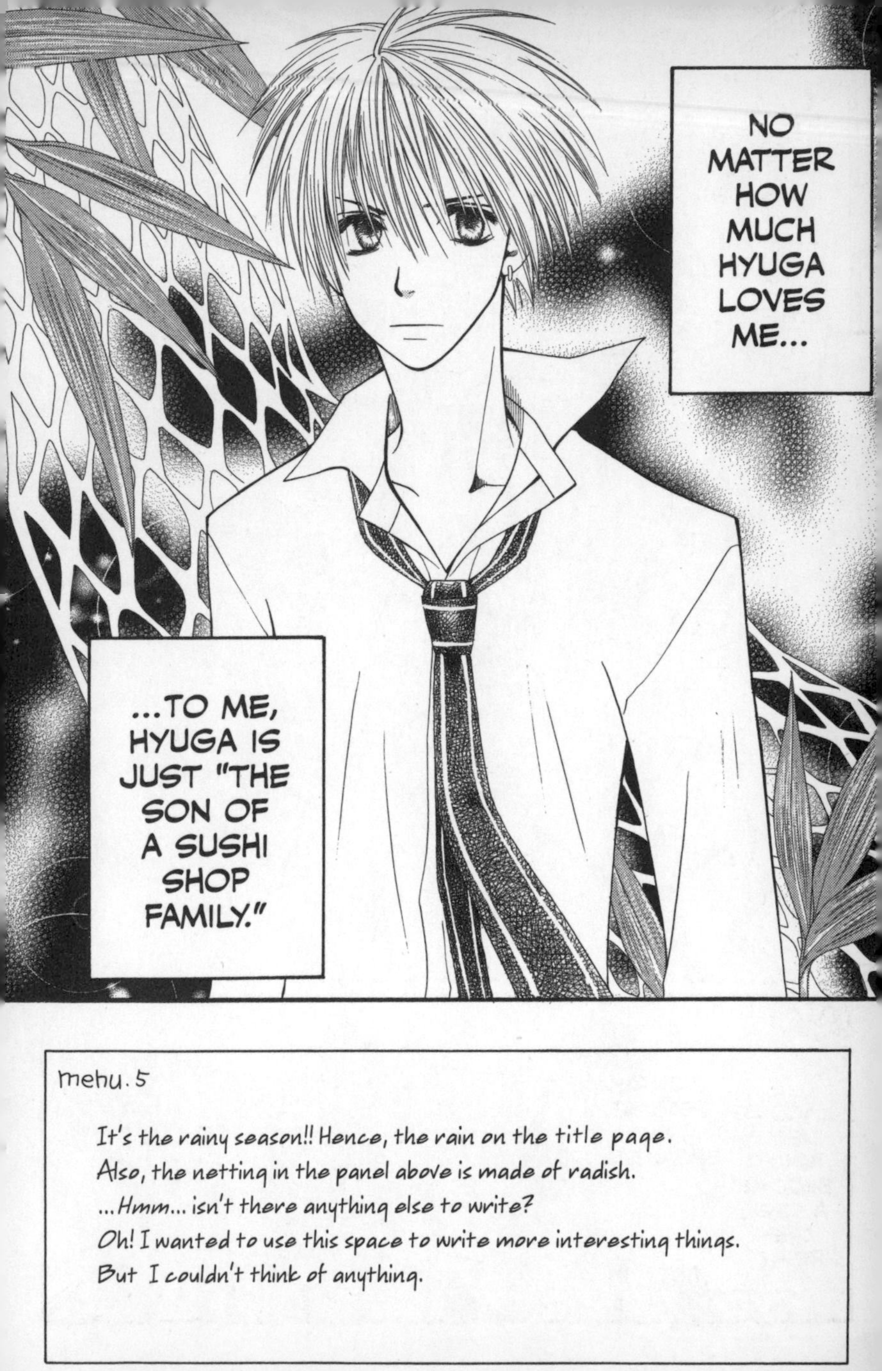
NO MATTER HOW MUCH HYUGA LOVES ME...
...TO ME, HYUGA IS JUST "THE SON OF A SUSHI SHOP FAMILY."

mehu. 5

It's the rainy season!! Hence, the rain on the title page.
Also, the netting in the panel above is made of radish.
...Hmm... isn't there anything else to write?
Oh! I wanted to use this space to write more interesting things.
But I couldn't think of anything.

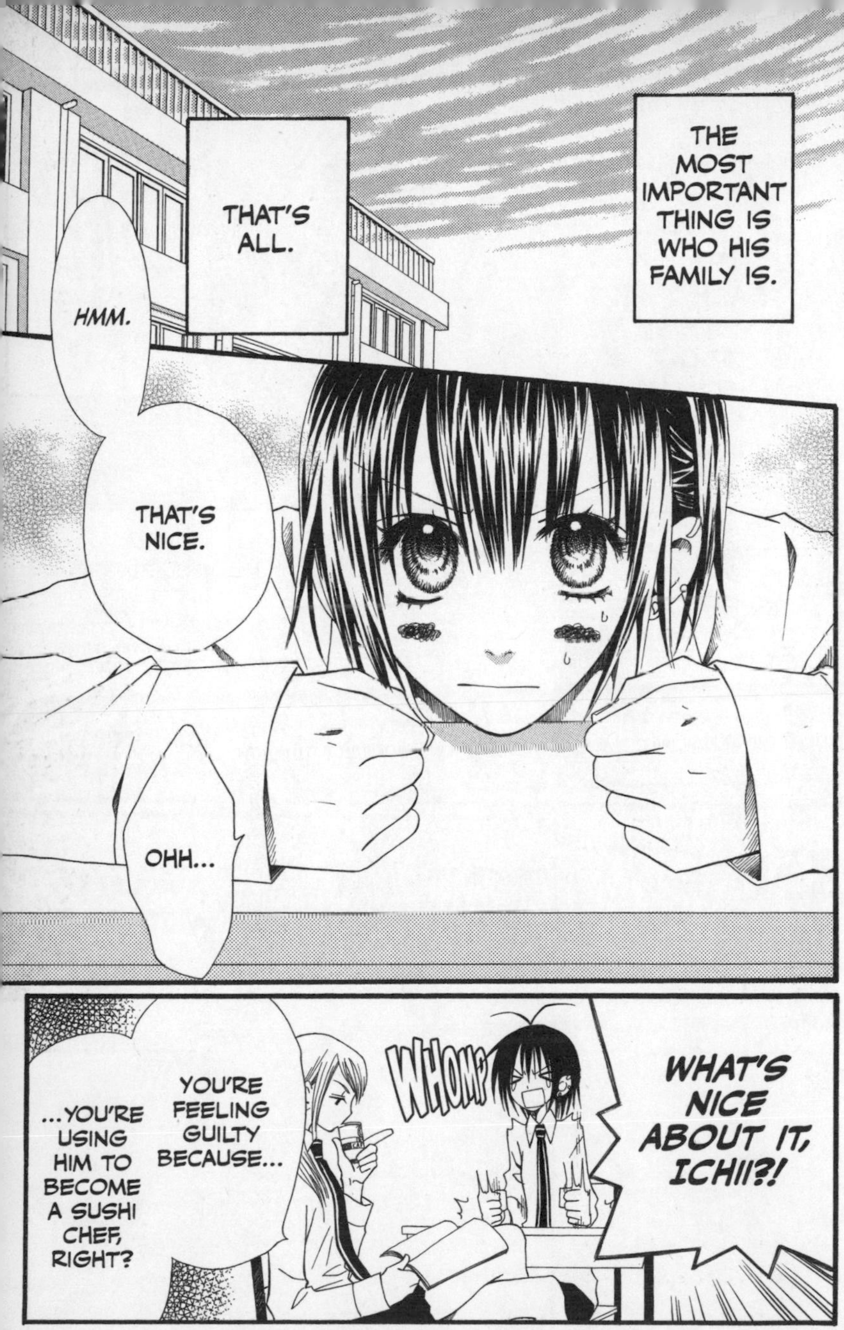
THE MOST IMPORTANT THING IS WHO HIS FAMILY IS.
THAT'S ALL.
HMM.
THAT'S NICE.
OHH...
WHAT'S NICE ABOUT IT, ICHII?!
WHOMP
YOU'RE FEELING GUILTY BECAUSE...
...YOU'RE USING HIM TO BECOME A SUSHI CHEF, RIGHT?

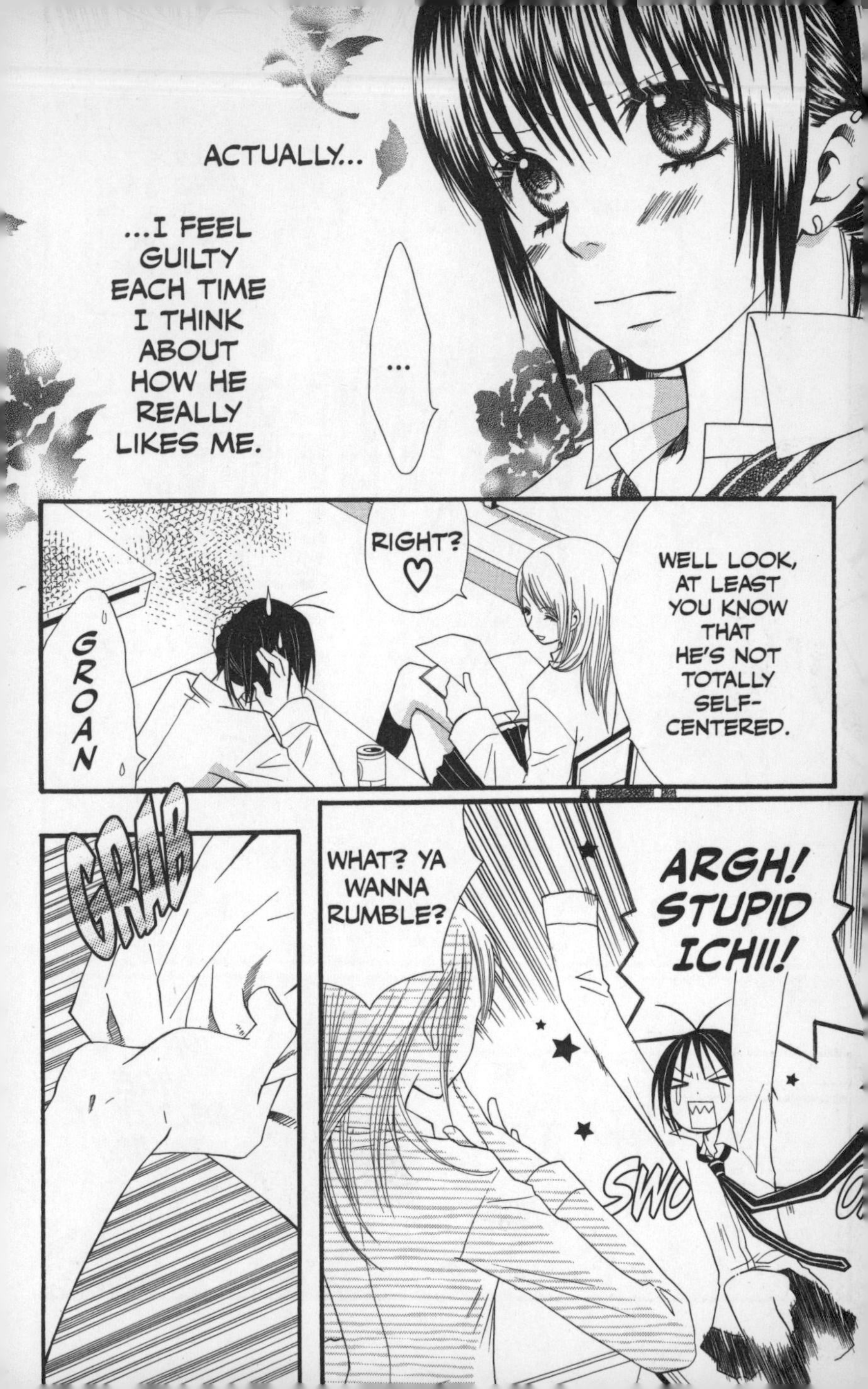

ACTUALLY...
...I FEEL GUILTY EACH TIME I THINK ABOUT HOW HE REALLY LIKES ME.
...
WELL LOOK, AT LEAST YOU KNOW THAT HE'S NOT TOTALLY SELF-CENTERED.
RIGHT? ♡
GROAN
ARGH! STUPID ICHII!
WHAT? YA WANNA RUMBLE?
GRAB

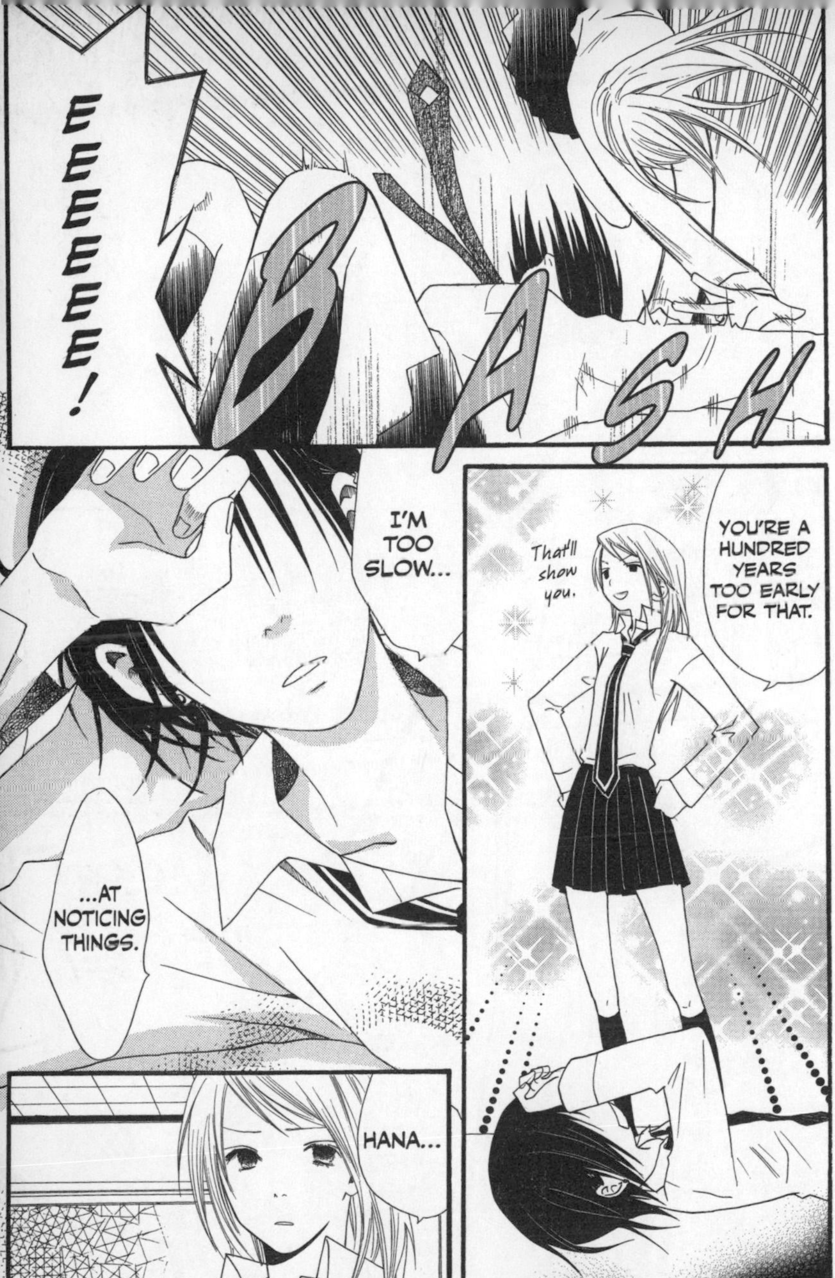
EEEEEEEEE!
BASH
YOU'RE A HUNDRED YEARS TOO EARLY FOR THAT.
That'll show you.
I'M TOO SLOW...
...AT NOTICING THINGS.
HANA...

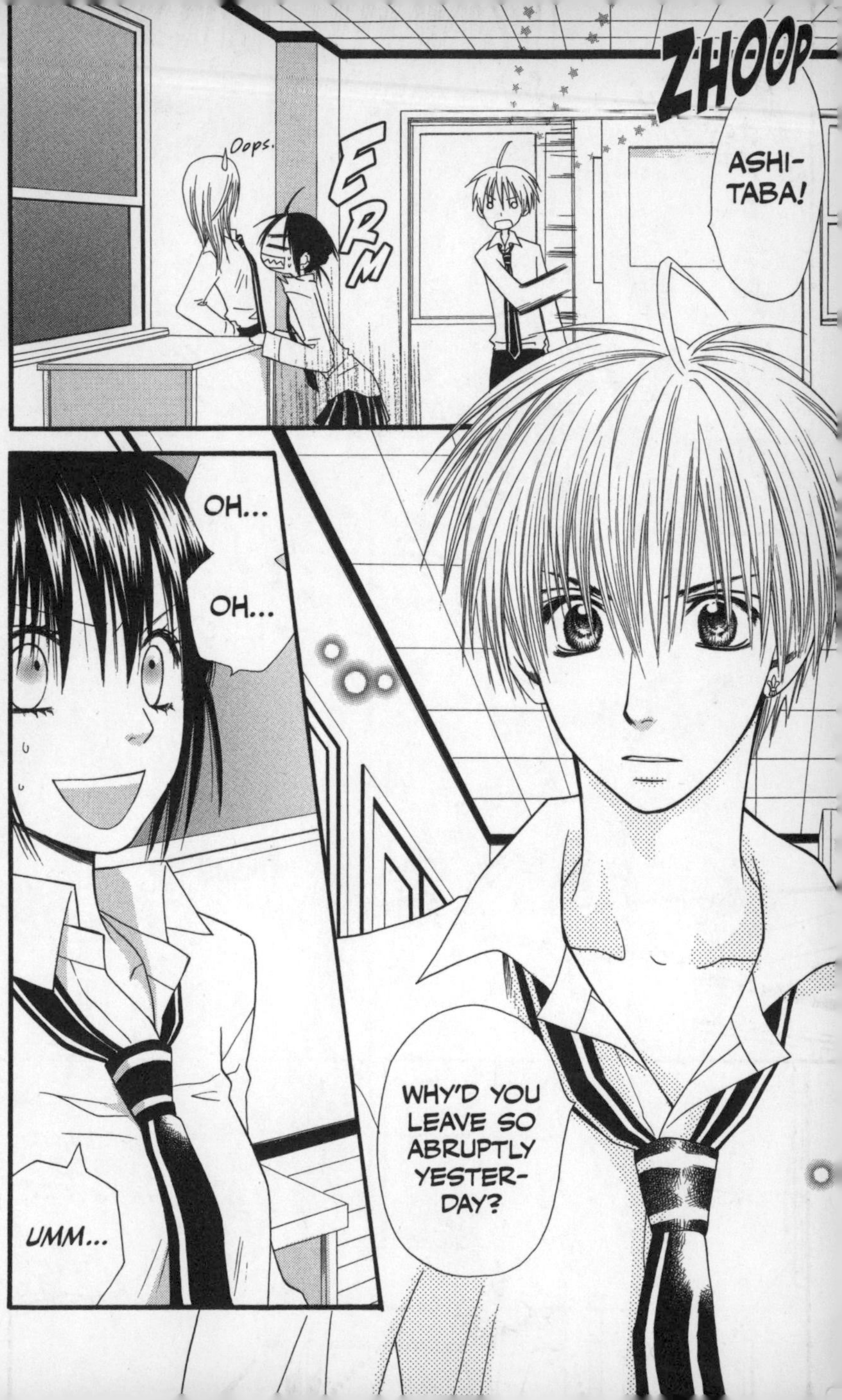
ZHOOP
ASHI-TABA!
ERM
Oops.
WHY'D YOU LEAVE SO ABRUPTLY YESTER-DAY?
OH...
OH...
UMM...

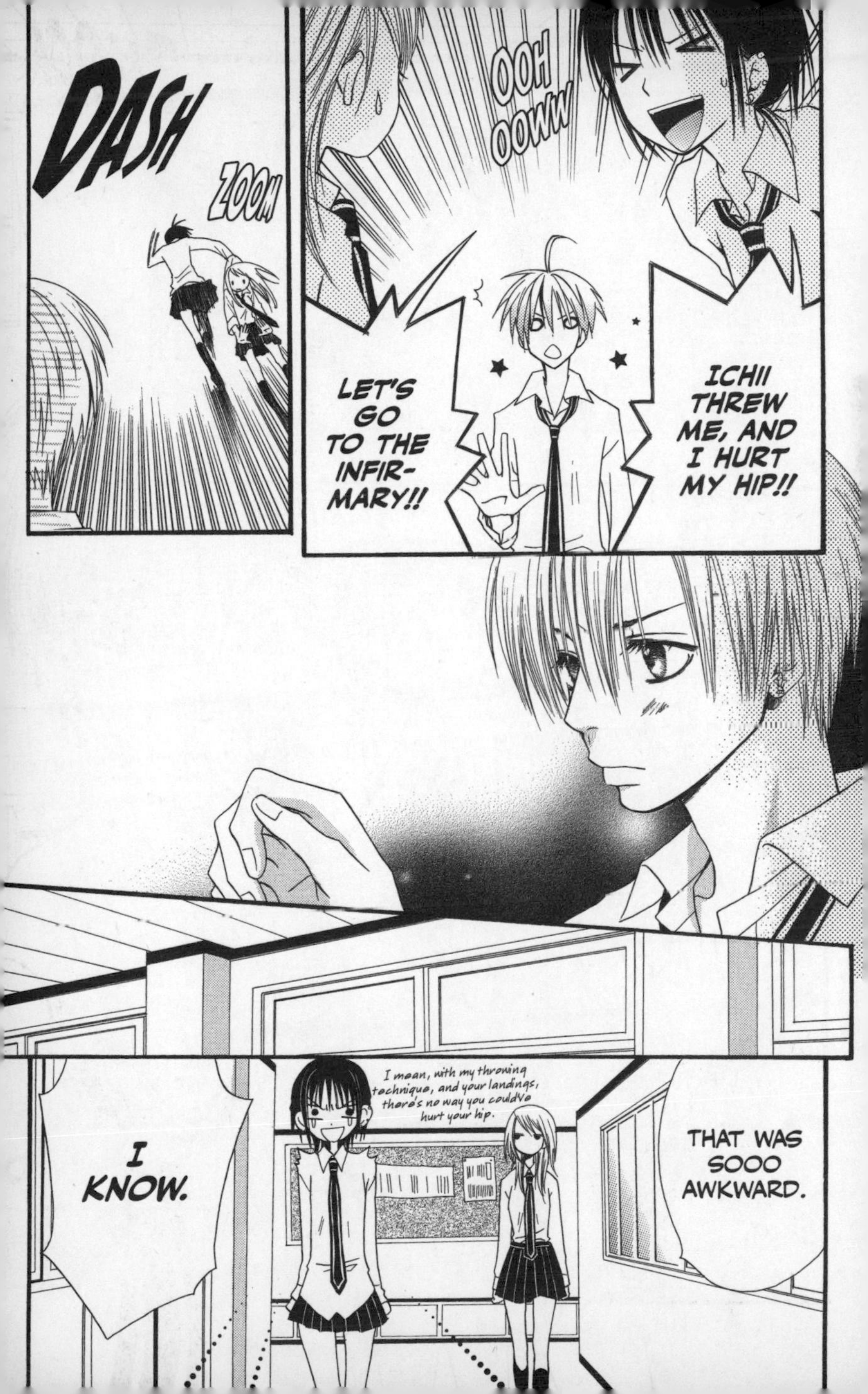
OOH OOWW
ICHII THREW ME, AND I HURT MY HIP!!
LET'S GO TO THE INFIRMARY!!
DASH
ZOOM
THAT WAS SOOO AWKWARD.
I mean, with my throwing technique, and your landings, there's no way you could've hurt your hip.
I KNOW.

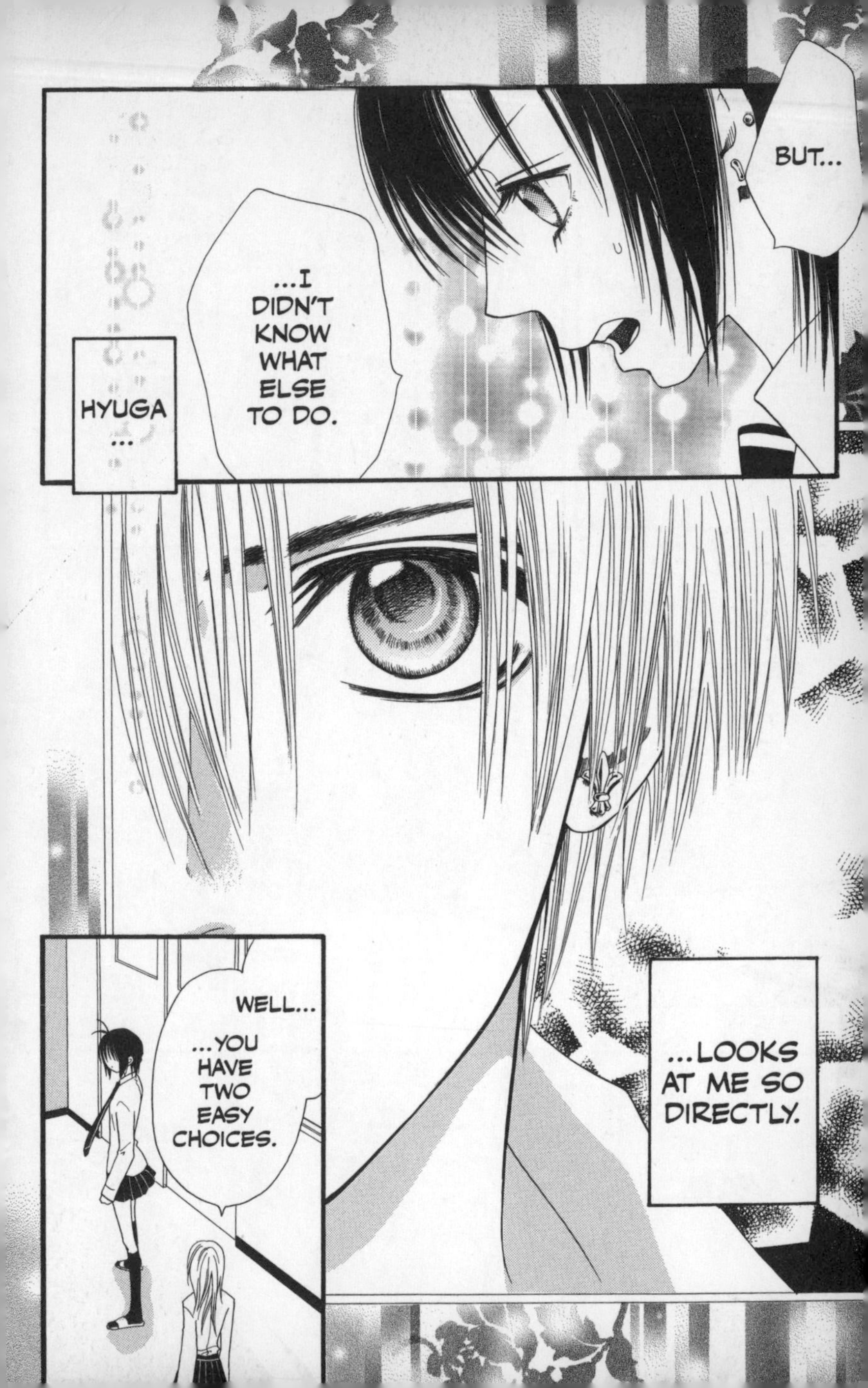
BUT...
...I DIDN'T KNOW WHAT ELSE TO DO.
HYUGA...
...LOOKS AT ME SO DIRECTLY.
WELL...
...YOU HAVE TWO EASY CHOICES.

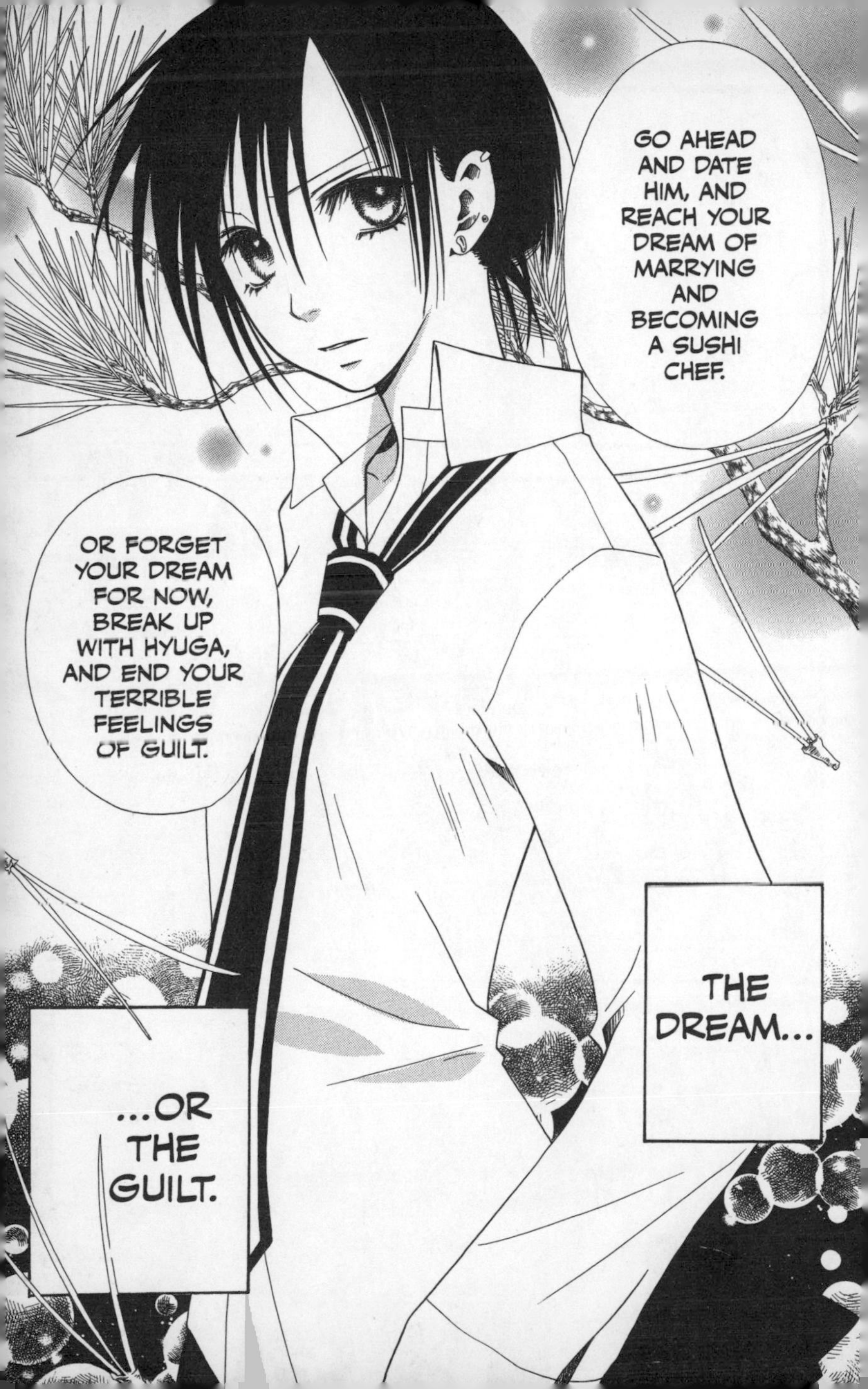
GO AHEAD AND DATE HIM, AND REACH YOUR DREAM OF MARRYING AND BECOMING A SUSHI CHEF.
OR FORGET YOUR DREAM FOR NOW, BREAK UP WITH HYUGA, AND END YOUR TERRIBLE FEELINGS OF GUILT.
THE DREAM...
...OR THE GUILT.

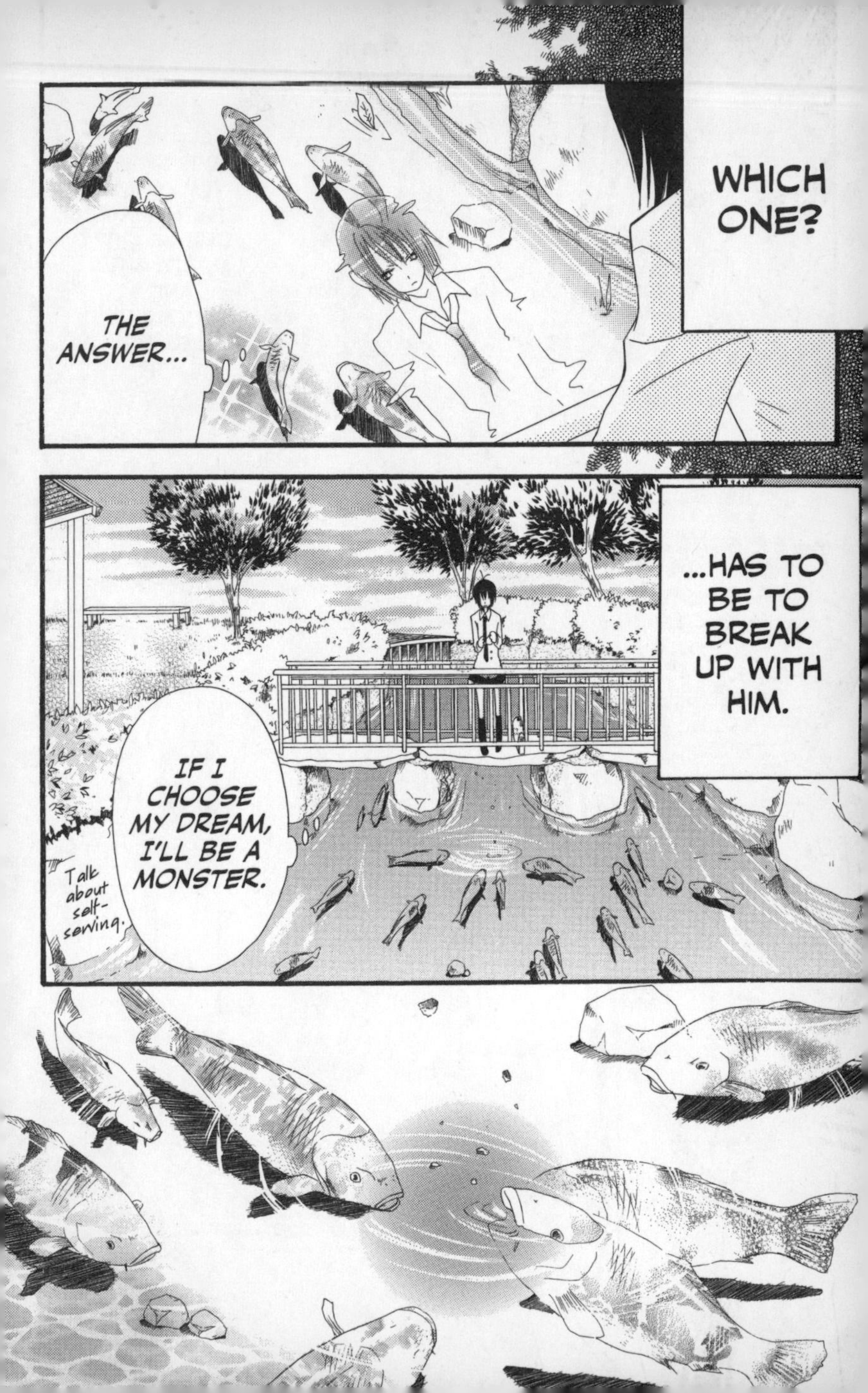
WHICH ONE?
THE ANSWER...
...HAS TO BE TO BREAK UP WITH HIM.
IF I CHOOSE MY DREAM, I'LL BE A MONSTER.
Talk about self-serving.

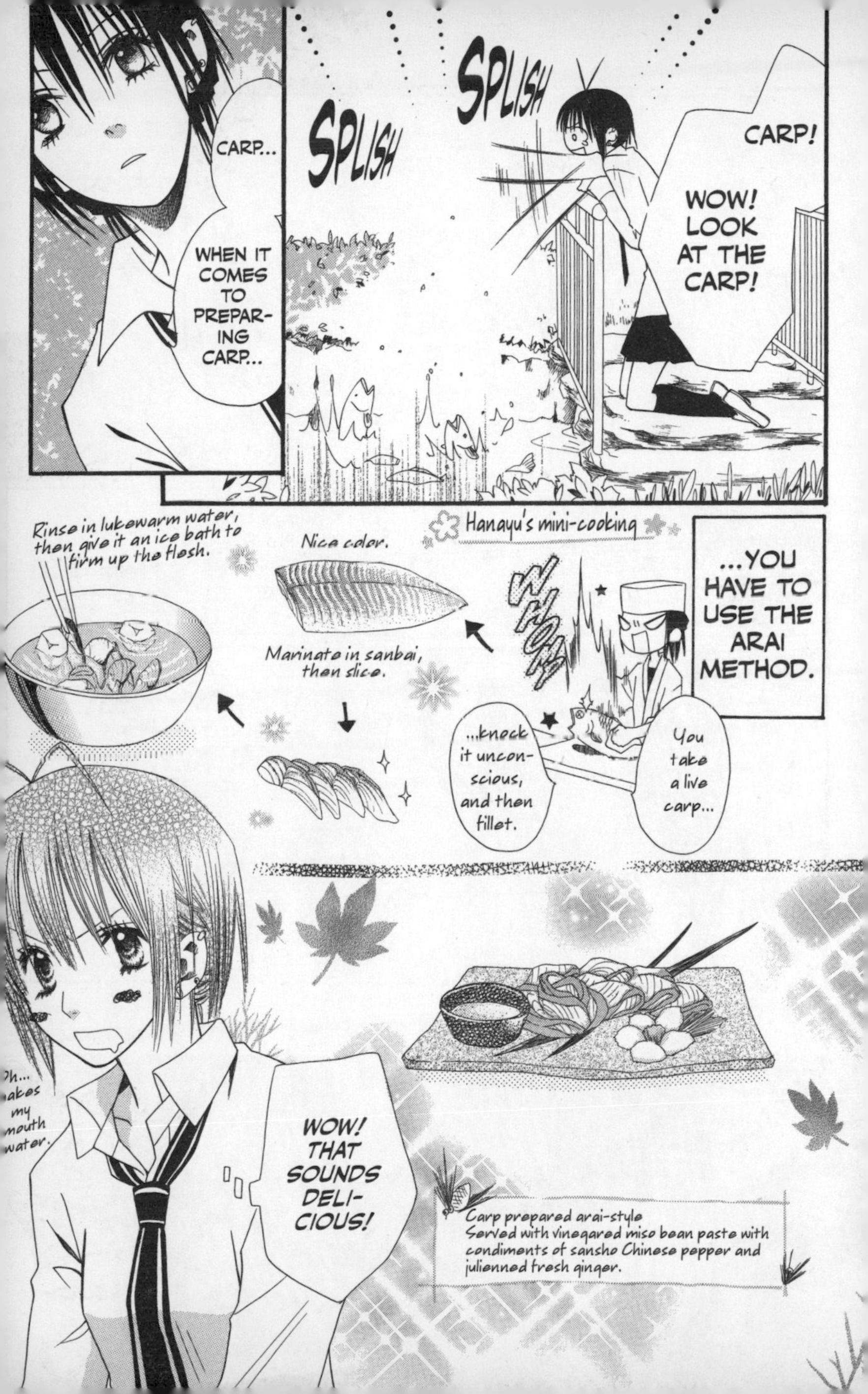
SPLISH
SPLISH
CARP!
WOW! LOOK AT THE CARP!
CARP...
WHEN IT COMES TO PREPARING CARP...
...YOU HAVE TO USE THE ARAI METHOD.
Hanayu's mini-cooking
You take a live carp...
...knock it unconscious, and then fillet.
Nice color.
Marinate in sanbai, then slice.
Rinse in lukewarm water, then give it an ice bath to firm up the flesh.
Carp prepared arai-style
Served with vinegared miso bean paste with condiments of sansho Chinese pepper and julienned fresh ginger.
WOW! THAT SOUNDS DELICIOUS!
h... akes my mouth water.

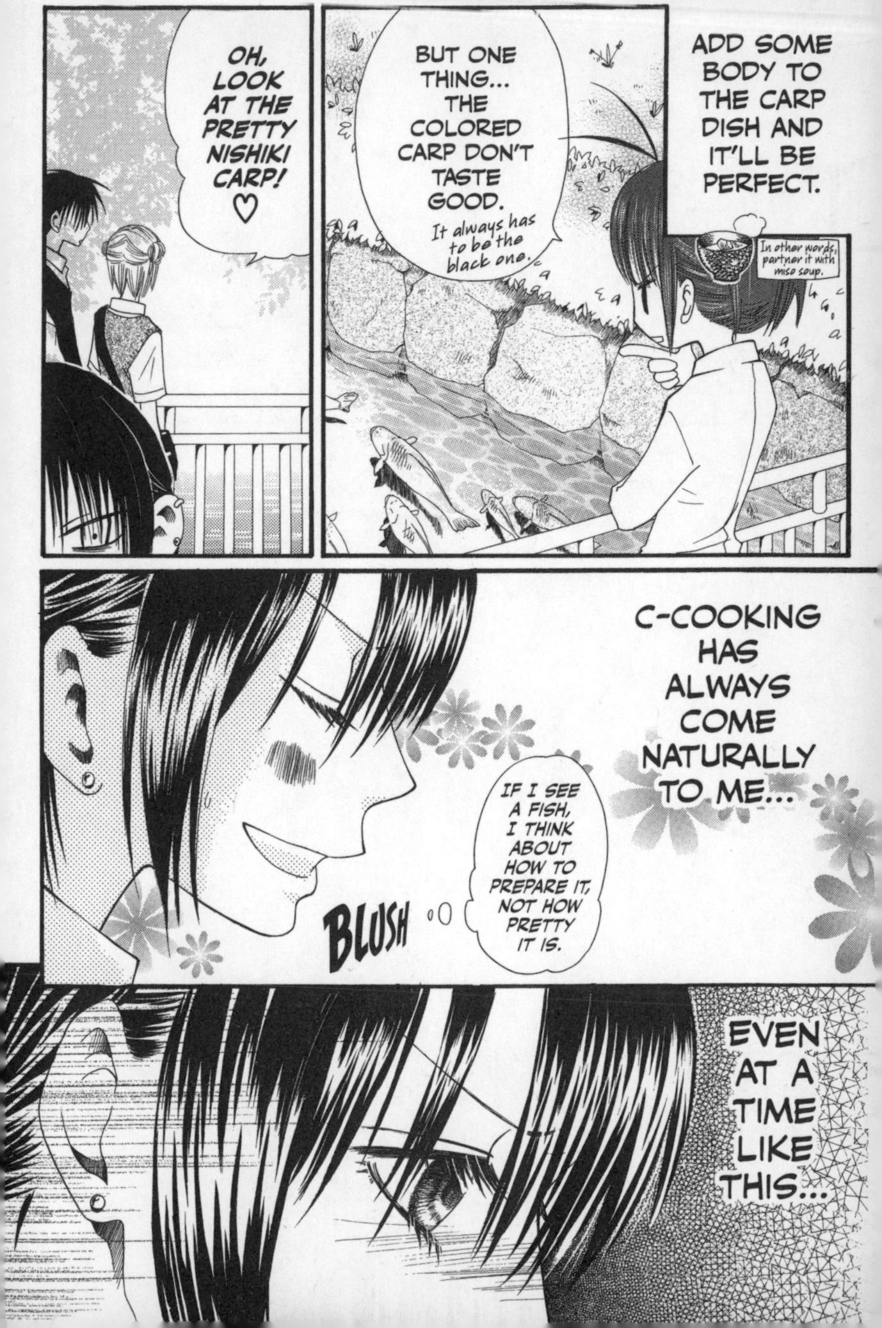
ADD SOME BODY TO THE CARP DISH AND IT'LL BE PERFECT.
In other words, partner it with miso soup.
BUT ONE THING... THE COLORED CARP DON'T TASTE GOOD.
It always has to be the black one.
OH, LOOK AT THE PRETTY NISHIKI CARP! ♡
C-COOKING HAS ALWAYS COME NATURALLY TO ME...
IF I SEE A FISH, I THINK ABOUT HOW TO PREPARE IT, NOT HOW PRETTY IT IS.
BLUSH
EVEN AT A TIME LIKE THIS...

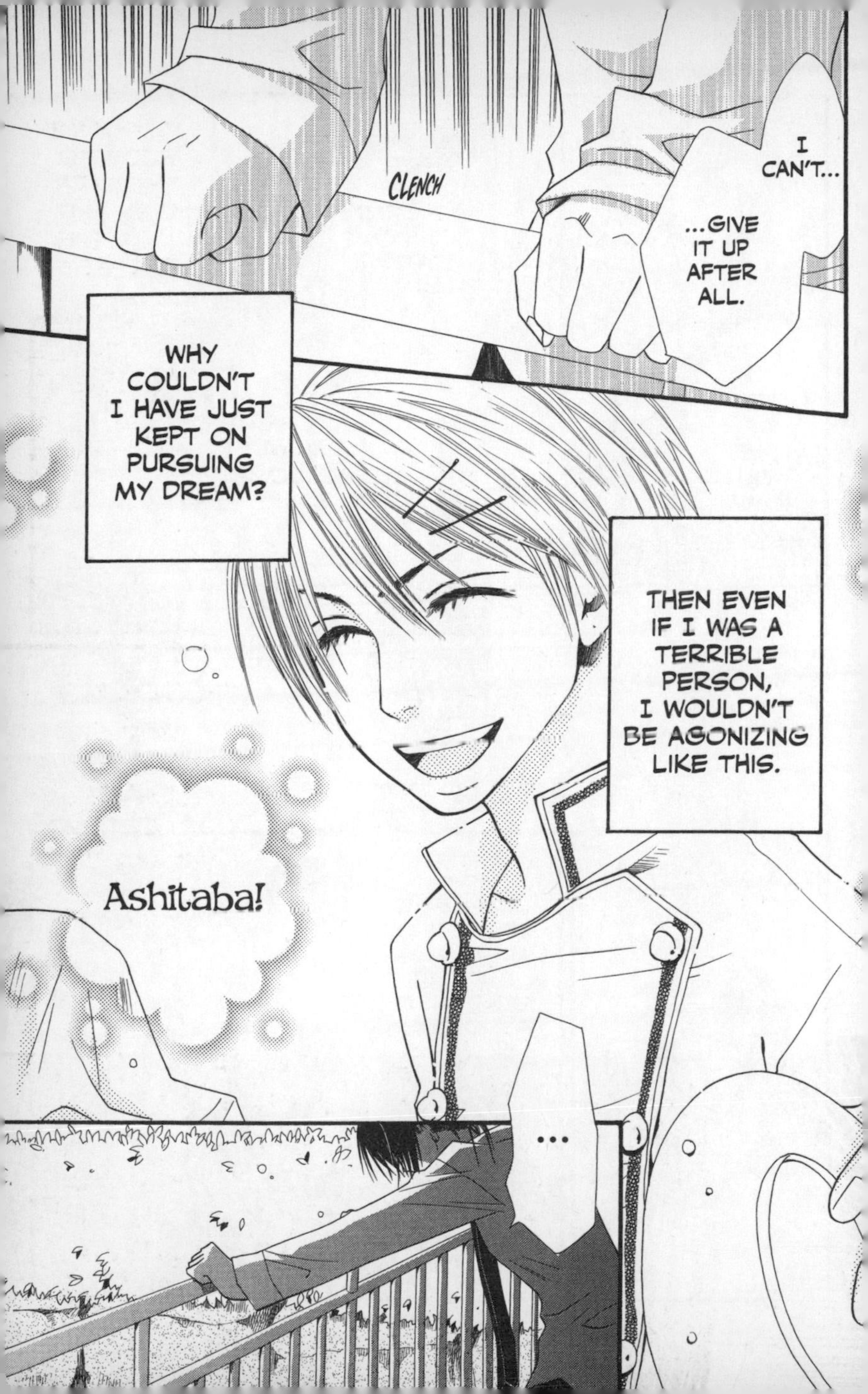
I CAN'T...
...GIVE IT UP AFTER ALL.
CLENCH
WHY COULDN'T I HAVE JUST KEPT ON PURSUING MY DREAM?
THEN EVEN IF I WAS A TERRIBLE PERSON, I WOULDN'T BE AGONIZING LIKE THIS.
Ashitaba!
...

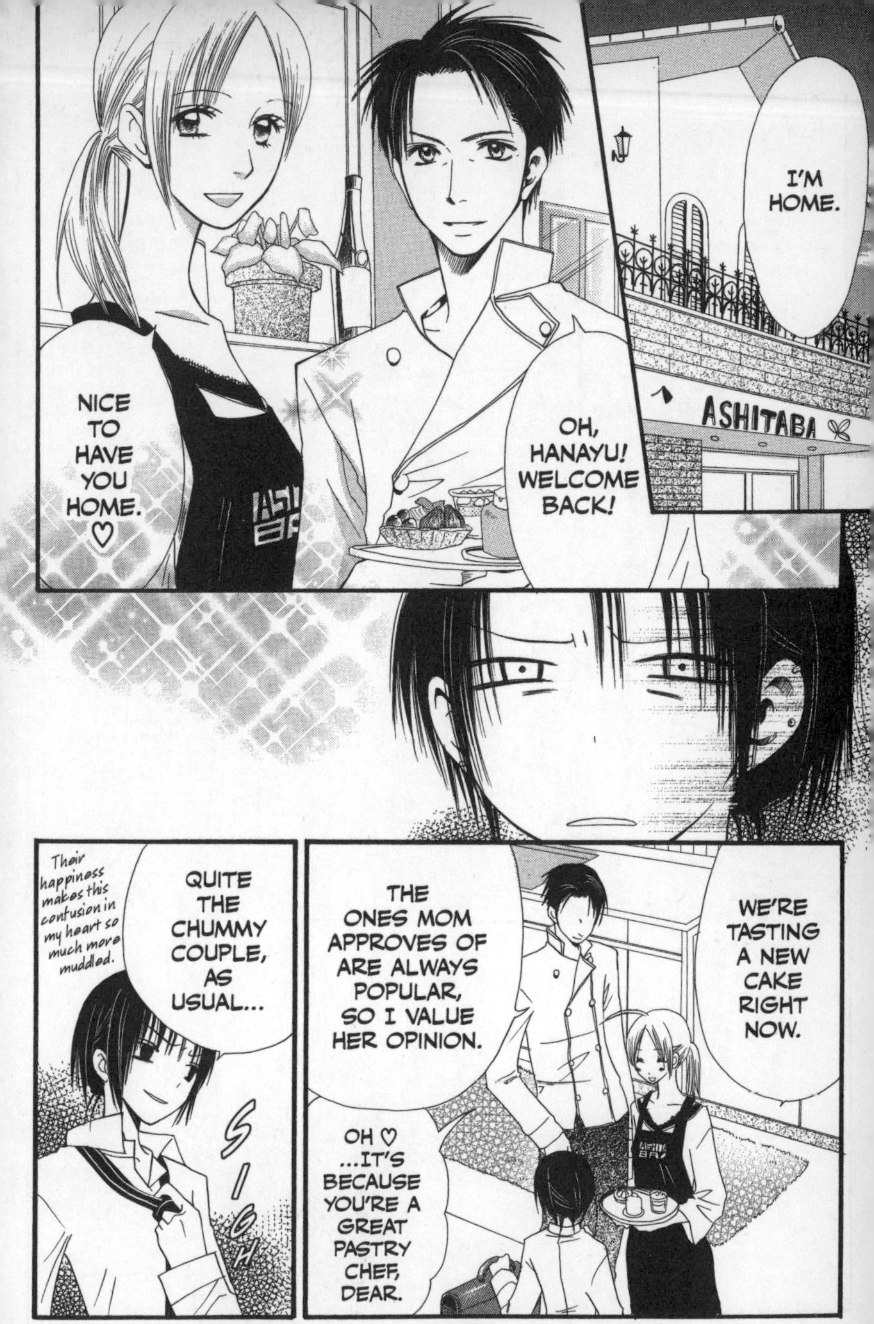
I'M HOME.
ASHITABA
OH, HANAYU! WELCOME BACK!
NICE TO HAVE YOU HOME. ♡
WE'RE TASTING A NEW CAKE RIGHT NOW.
THE ONES MOM APPROVES OF ARE ALWAYS POPULAR, SO I VALUE HER OPINION.
OH ♡ ...IT'S BECAUSE YOU'RE A GREAT PASTRY CHEF, DEAR.
QUITE THE CHUMMY COUPLE, AS USUAL...
Their happiness makes this confusion in my heart so much more muddled.
SIGH

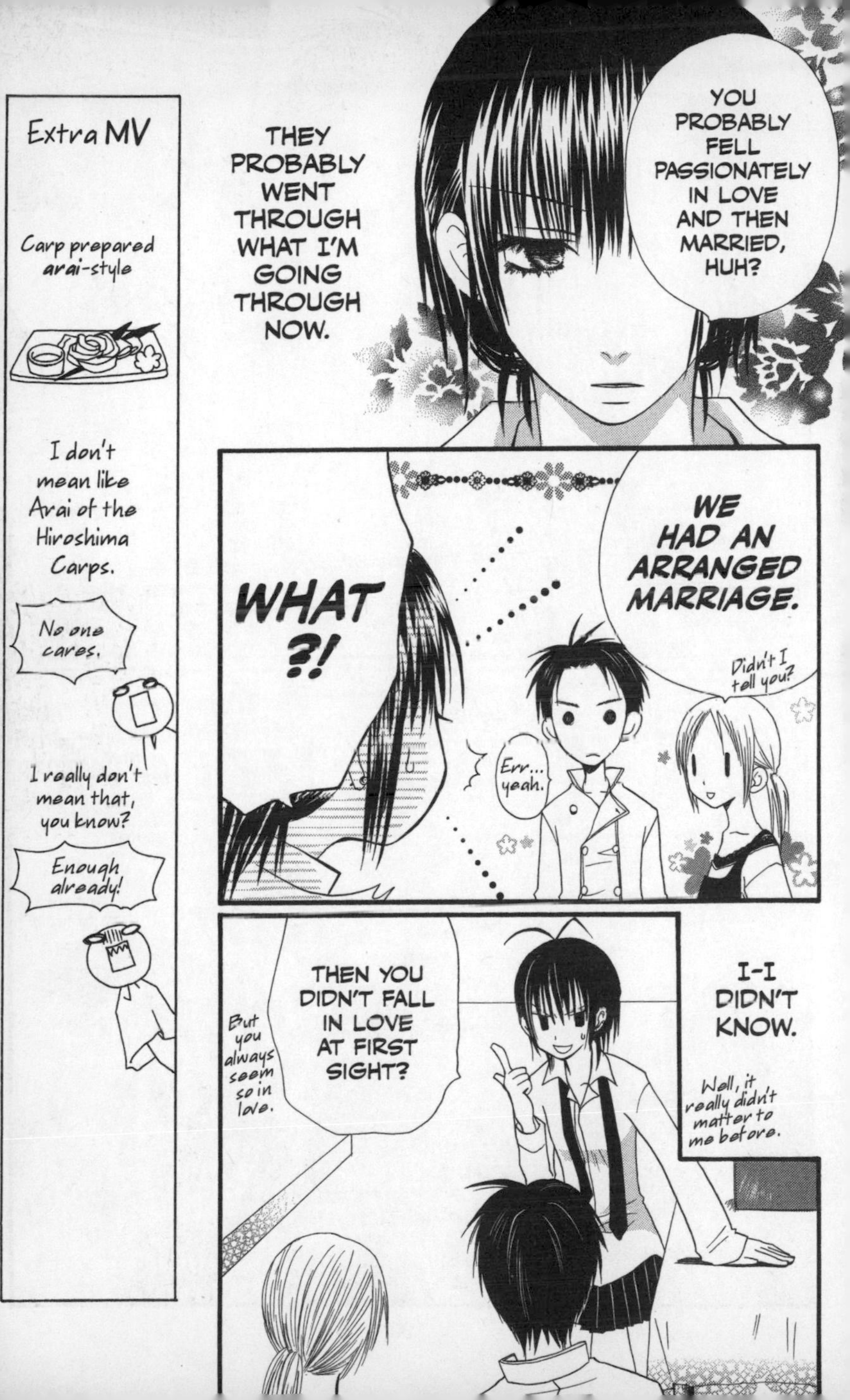
YOU PROBABLY FELL PASSIONATELY IN LOVE AND THEN MARRIED, HUH?
THEY PROBABLY WENT THROUGH WHAT I'M GOING THROUGH NOW.
WE HAD AN ARRANGED MARRIAGE.
Didn't I tell you?
WHAT ?!
Err... yeah.
I-I DIDN'T KNOW.
Well, it really didn't matter to me before.
THEN YOU DIDN'T FALL IN LOVE AT FIRST SIGHT?
But you always seem so in love.
Extra MV
Carp prepared arai-style
I don't mean like Arai of the Hiroshima Carps.
No one cares.
I really don't mean that, you know?
Enough already!

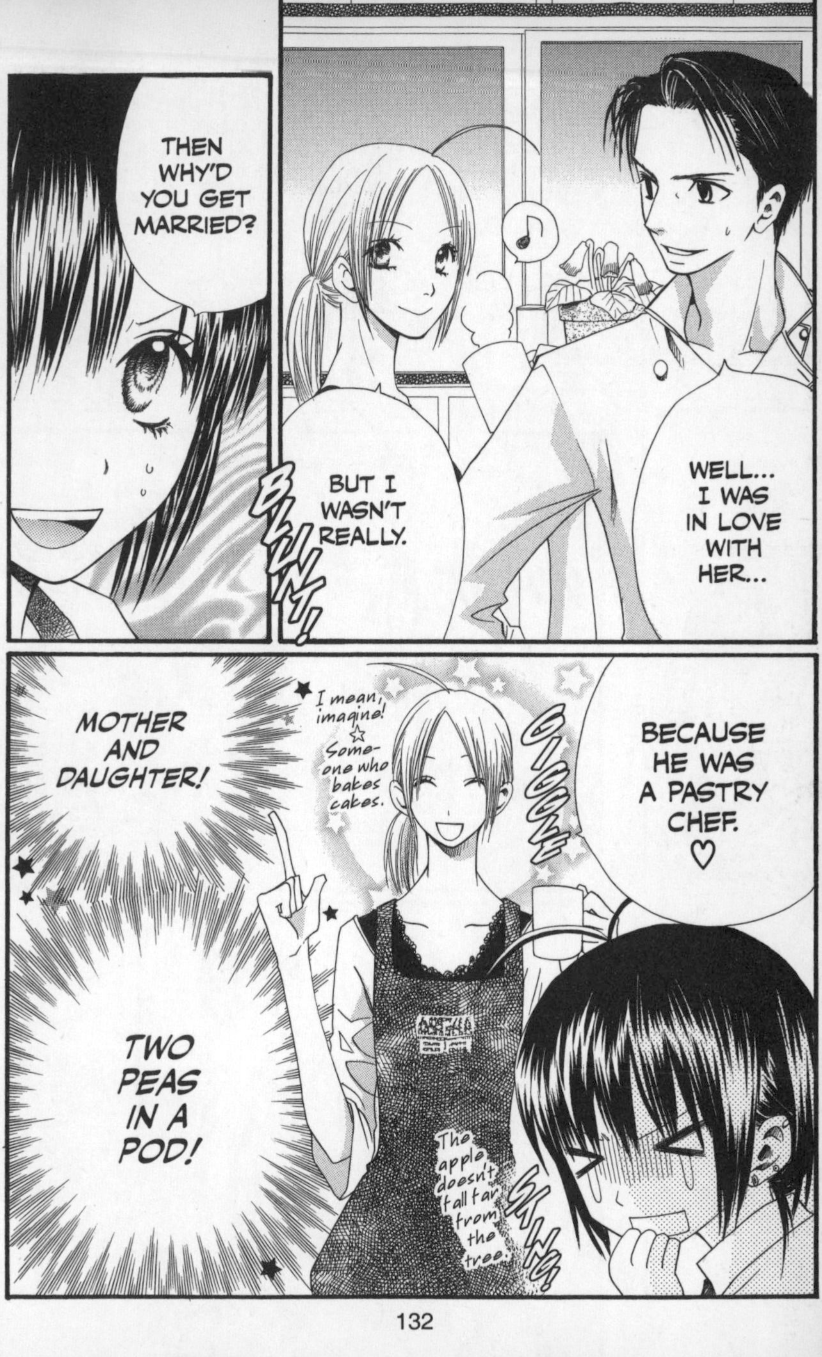
WELL... I WAS IN LOVE WITH HER...
BUT I WASN'T REALLY.
BLUNT!
THEN WHY'D YOU GET MARRIED?
BECAUSE HE WAS A PASTRY CHEF. ♡
GIGGLE
I mean, imagine! ☆ Someone who bakes cakes.
MOTHER AND DAUGHTER!
TWO PEAS IN A POD!
The apple doesn't fall far from the tree.
SWING!

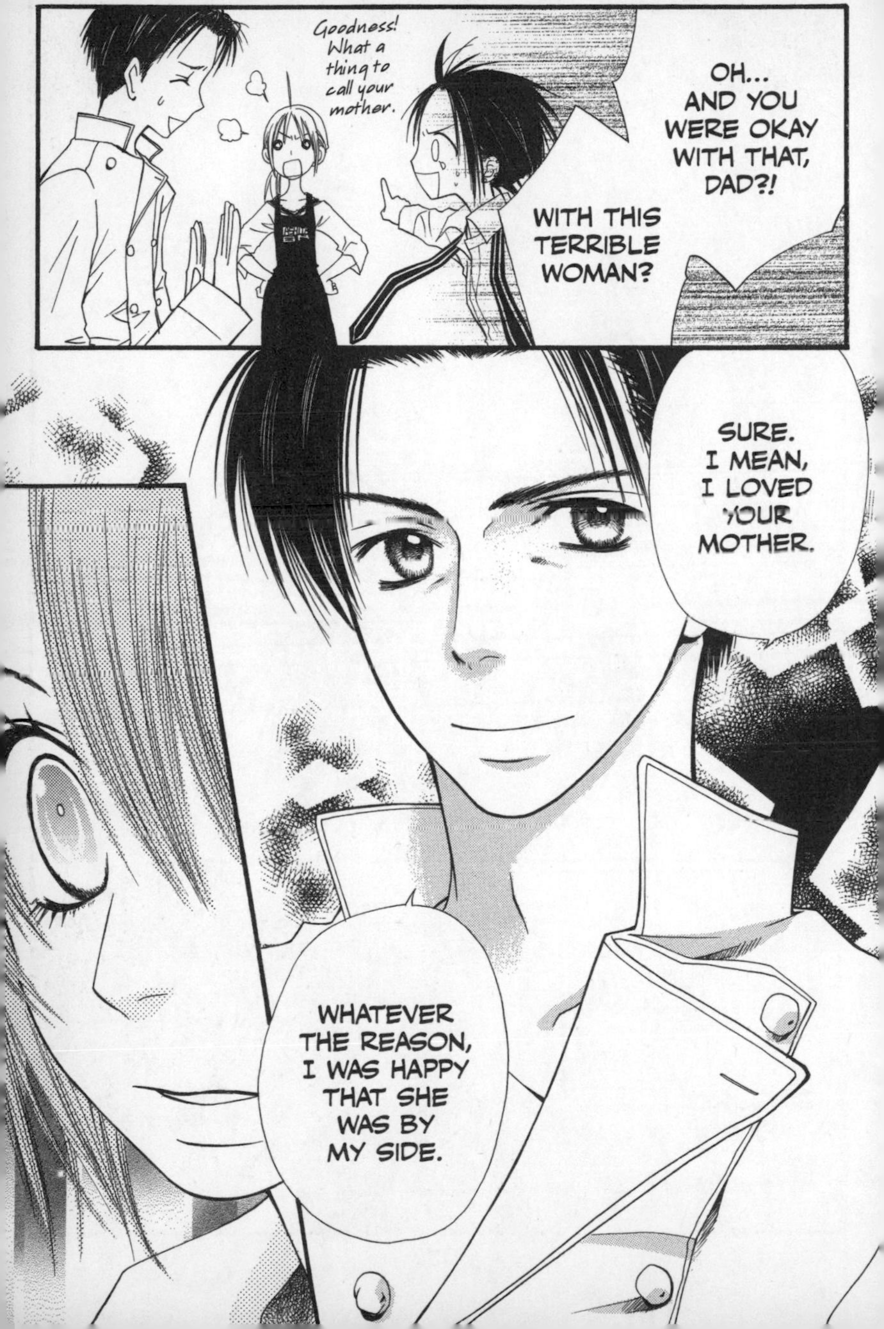
OH... AND YOU WERE OKAY WITH THAT, DAD?!
WITH THIS TERRIBLE WOMAN?
Goodness! What a thing to call your mother.
SURE. I MEAN, I LOVED YOUR MOTHER.
WHATEVER THE REASON, I WAS HAPPY THAT SHE WAS BY MY SIDE.

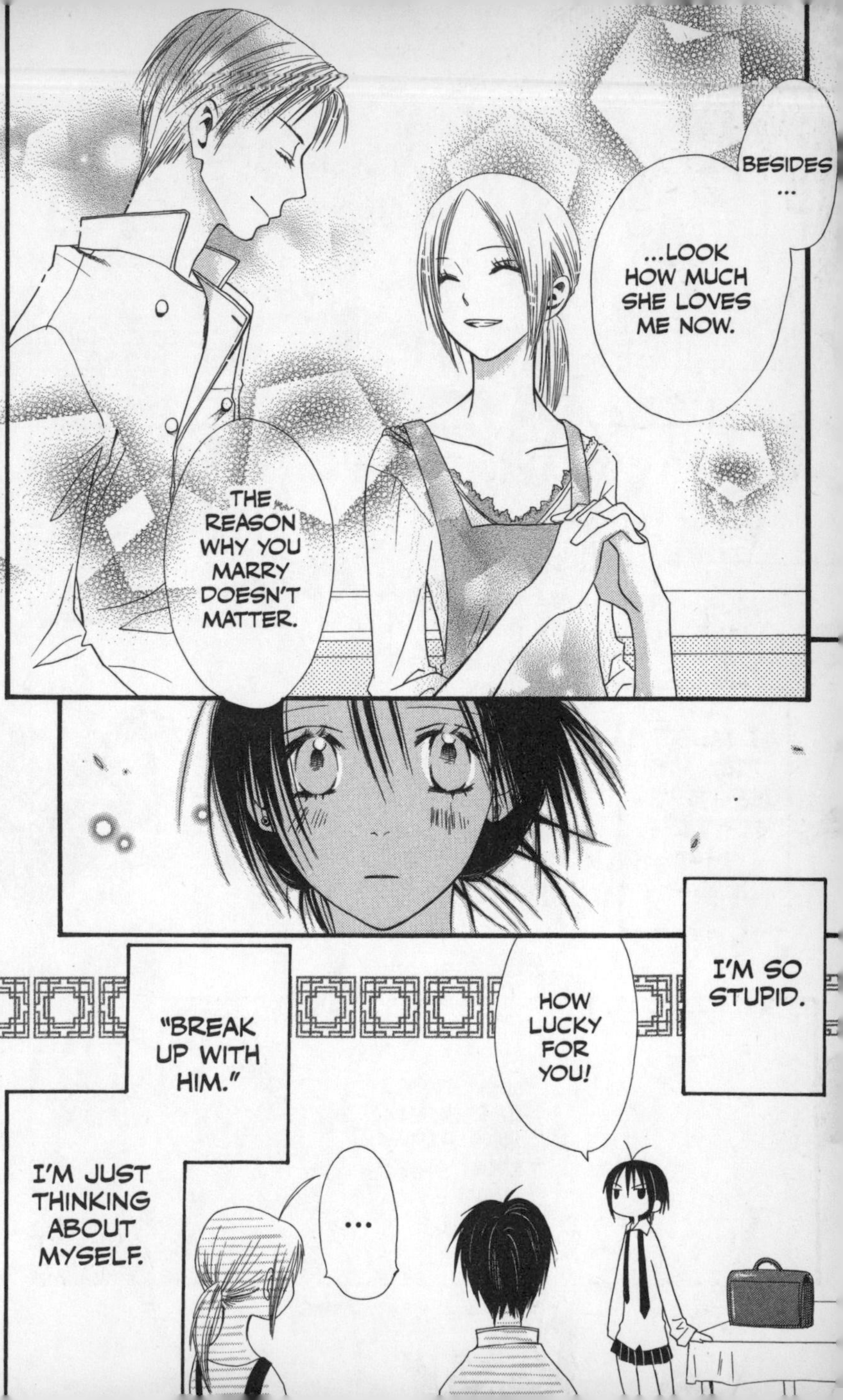
BESIDES...
...LOOK HOW MUCH SHE LOVES ME NOW.
THE REASON WHY YOU MARRY DOESN'T MATTER.
I'M SO STUPID.
HOW LUCKY FOR YOU!
"BREAK UP WITH HIM."
...
I'M JUST THINKING ABOUT MYSELF.

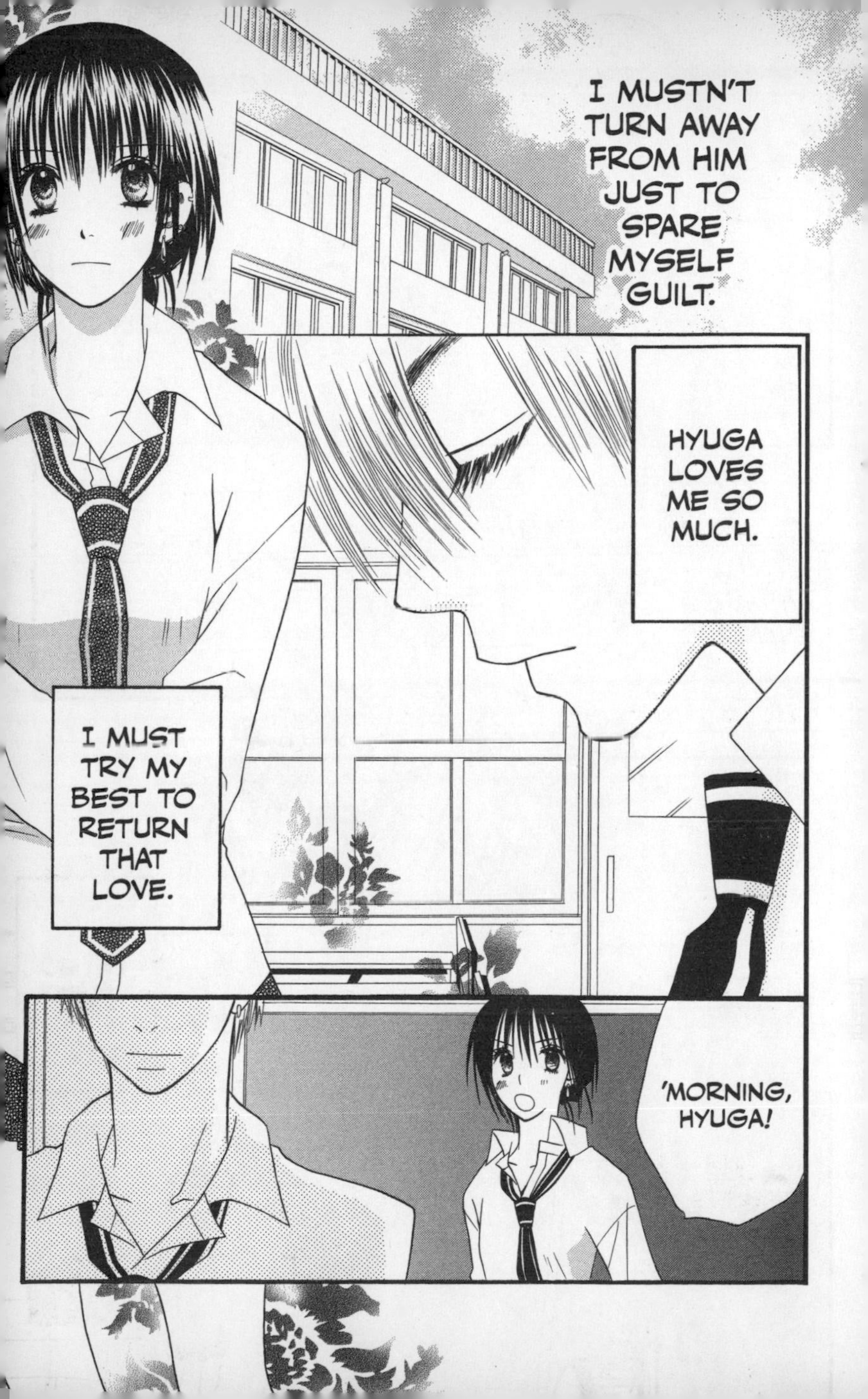
I MUSTN'T TURN AWAY FROM HIM JUST TO SPARE MYSELF GUILT.
HYUGA LOVES ME SO MUCH.
I MUST TRY MY BEST TO RETURN THAT LOVE.
'MORNING, HYUGA!

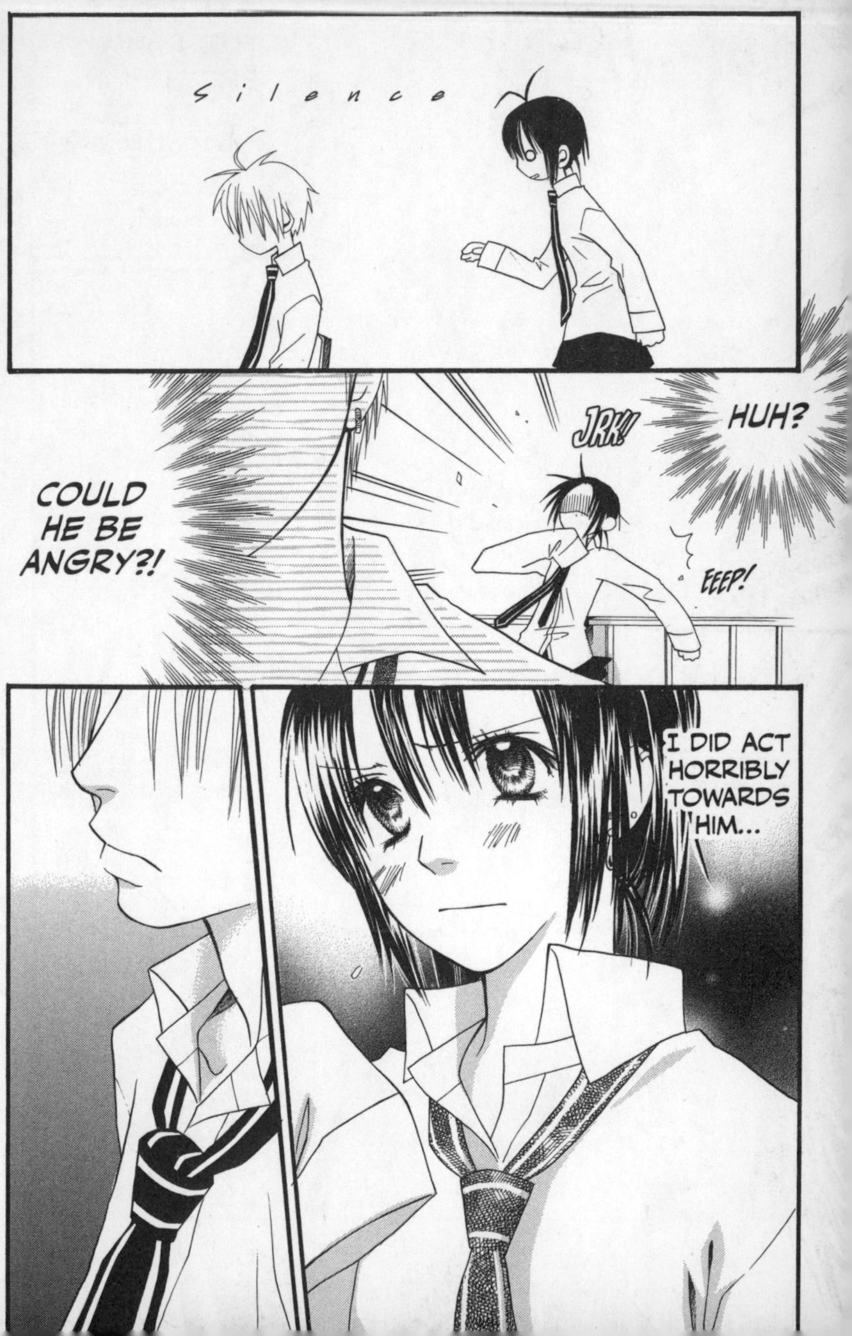
Silence
HUH?
JRK!!
EEEP!
COULD HE BE ANGRY?!
I DID ACT HORRIBLY TOWARDS HIM...

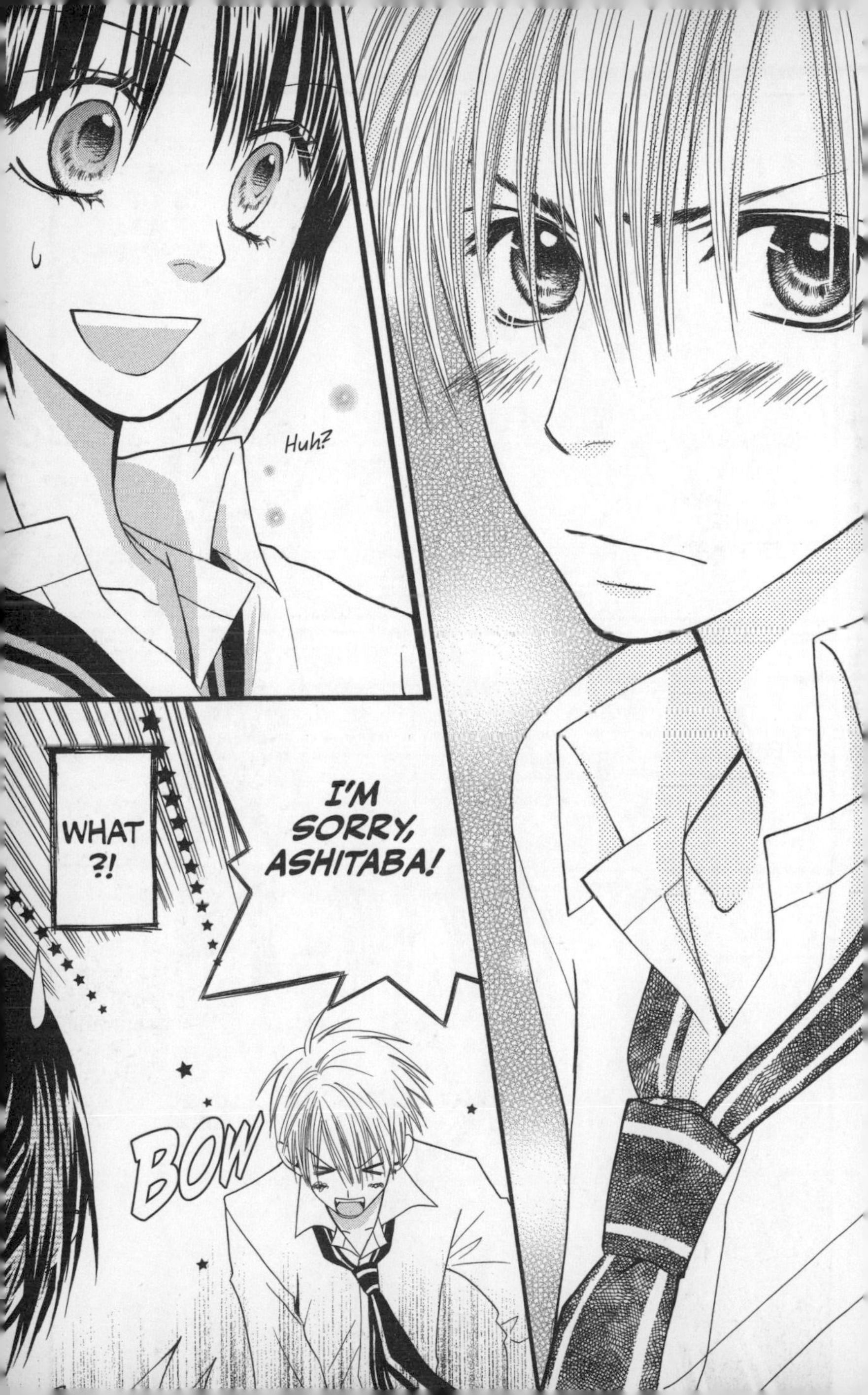
Huh?
I'M SORRY, ASHITABA!
WHAT ?!
BOW

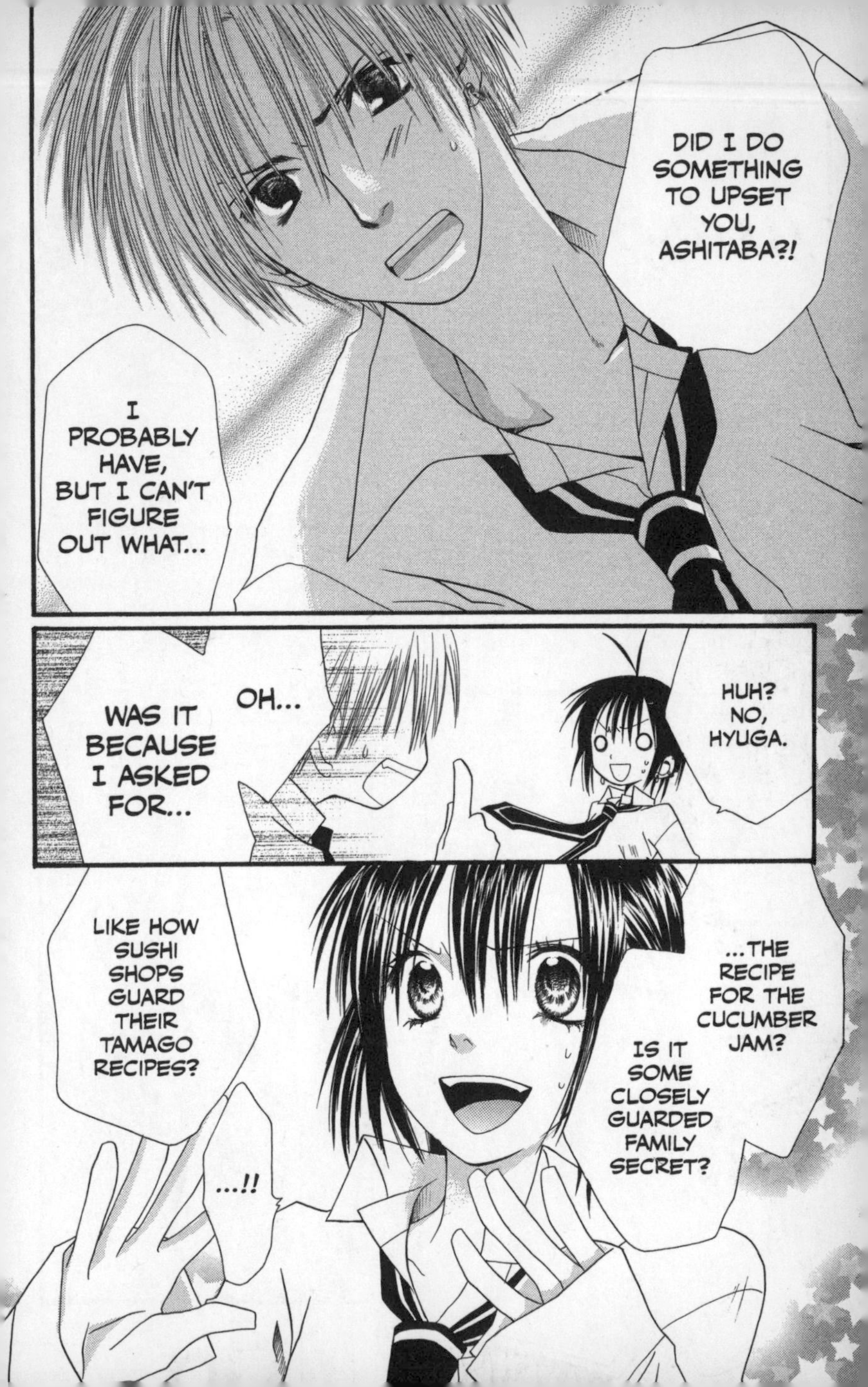
DID I DO SOMETHING TO UPSET YOU, ASHITABA?!
I PROBABLY HAVE, BUT I CAN'T FIGURE OUT WHAT...
HUH? NO, HYUGA.
OH...
WAS IT BECAUSE I ASKED FOR...
...THE RECIPE FOR THE CUCUMBER JAM?
IS IT SOME CLOSELY GUARDED FAMILY SECRET?
LIKE HOW SUSHI SHOPS GUARD THEIR TAMAGO RECIPES?
...!!

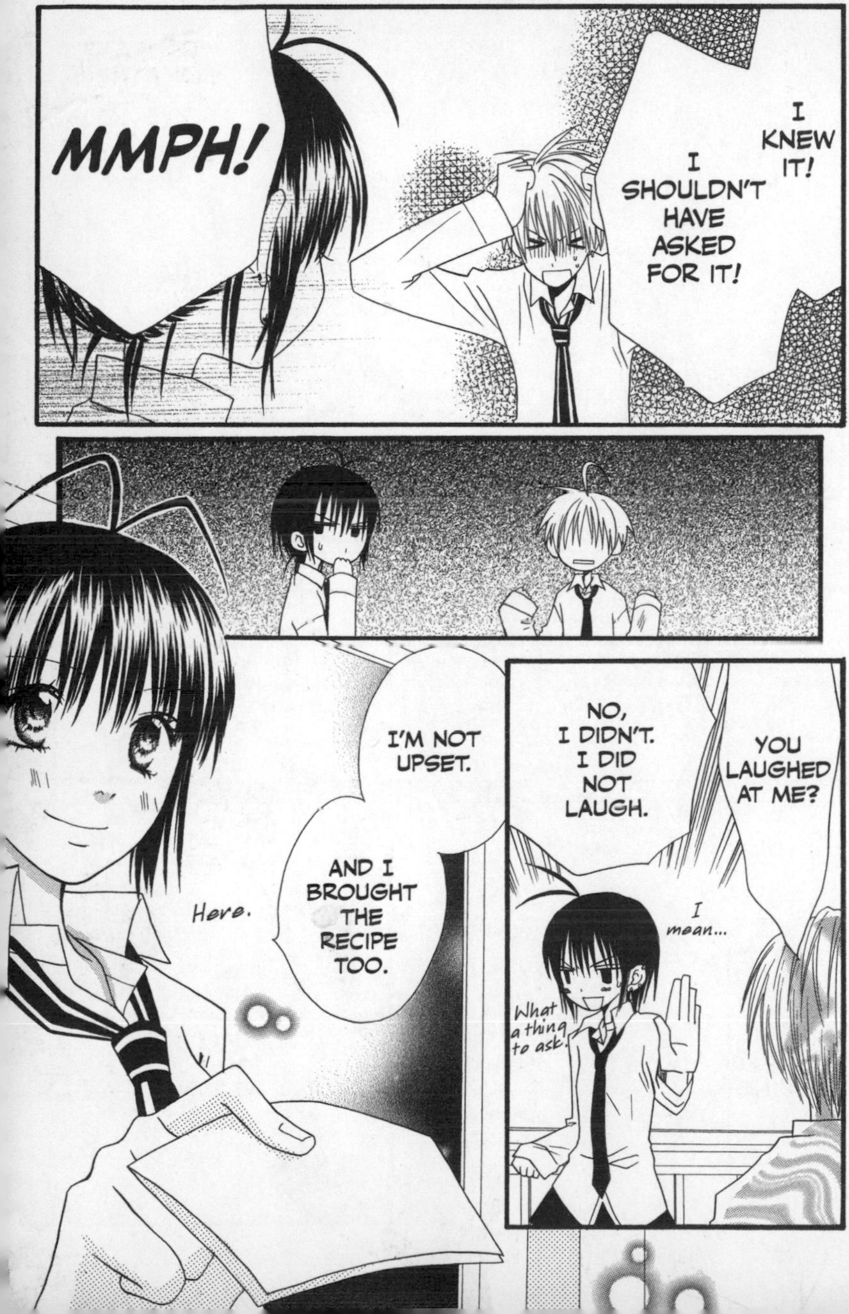
I KNEW IT!
I SHOULDN'T HAVE ASKED FOR IT!
MMPH!
YOU LAUGHED AT ME?
NO, I DIDN'T. I DID NOT LAUGH.
I mean...
What a thing to ask.
I'M NOT UPSET.
AND I BROUGHT THE RECIPE TOO.
Here.

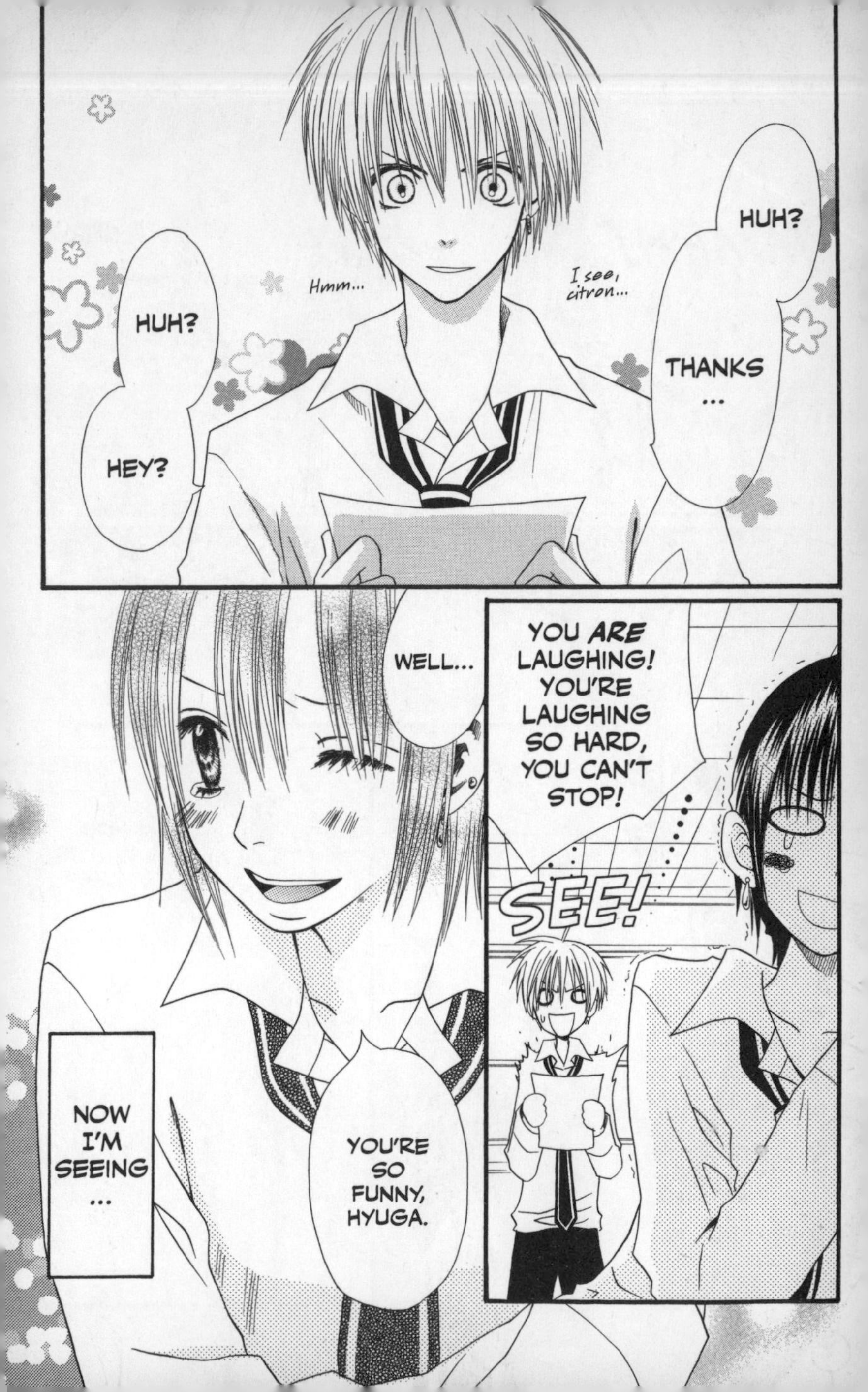
HUH?
THANKS...
I see, citron...
Hmm...
HUH?
HEY?
YOU *ARE* LAUGHING! YOU'RE LAUGHING SO HARD, YOU CAN'T STOP!
SEE!
WELL...
YOU'RE SO FUNNY, HYUGA.
NOW I'M SEEING...

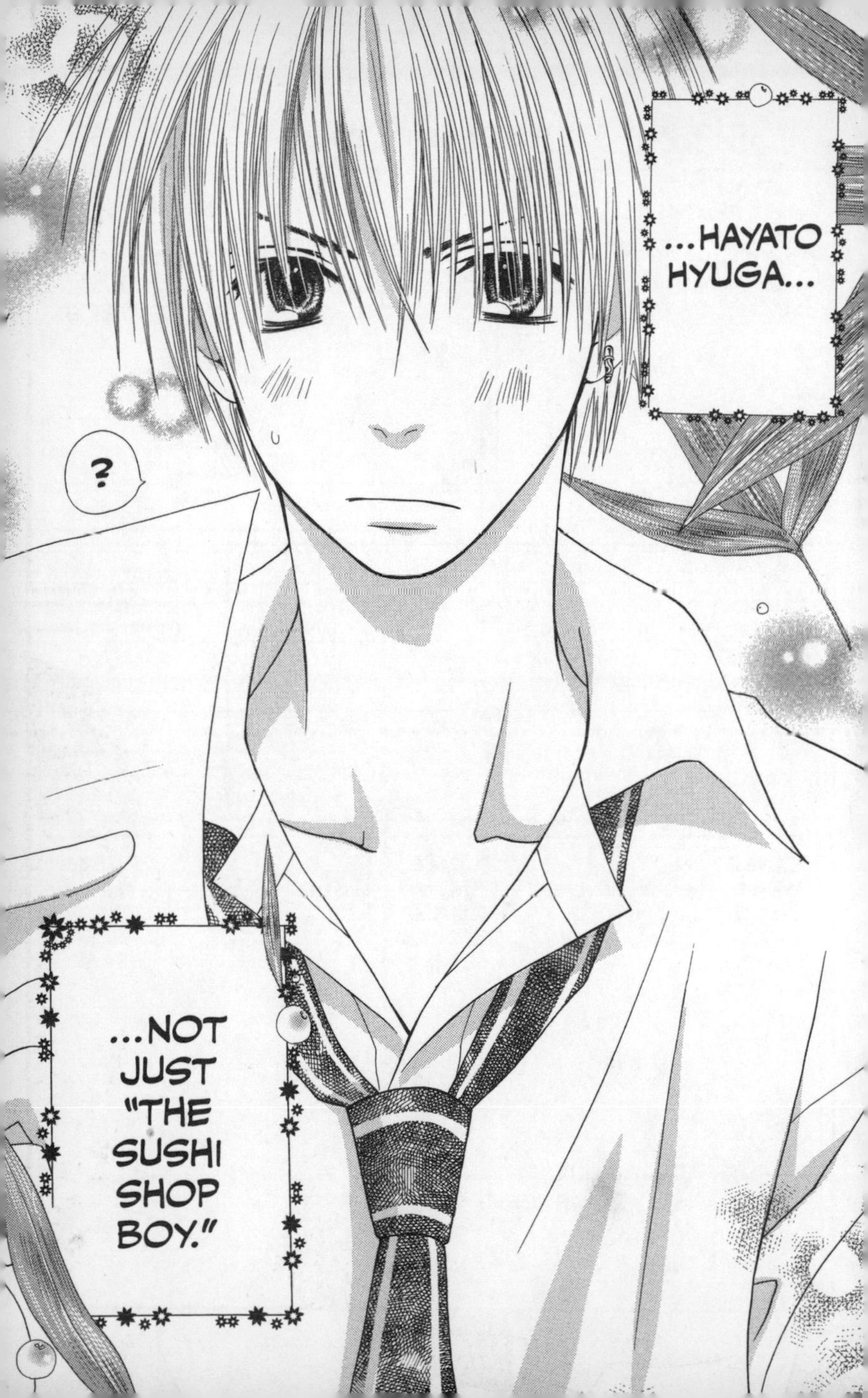
...HAYATO HYUGA...
?
...NOT JUST "THE SUSHI SHOP BOY."

SIDE DISH Mixed Vegetables 5

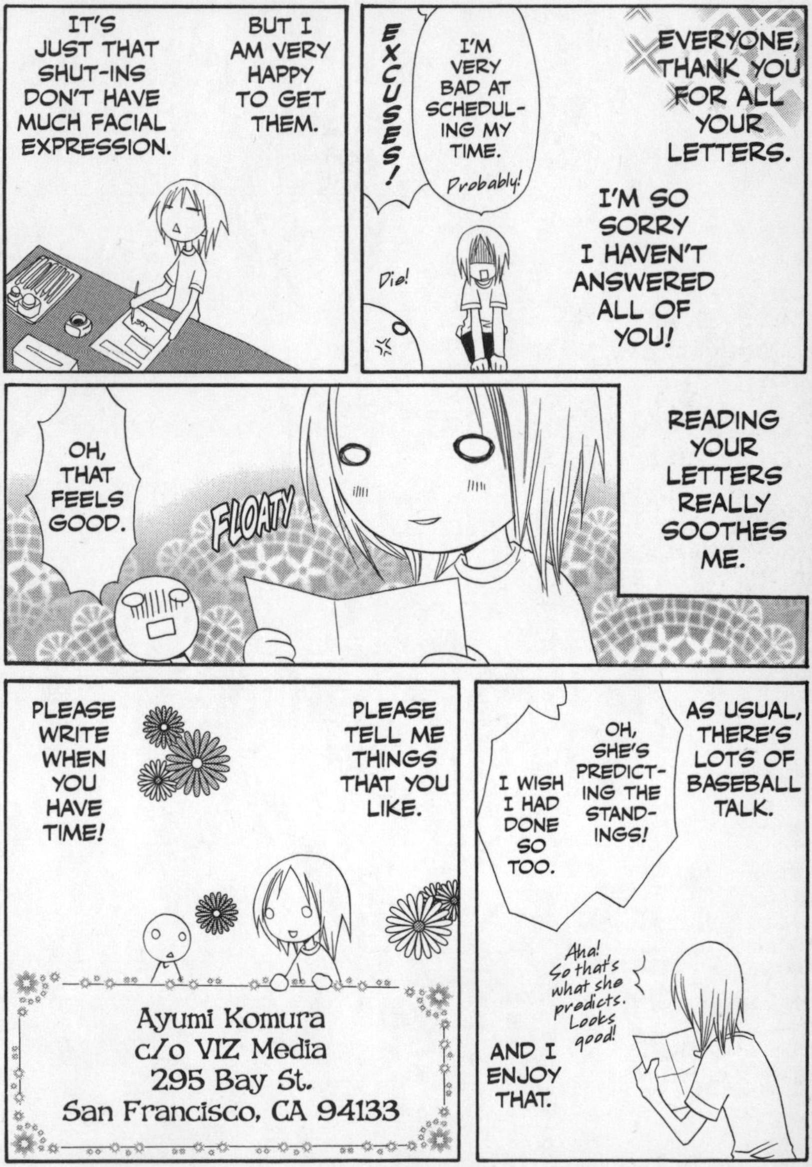
EVERYONE, THANK YOU FOR ALL YOUR LETTERS.
I'M SO SORRY I HAVEN'T ANSWERED ALL OF YOU!
I'M VERY BAD AT SCHEDULING MY TIME.
Probably!
EXCUSES!
Die!
BUT I AM VERY HAPPY TO GET THEM.
IT'S JUST THAT SHUT-INS DON'T HAVE MUCH FACIAL EXPRESSION.
READING YOUR LETTERS REALLY SOOTHES ME.
FLOATY
OH, THAT FEELS GOOD.
AS USUAL, THERE'S LOTS OF BASEBALL TALK.
OH, SHE'S PREDICTING THE STANDINGS!
I WISH I HAD DONE SO TOO.
Aha! So that's what she predicts. Looks good!
AND I ENJOY THAT.
PLEASE TELL ME THINGS THAT YOU LIKE.
PLEASE WRITE WHEN YOU HAVE TIME!
Ayumi Komura
c/o VIZ Media
295 Bay St.
San Francisco, CA 94133

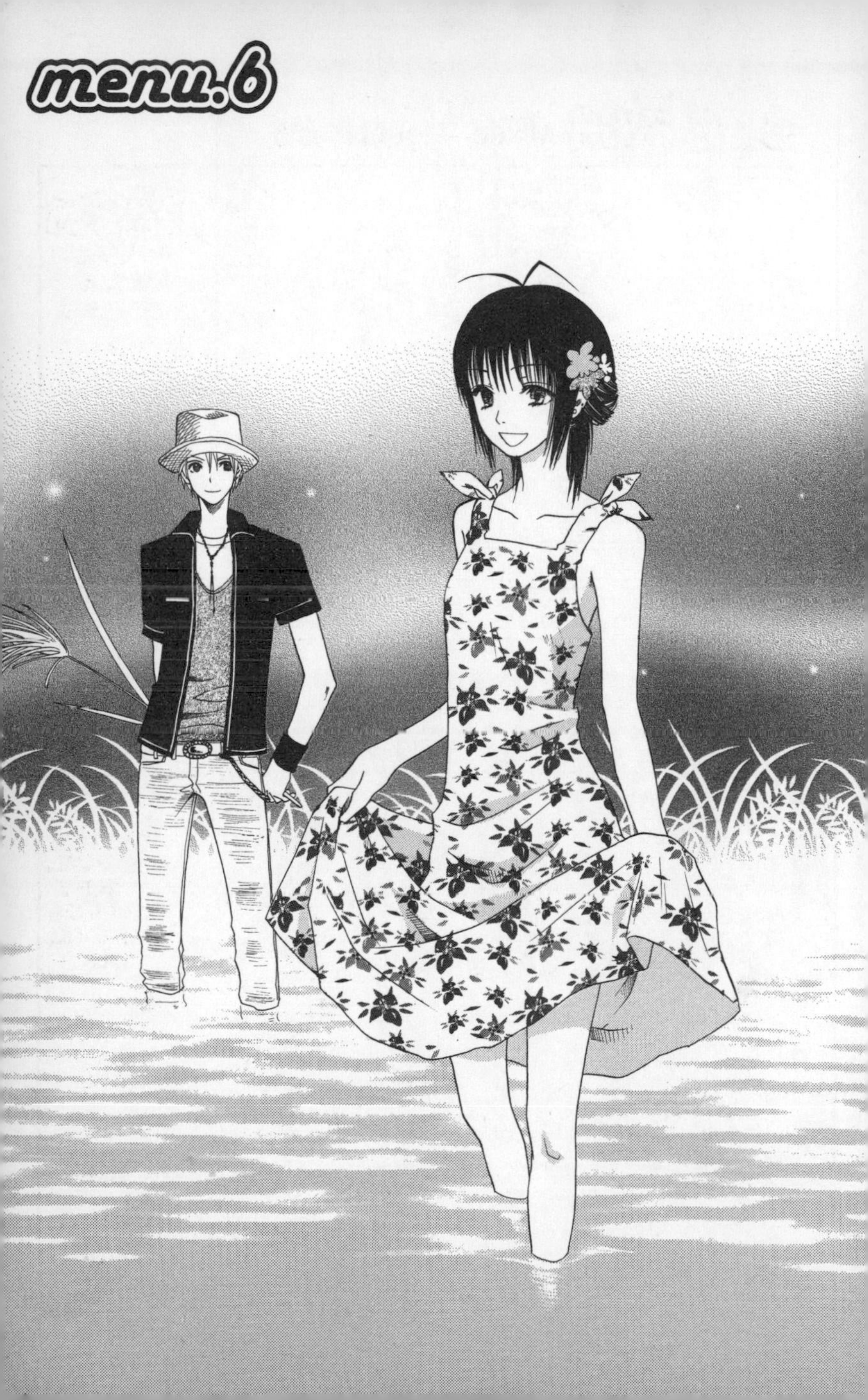
menu.6

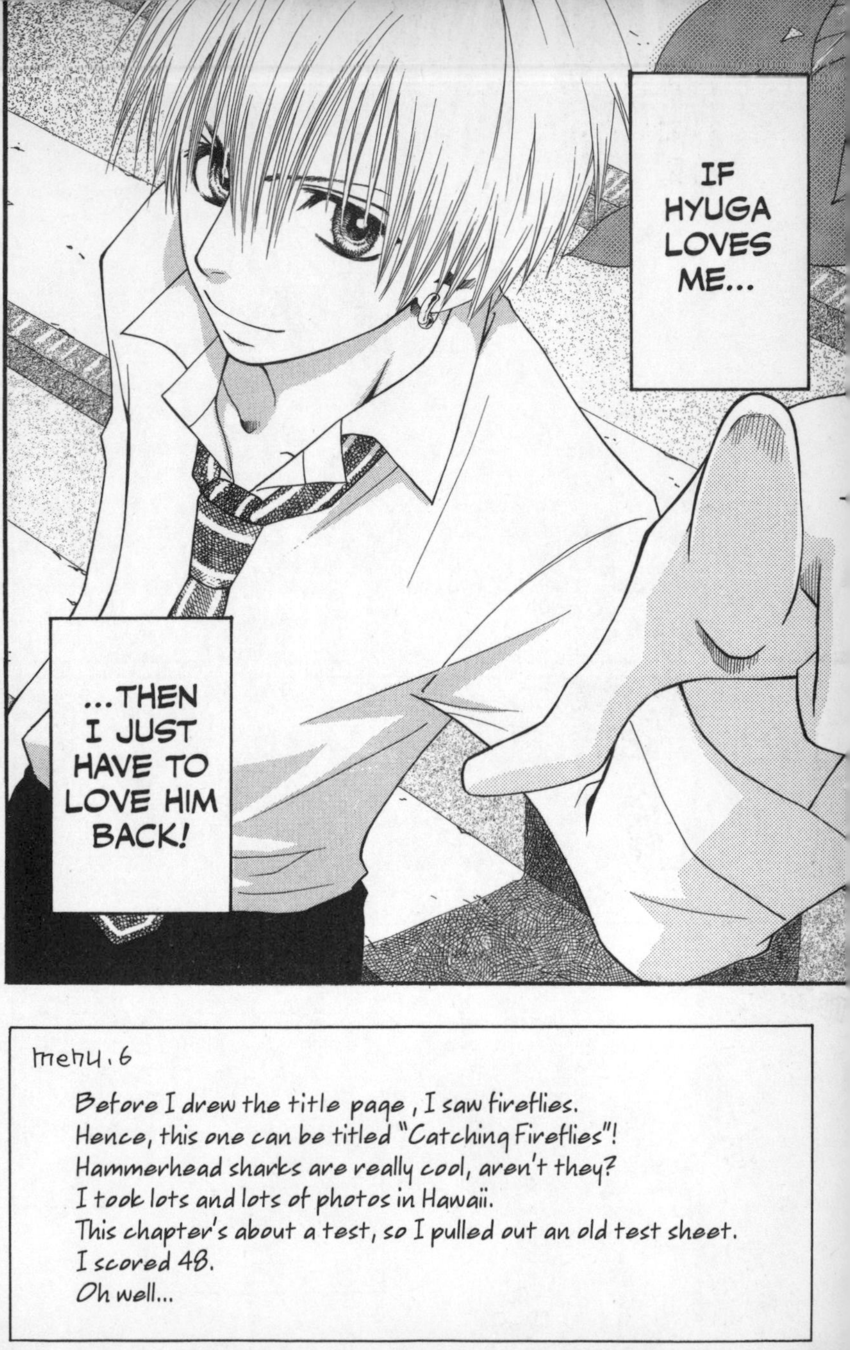
IF HYUGA LOVES ME...
...THEN I JUST HAVE TO LOVE HIM BACK!

menu.6

Before I drew the title page, I saw fireflies.
Hence, this one can be titled "Catching Fireflies"!
Hammerhead sharks are really cool, aren't they?
I took lots and lots of photos in Hawaii.
This chapter's about a test, so I pulled out an old test sheet.
I scored 48.
Oh well...

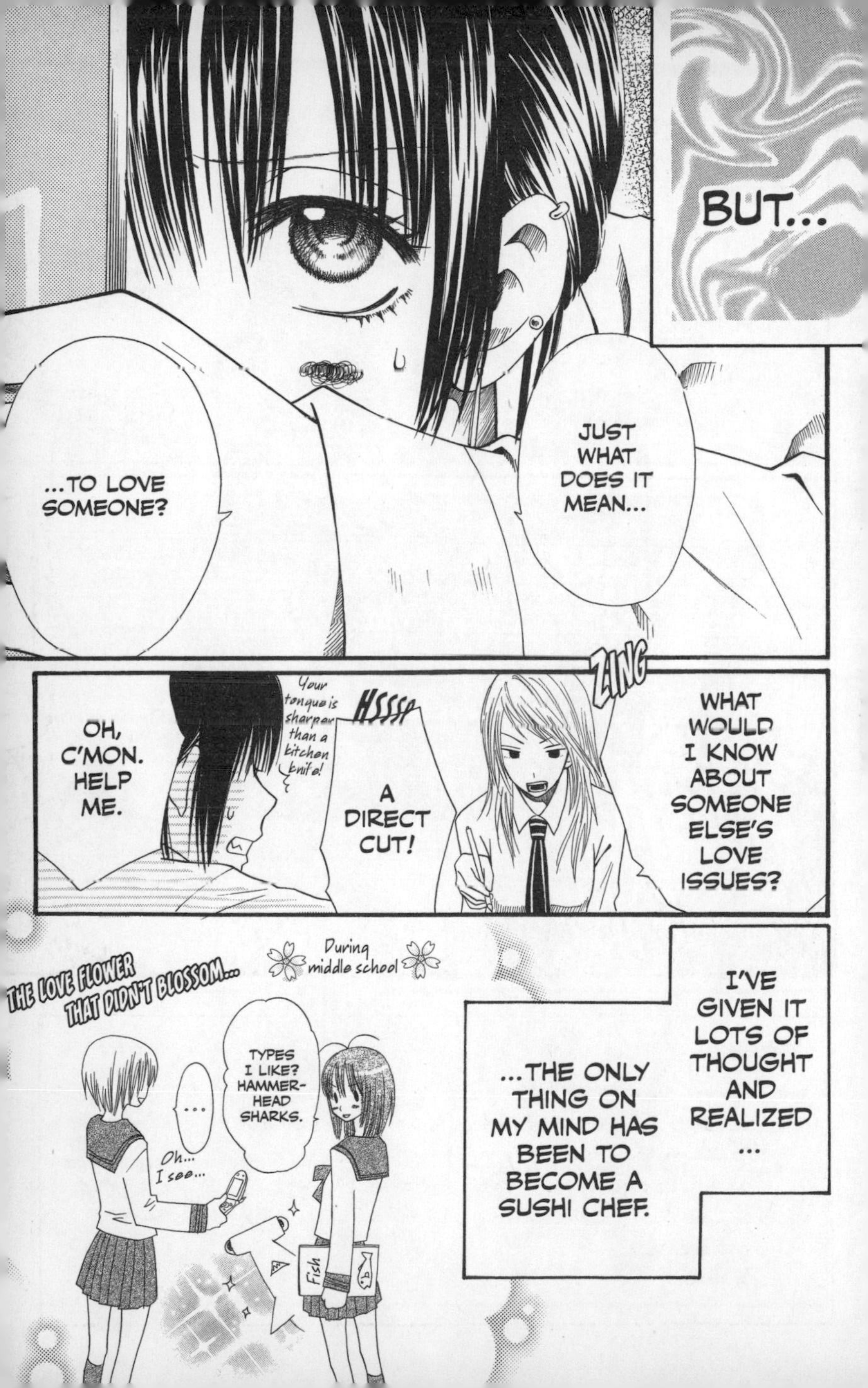
BUT...
JUST WHAT DOES IT MEAN...
...TO LOVE SOMEONE?
ZING
WHAT WOULD I KNOW ABOUT SOMEONE ELSE'S LOVE ISSUES?
HSSSP
A DIRECT CUT!
Your tongue is sharper than a kitchen knife!
OH, C'MON. HELP ME.
I'VE GIVEN IT LOTS OF THOUGHT AND REALIZED...
...THE ONLY THING ON MY MIND HAS BEEN TO BECOME A SUSHI CHEF.
THE LOVE FLOWER THAT DIDN'T BLOSSOM...
During middle school
TYPES I LIKE? HAMMERHEAD SHARKS.
...
Oh... I see...
Fish

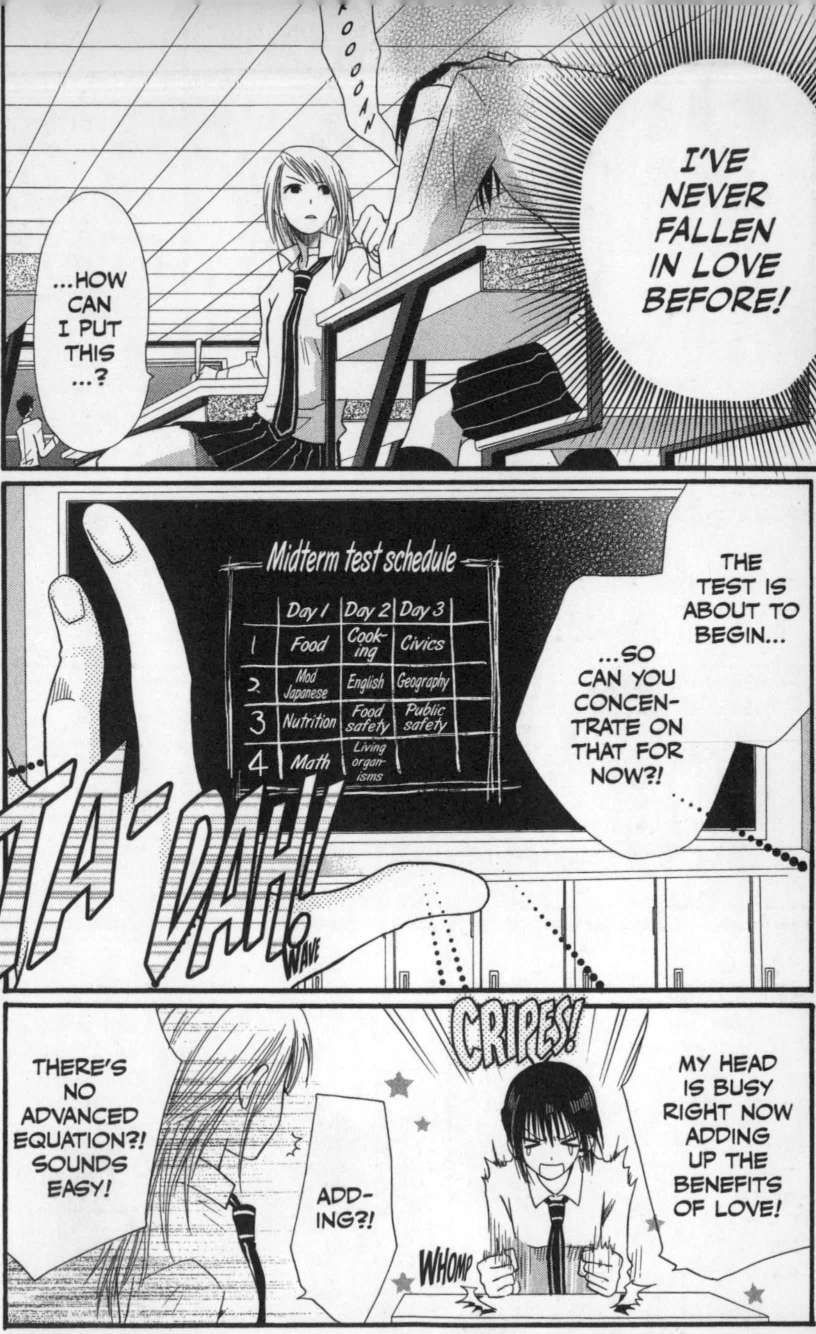
FOOOOOAN
I'VE NEVER FALLEN IN LOVE BEFORE!
...HOW CAN I PUT THIS ...?
THE TEST IS ABOUT TO BEGIN...
...SO CAN YOU CONCENTRATE ON THAT FOR NOW?!
Midterm test schedule
Day 1 Day 2 Day 3
1 Food Cooking Civics
2 Mod Japanese English Geography
3 Nutrition Food safety Public safety
4 Math Living organisms
TA-DAH!
WAVE
CRIPES!
MY HEAD IS BUSY RIGHT NOW ADDING UP THE BENEFITS OF LOVE!
WHOMP
ADDING?!
THERE'S NO ADVANCED EQUATION?! SOUNDS EASY!

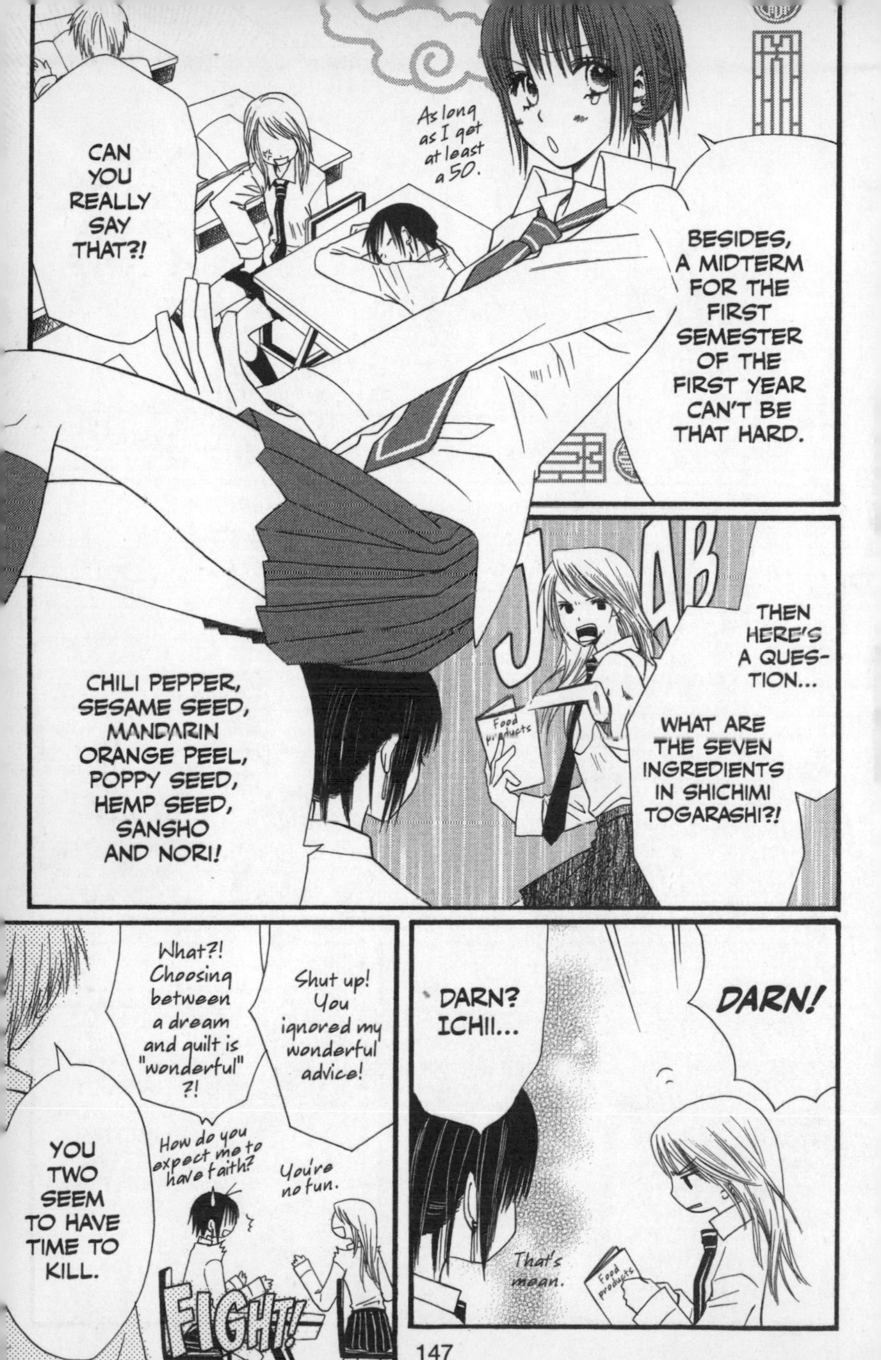

As long as I get at least a 50.
BESIDES, A MIDTERM FOR THE FIRST SEMESTER OF THE FIRST YEAR CAN'T BE THAT HARD.
CAN YOU REALLY SAY THAT?!
JAB
THEN HERE'S A QUES-TION...
WHAT ARE THE SEVEN INGREDIENTS IN SHICHIMI TOGARASHI?!
Food products
CHILI PEPPER, SESAME SEED, MANDARIN ORANGE PEEL, POPPY SEED, HEMP SEED, SANSHO AND NORI!
DARN!
DARN? ICHII...
That's mean.
Food products
Shut up! You ignored my wonderful advice!
What?! Choosing between a dream and guilt is "wonderful"?!
You're no fun.
How do you expect me to have faith?
YOU TWO SEEM TO HAVE TIME TO KILL.
FIGHT!

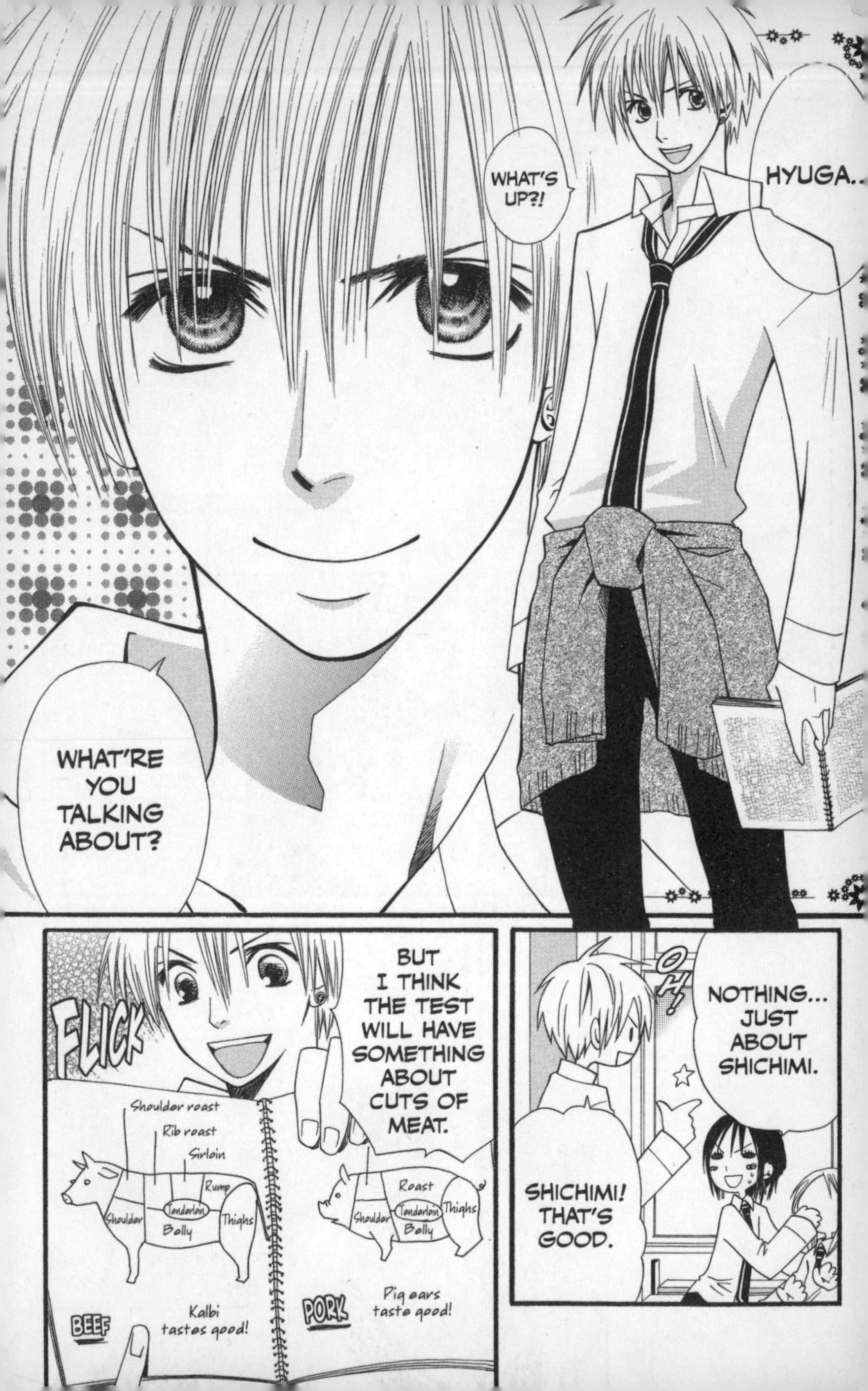
HYUGA..
WHAT'S UP?!
WHAT'RE YOU TALKING ABOUT?
NOTHING... JUST ABOUT SHICHIMI.
OH!
SHICHIMI! THAT'S GOOD.
BUT I THINK THE TEST WILL HAVE SOMETHING ABOUT CUTS OF MEAT.
FLICK
Shoulder roast
Rib roast
Sirloin
Rump
Tenderloin
Shoulder
Thighs
Belly
BEEF
Kalbi tastes good!
Roast
Shoulder
Tenderloin
Thighs
Belly
PORK
Pig ears taste good!

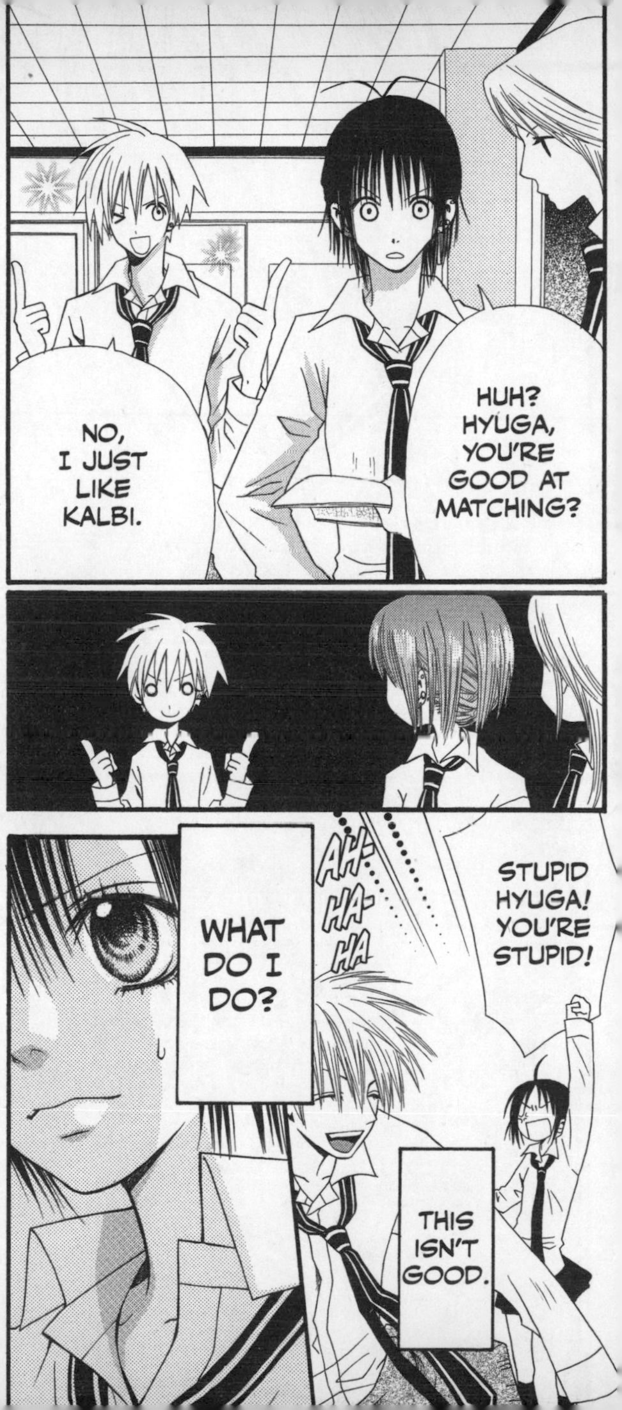
HUH? HYUGA, YOU'RE GOOD AT MATCHING?
NO, I JUST LIKE KALBI.
STUPID HYUGA! YOU'RE STUPID!
AH-HA-HA
WHAT DO I DO?
THIS ISN'T GOOD.

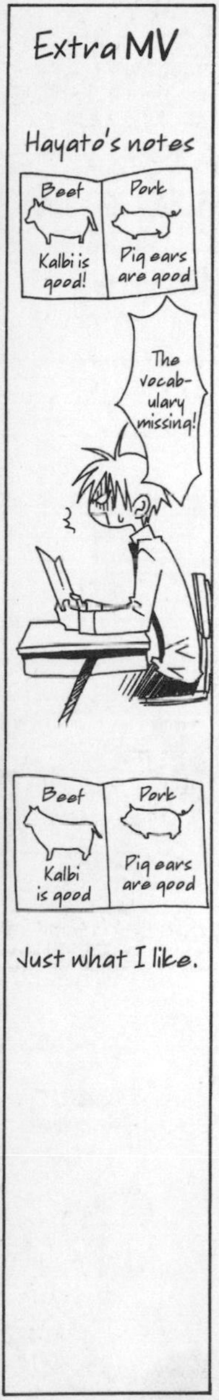
Extra MV
Hayato's notes
Beef
Pork
Kalbi is good!
Pig ears are good
The vocab-ulary missing!
Beef
Pork
Kalbi is good
Pig ears are good
Just what I like.

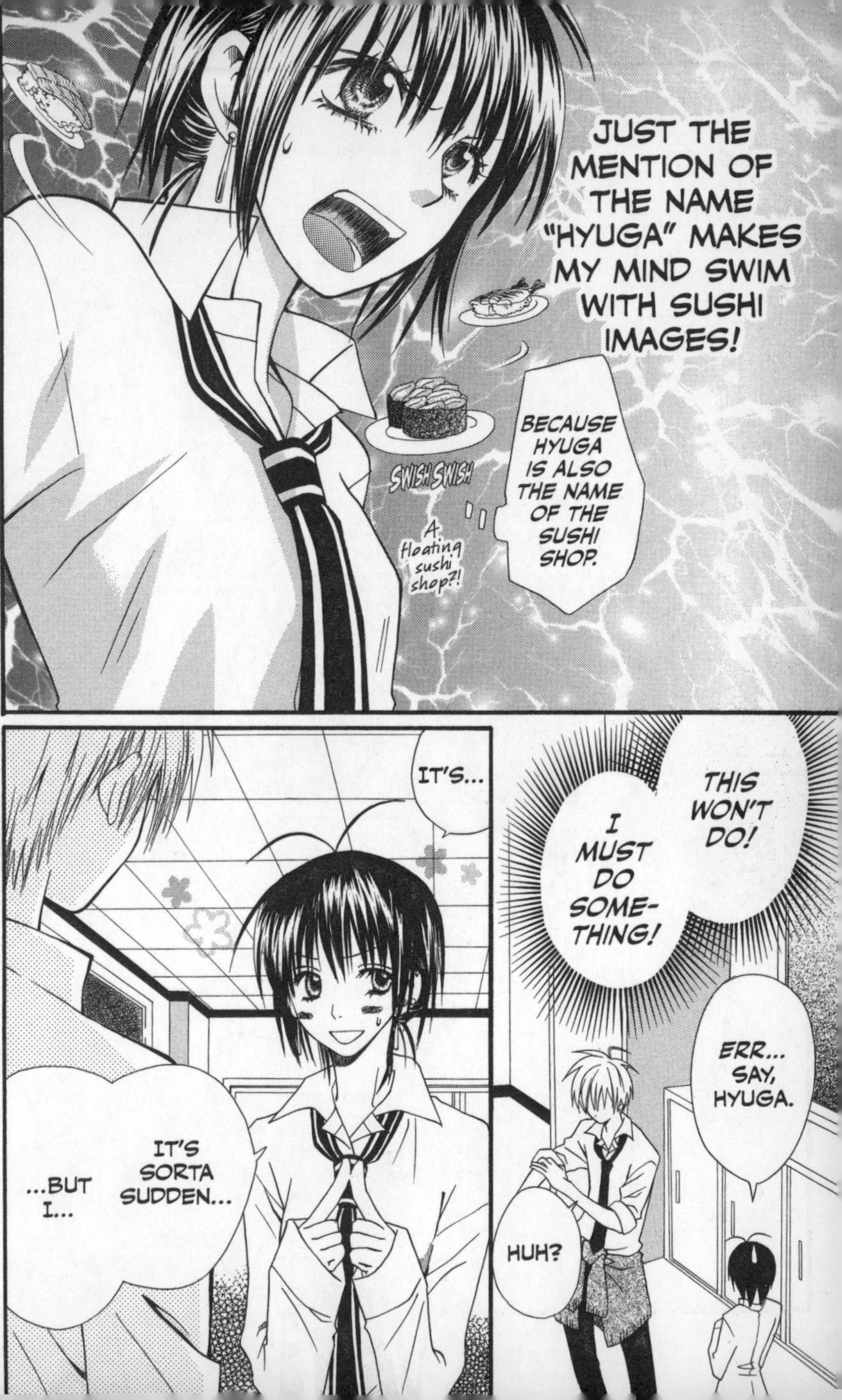

JUST THE MENTION OF THE NAME "HYUGA" MAKES MY MIND SWIM WITH SUSHI IMAGES!
BECAUSE HYUGA IS ALSO THE NAME OF THE SUSHI SHOP.
SWISH SWISH
A floating sushi shop?!
THIS WON'T DO!
I MUST DO SOME-THING!
ERR... SAY, HYUGA.
HUH?
IT'S...
IT'S SORTA SUDDEN...
...BUT I...

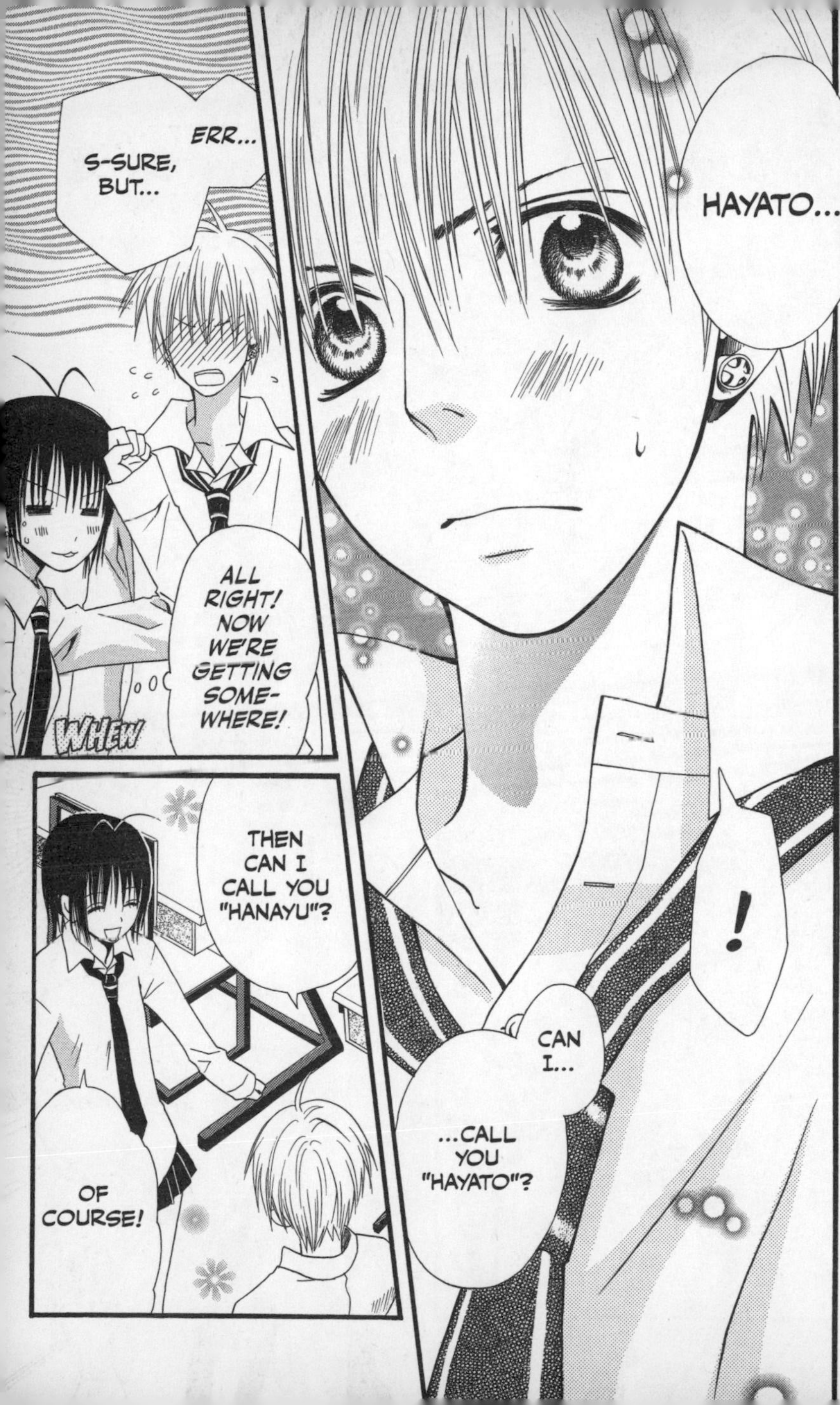
HAYATO...
!
CAN I...
...CALL YOU "HAYATO"?
ERR... S-SURE, BUT...
ALL RIGHT! NOW WE'RE GETTING SOME-WHERE!
WHEW
THEN CAN I CALL YOU "HANAYU"?
OF COURSE!

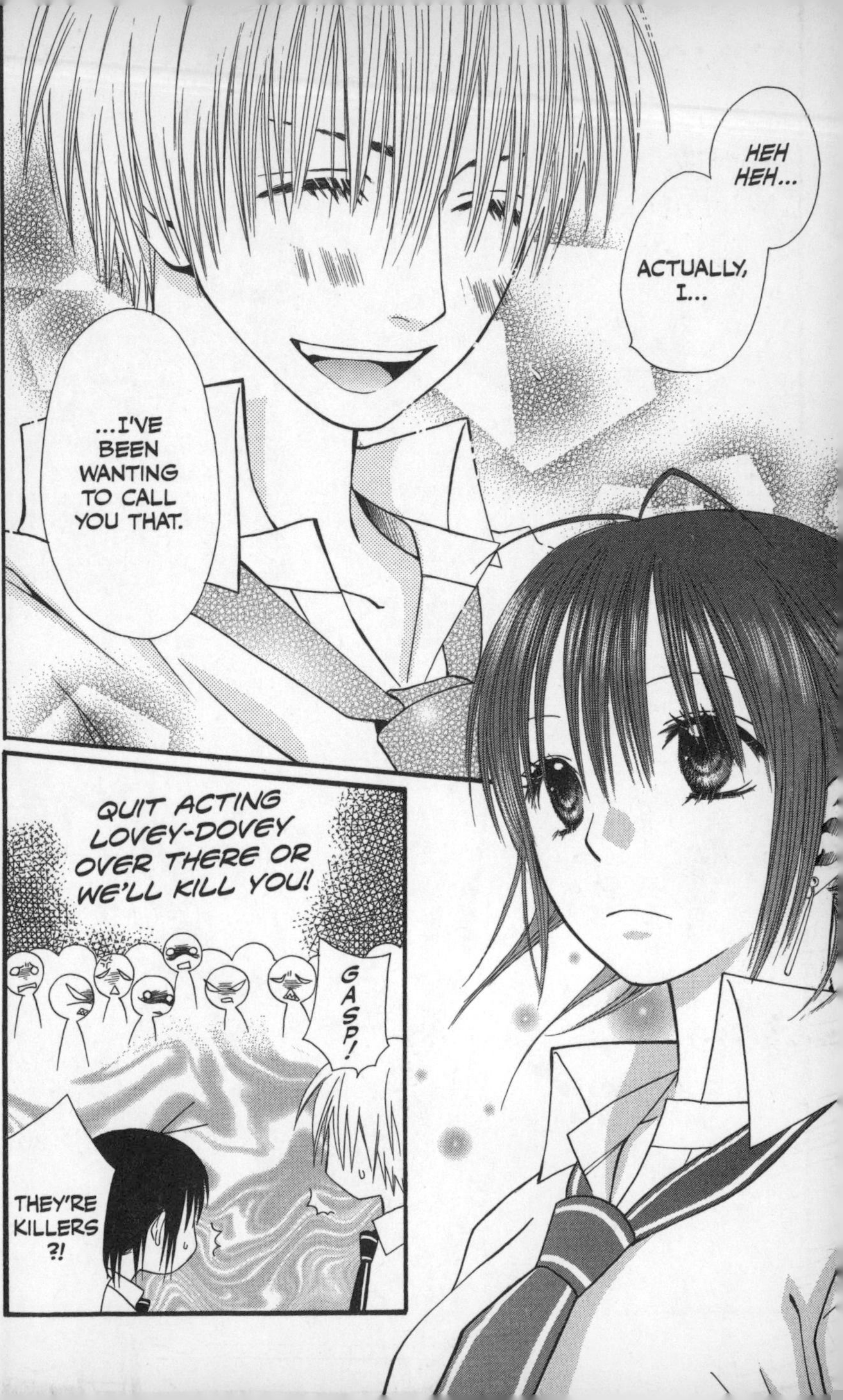
HEH HEH...
ACTUALLY, I...
...I'VE BEEN WANTING TO CALL YOU THAT.
QUIT ACTING LOVEY-DOVEY OVER THERE OR WE'LL KILL YOU!
GASP!
THEY'RE KILLERS ?!

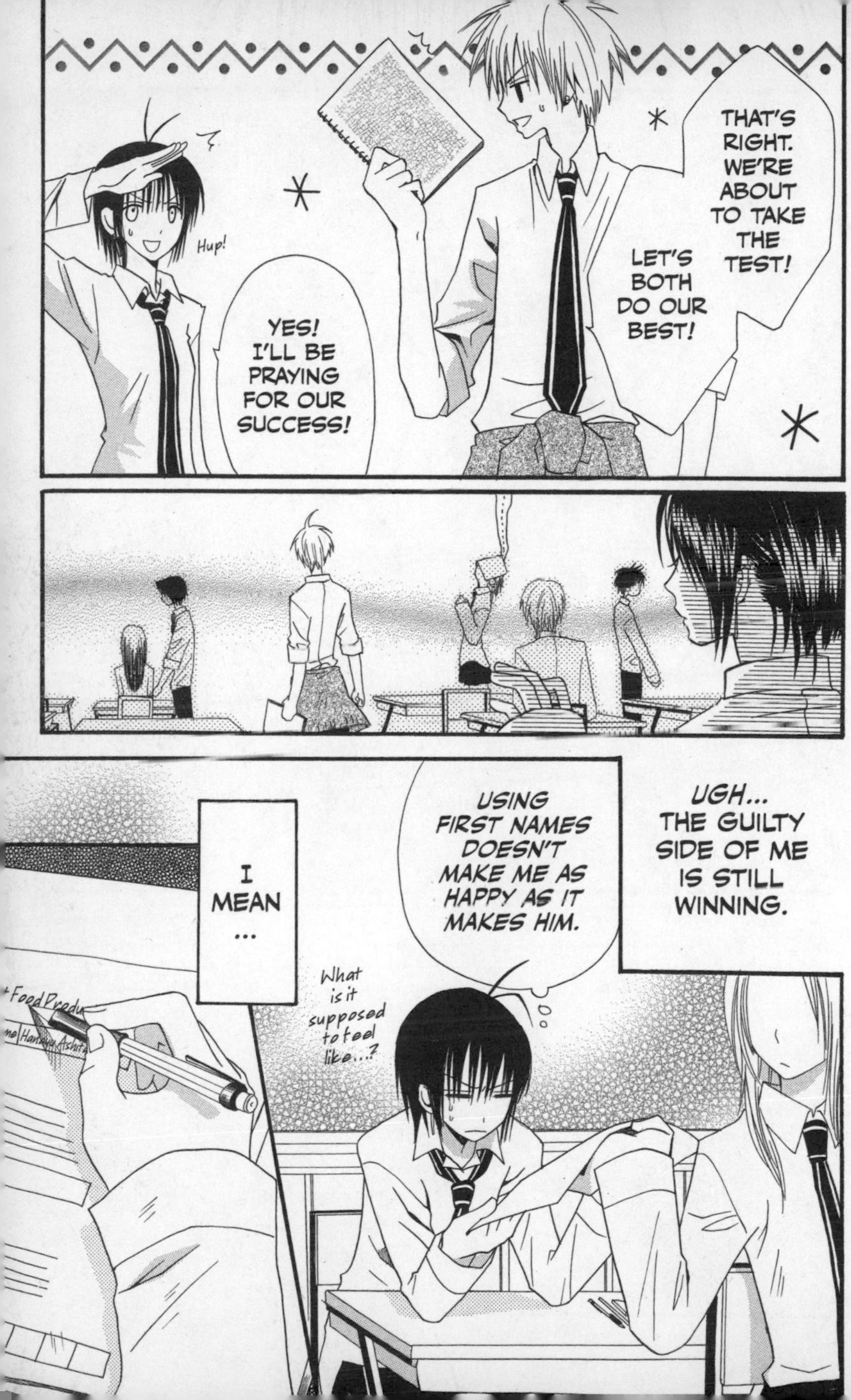
THAT'S RIGHT. WE'RE ABOUT TO TAKE THE TEST!
LET'S BOTH DO OUR BEST!
Hup!
YES! I'LL BE PRAYING FOR OUR SUCCESS!
UGH... THE GUILTY SIDE OF ME IS STILL WINNING.
USING FIRST NAMES DOESN'T MAKE ME AS HAPPY AS IT MAKES HIM.
I MEAN ...
What is it supposed to feel like...?

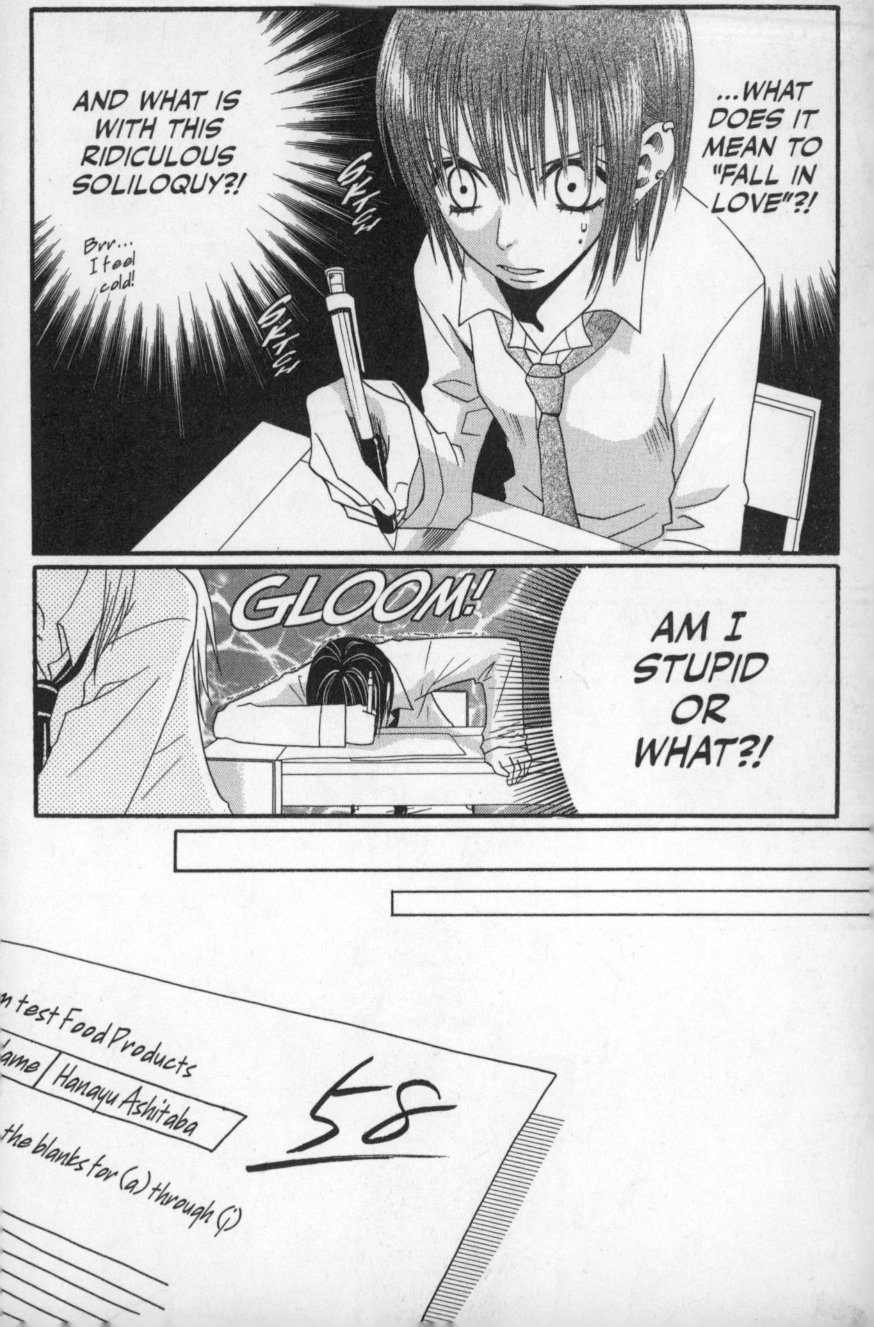
...WHAT DOES IT MEAN TO "FALL IN LOVE"?!
AND WHAT IS WITH THIS RIDICULOUS SOLILOQUY?!
Brr... I feel cold!
AM I STUPID OR WHAT?!
GLOOM!
n test Food Products
ame Hanayu Ashitaba
58
the blanks for (a) through (j)

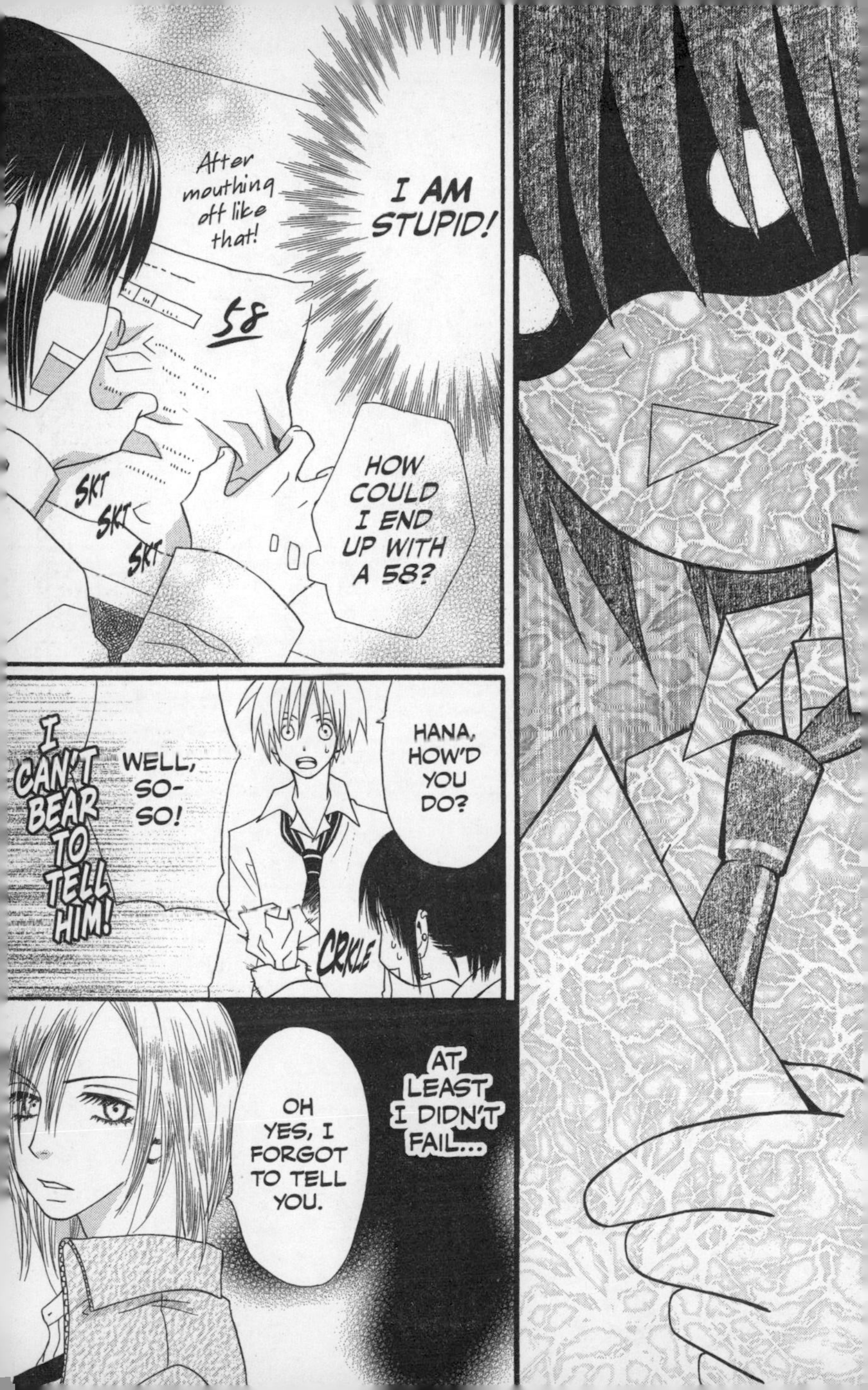
I AM STUPID!
After mouthing off like that!
58
HOW COULD I END UP WITH A 58?
SKT
SKT
SKT
HANA, HOW'D YOU DO?
WELL, SO-SO!
I CAN'T BEAR TO TELL HIM!
CRKLE
AT LEAST I DIDN'T FAIL...
OH YES, I FORGOT TO TELL YOU.

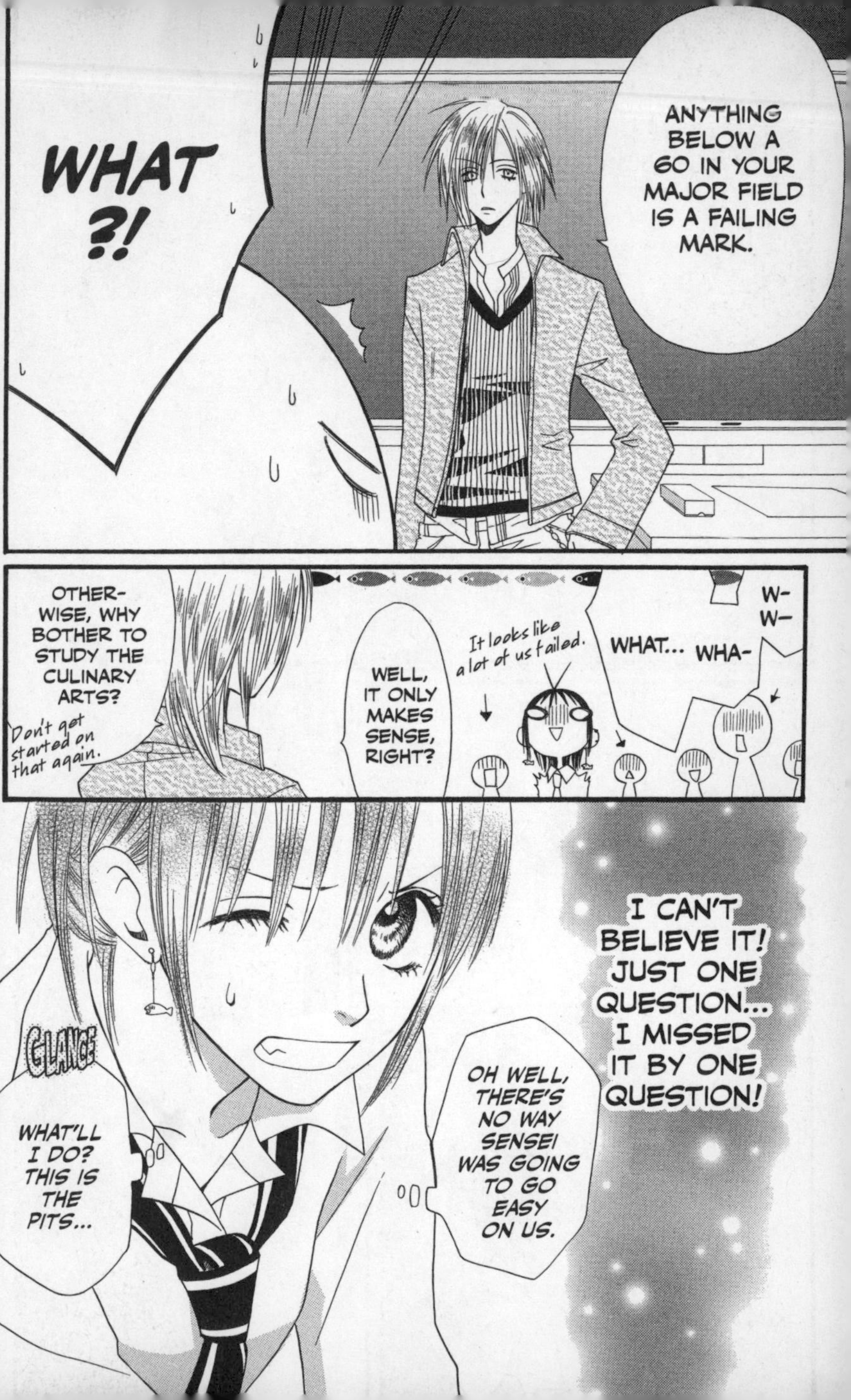

ANYTHING BELOW A 60 IN YOUR MAJOR FIELD IS A FAILING MARK.
WHAT ?!
W- W-
WHAT... WHA-
It looks like a lot of us failed.
WELL, IT ONLY MAKES SENSE, RIGHT?
OTHER-WISE, WHY BOTHER TO STUDY THE CULINARY ARTS?
Don't get started on that again.
I CAN'T BELIEVE IT! JUST ONE QUESTION... I MISSED IT BY ONE QUESTION!
OH WELL, THERE'S NO WAY SENSEI WAS GOING TO GO EASY ON US.
GLANCE
WHAT'LL I DO? THIS IS THE PITS...

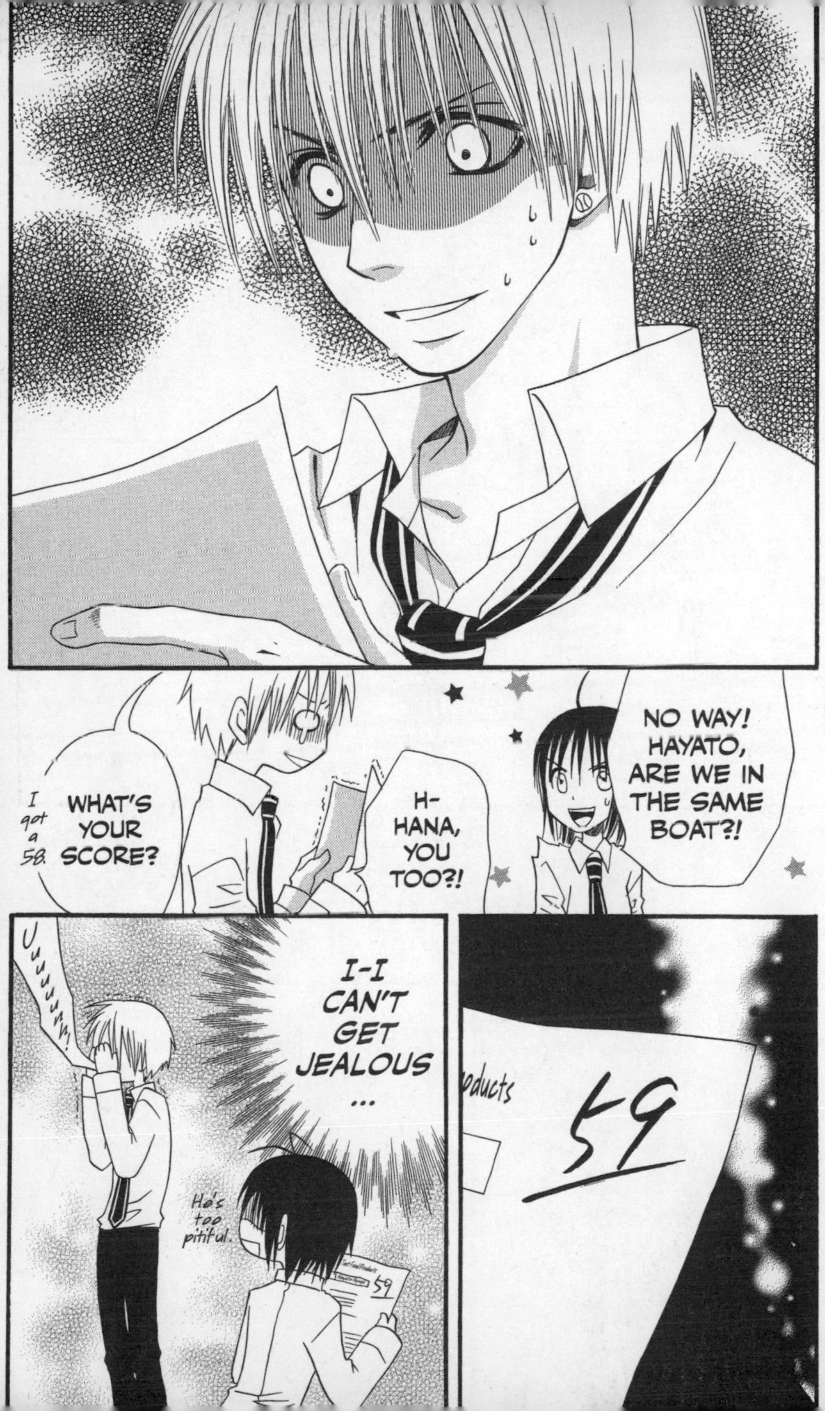
NO WAY! HAYATO, ARE WE IN THE SAME BOAT?!
H-HANA, YOU TOO?!
WHAT'S YOUR SCORE?
I got a 58.
59
I-I CAN'T GET JEALOUS ...
Uuuuuurn!
He's too pitiful.

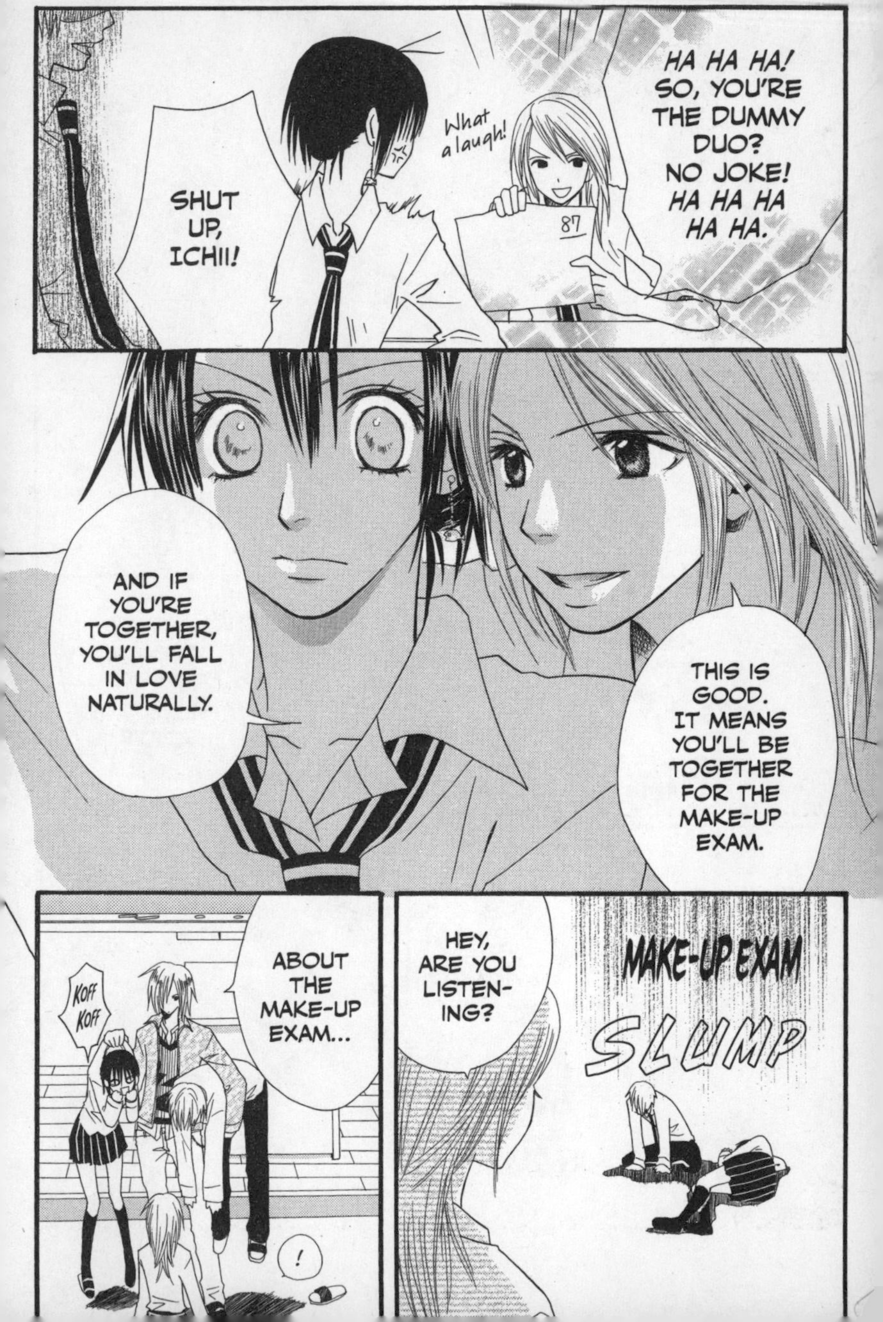
HA HA HA! SO, YOU'RE THE DUMMY DUO? NO JOKE! HA HA HA HA HA.
What a laugh!
87
SHUT UP, ICHII!
THIS IS GOOD. IT MEANS YOU'LL BE TOGETHER FOR THE MAKE-UP EXAM.
AND IF YOU'RE TOGETHER, YOU'LL FALL IN LOVE NATURALLY.
MAKE-UP EXAM
HEY, ARE YOU LISTEN-ING?
SLUMP
ABOUT THE MAKE-UP EXAM...
KOFF KOFF
!

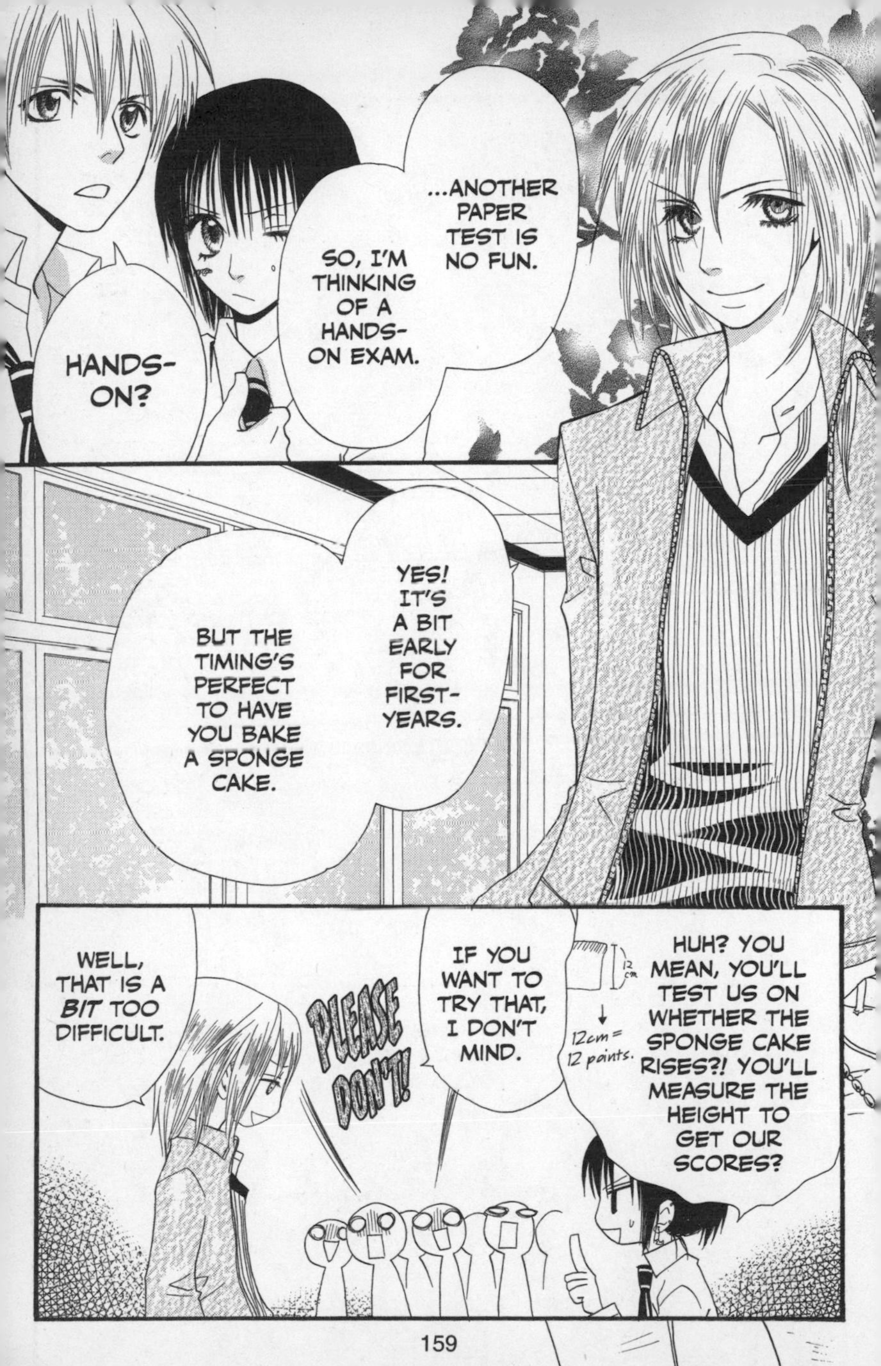
...ANOTHER PAPER TEST IS NO FUN.
SO, I'M THINKING OF A HANDS-ON EXAM.
HANDS-ON?
YES! IT'S A BIT EARLY FOR FIRST-YEARS.
BUT THE TIMING'S PERFECT TO HAVE YOU BAKE A SPONGE CAKE.
HUH? YOU MEAN, YOU'LL TEST US ON WHETHER THE SPONGE CAKE RISES?! YOU'LL MEASURE THE HEIGHT TO GET OUR SCORES?
12 cm
12cm = 12 paints.
IF YOU WANT TO TRY THAT, I DON'T MIND.
PLEASE DON'T!
WELL, THAT IS A *BIT* TOO DIFFICULT.

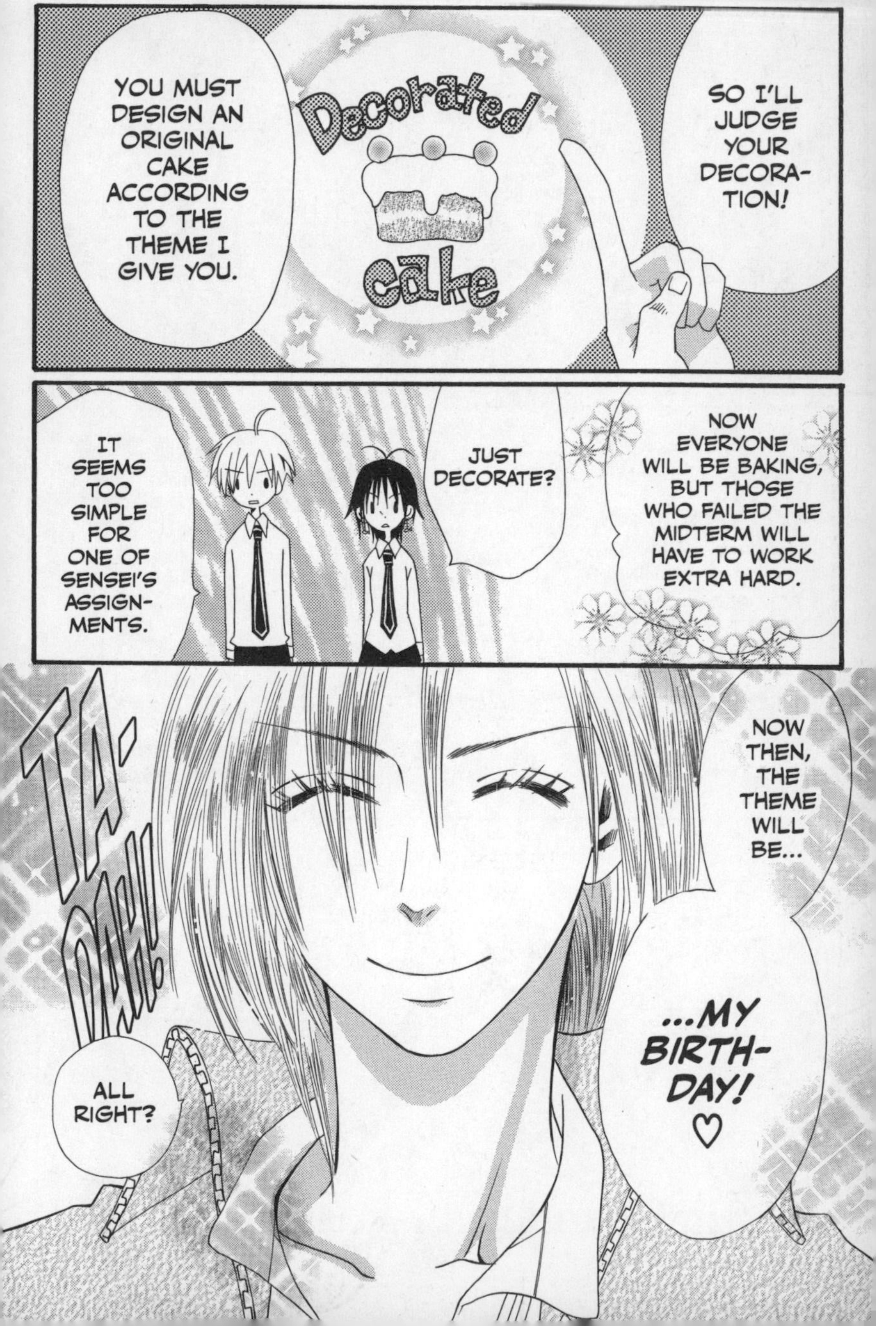
SO I'LL JUDGE YOUR DECORATION!
YOU MUST DESIGN AN ORIGINAL CAKE ACCORDING TO THE THEME I GIVE YOU.
Decorated cake
NOW EVERYONE WILL BE BAKING, BUT THOSE WHO FAILED THE MIDTERM WILL HAVE TO WORK EXTRA HARD.
JUST DECORATE?
IT SEEMS TOO SIMPLE FOR ONE OF SENSEI'S ASSIGNMENTS.
NOW THEN, THE THEME WILL BE...
TA-DAA!
...MY BIRTHDAY! ♡
ALL RIGHT?

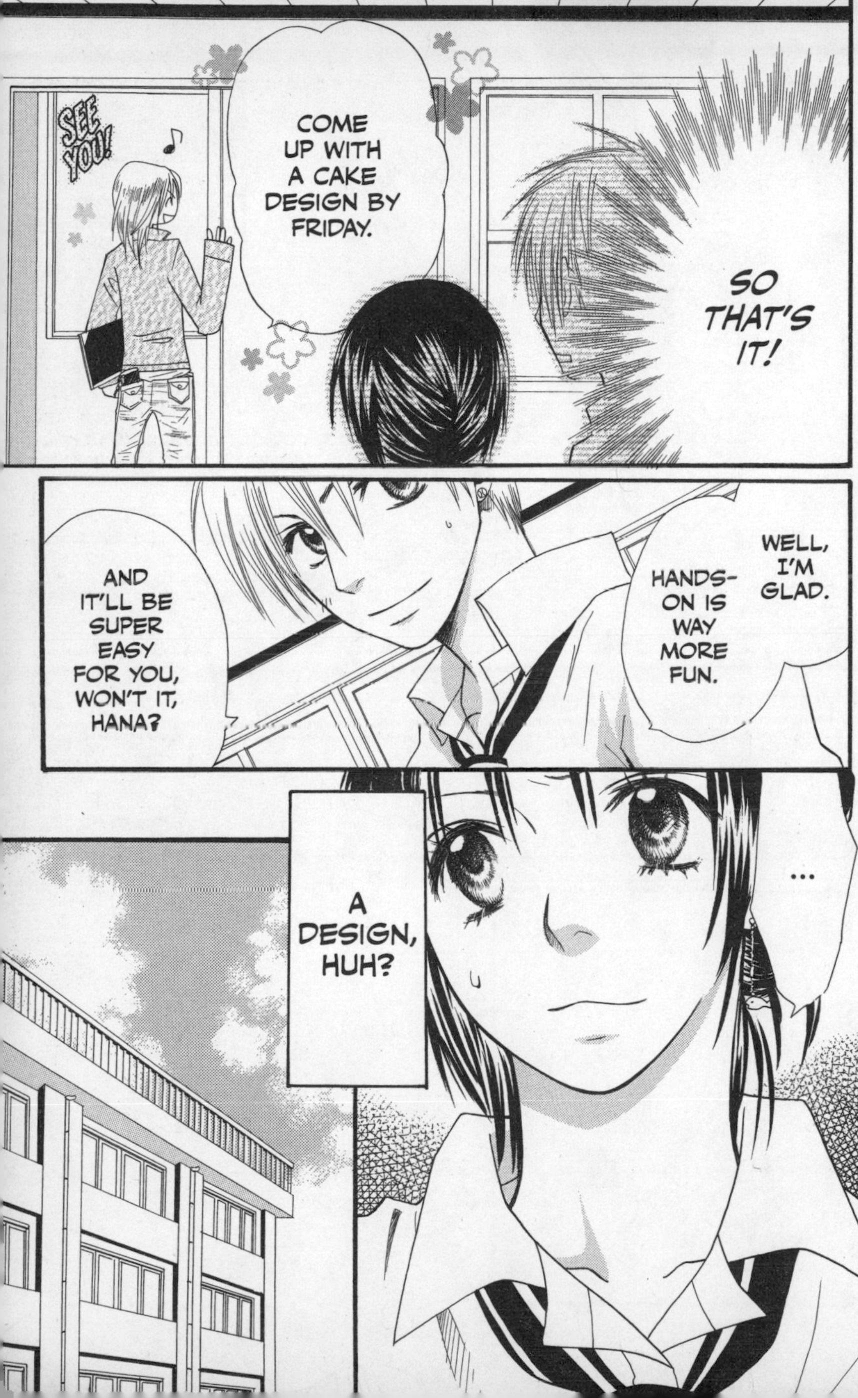
COME UP WITH A CAKE DESIGN BY FRIDAY.
SEE YOU!
SO THAT'S IT!
WELL, I'M GLAD.
HANDS-ON IS WAY MORE FUN.
AND IT'LL BE SUPER EASY FOR YOU, WON'T IT, HANA?
...
A DESIGN, HUH?

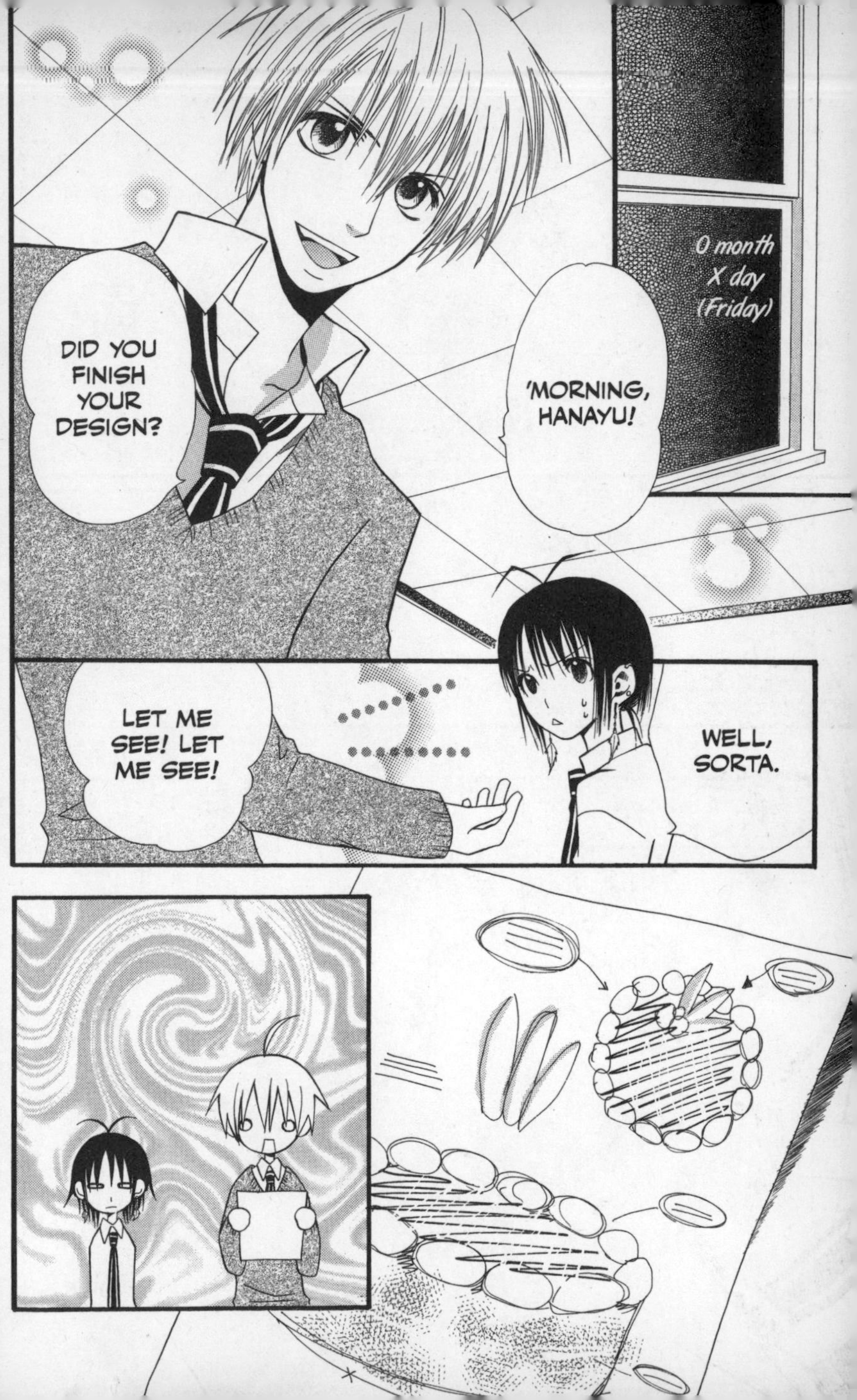
0 month X day (Friday)
'MORNING, HANAYU!
DID YOU FINISH YOUR DESIGN?
WELL, SORTA.
LET ME SEE! LET ME SEE!

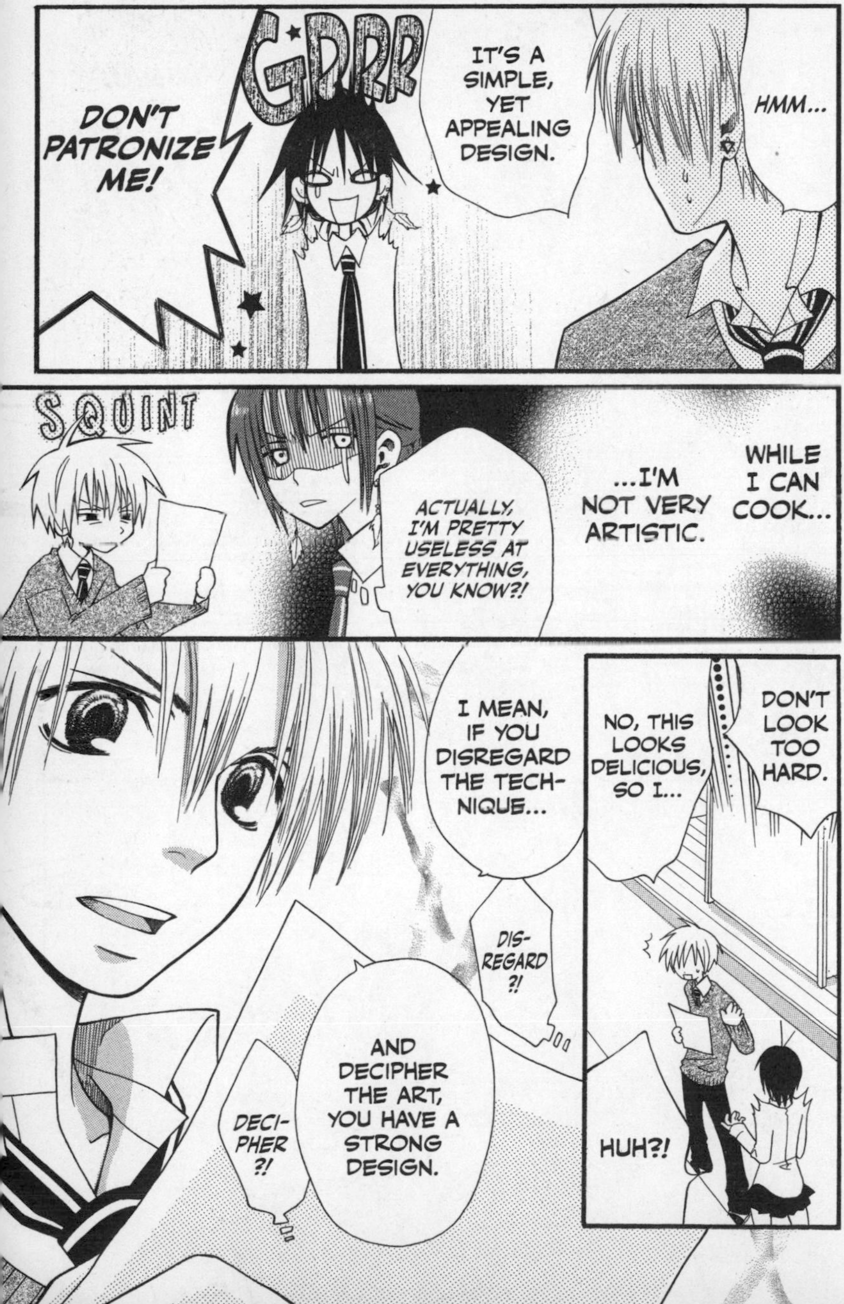
HMM...
IT'S A SIMPLE, YET APPEALING DESIGN.
GRRR
DON'T PATRONIZE ME!
WHILE I CAN COOK...
...I'M NOT VERY ARTISTIC.
ACTUALLY, I'M PRETTY USELESS AT EVERYTHING, YOU KNOW?!
SQUINT
DON'T LOOK TOO HARD.
NO, THIS LOOKS DELICIOUS, SO I...
HUH?!
I MEAN, IF YOU DISREGARD THE TECH-NIQUE...
DIS-REGARD?!
AND DECIPHER THE ART, YOU HAVE A STRONG DESIGN.
DECI-PHER?!

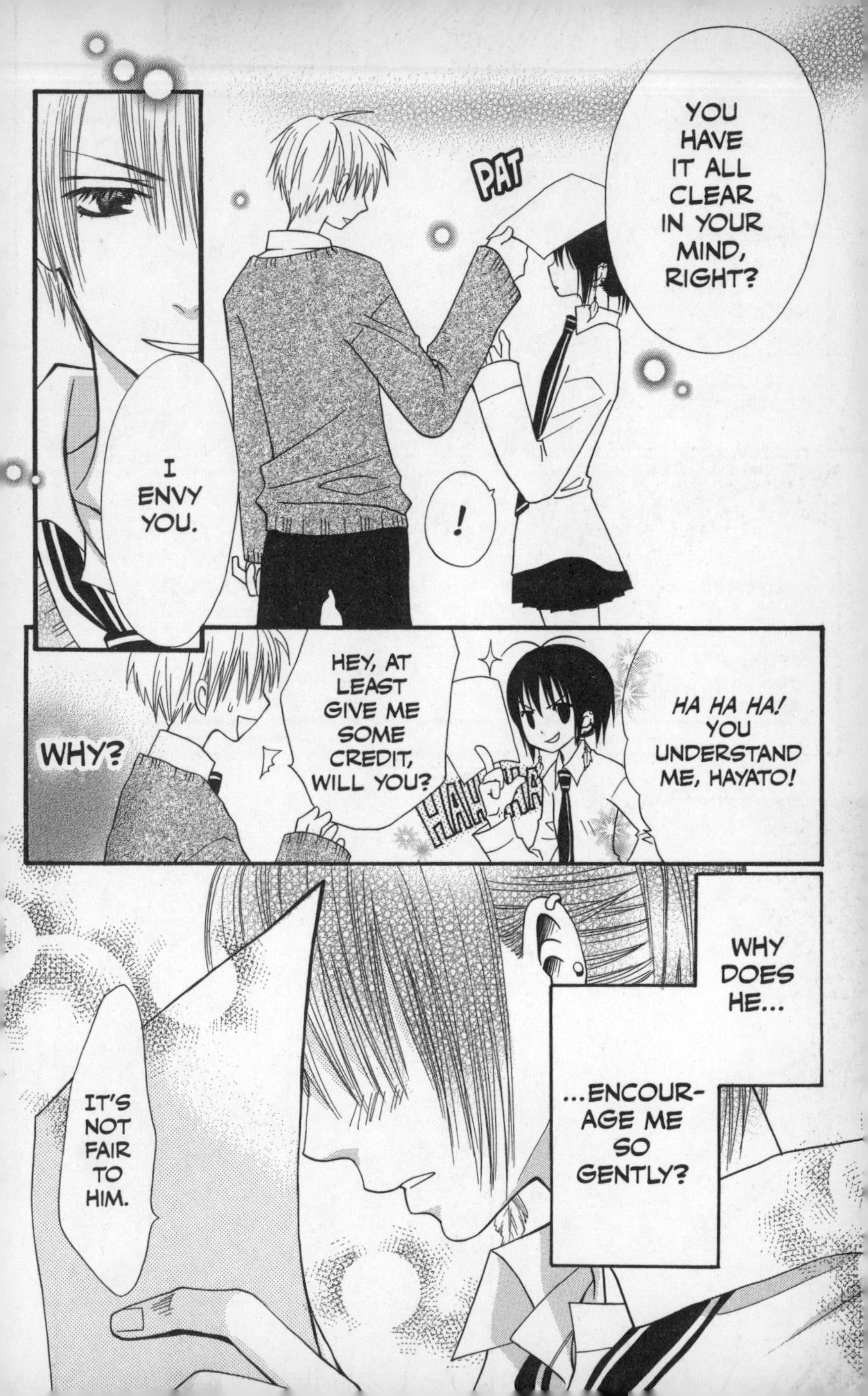
YOU HAVE IT ALL CLEAR IN YOUR MIND, RIGHT?
PAT
!
I ENVY YOU.
HA HA HA! YOU UNDERSTAND ME, HAYATO!
HEY, AT LEAST GIVE ME SOME CREDIT, WILL YOU?
WHY?
WHY DOES HE...
...ENCOUR-AGE ME SO GENTLY?
IT'S NOT FAIR TO HIM.

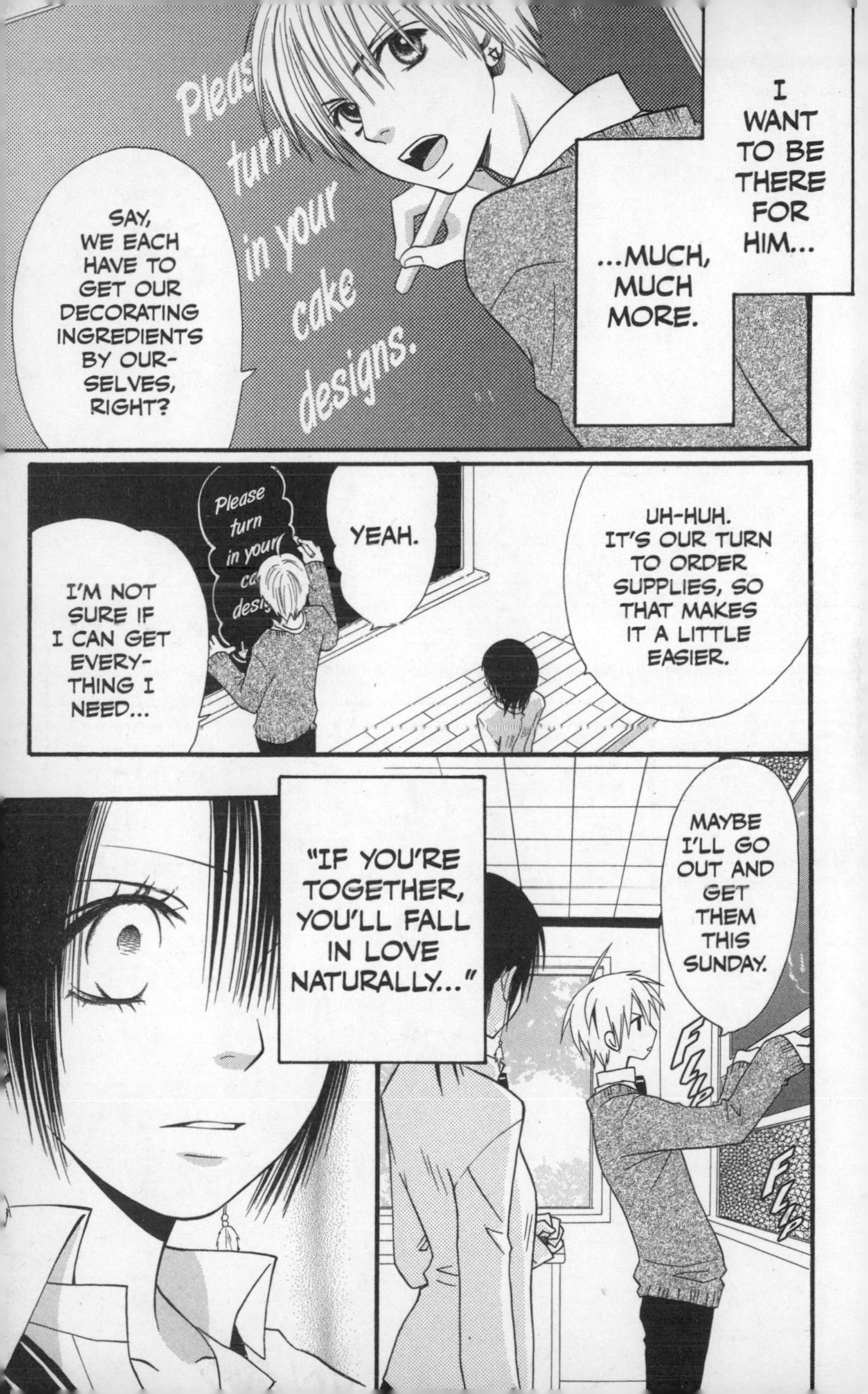
I WANT TO BE THERE FOR HIM...
...MUCH, MUCH MORE.
Please turn in your cake designs.
SAY, WE EACH HAVE TO GET OUR DECORATING INGREDIENTS BY OUR-SELVES, RIGHT?
UH-HUH. IT'S OUR TURN TO ORDER SUPPLIES, SO THAT MAKES IT A LITTLE EASIER.
YEAH.
I'M NOT SURE IF I CAN GET EVERY-THING I NEED...
MAYBE I'LL GO OUT AND GET THEM THIS SUNDAY.
FLIP
FLIP
"IF YOU'RE TOGETHER, YOU'LL FALL IN LOVE NATURALLY..."

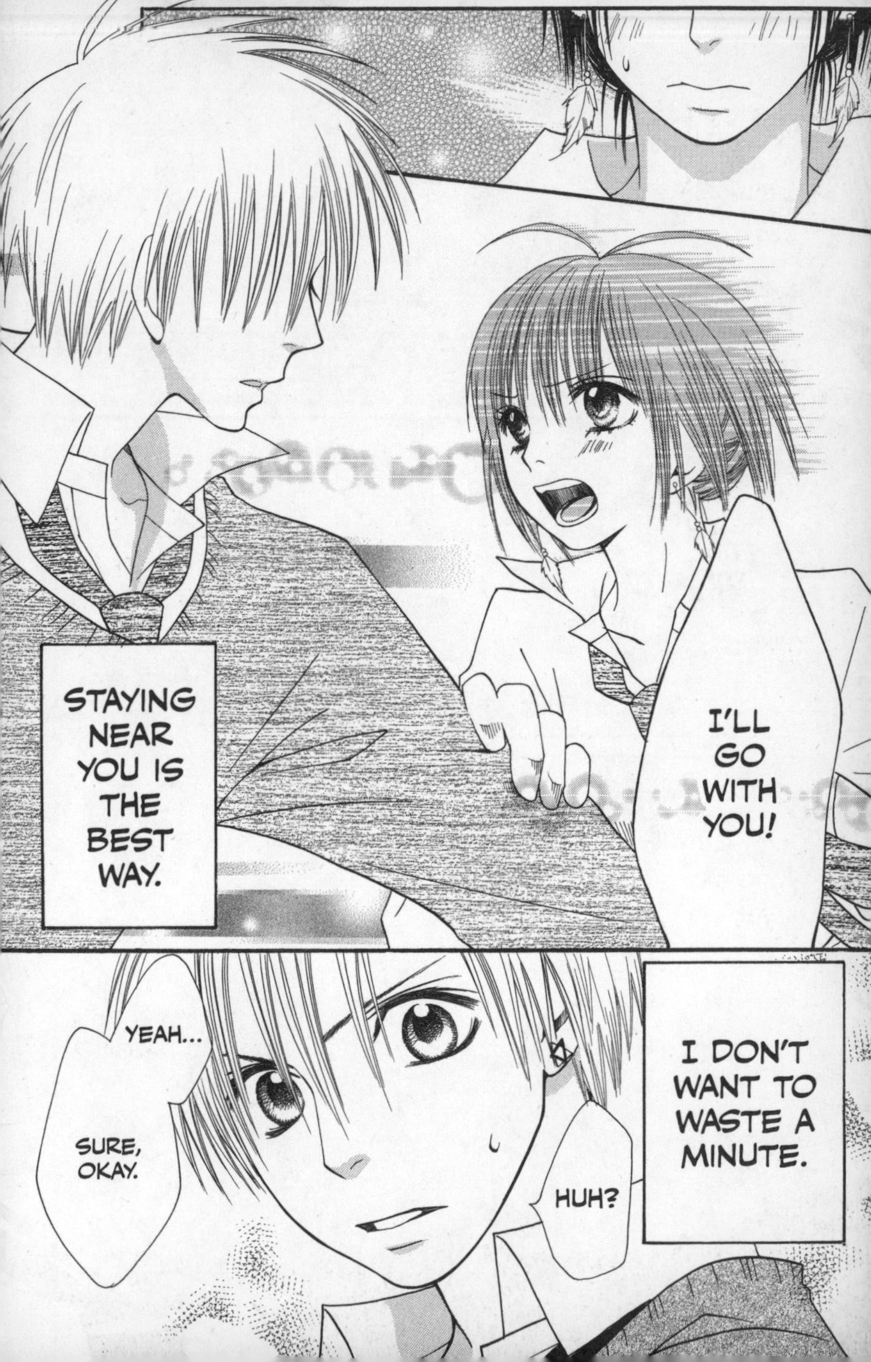
I'LL GO WITH YOU!
STAYING NEAR YOU IS THE BEST WAY.
I DON'T WANT TO WASTE A MINUTE.
HUH?
YEAH...
SURE, OKAY.

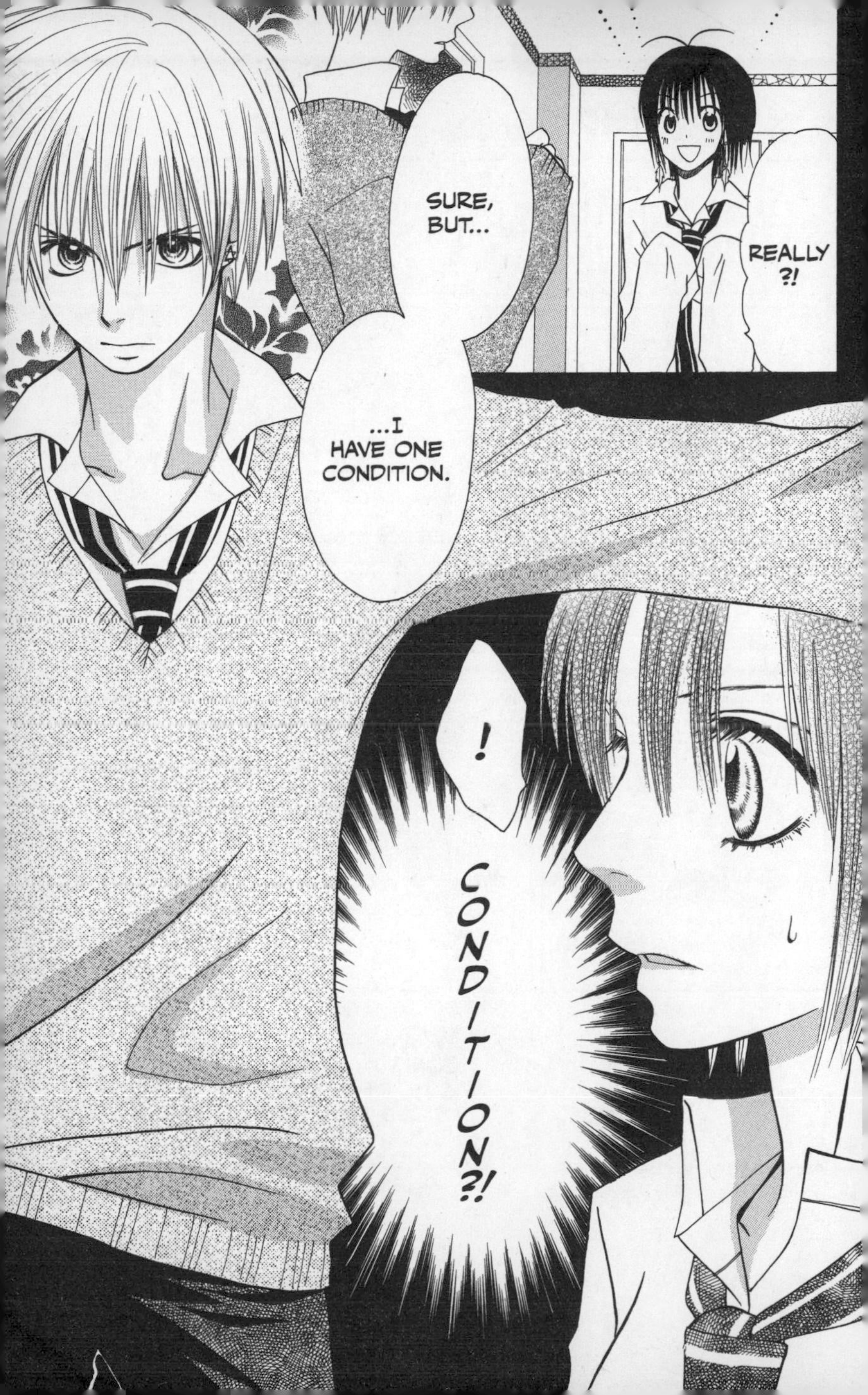
REALLY ?!
SURE, BUT...
...I HAVE ONE CONDITION.
!
CONDITION?!

SIDE DISH Mixed Vegetables 6

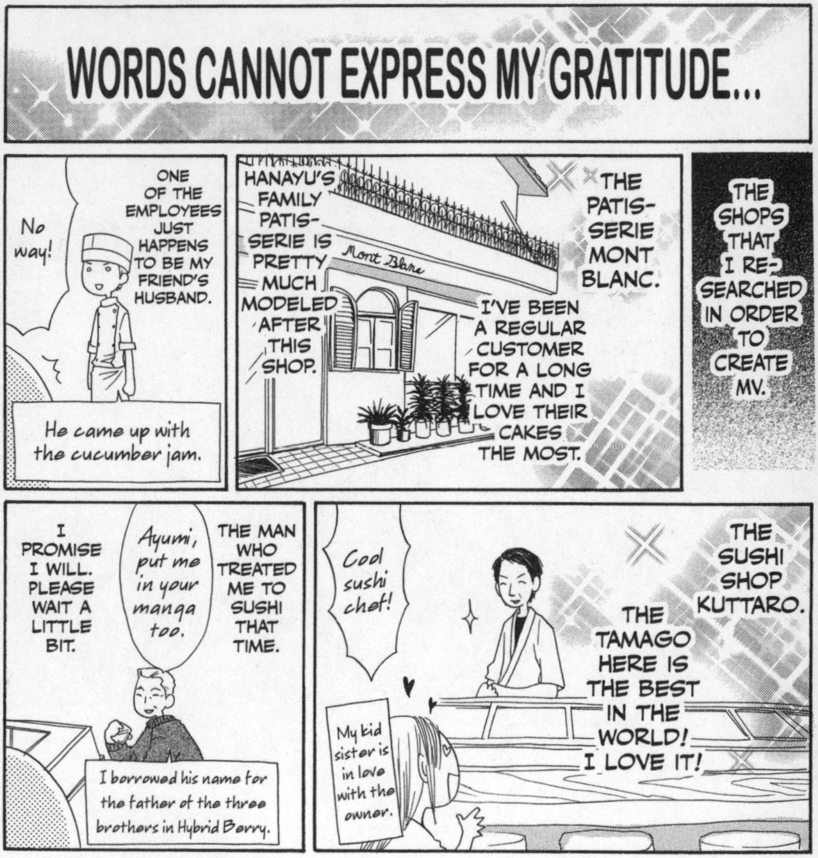
WORDS CANNOT EXPRESS MY GRATITUDE...
THE SHOPS THAT I RESEARCHED IN ORDER TO CREATE MV.
THE PATISSERIE MONT BLANC.
I'VE BEEN A REGULAR CUSTOMER FOR A LONG TIME AND I LOVE THEIR CAKES THE MOST.
HANAYU'S FAMILY PATISSERIE IS PRETTY MUCH MODELED AFTER THIS SHOP.
Mont Blanc
ONE OF THE EMPLOYEES JUST HAPPENS TO BE MY FRIEND'S HUSBAND.
No way!
He came up with the cucumber jam.
THE SUSHI SHOP KUTTARO.
THE TAMAGO HERE IS THE BEST IN THE WORLD! I LOVE IT!
Cool sushi chef!
My kid sister is in love with the owner.
THE MAN WHO TREATED ME TO SUSHI THAT TIME.
Ayumi, put me in your manga too.
I PROMISE I WILL. PLEASE WAIT A LITTLE BIT.
I borrowed his name for the father of the three brothers in Hybrid Berry.

AND THERE ARE OTHERS:

*MY EDITOR, WHO SENDS ME LOTS AND LOTS OF MATERIAL.

*MY FRIENDS, WHO SEND ME FOOD AND EMAIL ME.

*MY MANGA COMPATRIOTS, WHO CRITIQUE ME, ENCOURAGE ME, KID ME AND GOAD ME.

*MY FAMILY

AND ABOVE ALL...

...EVERY ONE OF YOU READERS!

THANK YOU SO MUCH FOR READING MY MANGA! PLEASE CONTINUE TO SUPPORT MV AND ME!

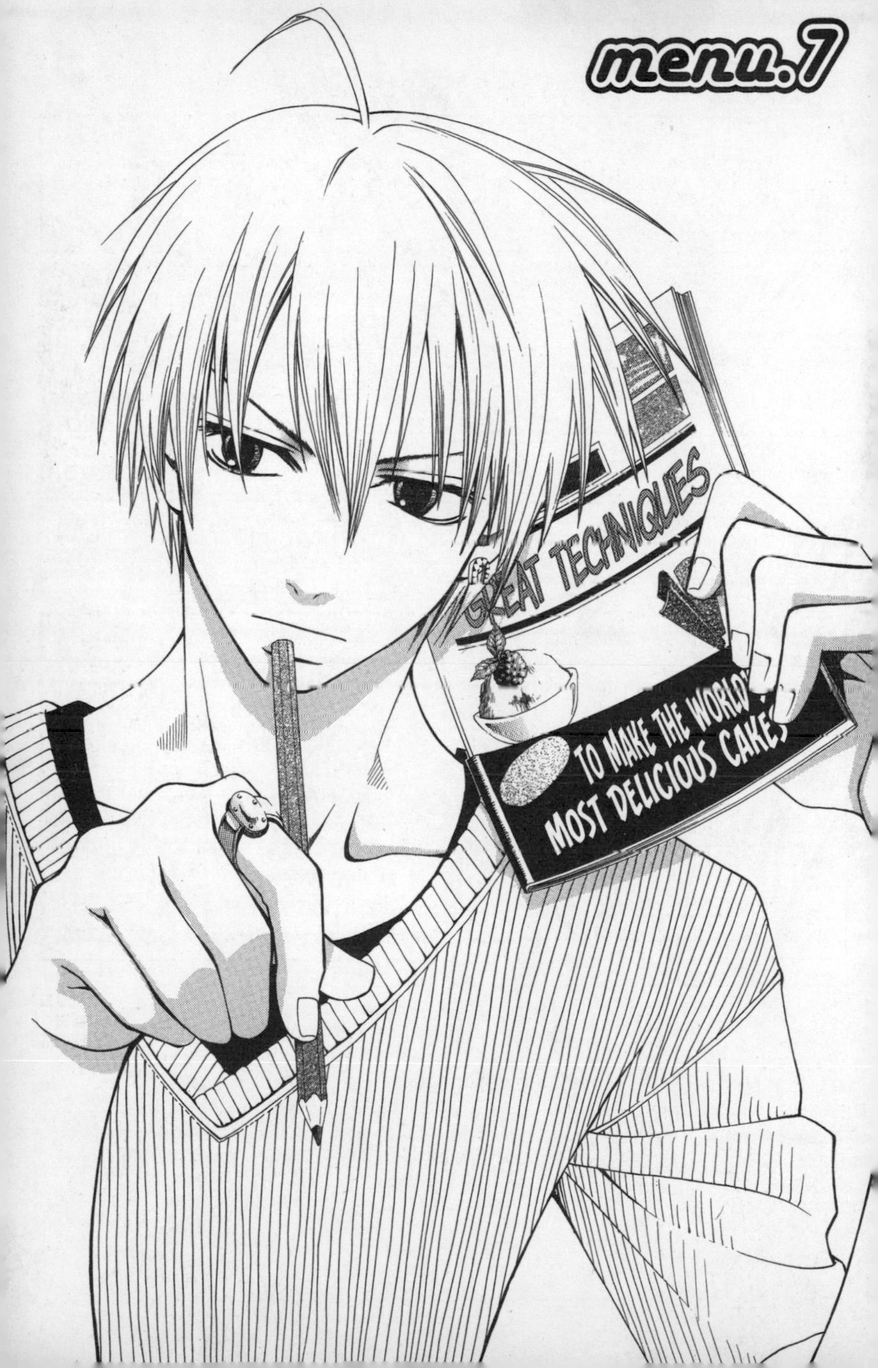
menu.7
GREAT TECHNIQUES
TO MAKE THE WORLD'
MOST DELICIOUS CAKES

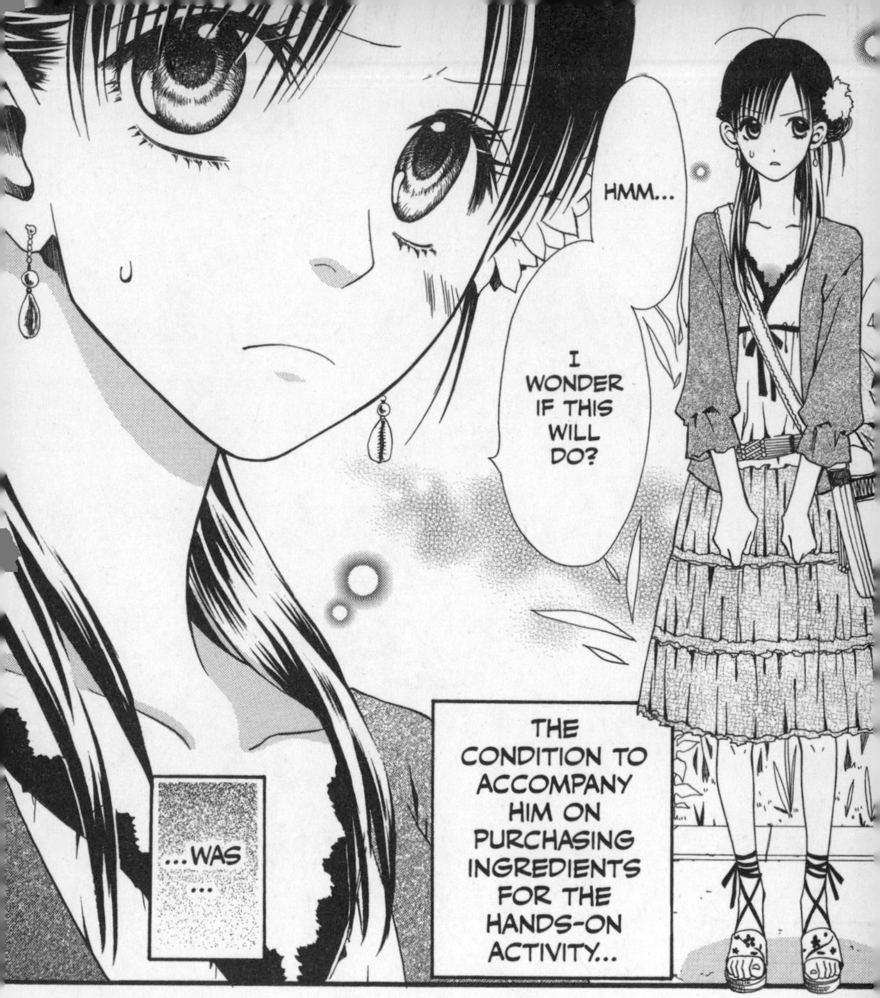
HMM...
I WONDER IF THIS WILL DO?
THE CONDITION TO ACCOMPANY HIM ON PURCHASING INGREDIENTS FOR THE HANDS-ON ACTIVITY...
...WAS ...

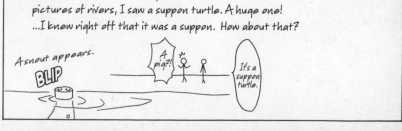

Menu 7

I mentioned this in a Margaret column, but when I went to take pictures of rivers, I saw a suppon turtle. A huge one! ...I knew right off that it was a suppon. How about that?

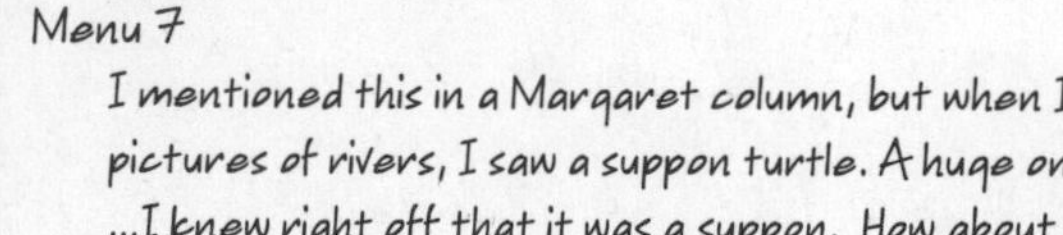
It's a suppon turtle.
A pig?!
A snout appears.
BLIP

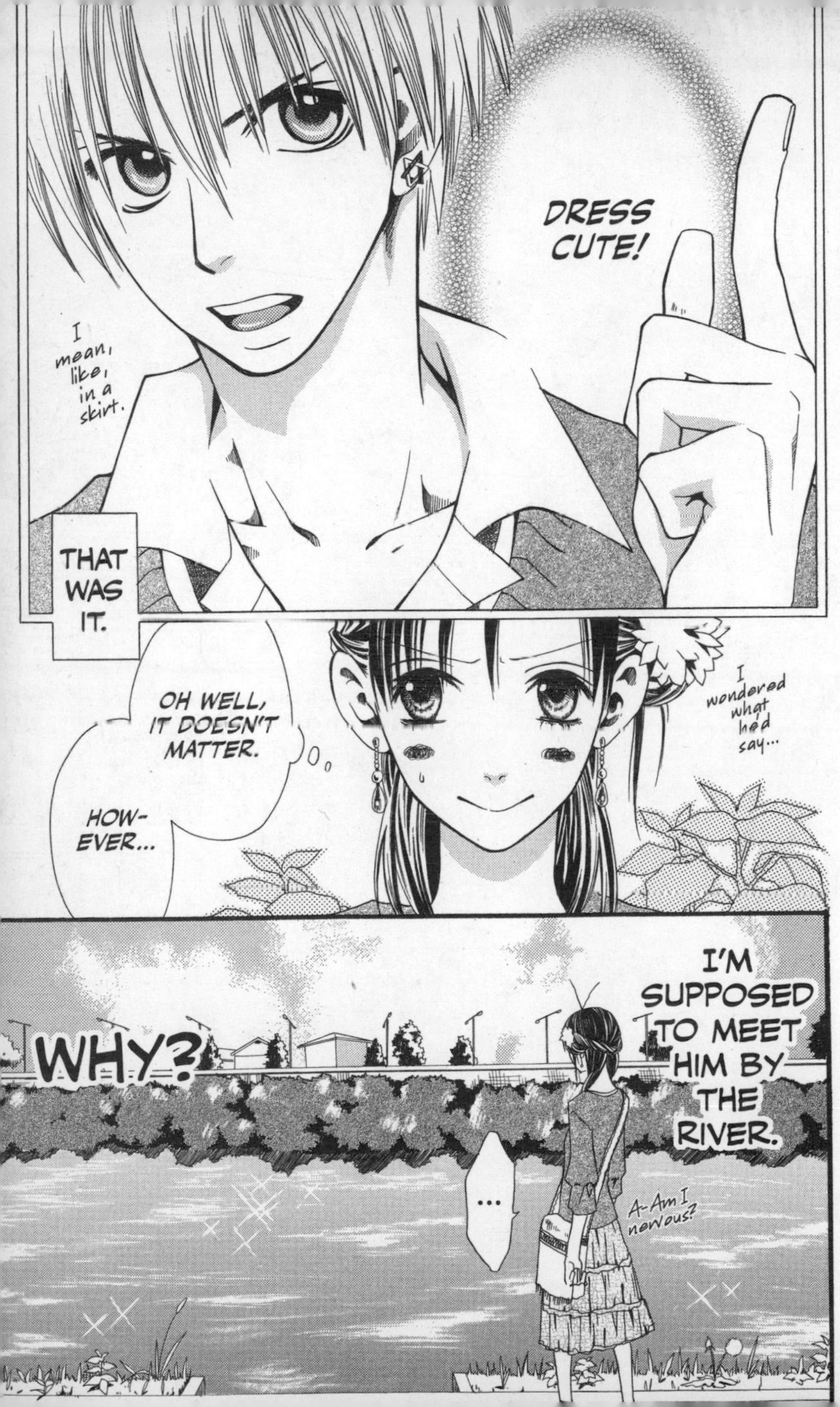
DRESS CUTE!
I mean, like, in a skirt.
THAT WAS IT.
I wondered what he'd say...
OH WELL, IT DOESN'T MATTER.
HOW-EVER...
I'M SUPPOSED TO MEET HIM BY THE RIVER.
A-Am I nervous?
...
WHY?

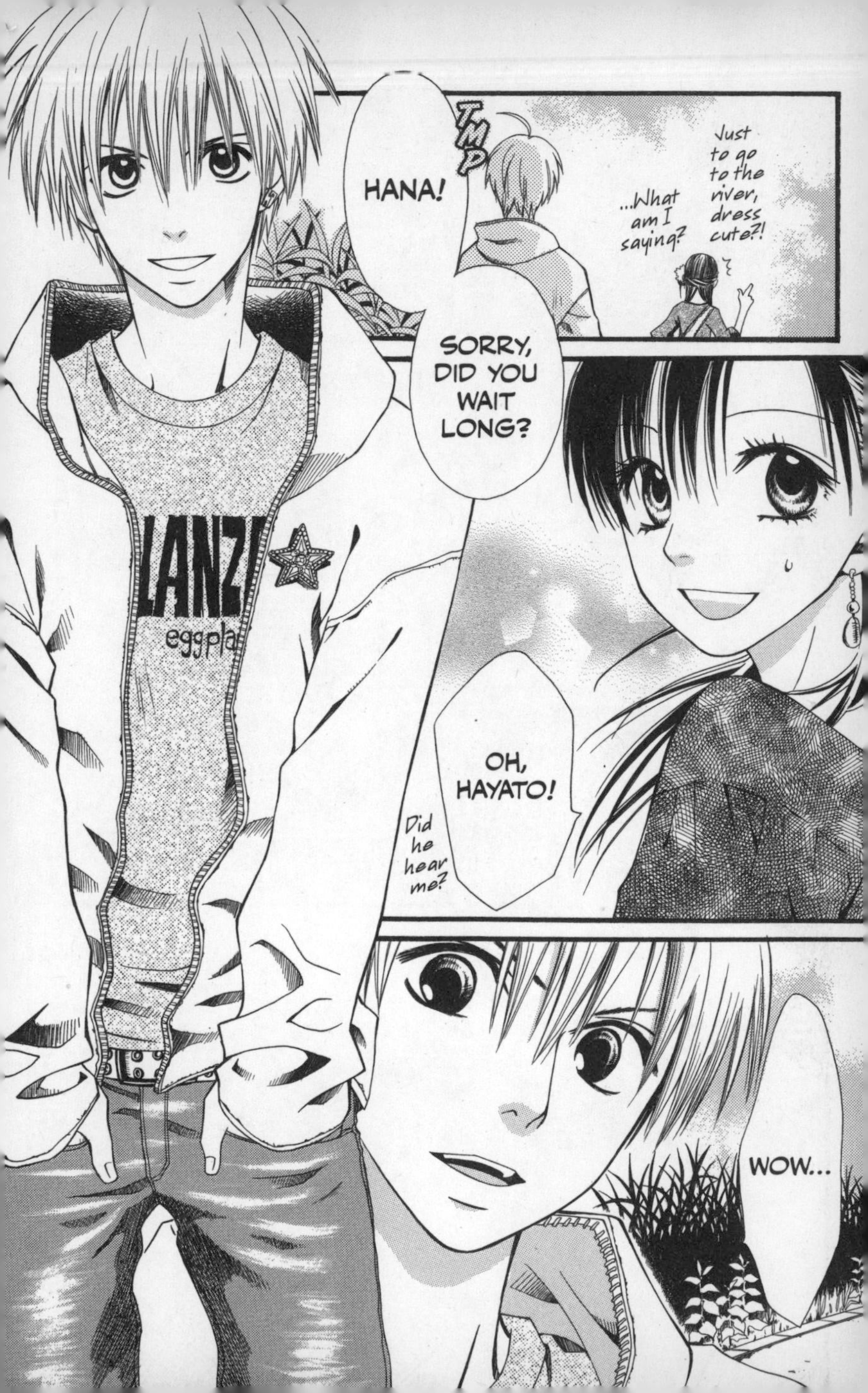
Just to go to the river, dress cute?!
...What am I saying?
TMP
HANA!
SORRY, DID YOU WAIT LONG?
OH, HAYATO!
Did he hear me?
WOW...

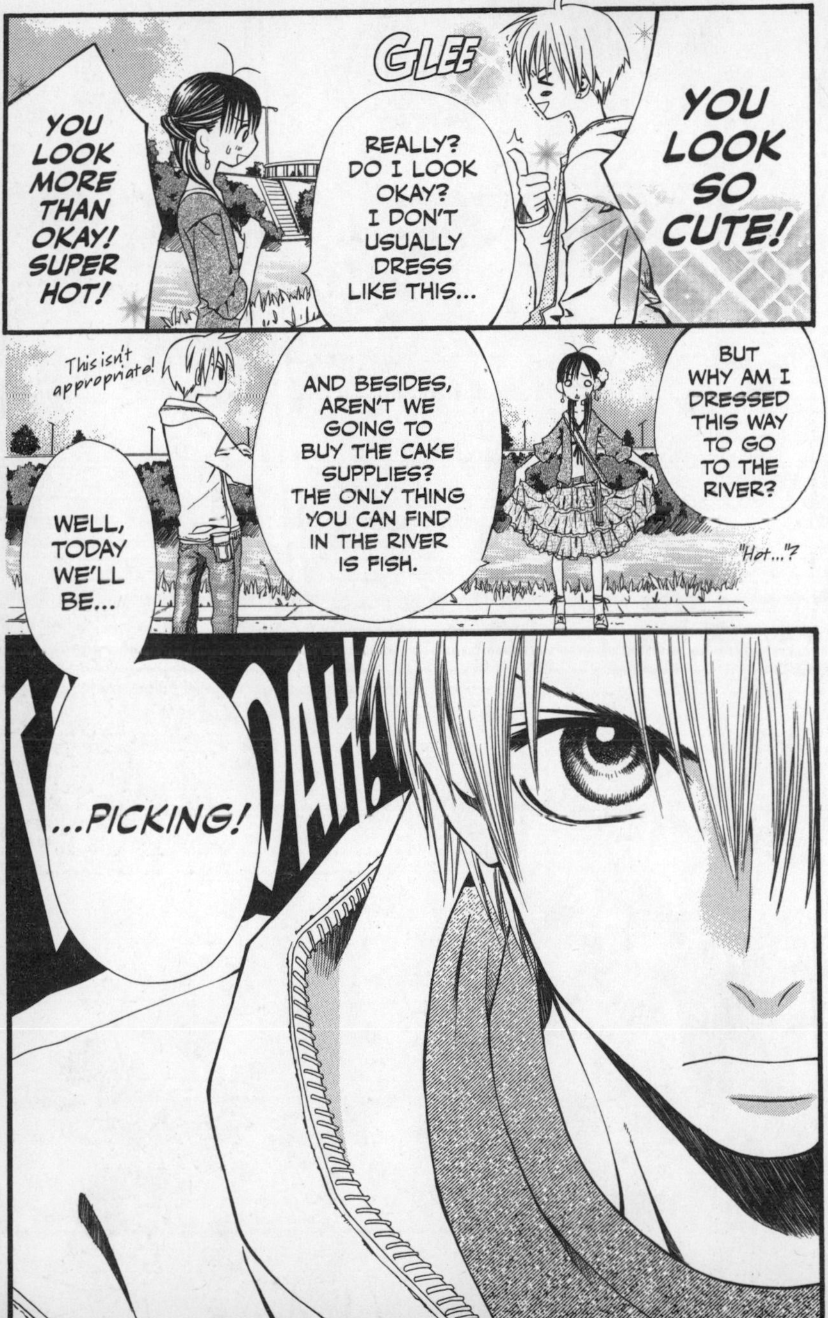
YOU LOOK SO CUTE!
GLEE
REALLY? DO I LOOK OKAY? I DON'T USUALLY DRESS LIKE THIS...
YOU LOOK MORE THAN OKAY! SUPER HOT!
BUT WHY AM I DRESSED THIS WAY TO GO TO THE RIVER?
"Hot..."?
AND BESIDES, AREN'T WE GOING TO BUY THE CAKE SUPPLIES? THE ONLY THING YOU CAN FIND IN THE RIVER IS FISH.
This isn't appropriate!
WELL, TODAY WE'LL BE...
...PICKING!

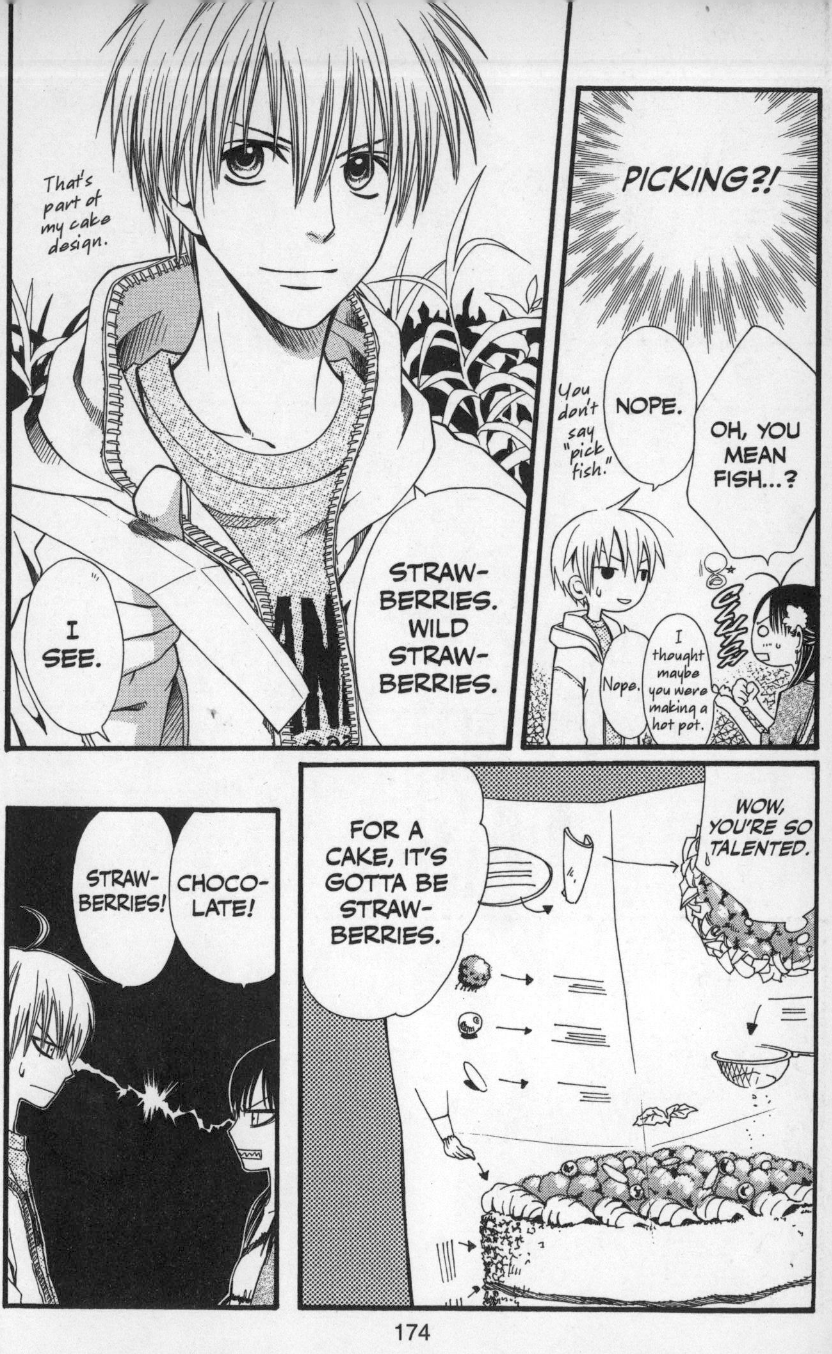
PICKING?!
OH, YOU MEAN FISH...?
NOPE.
You don't say "pick fish."
I thought maybe you were making a hot pot.
Nope.
STRAW-BERRIES. WILD STRAW-BERRIES.
That's part of my cake design.
I SEE.
WOW, YOU'RE SO TALENTED.
FOR A CAKE, IT'S GOTTA BE STRAW-BERRIES.
CHOCO-LATE!
STRAW-BERRIES!

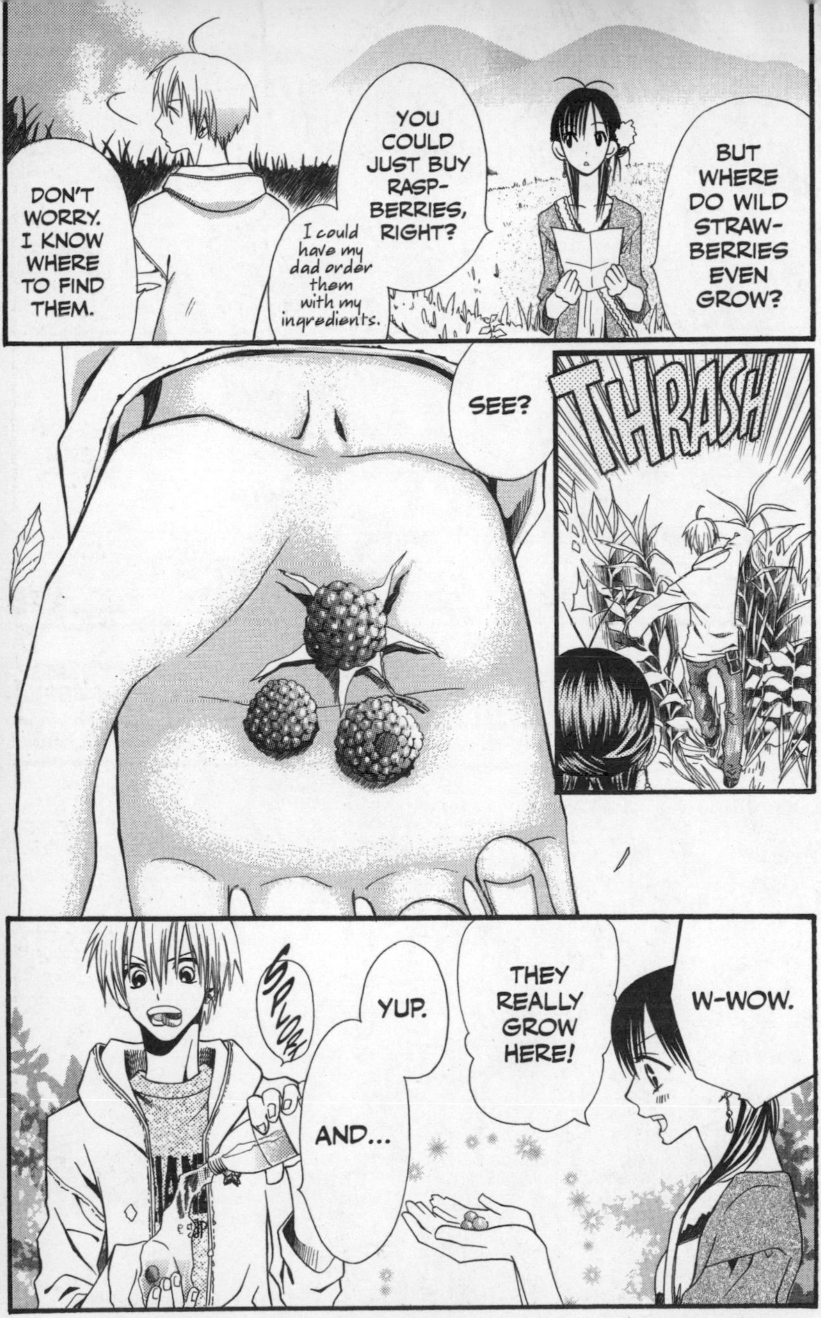
BUT WHERE DO WILD STRAW-BERRIES EVEN GROW?
YOU COULD JUST BUY RASP-BERRIES, RIGHT?
I could have my dad order them with my ingredients.
DON'T WORRY. I KNOW WHERE TO FIND THEM.
THRASH
SEE?
W-WOW.
THEY REALLY GROW HERE!
YUP.
AND...

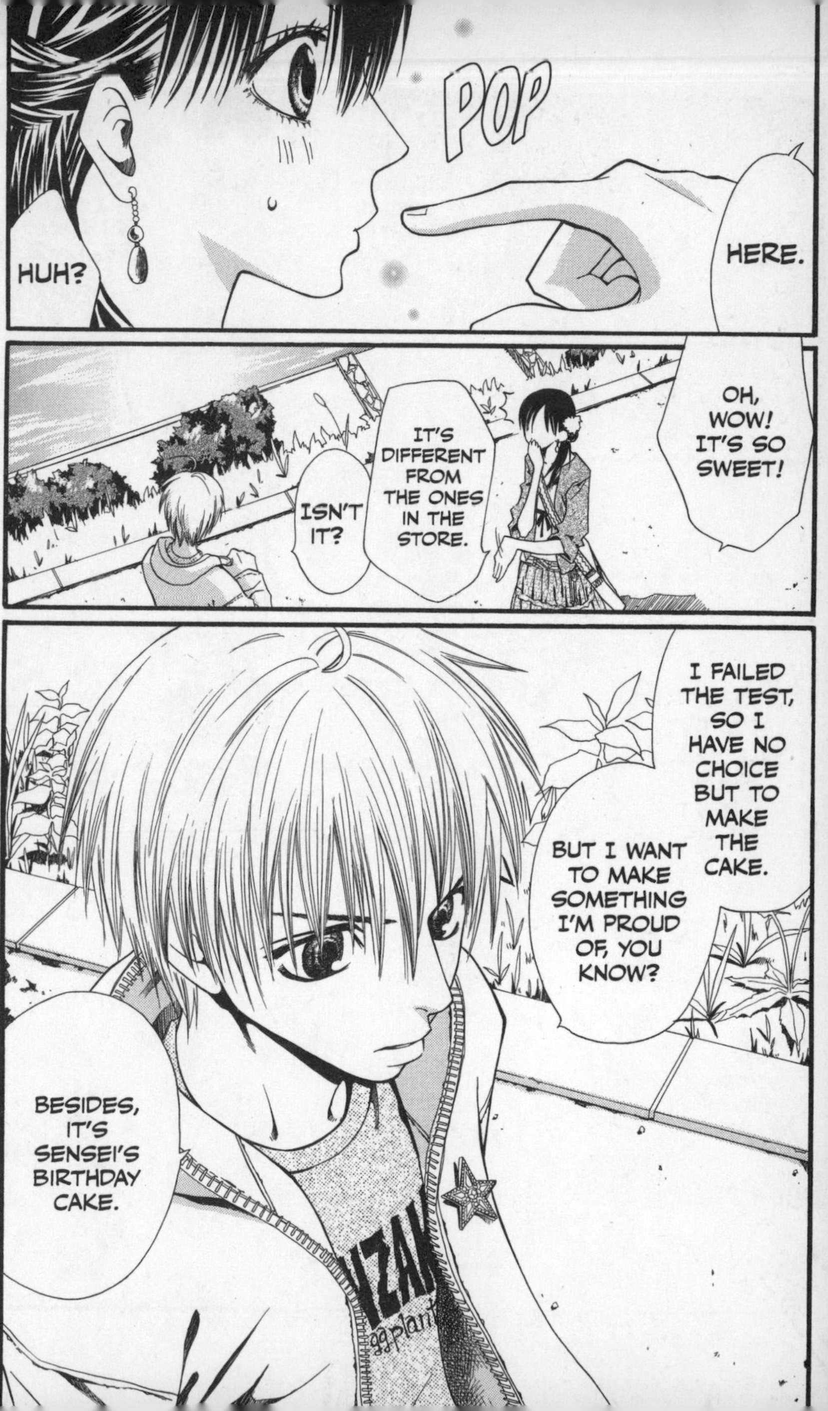
HERE.
POP
HUH?
OH, WOW! IT'S SO SWEET!
IT'S DIFFERENT FROM THE ONES IN THE STORE.
ISN'T IT?
I FAILED THE TEST, SO I HAVE NO CHOICE BUT TO MAKE THE CAKE.
BUT I WANT TO MAKE SOMETHING I'M PROUD OF, YOU KNOW?
BESIDES, IT'S SENSEI'S BIRTHDAY CAKE.

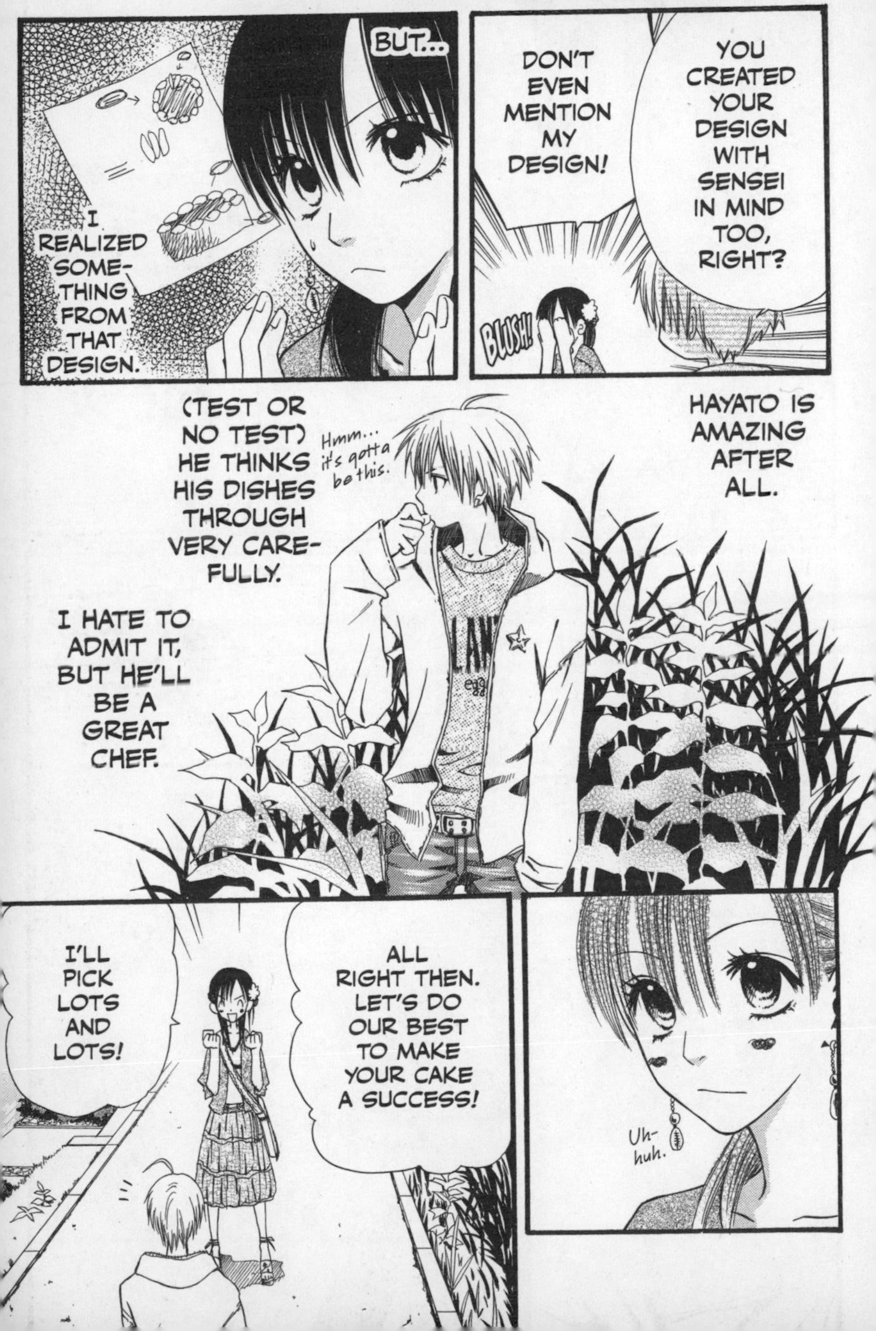

YOU CREATED YOUR DESIGN WITH SENSEI IN MIND TOO, RIGHT?
DON'T EVEN MENTION MY DESIGN!
BLUSH!
BUT...
I REALIZED SOME-THING FROM THAT DESIGN.
HAYATO IS AMAZING AFTER ALL.
Hmm... it's gotta be this.
(TEST OR NO TEST) HE THINKS HIS DISHES THROUGH VERY CARE-FULLY.
I HATE TO ADMIT IT, BUT HE'LL BE A GREAT CHEF.
Uh-huh.
ALL RIGHT THEN. LET'S DO OUR BEST TO MAKE YOUR CAKE A SUCCESS!
I'LL PICK LOTS AND LOTS!

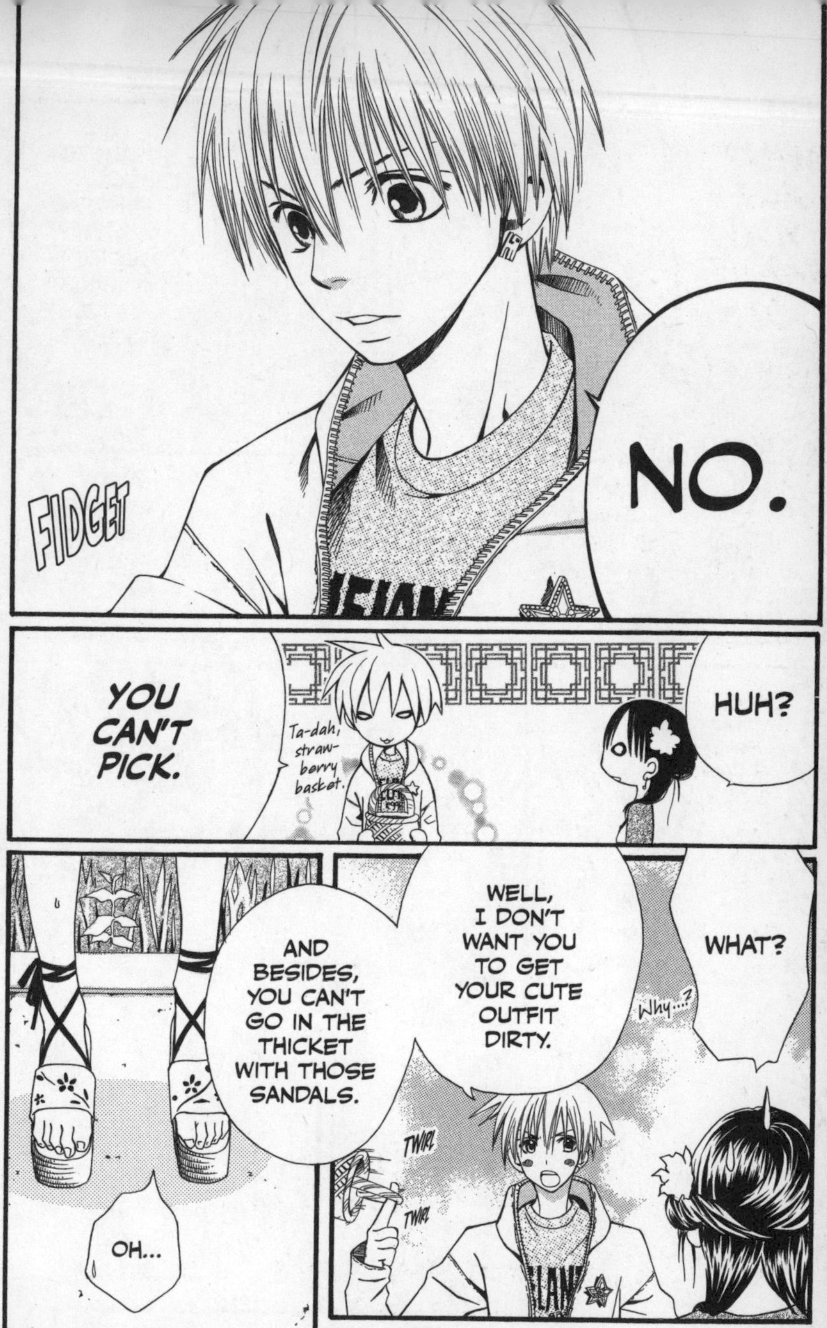

NO.
FIDGET
HUH?
Ta-dah, strawberry basket.
YOU CAN'T PICK.
WHAT?
Why...?
WELL, I DON'T WANT YOU TO GET YOUR CUTE OUTFIT DIRTY.
TWIRL
TWIRL
AND BESIDES, YOU CAN'T GO IN THE THICKET WITH THOSE SANDALS.
OH...

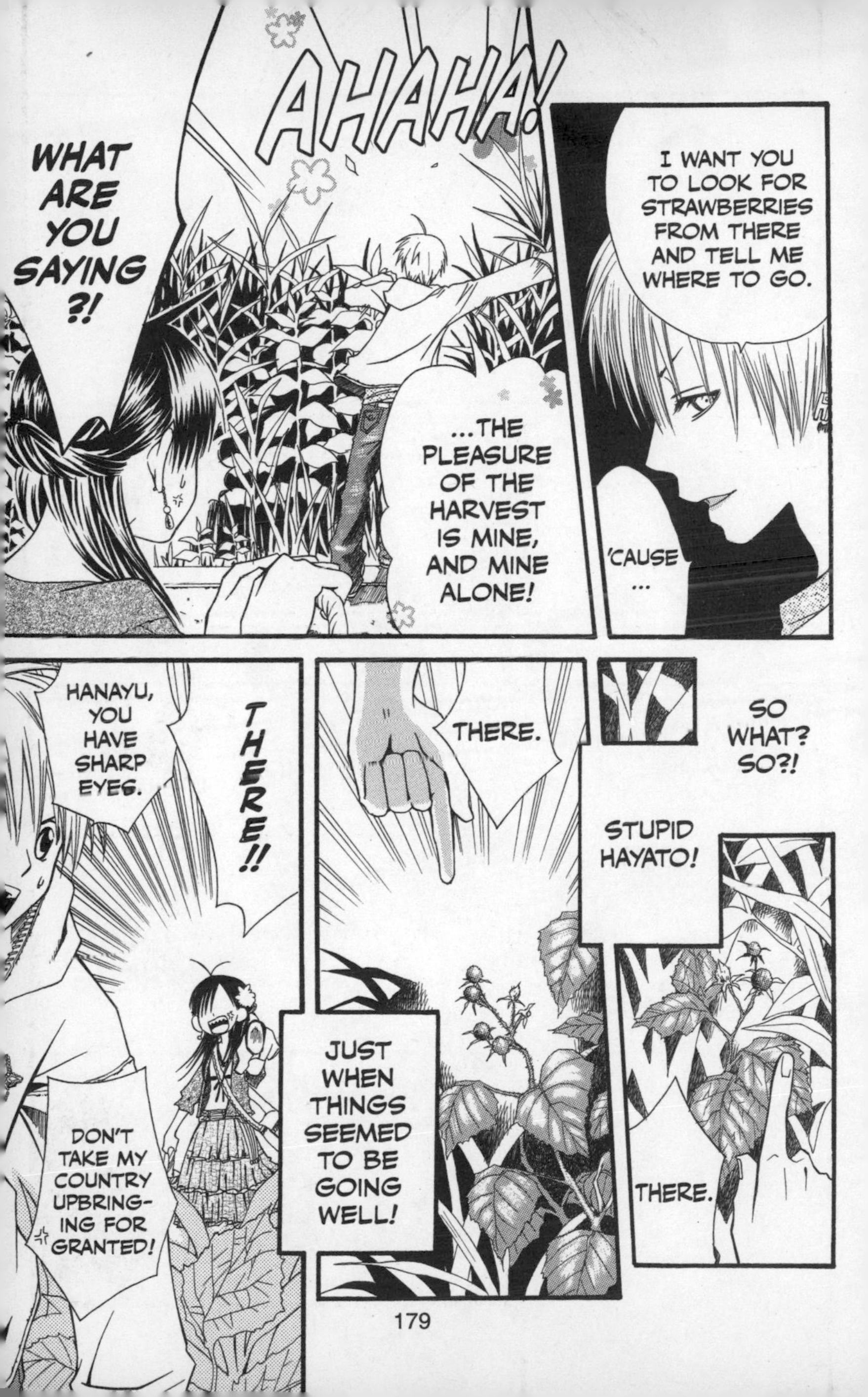

I WANT YOU TO LOOK FOR STRAWBERRIES FROM THERE AND TELL ME WHERE TO GO.
'CAUSE ...
...THE PLEASURE OF THE HARVEST IS MINE, AND MINE ALONE!
AHAHA!
WHAT ARE YOU SAYING?!
SO WHAT? SO?!
STUPID HAYATO!
THERE.
THERE.
JUST WHEN THINGS SEEMED TO BE GOING WELL!
HANAYU, YOU HAVE SHARP EYES.
THERE!!
DON'T TAKE MY COUNTRY UPBRINGING FOR GRANTED!

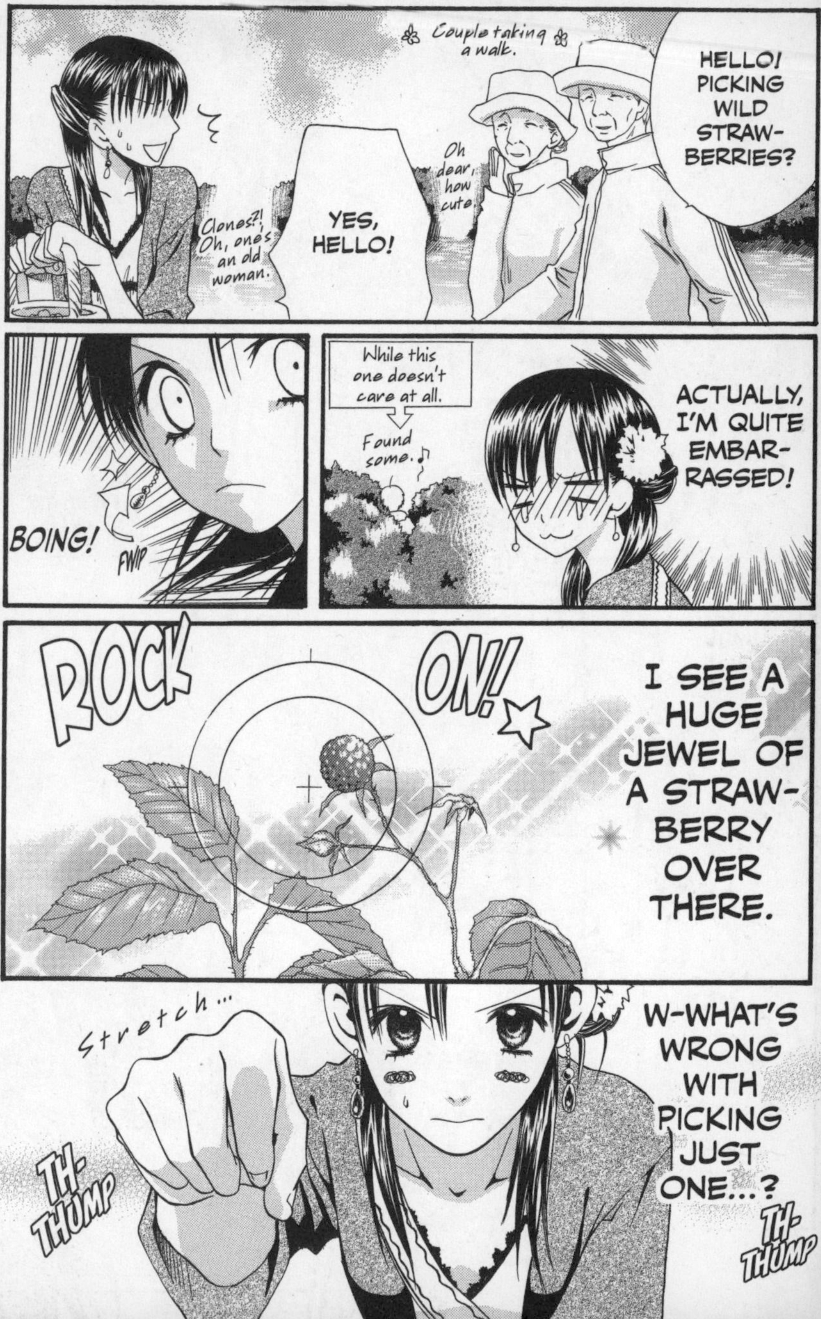
HELLO! PICKING WILD STRAWBERRIES?
Couple taking a walk.
Oh dear, how cute.
YES, HELLO!
Clones?! Oh, one's an old woman.
ACTUALLY, I'M QUITE EMBARRASSED!
While this one doesn't care at all.
Found some. ♪
BOING!
FWIP
I SEE A HUGE JEWEL OF A STRAWBERRY OVER THERE.
ROCK ON!
W-WHAT'S WRONG WITH PICKING JUST ONE...?
TH-THUMP
Stretch...
TH-THUMP

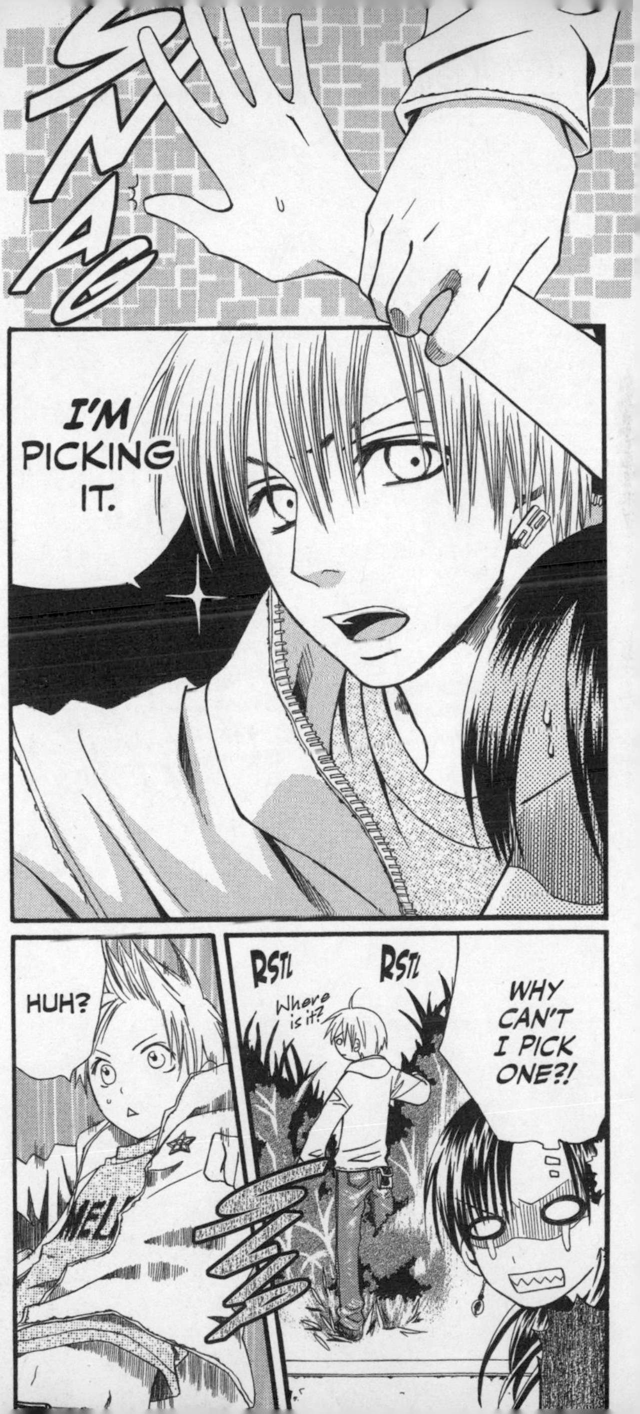
SNAG
I'M PICKING IT.
RSTL
RSTL
Where is it?
WHY CAN'T I PICK ONE?!
HUH?

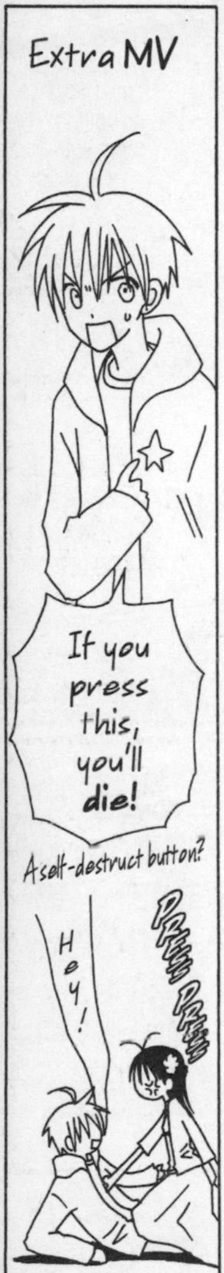
Extra MV
If you press this, you'll die!
A self-destruct button?
Hey!
PRESS PRESS

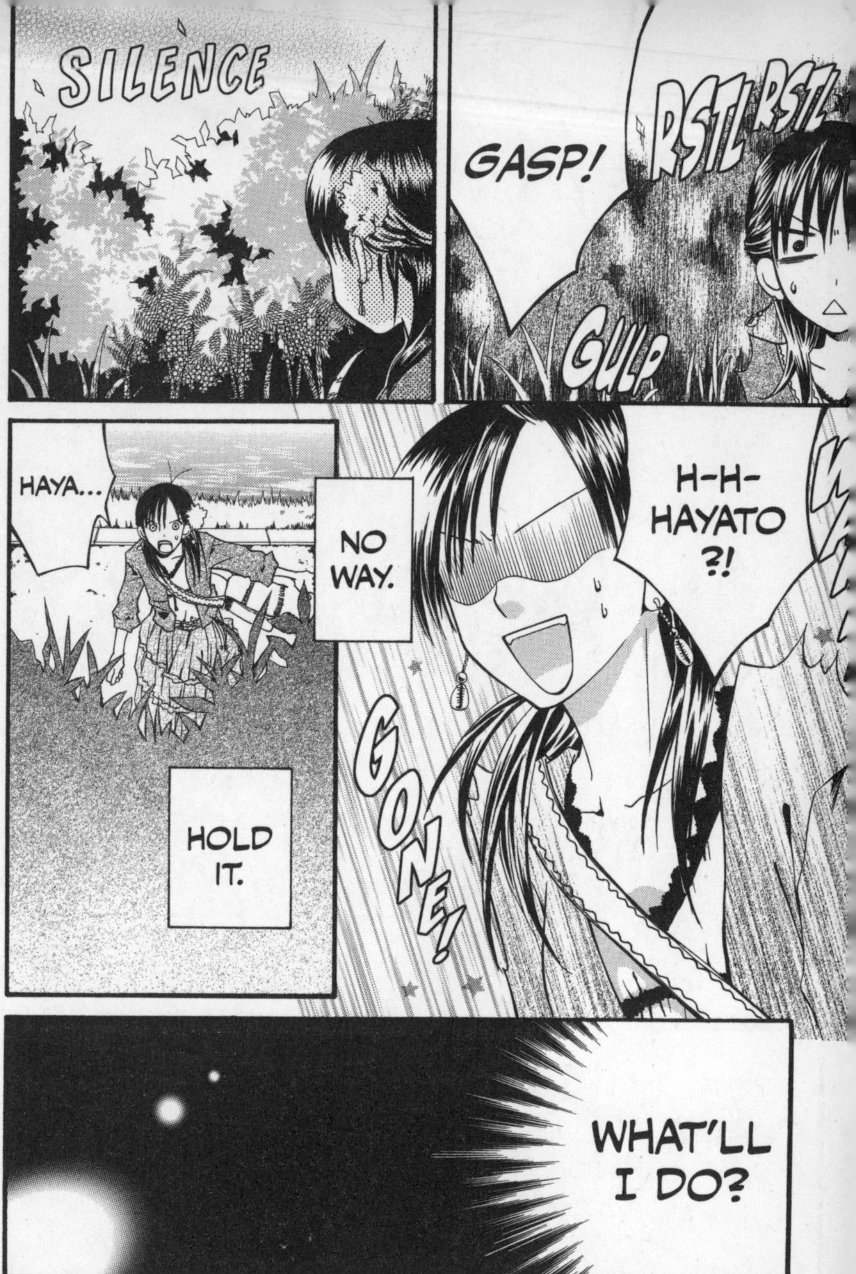
RSTL RSTL
GASP!
GULP
SILENCE
H-H-HAYATO ?!
NO WAY.
GONE!
HAYA...
HOLD IT.
WHAT'LL I DO?

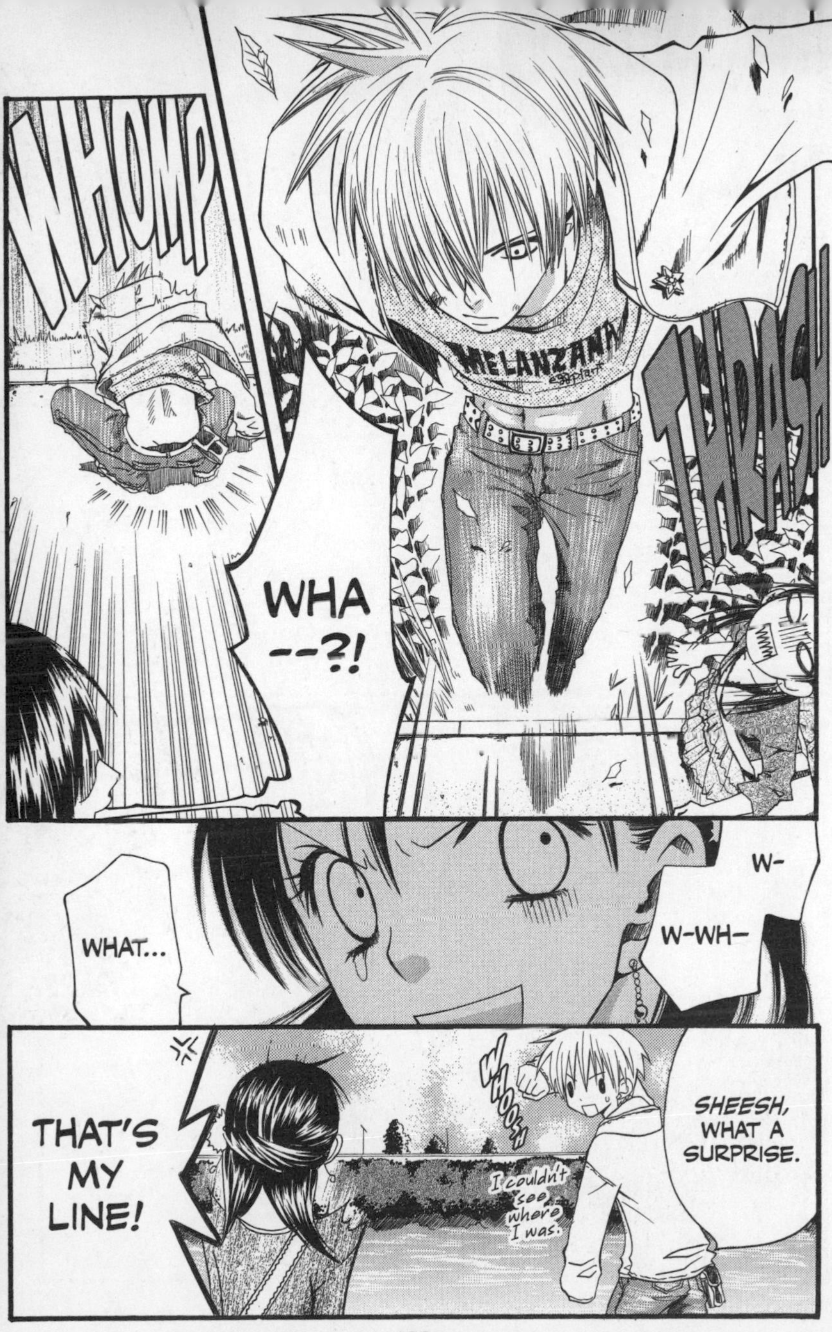
THRASH
MELANZANA
eggplant
WHOMP
WHA--?!
W-
W-WH-
WHAT...
SHEESH, WHAT A SURPRISE.
WHOOSH
I couldn't see where I was.
THAT'S MY LINE!

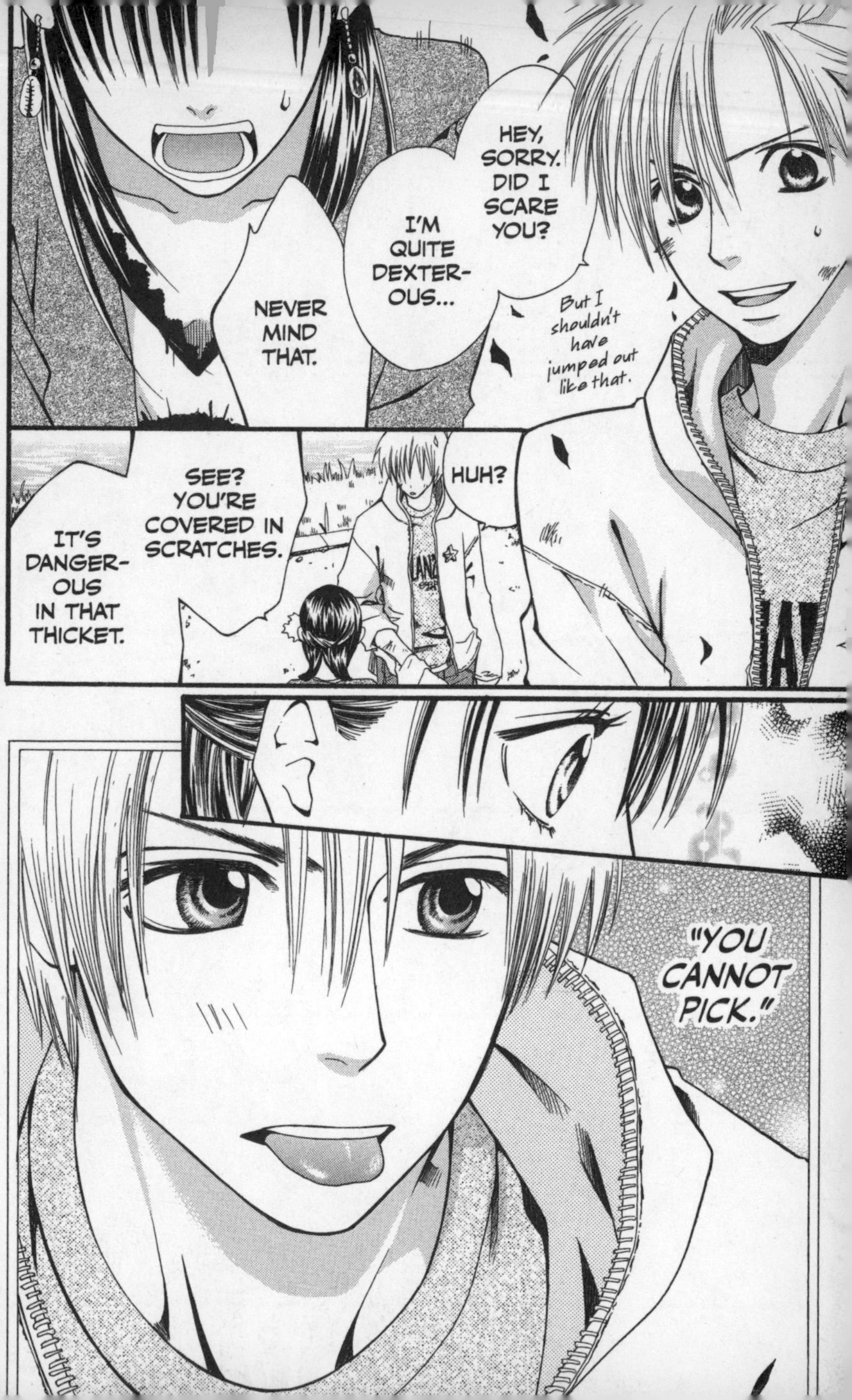

HEY, SORRY. DID I SCARE YOU?
But I shouldn't have jumped out like that.
I'M QUITE DEXTER-OUS...
NEVER MIND THAT.
HUH?
SEE? YOU'RE COVERED IN SCRATCHES.
IT'S DANGER-OUS IN THAT THICKET.
"YOU CANNOT PICK."

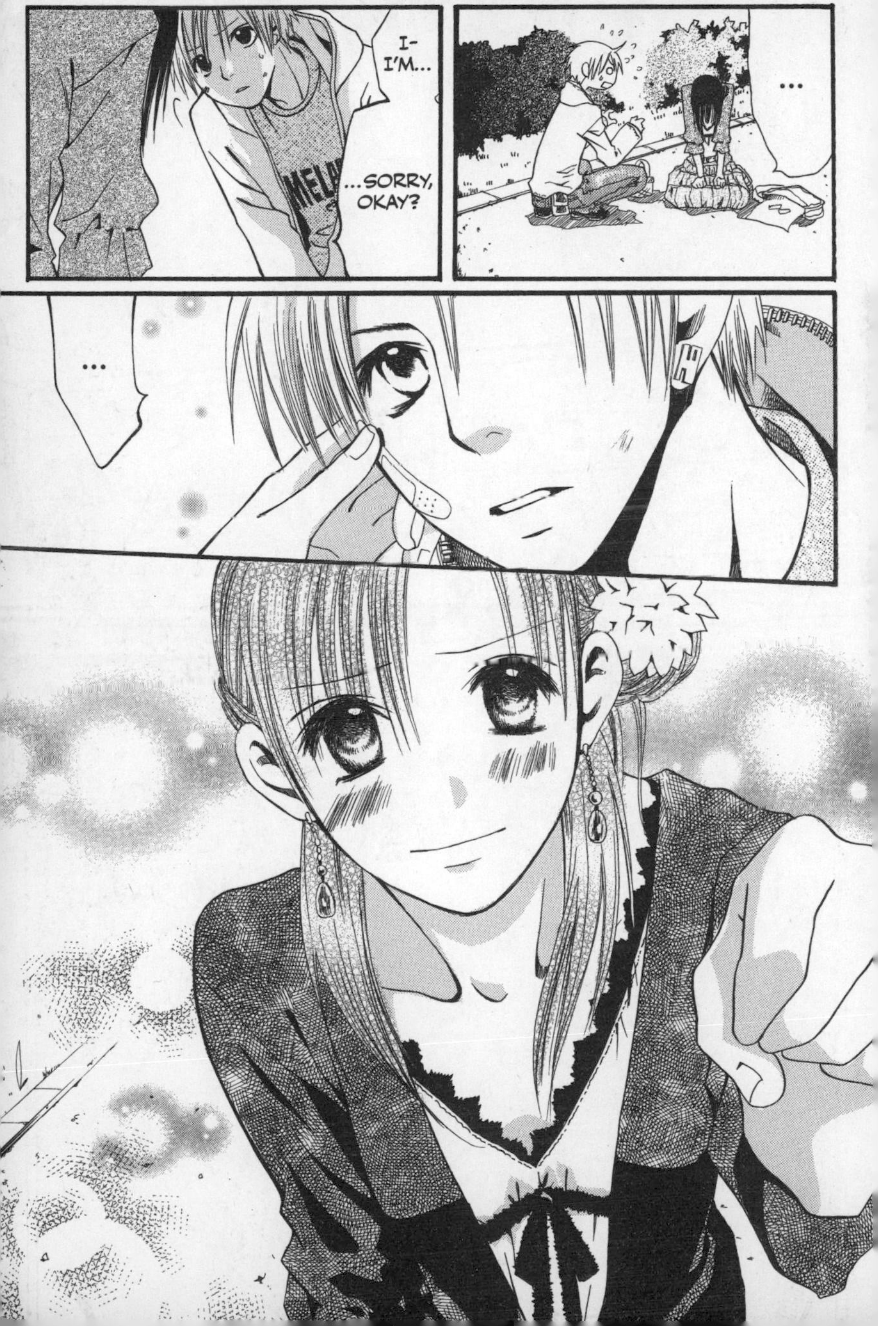
...
I- I'M...
...SORRY, OKAY?
...

HANA...

HEH!

OOPS, I'M SORRY.

HEY!

OWWEEE!

PINCH

YIKES?!

HUH?

BEWARE OF SNAKES!!

DANGER

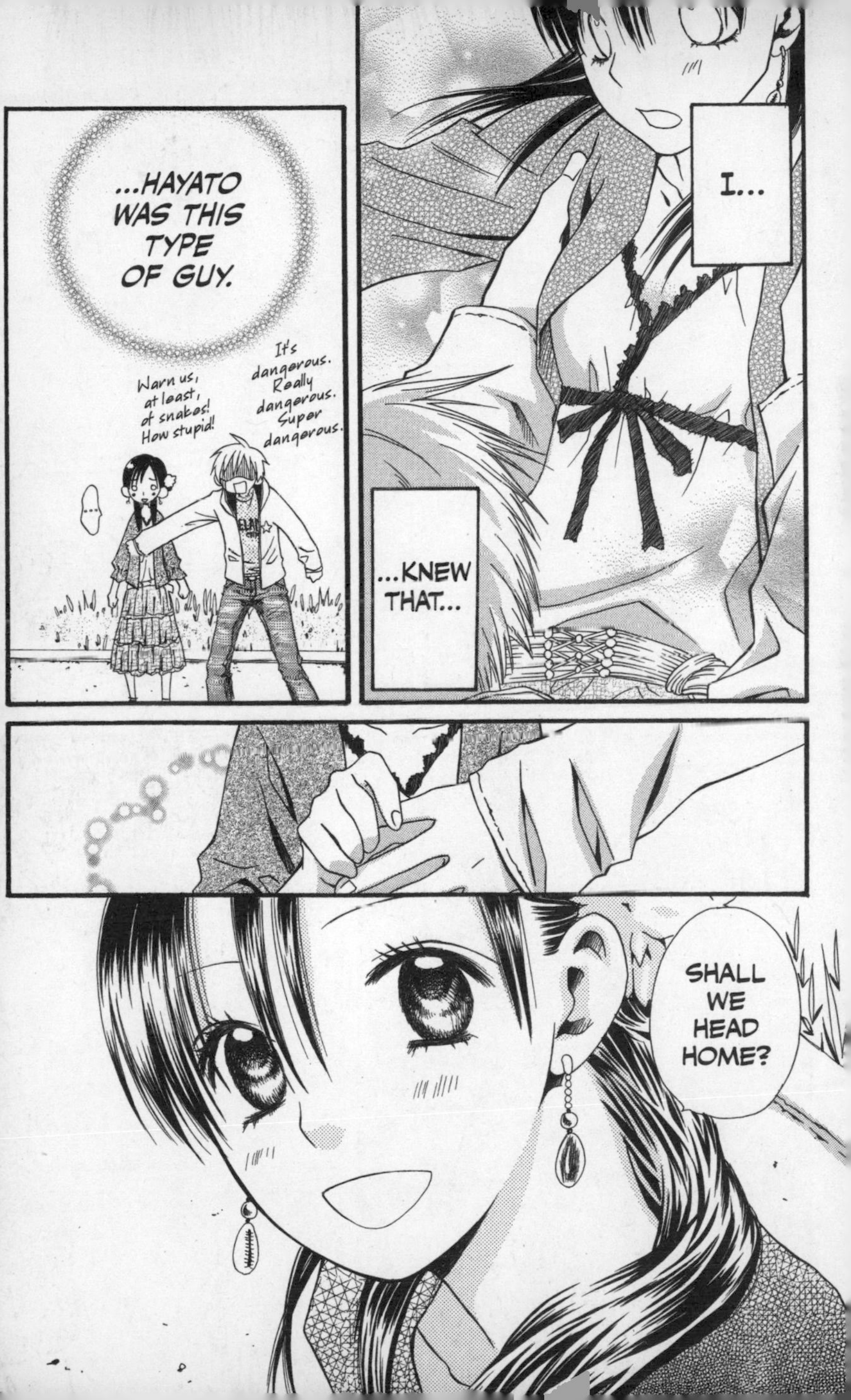
I...
...KNEW THAT...
...HAYATO WAS THIS TYPE OF GUY.
It's dangerous. Really dangerous. Super dangerous.
Warn us, at least, of snakes! How stupid!
...
SHALL WE HEAD HOME?

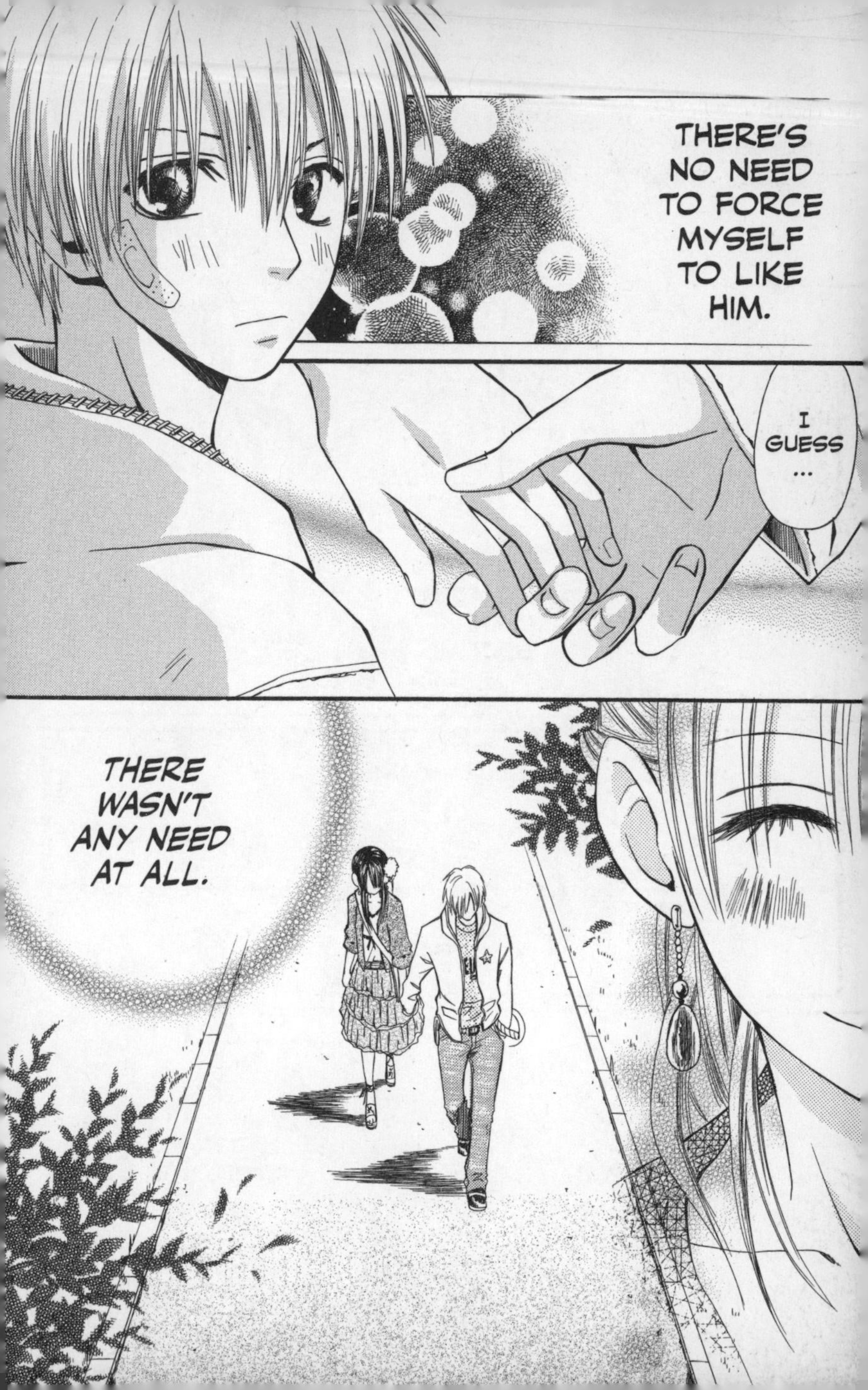
THERE'S NO NEED TO FORCE MYSELF TO LIKE HIM.
I GUESS ...
THERE WASN'T ANY NEED AT ALL.

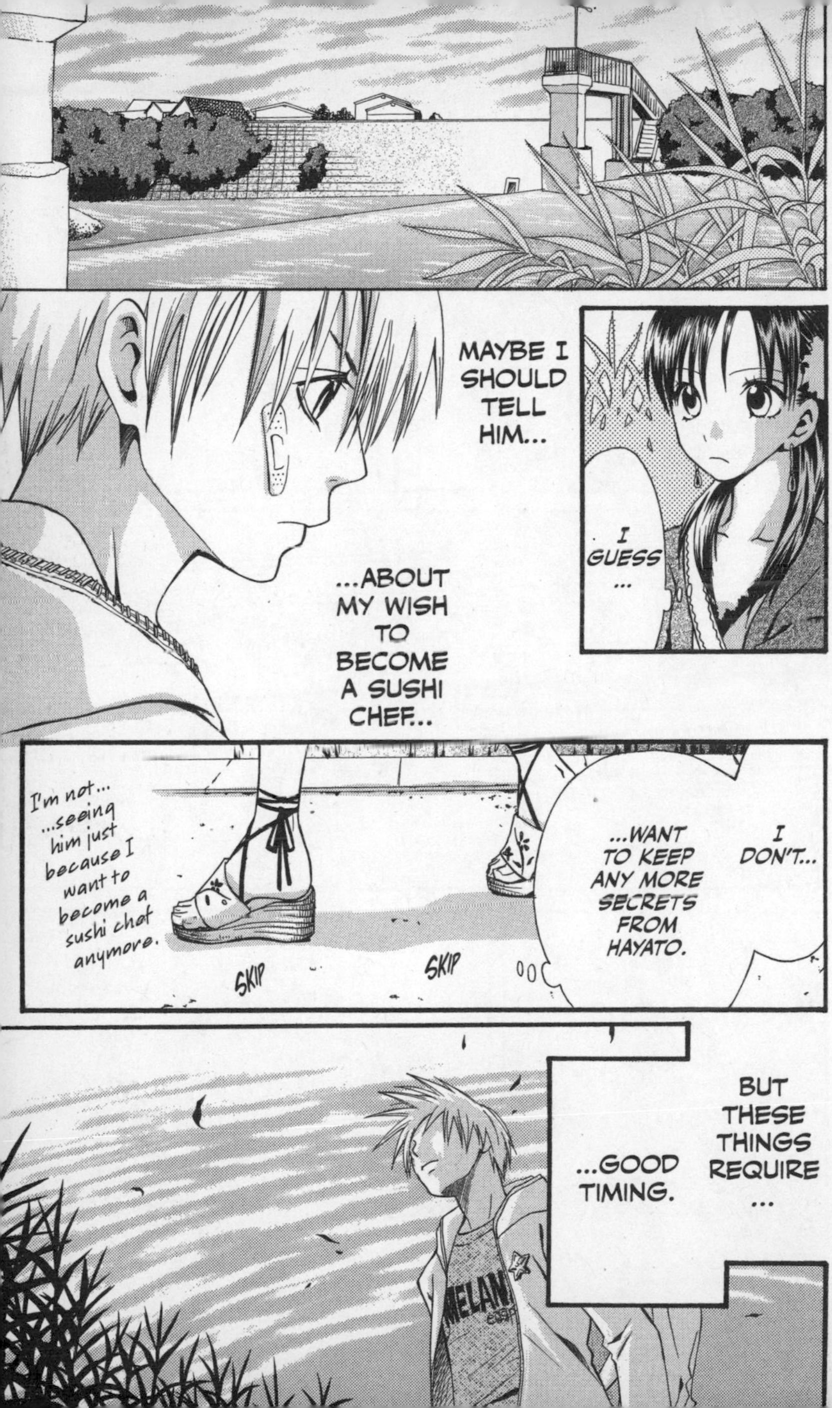
MAYBE I SHOULD TELL HIM...
I GUESS...
...ABOUT MY WISH TO BECOME A SUSHI CHEF...
I DON'T...
...WANT TO KEEP ANY MORE SECRETS FROM HAYATO.
I'm not... ...seeing him just because I want to become a sushi chef anymore.
SKIP
SKIP
BUT THESE THINGS REQUIRE...
...GOOD TIMING.

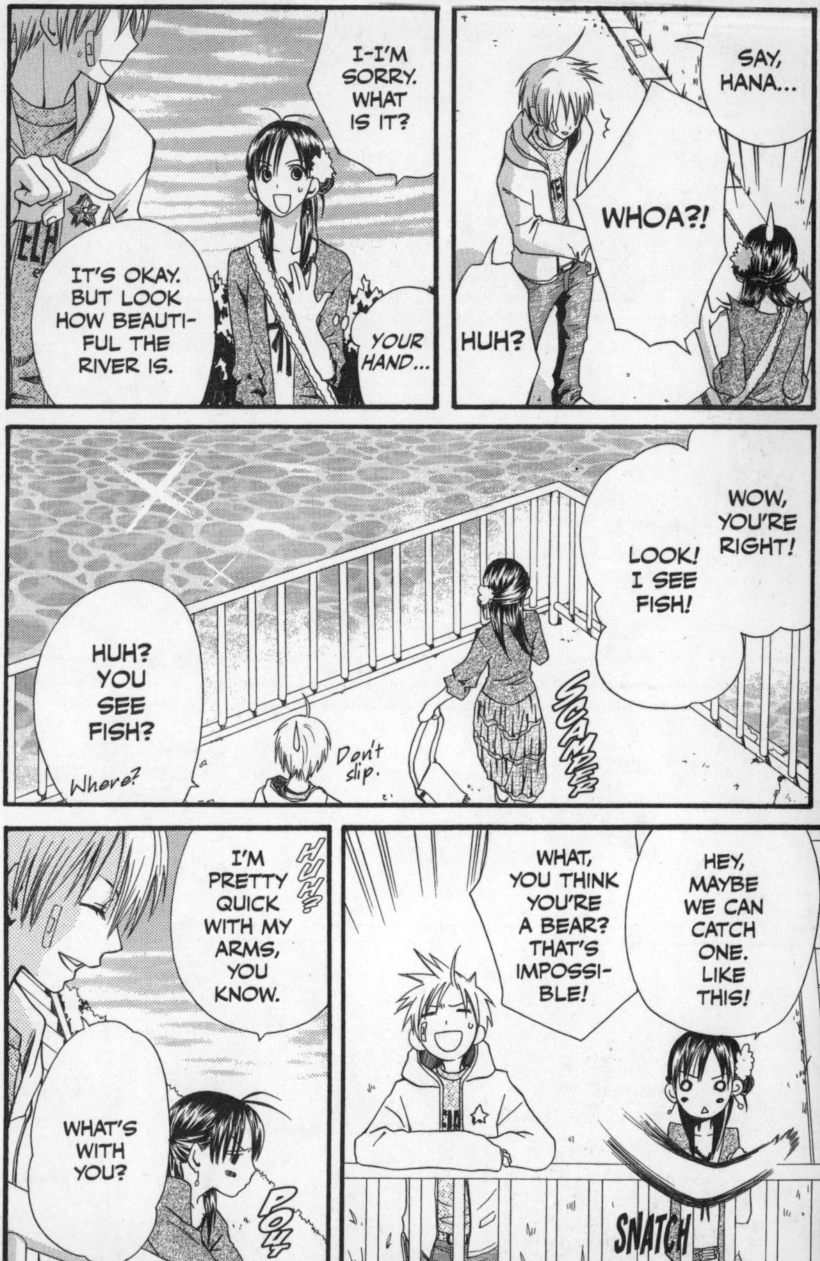
SAY, HANA...
WHOA?!
HUH?
I-I'M SORRY. WHAT IS IT?
YOUR HAND...
IT'S OKAY. BUT LOOK HOW BEAUTIFUL THE RIVER IS.
WOW, YOU'RE RIGHT!
LOOK! I SEE FISH!
SCAMPER
Don't slip.
HUH? YOU SEE FISH?
Where?
HEY, MAYBE WE CAN CATCH ONE. LIKE THIS!
WHAT, YOU THINK YOU'RE A BEAR? THAT'S IMPOSSIBLE!
SNATCH
HUH HUH
I'M PRETTY QUICK WITH MY ARMS, YOU KNOW.
WHAT'S WITH YOU?
POW

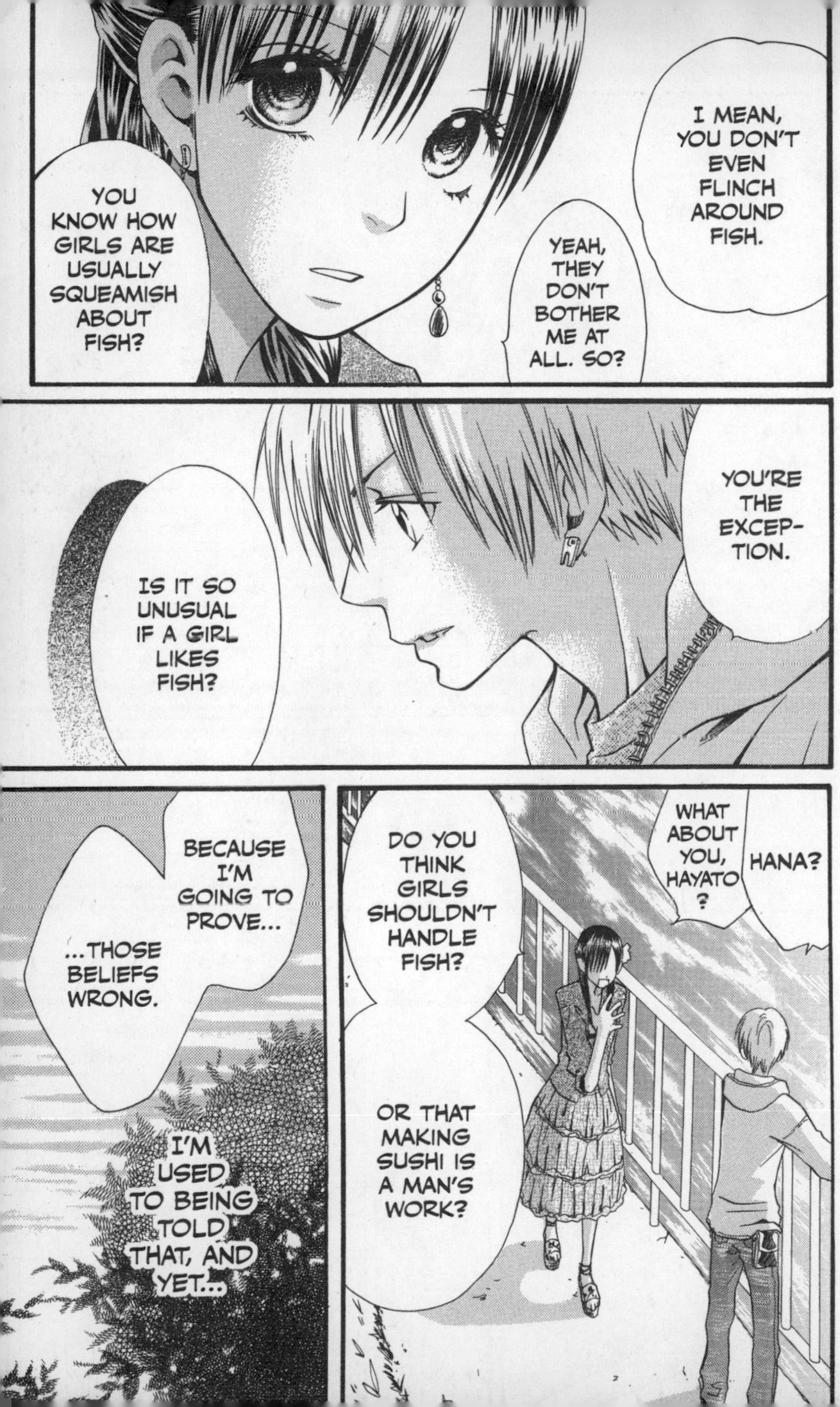
I MEAN, YOU DON'T EVEN FLINCH AROUND FISH.
YEAH, THEY DON'T BOTHER ME AT ALL. SO?
YOU KNOW HOW GIRLS ARE USUALLY SQUEAMISH ABOUT FISH?
YOU'RE THE EXCEPTION.
IS IT SO UNUSUAL IF A GIRL LIKES FISH?
HANA?
WHAT ABOUT YOU, HAYATO?
DO YOU THINK GIRLS SHOULDN'T HANDLE FISH?
OR THAT MAKING SUSHI IS A MAN'S WORK?
BECAUSE I'M GOING TO PROVE...
...THOSE BELIEFS WRONG.
I'M USED TO BEING TOLD THAT, AND YET...

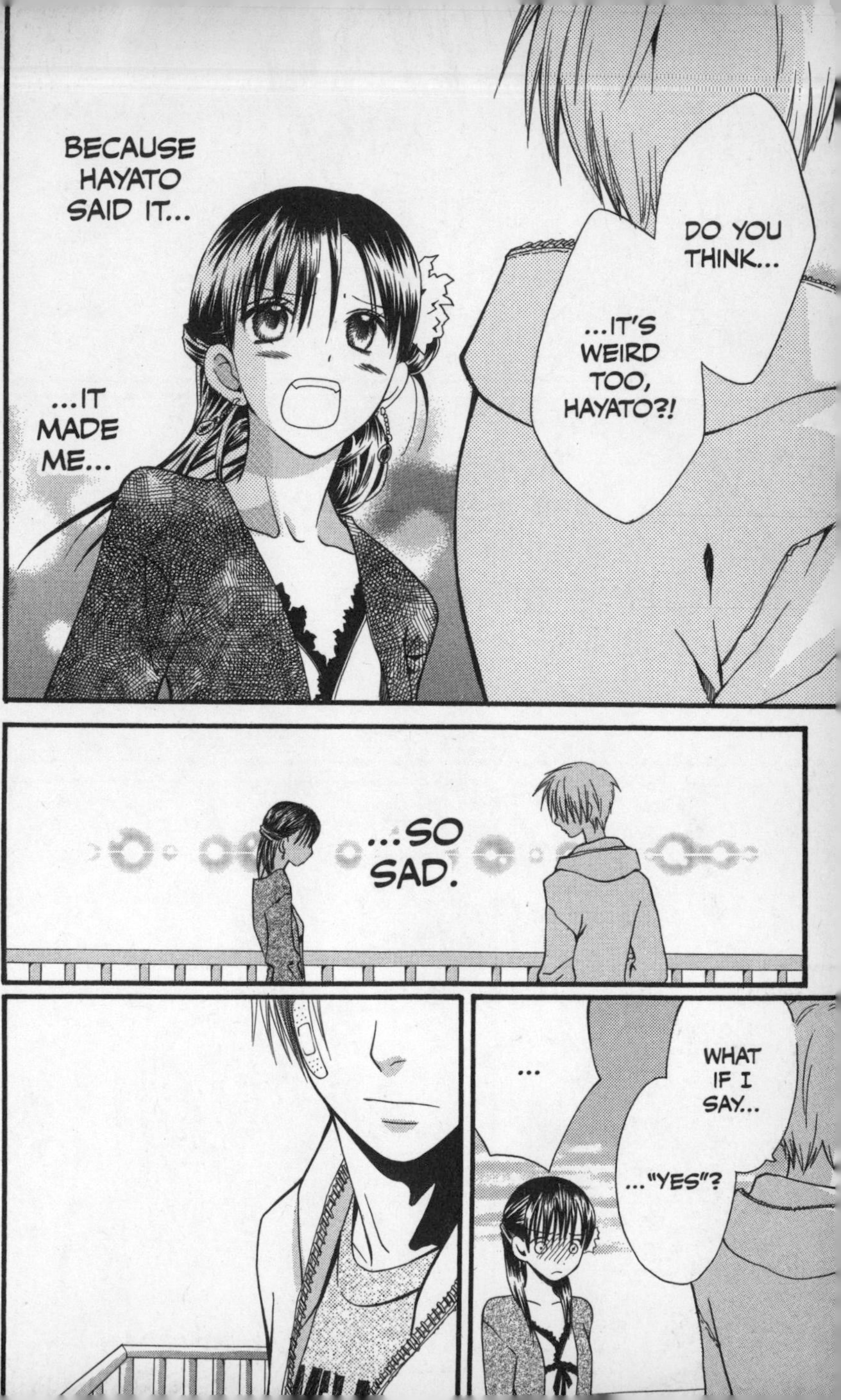
DO YOU THINK...
...IT'S WEIRD TOO, HAYATO?!
BECAUSE HAYATO SAID IT...
...IT MADE ME...
...SO SAD.
WHAT IF I SAY...
..."YES"?
...

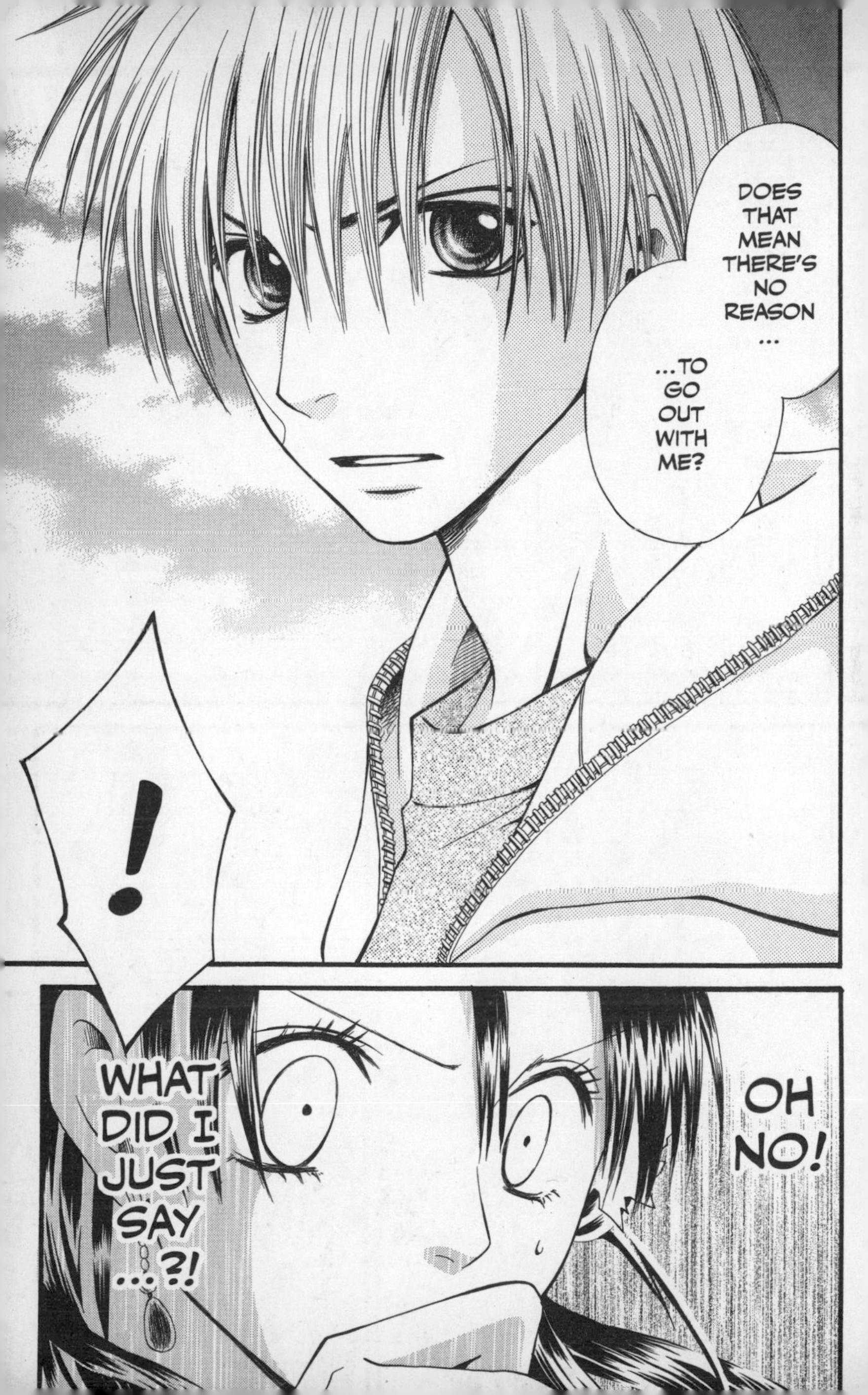
DOES THAT MEAN THERE'S NO REASON...
...TO GO OUT WITH ME?
!
OH NO!
WHAT DID I JUST SAY...?!

Bonus Manga
"Tell Us, Matsuzaka Sensei!"

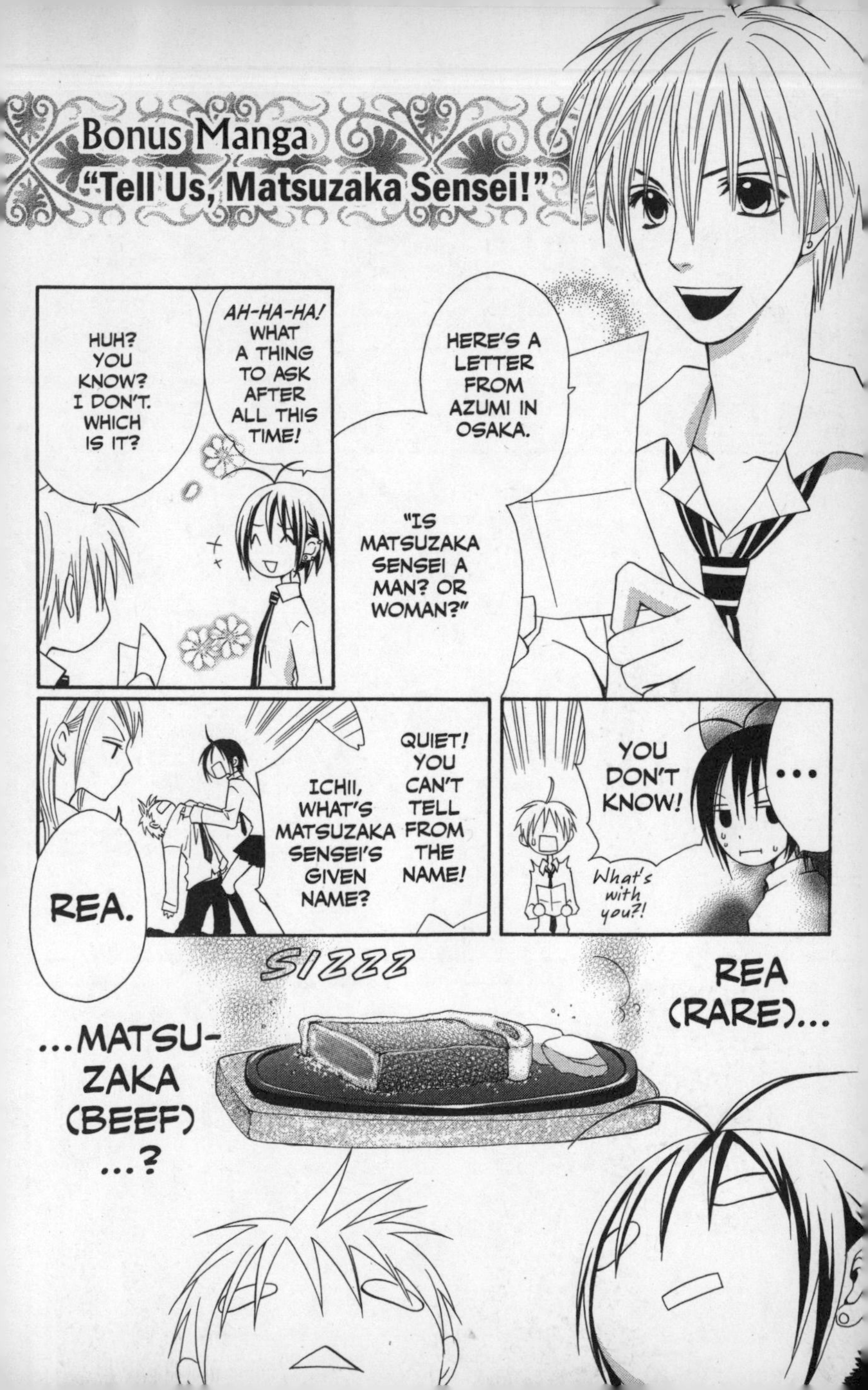
HERE'S A LETTER FROM AZUMI IN OSAKA.
"IS MATSUZAKA SENSEI A MAN? OR WOMAN?"
AH-HA-HA! WHAT A THING TO ASK AFTER ALL THIS TIME!
HUH? YOU KNOW? I DON'T. WHICH IS IT?
YOU DON'T KNOW!
...
What's with you?!
QUIET! YOU CAN'T TELL FROM THE NAME!
ICHII, WHAT'S MATSUZAKA SENSEI'S GIVEN NAME?
REA.
SIZZZ
REA (RARE)...
...MATSU-ZAKA (BEEF) ...?

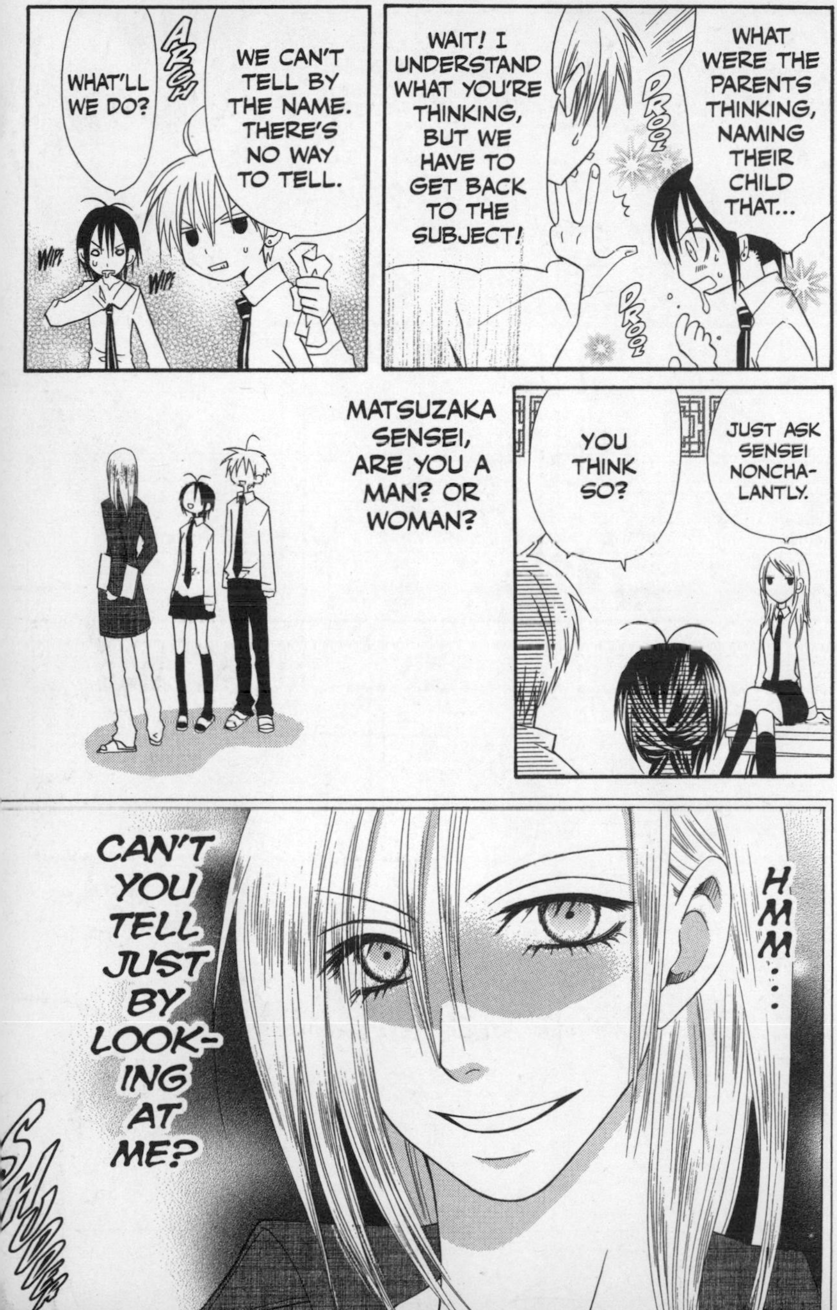
WHAT WERE THE PARENTS THINKING, NAMING THEIR CHILD THAT...
DROOL
WAIT! I UNDERSTAND WHAT YOU'RE THINKING, BUT WE HAVE TO GET BACK TO THE SUBJECT!
DROOL
WE CAN'T TELL BY THE NAME. THERE'S NO WAY TO TELL.
ARGH
WHAT'LL WE DO?
WIPE
WIPE
JUST ASK SENSEI NONCHALANTLY.
YOU THINK SO?
MATSUZAKA SENSEI, ARE YOU A MAN? OR WOMAN?
HMM...
CAN'T YOU TELL JUST BY LOOKING AT ME?

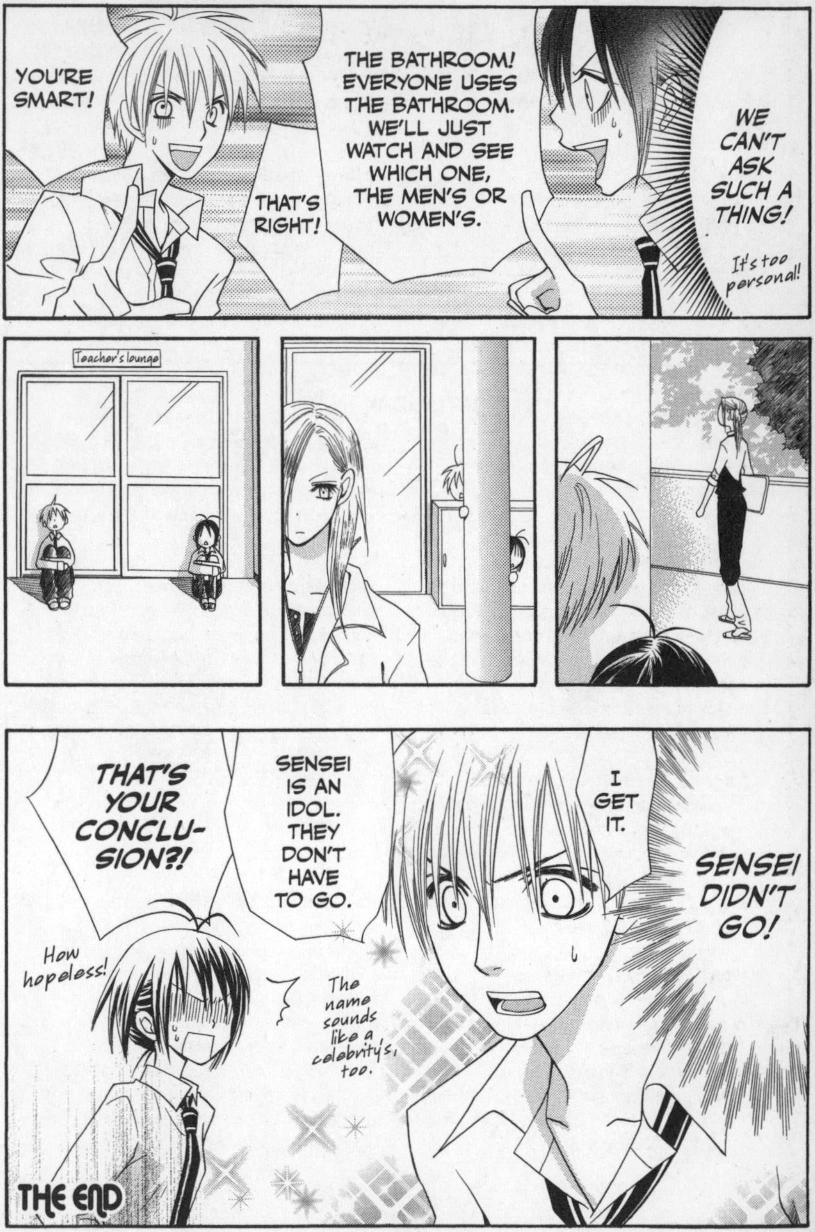
WE CAN'T ASK SUCH A THING!
It's too personal!
THE BATHROOM! EVERYONE USES THE BATHROOM. WE'LL JUST WATCH AND SEE WHICH ONE, THE MEN'S OR WOMEN'S.
THAT'S RIGHT!
YOU'RE SMART!
Teacher's lounge
SENSEI DIDN'T GO!
I GET IT.
SENSEI IS AN IDOL. THEY DON'T HAVE TO GO.
THAT'S YOUR CONCLUSION?!
The name sounds like a celebrity's, too.
How hopeless!
THE END

Side Dish—End Notes

For those who want to know a little more about the menu.

Page 7, panel 1: Saurel
An oily fish in the mackerel family, caught in August off the Izu Peninsula and considered a good fish for sashimi (thin slices of seafood served with a dip and simple garnish).

Page 7, panel 1: Ikizukuri platter
The sushi tradition of preparing sashimi while the fish/shellfish is still alive. The customer selects their fish and the sashimi chef fillets and guts it, serving it to the customer with the heart still beating.

Page 8, panel 3: Dorayaki
A sweet Japanese snack food that consists of two small sweet pancakes sandwiching a layer of sweet bean jam. The beans—usually a dark red bean known as azuki—are mashed into a paste and sweetened with honey or sugar. In the Kansai region, dorayaki is often called *mikasa*.

Page 17, panel 1: Sake bottles
The labels on these sake bottles bear the names of patrons, like the VIP bottle service in an American bar.

Page 21, panel 1: Sushidokoro
This means "sushi place."

Page 64, panel 3: Kaedama
A system for enjoying a second helping of noodles when eating ramen. When ordering kaedama, you eat your noodles, leave most of the broth, and order more noodles for the leftover broth. Doing this, you get double the noodles for less than the price of two orders.

Page 66, author note: Yaminabe
A hodgepodge hot pot where anything and everything is thrown in to be cooked. It's a useful way of getting rid of leftovers. The *yami* means "dark or mysterious," and refers to the surprises you might encounter while eating.

Page 78, panel 3: Unagi knife
Unagi are eel, and Tokyo sushi chefs never clean the eel from the belly due to unpleasant connotations to *harakiri* (ritual suicide). Instead, they clean the eel from the head. However, the Osaka and Kyoto style is to clean the eel from the belly.

Page 92, author note: Sweetfish
Also known as *ayu*, it is a delicate saltwater fish with slightly golden, olive skin and a white belly. The sweetfish gets its name from a sweet-tasting flesh, which the author likens to watermelon. Others attribute a cucumber aroma to the fish.

Page 92, author note: Char
A member of the trout and salmon family. Char have light spots, unlike the black-spotted trout.

Page 116, author note: Furikake
A condiment that contains dried seaweed, dried bonito (shrimp flakes), bits of dried salmon, etc. that you sprinkle onto hot rice.

Page 116, author note: Udon
Thick wheat noodles, usually served in broth with various accompaniments like green onions, tempura, or fish cake. Udon is also served chilled or stir-fried.

Page 127, panel 3: Arai
Literally means "to wash." The technique is usually employed when preparing sashimi from freshwater fish. The fish flesh is washed in a bowl of cool water to get rid of "muddiness" and excess oil and then dunked in ice water for one minute. The ice water plunge firms up the fish flesh.

Page 127, panel 3: Sogigiri
A method of cutting fish or meat very thinly. Here, the fillet is cut in three horizontal pieces, then sliced vertically into many thin pieces.

Page 127, panel 4: Miso
Fermented paste (usually from soybeans) used to make broths, sauces, spreads, and to pickle vegetables and meat. Miso comes in a variety of types, with *shiromiso* (white miso) and *akamiso* (red miso) the most common. Miso is considered a very healthy food, and it has even been suggested that miso helps protect against radiation sickness. The sauce made from vinegar and miso paste is called *sumiso*.

Page 127, panel 4: Sansho
Greenish-brown spice from the pods of the sansho tree, similar to pepper. Used in Japanese dishes not for heat but for its aromatic qualities. Sansho is thought to be a relative of the Szechuan pepper.

Page 127, panel 4: Julienne
A culinary term used to describe vegetables or other food that has been sliced in matchstick proportions, usually measuring 1/8-inch thick.

Page 128, panel 2: Nishiki
Literally means "brocade." Nishiki carp are a colorful mixture of orange, gold, and red.

Page 131, author note: Arai of the Hiroshima Carps
Hiroshima Carps is a pro baseball team and Arai is their first baseman.

Page 138, panel 3: Tamago
A thick omelet-like egg preparation cooked in a special pan. Sushi shops are often rated by how good their tamago recipe is.

Page 147, panel 2: Shichimi togarashi
A Japanese spice blend made up of seven spices, with the main spice being chili pepper. Other spices include sansho, nori, dried mandarin orange peel, sesame seed, hemp seed, and poppy seed. Another variation might include rapeseed (similar to mustard seed), shiso seed (member of the mint family), yuzu peel, ginger, and mulberry.

Page 147, panel 2: Nori
Nori is dried laver seaweed. It is most commonly known as the seaweed wrap on sushi, but it is also used shredded or flaked in a variety of other dishes.

Page 148, panel 3: Kalbi
A Korean barbecue dish where beef short ribs (sometimes pork) are marinated in a pear juice-based sauce. The Japanese version of the kalbi marinade is closer to teriyaki sauce found in America.

Page 170, panel 2: Suppon
A large, freshwater snapping turtle prized for its meat.

Page 174, panel 1: Hot Pot
Hana says *ishi-kari-nabe*, a type of hot pot with salmon and vegetables. The kari means "to hunt/harvest/pick" and refers to fish obtained by hunting.

Page 194, panel 4: Rea.
The first kanji (玲) means "the sound of jewels" and the second (亜) represents the first letter in the alphabet.

I'm happy that, once again, our paths are crossing because of comics.
But it's embarrassing, so please don't read on!
No, wait, please read it after all!
(That's sort of how I'm feeling right now.)

-Ayumi Komura

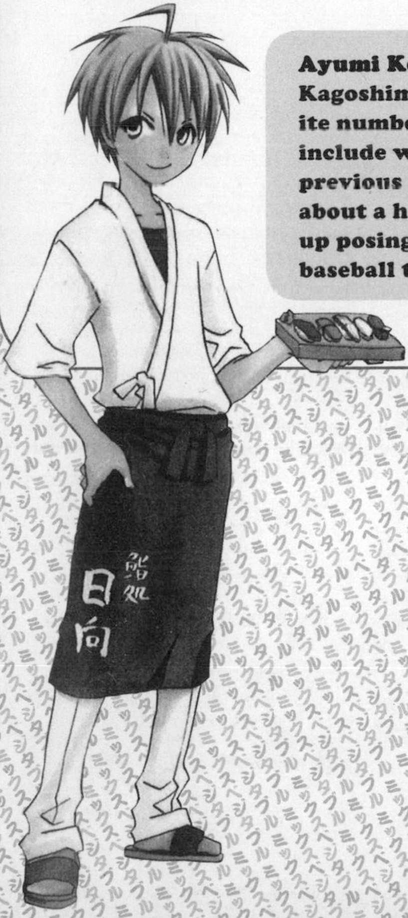
鮨処
日向

Ayumi Komura was born in Kagoshima Prefecture. Her favorite number is 22, and her hobbies include watching baseball. Her previous title is *Hybrid Berry*, about a high school girl who ends up posing as a boy on her school's baseball team.

MIXED VEGETABLES
VOL. 1
The Shojo Beat Manga Edition

STORY AND ART BY
AYUMI KOMURA

English Translation /JN Productions
English Adaptation/Stephanie V.W. Lucianovic
Touch-up Art & Lettering/Gia Cam Luc
Design/Yukiko Whitley
Editor/Pancha Diaz

Editor in Chief, Books/Alvin Lu
Editor in Chief, Magazines/Marc Weidenbaum
VP of Publishing Licensing/Rika Inouye
VP of Sales/Gonzalo Ferreyra
Sr. VP of Marketing/Liza Coppola
Publisher/Hyoe Narita

Printed in Canada

Published by VIZ Media, LLC
P.O. Box 77010
San Francisco, CA 94107

Shojo Beat Manga Edition
10 9 8 7 6 5 4 3 2 1
First printing, September 2008

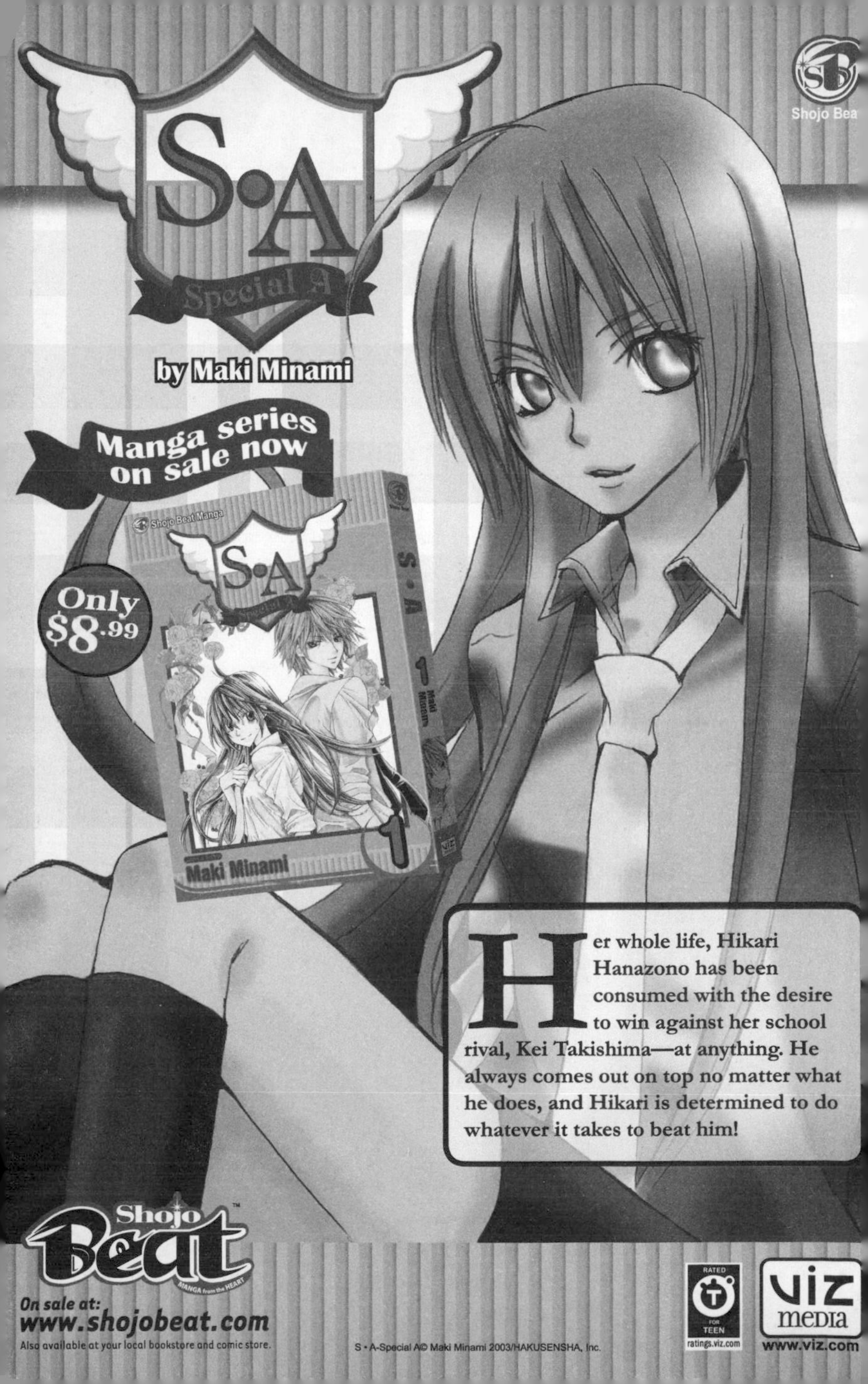

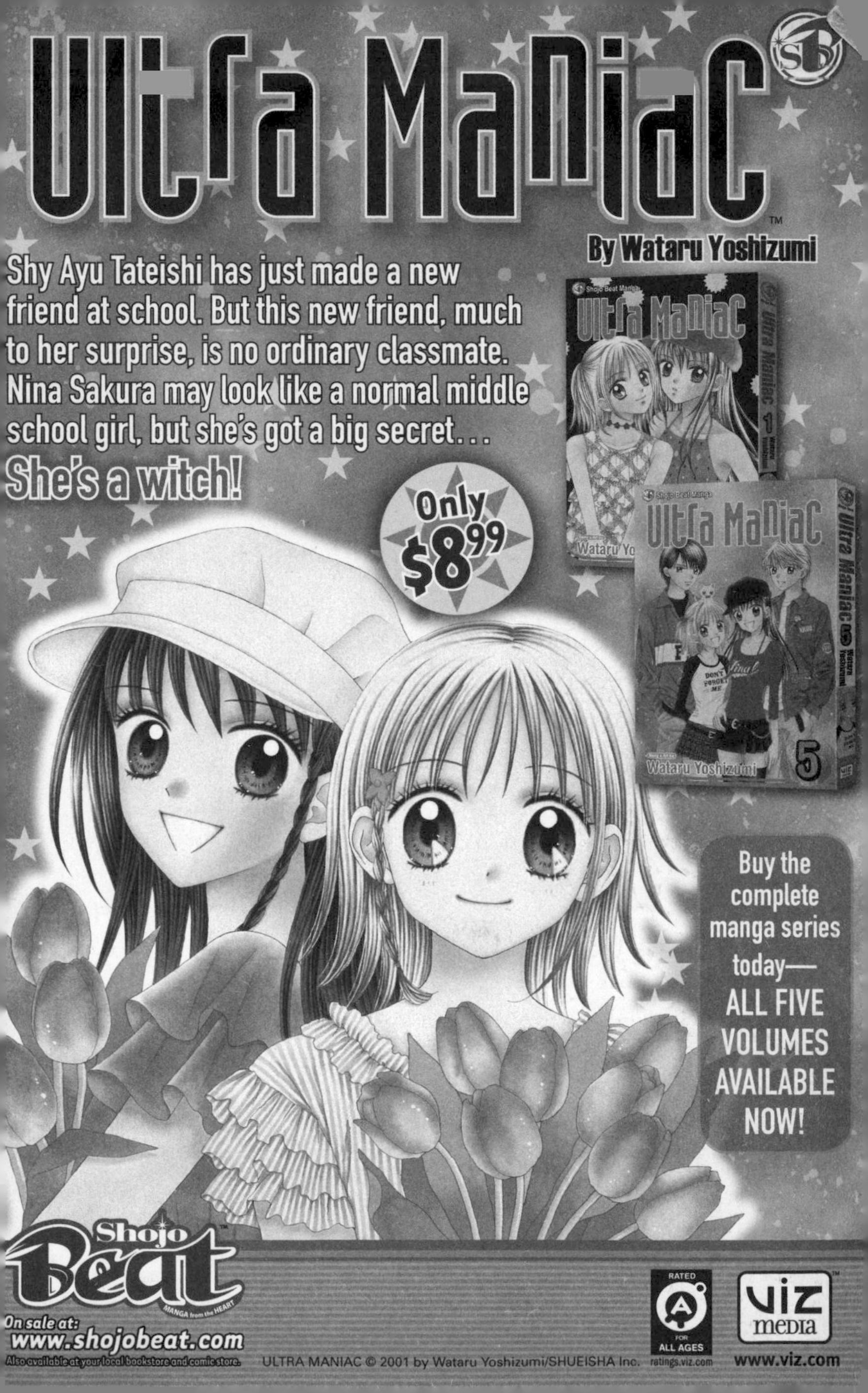

Ultra Maniac™
By Wataru Yoshizumi
Shy Ayu Tateishi has just made a new friend at school. But this new friend, much to her surprise, is no ordinary classmate. Nina Sakura may look like a normal middle school girl, but she's got a big secret...
She's a witch!
Only $8.99
Buy the complete manga series today—ALL FIVE VOLUMES AVAILABLE NOW!
Shojo Beat™
MANGA from the HEART
On sale at:
www.shojobeat.com
Also available at your local bookstore and comic store.
ULTRA MANIAC © 2001 by Wataru Yoshizumi/SHUEISHA Inc.
RATED A FOR ALL AGES
ratings.viz.com
VIZ media
www.viz.com

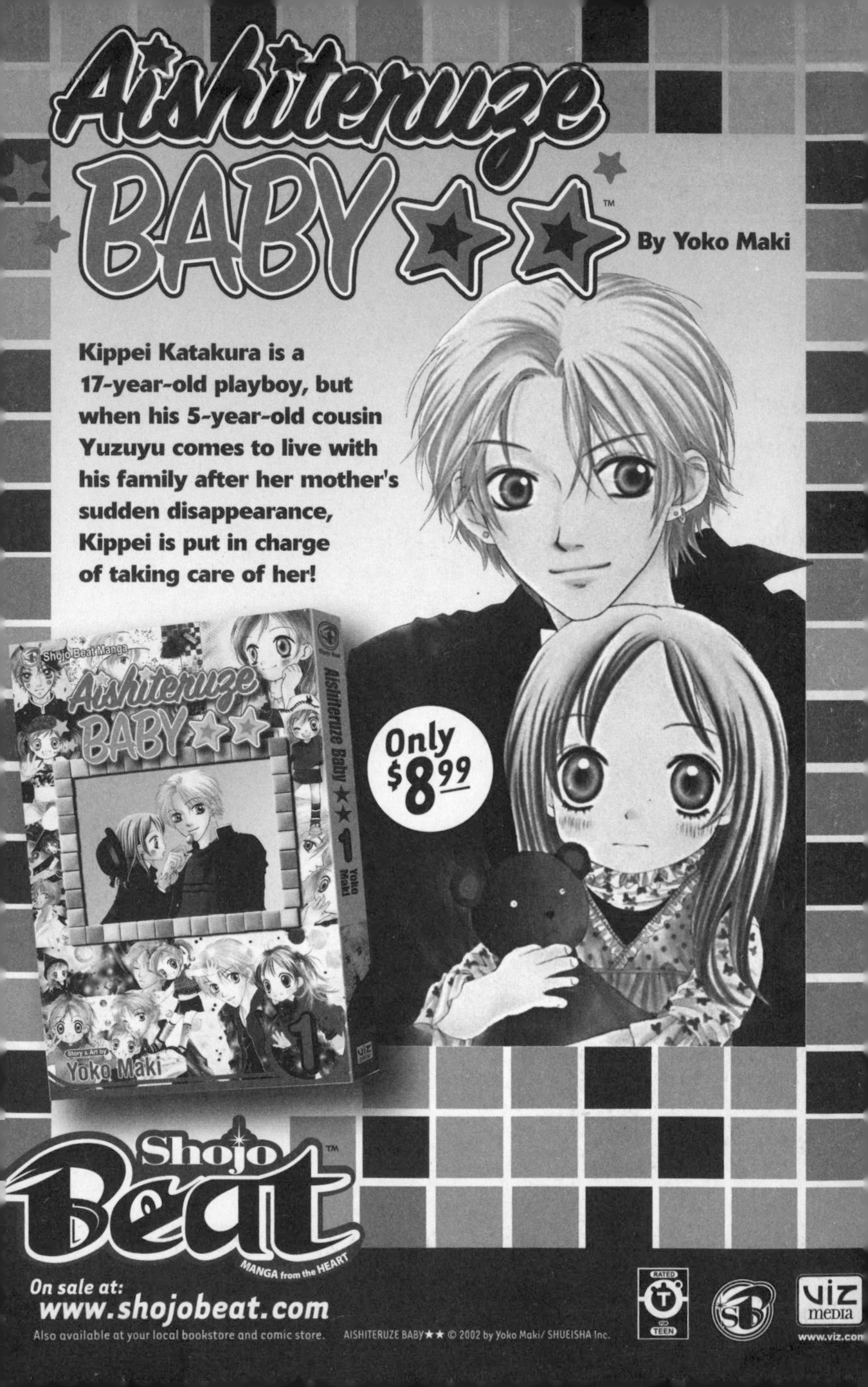

Aishiteruze BABY★★™
By Yoko Maki
Kippei Katakura is a 17-year-old playboy, but when his 5-year-old cousin Yuzuyu comes to live with his family after her mother's sudden disappearance, Kippei is put in charge of taking care of her!
Only $8.99
Shojo Beat Manga
Aishiteruze BABY★★
Aishiteruze Baby ★★ 1 Yoko Maki
Story & Art by Yoko Maki
Shojo Beat™
MANGA from the HEART
On sale at:
www.shojobeat.com
Also available at your local bookstore and comic store.
AISHITERUZE BABY★★ © 2002 by Yoko Maki/ SHUEISHA Inc.
RATED T TEEN
VIZ MEDIA
www.viz.com

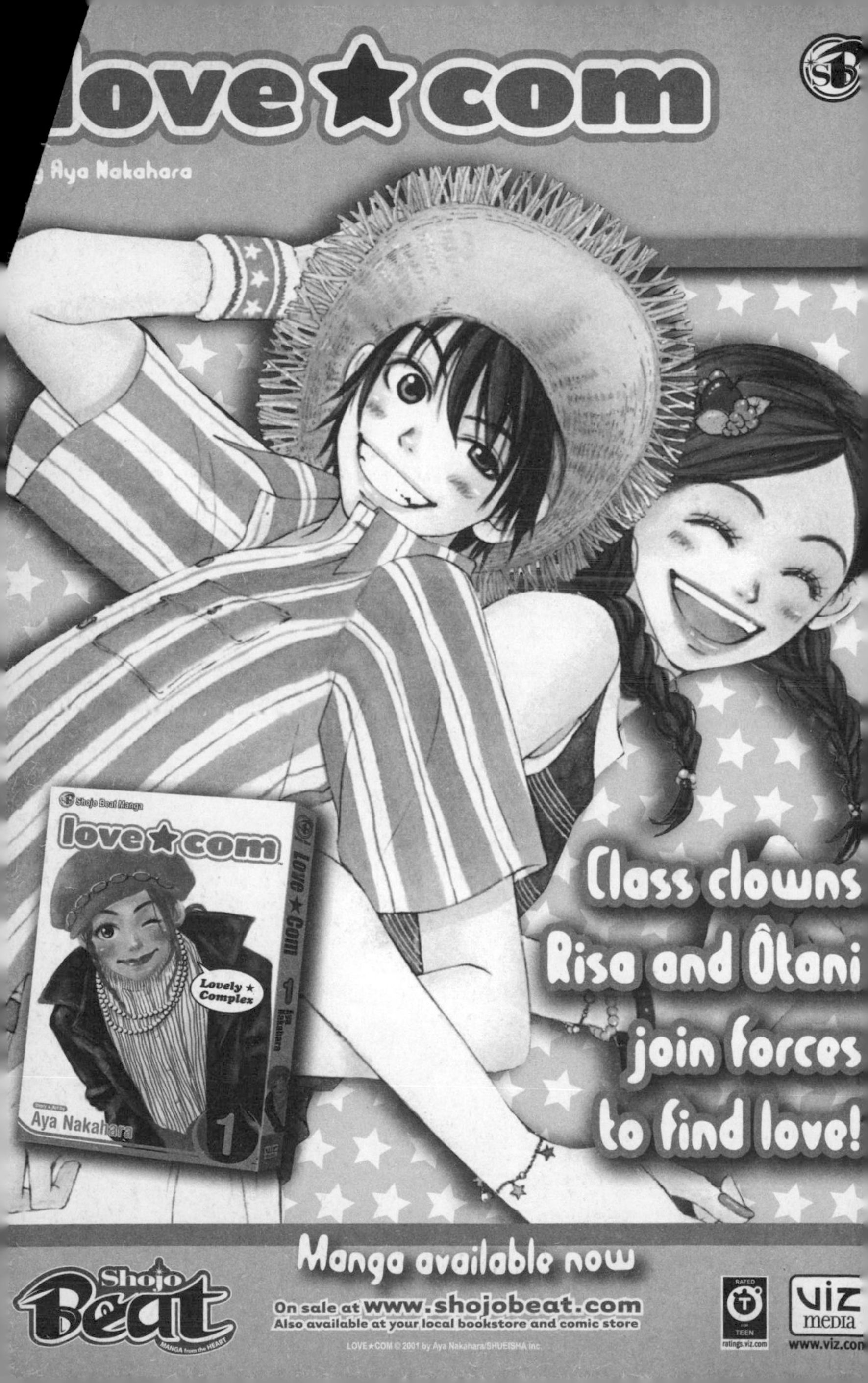
love★com
by Aya Nakahara
Shojo Beat Manga
love★com
Lovely ★ Complex
Love★Com 1
Story & Art by Aya Nakahara
1
Class clowns Risa and Ôtani join forces to find love!
Manga available now
Shojo Beat
MANGA from the HEART
On sale at www.shojobeat.com
Also available at your local bookstore and comic store
RATED T TEEN
ratings.viz.com
VIZ media
www.viz.com
LOVE★COM © 2001 by Aya Nakahara/SHUEISHA Inc.

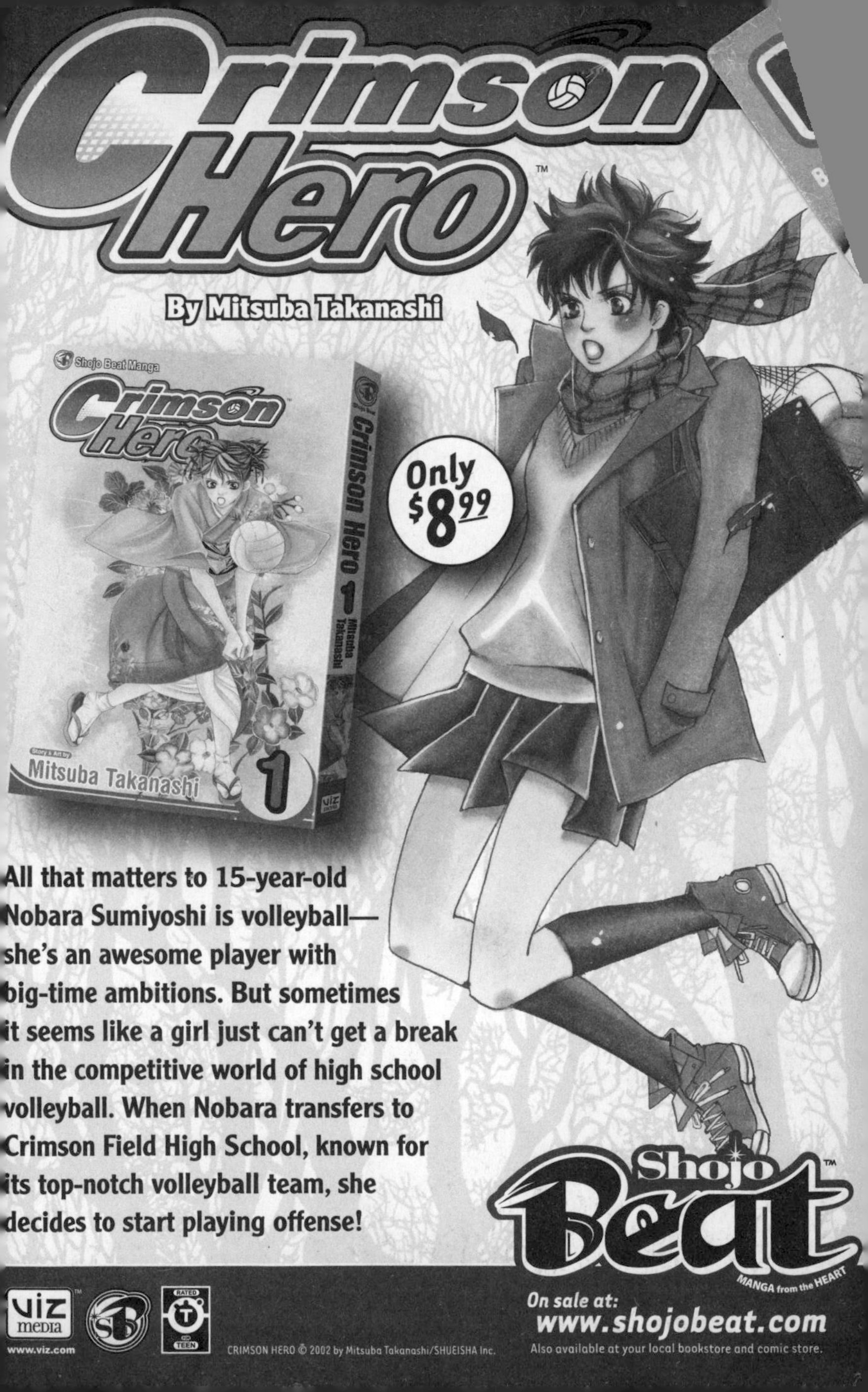
Crimson Hero™
By Mitsuba Takanashi
Shojo Beat Manga
Crimson Hero
Story & Art by
Mitsuba Takanashi
1
Crimson Hero 1
Mitsuba Takanashi
Only $8.99
All that matters to 15-year-old Nobara Sumiyoshi is volleyball—she's an awesome player with big-time ambitions. But sometimes it seems like a girl just can't get a break in the competitive world of high school volleyball. When Nobara transfers to Crimson Field High School, known for its top-notch volleyball team, she decides to start playing offense!
Shojo Beat™
MANGA from the HEART
On sale at:
www.shojobeat.com
Also available at your local bookstore and comic store.
viz media
www.viz.com
RATED T TEEN
CRIMSON HERO © 2002 by Mitsuba Takanashi/SHUEISHA Inc.

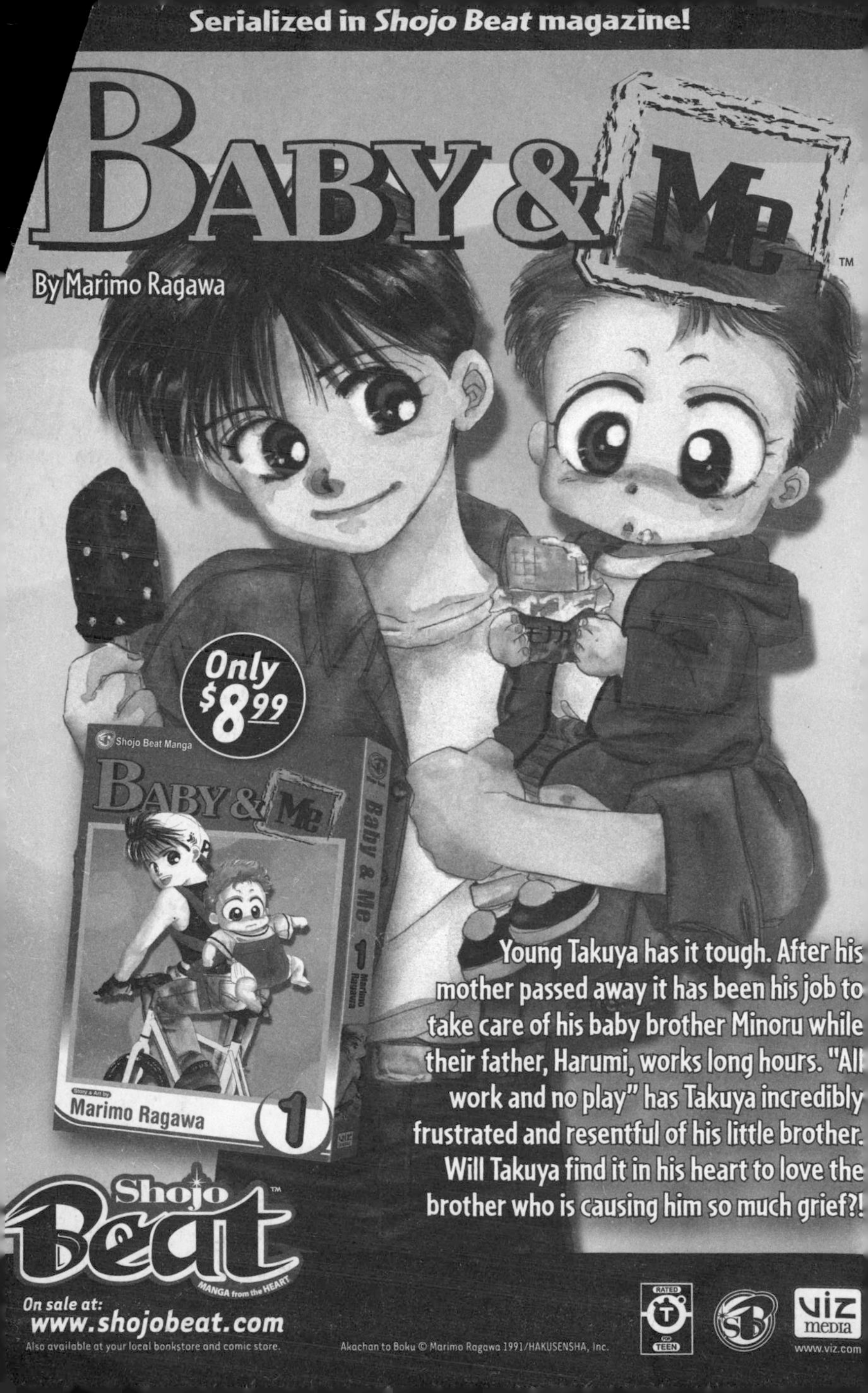
Serialized in Shojo Beat magazine!
BABY & ME™
By Marimo Ragawa
Only $8.99
Shojo Beat Manga
BABY & ME
Baby & Me 1 Marimo Ragawa
Story & Art by
Marimo Ragawa
1
Young Takuya has it tough. After his mother passed away it has been his job to take care of his baby brother Minoru while their father, Harumi, works long hours. "All work and no play" has Takuya incredibly frustrated and resentful of his little brother. Will Takuya find it in his heart to love the brother who is causing him so much grief?!
Shojo Beat™
MANGA from the HEART
On sale at:
www.shojobeat.com
Also available at your local bookstore and comic store.
Akachan to Boku © Marimo Ragawa 1991/HAKUSENSHA, Inc.
RATED T FOR TEEN
viz media
www.viz.com

Tell us what you think about Shojo Beat Mang

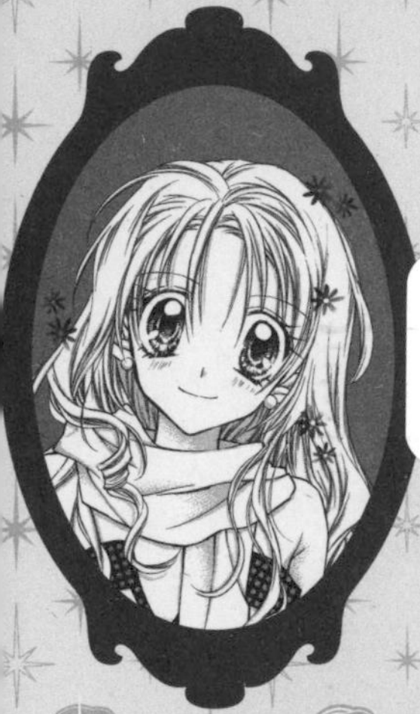

Our survey is now available online. Go to:

shojobeat.com/mangasurvey

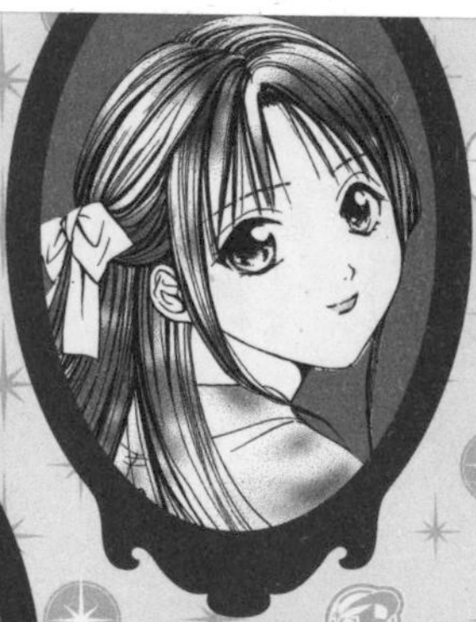

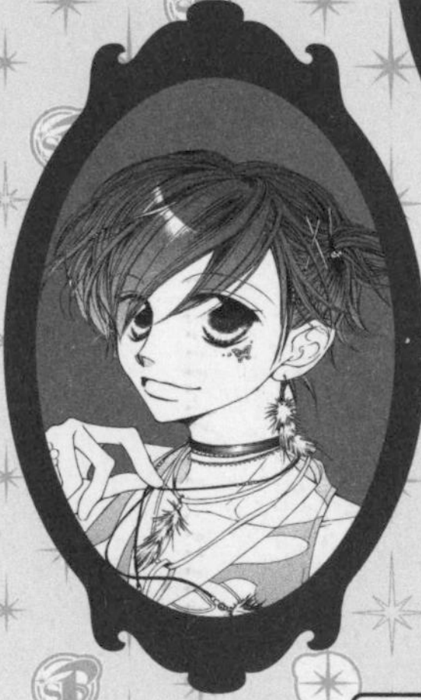

Help us make our product offerings better!

VIZ media

Shojo Beat MANGA from the HEART

THE REAL DRAMA BEGINS IN...

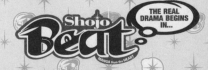